Introduction to Graphics Programming for Windows® 95

Vector Graphics Using C++

Introduction to Graphics Programming for Windows® 95

Vector Graphics Using C++

MICHAEL J. YOUNG

AP PROFESSIONAL

Boston San Diego New York
London Sydney Tokyo Toronto

AP PROFESSIONAL
1300 Boylston Street, Chestnut Hill, MA 02167

An imprint of ACADEMIC PRESS, INC.
A Division of HARCOURT BRACE & COMPANY

United Kingdom Edition published by
ACADEMIC PRESS LIMITED
24–28 Oval Road, London NW1 7DX

Library of Congress Cataloging-in-Publication Data
Young, Michael J.
    Introduction to graphics programming for Windows 95 : vector
graphics using C++ / Michael J. Young
        p.   cm.
    Includes index.
    ISBN 0-12-773350-7 -- ISBN 0-12-773351-5 (disk)
    1. Computer graphics   2. C++ (Computer program language)
3. Microsoft Windows.   I. Title.
T385.Y695   1995
006.6'765--dc20   95-37048
                                                            CIP

Printed in the United States of America
95 96 97 98 IP 9 8 7 6 5 4 3 2 1

CONTENTS

Chapter 2 Drawing Graphics in Windows 95 — 35

Chapter 3 Drawing Straight Lines and Curves — 51

Chapter 4 Drawing Closed Figures — 107

Chapter 5 Using Regions, Paths, and Clipping   **183**

Chapter 6 Transforming Graphics   **211**

Chapter 7 Printing Graphics   **289**

INTRODUCTION

Windows has always been an excellent platform for developing and running graphics applications. The latest version, Windows 95, provides even more graphics features. For example, Windows 95 adds free-form curves (Bézier curves), paths (for drawing complex graphics more easily and for generating graphics effects), and enhanced metafiles (for storing graphics in a device-independent format).

Although mastering Windows 95 graphics programming can be a major undertaking, this book is designed to give you a good head start. To benefit from this book, you need to know the basics of C++ programming, but you do not need to have prior graphics or Windows programming experience (the specific requirements are described later in the Introduction).

The following are some of the important features of the book:

1. **The book focuses on vector graphics.**   With vector graphics, you call Windows drawing functions to create drawings that are scalable, device-independent, and consist of collections of discrete graphic figures that can be individually selected and modified. Most sophisticated drawing programs use vector graphics. In contrast, with bitmapped graphics (also known as raster graphics), you store and manipulate the values of the pixels (dots) that are used to display text and graphics on

the device surface. Although often more efficient than vector graphics, bitmapped graphics techniques are much more device-dependent and offer fewer options for scaling and editing drawings.

FYI

For a treatment of bitmapped graphics as well as graphics animation, see the book *Windows Animation Programming with C++*, by Michael J. Young, published by AP PROFESSIONAL.

2. **The book is written specifically for Windows 95.** However, because the graphics features of Windows 95 are largely a subset of those provided by Windows NT, you can use what you learn in this book for writing Windows NT programs. Throughout this book, the term *Windows* refers to Windows 95 unless it is otherwise qualified.

3. **The programming examples use C++.** In addition to learning basic graphics programming techniques, you will learn how to use the features of C++, primarily classes, for organizing your graphics programs. Not only is C++ the most powerful programming language commonly available for Windows programming, but also C++ classes are ideally suited for encapsulating the code and data required to draw vector graphics.

4. **The book presents a substantial example drawing program.** This vector drawing program, called DrawIt, employs almost all of the graphics techniques discussed in the book. It allows you to see how each programming technique is used within the context of a complete, working program, and also shows how C++ classes and virtual functions can be used to simplify a graphics program, minimize the duplication of code, and make the program easy to enhance.

THE CONTENTS OF THE BOOK

Chapters 1 and 2 provide basic background information and form the foundation of the book. Chapter 1 discusses the basics of Windows programming so that you will be able to understand the example programs given in the book. It also presents a Windows program template, which uses C++ classes and forms the basis of the other example programs. Chapter 2 explains the basic steps required to display graphics in a window or on another device, and provides an overview of the techniques that are presented in the remaining chapters.

Chapters 3 and 4 form the heart of the book. In these chapters, you will learn how to use the Windows graphics drawing functions that are the basis of vector graphics. In Chapter 3, you will learn how to draw straight lines and curves, and in Chapter 4, you will learn how to draw closed figures such as rectangles and ellipses.

The remaining chapters cover more specialized and advanced topics. Chapter 5 shows how to use Windows regions, paths, and clipping to create complex drawings and generate unique graphic effects. Chapter 6 explains how to transform graphics—that is, how to modify the size, orientation, position, or shape of graphic figures. Chapter 7 explains the techniques that are required to print graphics and manage print jobs. Finally, Chapter 8 shows you how to use enhanced metafiles to store vector graphics in memory and on disk.

The DrawIt Program

One of the most important features of this book is the DrawIt vector graphics program that it presents. This example program bridges the gap between the theoretical and the practical. By studying the code, you can learn how to use the graphics techniques in building an actual program.

The book presents five different versions of DrawIt. DrawIt Version 1, which is given in Chapter 3, allows you to draw only straight and curved lines (which are the topic of that chapter). Each subsequent version of DrawIt adds features that correspond to the topic of the chapter in which it is presented. Table 1 summarizes the different program versions.

Table 1: DrawIt Versions

DrawIt Version	Chapter Where Presented	Important Features Added
Version 1	3	Setting drawing attributes; creating pens; drawing lines, arcs, Bézier curves, and polylines
Version 2	4	Setting the polygon filling mode and brush origin, creating brushes, drawing closed figures, selecting and moving figures
Version 3	6	Scaling figures
Version 4	7 (not printed in book)	Printing drawings
Version 5	8	Saving drawings in disk files, in enhanced metafile format

The chapters contain many references to the DrawIt code. The C++ source code for each version (except Version 4, which has relatively few modifications) is printed at the end of the chapter in which that version is presented. Also, the complete source code for each version is provided on the companion disk.

TIP

The source code for the DrawIt program contains numerous comments. Studying the code should reveal many programming techniques beyond those covered in the book. Also, you might want to load the appropriate source code files into an editor while you are reading the book to make it easier to find and view the specific functions that are discussed.

THE CONTENTS OF THE COMPANION DISK

The companion disk provided with this book contains the following files:

- The executable file for each example program.

- The complete source code for each example program, so that you can study the code, modify it, or use it as the basis for your own programs.

- A project file for each example program, so that you can open and modify the program in Microsoft Visual C++ 2.0. (If you are using a different development environment, you can create your own project file, as explained in Chapter 1.)

- An Install program for decompressing the companion disk files and copying them to your hard disk. For instructions on installing the companion disk, see Appendix A.

REQUIREMENTS

The following are the basic requirements for getting the most out of this book:

- To understand the programming techniques (especially those used in DrawIt) you should have a basic knowledge of C++, including classes, inheritance, and virtual functions.

- To run the example programs, you need Windows 95.

- To modify the example programs, you need a development environment that can generate 32-bit applications for Windows 95 (such as Microsoft Visual C++ version 2.0 or later, or Borland C++ version 4.5 or later). The code was kept as general and portable as possible, and it does *not* use any proprietary class libraries. Therefore, you should be able to use *any* of these development environments, making at most minor changes to the source code. (The code was developed using Microsoft Visual C++ 2.0.)

- To obtain additional information on the Windows functions that are discussed or mentioned in the book, you should have ready access to the documentation on the Win32 Application Program Interface, in online or printed form (this documentation should be included with your development environment).

CHAPTER 1

WRITING A WINDOWS 95 PROGRAM

This chapter explains the bare essentials of Windows 95 programming in C++. The goal of the chapter is to teach you just enough so that you will be able to understand the basic Windows programming techniques in the example programs given in the following chapters, even if you have had little or no Windows programming experience.

The chapter teaches these techniques by presenting a simple Windows 95 program named Template, which forms the basis for the example programs given in the following chapters (notably, the DrawIt vector drawing program). Template displays a text message within a small, fixed-size window and has a single pull-down menu labeled Options. The Options menu contains an About... command that displays an About dialog box, and an Exit command that terminates the program. Template also has a custom program icon. The program window is shown in Figure 1.1.

The chapter begins with an overview of the basic steps for creating and building the Template program. It then shows how to design the program resources—the menu, the dialog box, and the icon. Finally, the chapter describes the C++ program source code, explaining the overall flow of program control and how the program performs each of its main tasks.

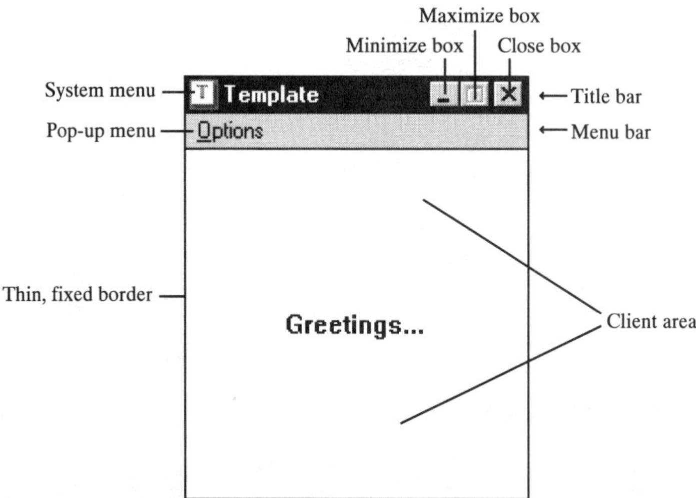

Figure 1.1:   The Template program window

THE STEPS FOR CREATING AND BUILDING THE PROGRAM

The following is a general description of the main steps required to create and build the Template program, using an integrated Windows development environment such as Microsoft Visual C++ version 2.0 or later or Borland C++ version 4.5 or later. (Your development environment must be capable of building 32-bit Windows 95 applications, using the Win32 application program interface, which will be explained later.) The remainder of the chapter will provide additional details on performing these steps. Also, see the documentation on your development environment for information on the specific commands used by your programming tools.

1. Create a folder on your hard disk to be used exclusively for storing the Template program files. This folder will be referred to as the *project folder*. Because a Windows program has a large number of source and output files, it is wise to store the files for each program or program version within a separate folder.

2. Use the integrated development environment to create a *resource-definition file* named Template.rc. Then use the appropriate resource editors to add the definitions for the individual program resources—the menu, the icon, and the About dialog box—to this resource-defini-

tion file. Store all files within the project folder you created in step 1. The next section in this chapter explains how to perform these tasks.

3. Use the text editor provided by the development environment to create the C++ program source files: Template.cpp, App.h, MainWnd.h, MainWnd.cpp, AboutDlg.h, and AboutDlg.cpp. These files are listed and explained later in the chapter, in the section "The C++ Source Code." Be sure to store the files in the project folder.

    To create a new C++ source file using Microsoft Visual C++ 2.0, choose the New... command on the File menu and select the Code/Text file type.

4. In the development environment, create a *project file* for Template. A project file stores a complete set of instructions for building or rebuilding a program. Be sure to create a project file that is suitable for generating a standard 32-bit Windows 95 program. Also, assign "Template" as the name of the project file (the default file extension used for project files depends upon the particular development environment), and save the project file within the project folder you created in step 1. You should add the following source files to the project: AboutDlg.cpp, MainWnd.cpp, Template.cpp, and Template.rc (all header files referenced by these source files are automatically included in the project).

    To create a project file in Visual C++ 2.0, choose the New... command on the File menu and select the Project file type. In the New Project dialog box, enter "Template" as the project name and the folder you created in step 1 as the project folder. The project file will be named Template.mak. Select the Application project type and the Win32 platform; these choices will assign settings to the project file that are suitable for generating a standard Windows 95 executable program (you do *not* want to use the AppWizard code generator or the Microsoft Foundation Classes class library). In the Project Files dialog box, add the files listed in the previous paragraph.

5. Build the project and run the program.

    In Visual C++ 2.0, you should first select either the debug version of the program (which includes debugging information) or the release version (which is fully optimized) in the Target: list box of the project window. Then choose the "Build Template.exe" command on the Project menu. When the executable program file, Template.exe, has been created, choose the "Execute Template.exe" command on the Project menu to run it. (To run the program in the debugger, choose the Go command on the Debug menu.)

Any time you wish to modify the Template program, you can open the project file in your development environment, make the desired changes, and then rebuild the program.

Table 1.1 lists all of the Template source files, both those that you manually enter into a text editor and those generated by the development tools. These source files are typical of the files required to generate a simple Windows program, although some Windows programs require additional source file types. Note that a complete set of these files—as well as the Template.exe executable program file—is included on the companion disk provided with this book. For instructions on installing the companion disk files, see Appendix A. Once you have installed the disk, the Template files will be found within the \Template subfolder of the hard-disk folder in which you installed the companion disk. The project file provided on the companion disk, Template.mak, is specifically for Visual C++ version 2.0. If you are using a different development environment and if you want to modify the program, you will need to create your own project file (see step 4 above).

DESIGNING THE RESOURCES

A resource-definition file contains definitions for a program's resources—menus, icons, dialog boxes, bitmaps, strings, and so on. As mentioned in the previous section, you need to create a resource-definition file for the Template program that is named Template.rc and save it in the project folder. You must then use the appropriate resource editors to add definitions for the program menu, icon, and About dialog box. The following sections briefly explain how to add these definitions.

Note that when you define the resources, you must assign a unique identifier to each resource and to each element that the resource contains. The C++ source code uses the identifiers to access the resources. The resource editors normally generate a resource header file containing constant definitions for these identifiers; this header file is included both in the resource-definition file and in the C++ source files. You should make sure that the resource header file is named Resource.h.

To create a resource-definition file in Visual C++ 2.0, choose the New... command on the File menu, and then select the Resource Script file type. Visual C++ will open a resource window; as you add resources to the file, they will be displayed in a graph within this window. To save the resource-definition file, choose the Save command on the File menu and save the file under the name Template.rc in the project folder that you created. The Visual C++ resource editors will automatically create a resource header file named

Table 1.1: The source files for the Template program

Source File	Purpose	How Created
AboutDlg.cpp	Implementation file for the About dialog box class (`CAboutDlg`)	Entered manually in the text editor
AboutDlg.h	Header file for the About dialog box class (`CAboutDlg`)	Entered manually in the text editor
App.h	Header file for the application class (`CApp`)	Entered manually in the text editor
Icon1.ico	Stores the program icon (referenced by the Template.rc resource definition file)	Generated by the icon resource editor
MainWnd.cpp	Implementation file for the main window class (`CMainWnd`)	Entered manually in the text editor
MainWnd.h	Header file for the main window class (`CMainWnd`)	Entered manually in the text editor
Resource.h	Resource header file; defines the constants for program resources (this file is included in Template.rc and C++ source files)	Generated by the resource editors
Template.cpp	C++ source file that defines the program entry function, `WinMain`, and objects of the program classes	Entered manually in the text editor
Template.mak	Project file (Visual C++ uses the .mak extension, Borland C++ uses the .ide extension, and other development environments may assign different file extensions)	Generated by the integrated development environment
Template.rc	Resource-definition file; defines the program menu, icon, and About dialog box	Generated by the resource editors

Resource.h and will include it in the resource-definition file (as you will see later, you must manually include Resource.h in the C++ source files).

FYI   When you build the program, the development environment runs a utility known as a *resource compiler*, which processes the resource-definition file and adds the resource data to the executable program file.

Designing the Menu

Use the menu editor provided by your development environment to design the Template program menu and to store the menu definition within the resource-definition file. Table 1.2 lists the properties of the menu itself and of each of the items you need to add to the menu. Figure 1.2 shows the completed menu (as it appears in the Visual C++ 2.0 menu editor).

To open the menu editor in Visual C++ 2.0, make sure that the resource window is active, choose the New… command on the Resource menu, and specify the Menu resource type (if the resource window is not active when you choose New…, Visual C++ will create a *new* resource-definition file and add the menu to it).

Designing the Icon

Use the icon editor to design the program icon and add it to the resource-definition file. You should give the icon resource the identifier IDI_ICON1. Note that when you create an icon resource, you can define several versions of the image, each of which is appropriate for a particular type of device or display situation. For the Template program, you need to define only a standard color image with a size of 32 by 32 pixels. Figure 1.3 shows the program icon as it appears in the Visual C++ 2.0 icon editor.

FYI	The icon data is stored in a separate icon file (which Visual C++ names Icon1.ico). The resource-definition file contains an ICON statement that references this file and causes the icon data to be included in the program's resource data.

To open the icon editor in Visual C++ 2.0, activate the resource window, choose the New… command on the Resource menu, and specify the Icon resource type (the icon editor is part of a general Visual C++ facility known as the *graphic editor*).

Designing the Dialog Box

Finally, use the dialog editor to design the About dialog box and add it to the resource-definition file. Each of the items within a dialog box is known as a *control*. Table 1.3 lists the properties of the dialog box and each control you need to add to it. Note that Table 1.3 gives only the *nondefault* properties for each item—that is, the properties you must explicitly set or change from their default values; you should leave the values of all other properties unchanged.

Table 1.2: Properties of the Template program menu and of the items in the menu

Item	Identifier	Caption	Other Properties
Menu	IDR_MENU1	None	None
Options pop-up menu	None	&Options	Pop-up
About menu command	ID_OPTIONS_ABOUT	&About...	None
Horizontal separator	None	None	Separator
Exit menu command	ID_OPTIONS_EXIT	&Exit	None

The completed About dialog box, as it appears in the Visual C++ 2.0 dialog editor, is shown in Figure 1.4. Note that because the picture control in the center of the dialog box is assigned the identifier of the program icon (IDI_ICON1), the program icon will be displayed when the dialog box is shown at program run time; the icon displayed in the icon editor is only a place holder. Figure 1.6, given later in the chapter, shows the dialog box as it appears at run time.

To open the dialog editor in Visual C++ 2.0, activate the resource window, choose the New... command on the Resource menu, and select the Dialog resource type.

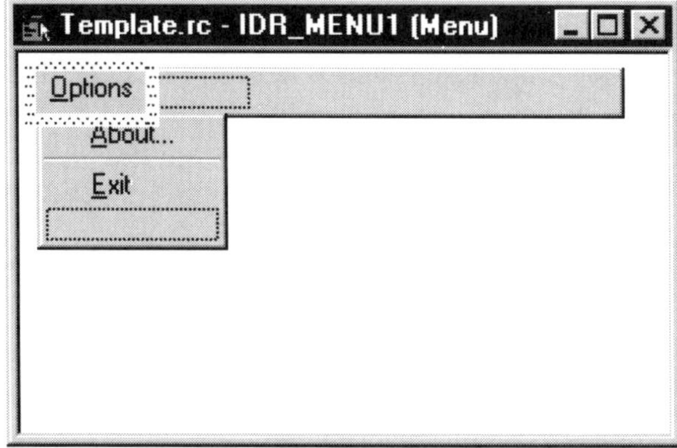

Figure 1.2:   The completed Template program menu as it appears in the Visual C++ menu editor

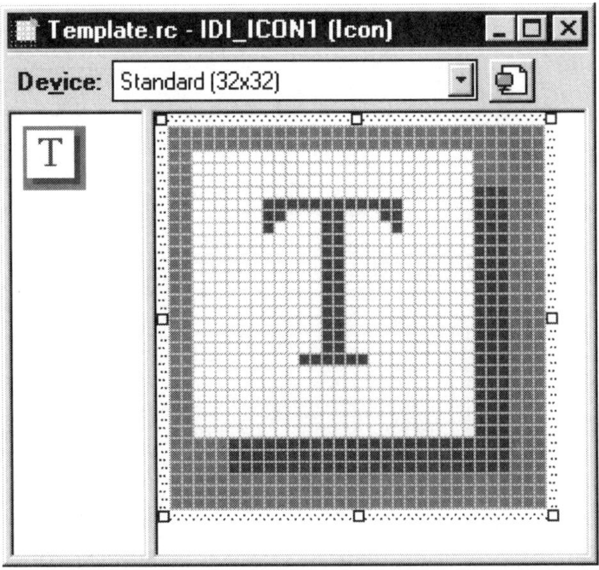

Figure 1.3:   The Template program icon as it appears in the Visual C++ 2.0 icon editor

THE C++ SOURCE CODE

The C++ source code files are listed at the end of this section. Template.cpp defines the program entry function, WinMain, and also declares a global instance of each of the three program classes that handle the primary program tasks. The *application class*, `CApp`, stores information on the application as a whole; this class is defined in App.h. The *main window class*, `CMainWnd`,

Table 1.3: Nondefault properties of the About dialog box and its controls

Item	*Identifier*	*Other Nondefault Properties*
Dialog box	`IDD_ABOUT`	Caption: `About`
Static text control	`IDD_STATIC`	Caption: `Windows 95` `Program Template` Text align: `Center`
Picture control	`IDC_STATIC`	Type: `Icon`
Push-button control	`IDOK`	Icon: `IDI_ICON1` Caption: `OK` `Default Button`

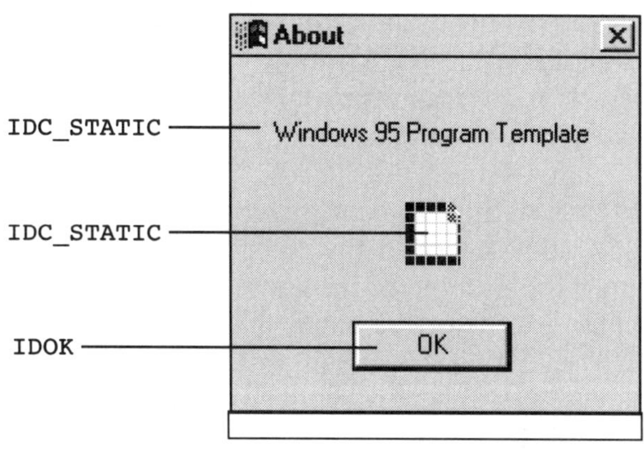

Figure 1.4:   The About dialog box as it appears in the Visual C++ 2.0 dialog editor

creates and displays the program window and handles the messages sent to this window (messages will be explained later); this class is defined in MainWnd.h and is implemented in MainWnd.cpp. The *About dialog box class*, `CAboutDlg`, displays the About dialog box and handles the messages sent to it; this class is defined in AboutDlg.h and is implemented in AboutDlg.cpp. Table 1.4 summarizes the features of the program classes.

Notice that each of the .cpp files begins with a statement that includes the file Windows.h:

```
#define STRICT
#include <windows.h>
```

Table 1.4: The Template program classes

Class	Header and Implementation Files	Purpose
CApp	App.h	Application class: stores information on the program
CMainWnd	MainWnd.h MainWnd.cpp	Main window class: manages the main program window
CAboutDlg	AboutDlg.h AboutDlg.cpp	About dialog box class: manages the About dialog box

Windows.h is the standard header file that you must include in a program that calls the functions provided by the Windows 95 system. These functions provide extensive support for Windows programs and are known collectively as the *Win32 application program interface*, or API. Windows.h (and the header files that it includes) contains prototypes for all of the API functions, as well as a collection of useful type definitions and macros. Defining the constant STRICT before including Windows.h causes the compiler to enforce strict type checking, which can reduce the number of programming errors and help ensure that the code will be portable to future versions of Windows and Windows NT.

Template.cpp defines a global object of each of the three program classes:

```
// header files for main program classes:
#include "app.h"
#include "mainwnd.h"
#include "aboutdlg.h"

// main program objects:
CApp       App;
CMainWnd   MainWnd;
CAboutDlg AboutDlg;
```

The other two .cpp files contain `extern` declarations for these objects so that they can be accessed. That is, MainWnd.cpp and AboutDlg.cpp include the following code:

```
#include "app.h"
#include "mainwnd.h"
#include "aboutdlg.h"

extern CApp       App;
extern CMainWnd   MainWnd;
extern CAboutDlg AboutDlg;
```

The following are the C++ source code listings for the Template program. The remaining sections of the chapter explain the workings of these files.

Listing 1.1:   Template.cpp

```
///////////////////////////////////////////////////////////////////////////////
//                                                                           //
// Template.cpp: Main program object declarations and WinMain                //
//               program entry function.                                     //
//                                                                           //
///////////////////////////////////////////////////////////////////////////////

#define STRICT
#include <windows.h>
```

```cpp
// header files for main program classes:
#include "app.h"
#include "mainwnd.h"
#include "aboutdlg.h"

// main program objects:
CApp       App;
CMainWnd   MainWnd;
CAboutDlg  AboutDlg;

//////////////////////////////////////////////////////////////////////////////
// program entry function:                                                   //
//////////////////////////////////////////////////////////////////////////////

int APIENTRY WinMain
  (HINSTANCE HInstCurrent,
   HINSTANCE HInstPrevious,
   LPSTR     CmdLine,
   int  CmdShow)
   {

   // store program informaton in application object:
   App.Initialize (HInstCurrent, CmdLine);

   // register class for main program window:
   if (!MainWnd.RegisterClass ())
      return 0;

   // create and display main program window:
   if (!MainWnd.Create ())
      return 0;

   // main message loop:
   MSG Msg;
   while (GetMessage (&Msg, NULL, NULL, NULL))
      {
      TranslateMessage (&Msg);
      DispatchMessage (&Msg);
      }

   // return "application-defined exit code":
   return Msg.wParam;
   }
```

Listing 1.2:   App.h

```cpp
//////////////////////////////////////////////////////////////////////////////
//                                                                           //
// App.h: Header file for application class.                                  //
//                                                                           //
//////////////////////////////////////////////////////////////////////////////
```

```cpp
class CApp
{
public:
   HINSTANCE mHInstance; // handle of program instance
   LPSTR     mCmdLine;   // pointer to program command line

   void Initialize (HINSTANCE HInstCurrent, LPSTR CmdLine)
   // saves application values
      {
      mHInstance = HInstCurrent;
      mCmdLine = CmdLine;
      }
      };
```

Listing 1.3:   MainWnd.h

```cpp
////////////////////////////////////////////////////////////////////////////
//                                                                        //
// MainWnd.h: Header file for main window class.                          //
//                                                                        //
////////////////////////////////////////////////////////////////////////////

// dimensions of main program window:
#define WINWIDTH  186
#define WINHEIGHT 224

class CMainWnd
{
public:
   HWND mHWnd; // main window handle

   BOOL Create (void);
   BOOL RegisterClass (void);

   // message-handling functions:
   LRESULT OnDestroy (void);
   LRESULT OnOptionsAbout (void);
   LRESULT OnOptionsExit (void);
   LRESULT OnPaint (void);
};
```

Listing 1.4:   MainWnd.cpp

```cpp
////////////////////////////////////////////////////////////////////////////
//                                                                        //
// MainWnd.cpp: Implementation file for main window class.                //
//                                                                        //
////////////////////////////////////////////////////////////////////////////
```

```cpp
#define STRICT
#include <windows.h>
#include "resource.h"

#include "app.h"
#include "mainwnd.h"
#include "aboutdlg.h"

extern CApp      App;
extern CMainWnd  MainWnd;
extern CAboutDlg AboutDlg;

LRESULT CALLBACK MainWndProc (HWND HWnd, UINT Msg, WPARAM WParam,
   LPARAM LParam);

//////////////////////////////////////////////////////////////////////
// CMainWnd public member functions:                                 //
//////////////////////////////////////////////////////////////////////

BOOL CMainWnd::Create (void)
// creates and displays main program window; returns TRUE on
// success or FALSE on error
   {
    // create main program window and save handle:
   mHWnd = CreateWindow
      ("DemoClass",
      "Template",
      WS_OVERLAPPED | WS_SYSMENU | WS_MINIMIZEBOX,
      CW_USEDEFAULT,
      CW_USEDEFAULT,
      WINWIDTH,
      WINHEIGHT,
      NULL,
      NULL,
      App.mHInstance,
      NULL);
    if (!mHWnd)
      return FALSE;

   // display window:
   ShowWindow
      (mHWnd,
      SW_SHOWDEFAULT);

   return TRUE;
   }

BOOL CMainWnd::RegisterClass (void)
// registers class for main program window; returns TRUE on
// success or FALSE on error
   {
   WNDCLASS WC;
```

```cpp
// specify class information:
WC.style = 0;
WC.lpfnWndProc = MainWndProc;
WC.cbClsExtra = 0;
WC.cbWndExtra = 0;
WC.hInstance = App.mHInstance;
WC.hIcon = LoadIcon (App.mHInstance,
   MAKEINTRESOURCE (IDI_ICON1));
WC.hCursor = LoadCursor (NULL, IDC_ARROW);
WC.hbrBackground = (HBRUSH)GetStockObject (WHITE_BRUSH);
WC.lpszMenuName = MAKEINTRESOURCE (IDR_MENU1);
WC.lpszClassName = "DemoClass";

// register class:
return (BOOL)::RegisterClass (&WC);
}

/////////////////////////////////////////////////////////////////////////////
// window procedure for main window:                                        //
/////////////////////////////////////////////////////////////////////////////

LRESULT CALLBACK MainWndProc
  (HWND   HWnd,
   UINT   Msg,
   WPARAM WParam,
   LPARAM LParam)
  {
  switch (Msg)
    {
    case WM_COMMAND: // user chose a menu command
       switch (LOWORD (WParam))
          {
          case ID_OPTIONS_ABOUT: // user chose Options/About
             return MainWnd.OnOptionsAbout ();

       case ID_OPTIONS_EXIT:         // user chose Options/Exit
          return MainWnd.OnOptionsExit ();

       default:
          // default processing for other commands:
          return DefWindowProc (HWnd, Msg, WParam, LParam);
       }

    case WM_DESTROY:  // DestroyWindow was called
       return MainWnd.OnDestroy ();

    case WM_PAINT: // window needs painting or repainting
       return MainWnd.OnPaint ();

    default:
       // default processing for all other messages:
       return DefWindowProc (HWnd, Msg, WParam, LParam);
    }
  }
```

```cpp
/////////////////////////////////////////////////////////////////////////
// CMainWnd message handling member functions:                          //
/////////////////////////////////////////////////////////////////////////

LRESULT CMainWnd::OnDestroy (void)
// processes WM_DESTROY messages
   {
   PostQuitMessage (0);   // post a WM_QUIT message to
   return NULL;           // cause message loop to exit
   }

LRESULT CMainWnd::OnOptionsAbout (void)
// processes WM_COMMAND / ID_OPTIONS_ABOUT messages
   {
   AboutDlg.Show ();    // display About dialog box
   return NULL;
   }

LRESULT CMainWnd::OnOptionsExit (void)
// processes WM_COMMAND / ID_OPTIONS_EXIT messages
   {
   DestroyWindow (mHWnd);    // destroy main window
   return NULL;
   }

LRESULT CMainWnd::OnPaint (void)
// processes WM_PAINT messages
   {
   HDC HDCPaint;               // client area device-context handle
   PAINTSTRUCT PaintStruct; // paint information
   RECT Rect;                  // dimensions of client area

   // initiate painting and obtain a device context:
   HDCPaint = BeginPaint (mHWnd, &PaintStruct);

   // get dimensions of client area of main window:
   GetClientRect (mHWnd, &Rect);

   // display text centered within client area:
   DrawText
      (HDCPaint,
      "Greetings...",
      -1,
      &Rect,
      DT_CENTER | DT_SINGLELINE | DT_VCENTER);

   // terminate painting and release device context:
   EndPaint (mHWnd, &PaintStruct);
   return NULL;
   }
```

Listing 1.5:   AboutDlg.h

```cpp
////////////////////////////////////////////////////////////////////////
//                                                                    //
// AboutDlg.h: Header file for About dialog box class.                //
//                                                                    //
////////////////////////////////////////////////////////////////////////

class CAboutDlg
{
public:
   int Show (void);

   // message-handling functions:
   BOOL OnCancel (HWND HDlg);
   BOOL OnCtlColor (HDC HDc);
   BOOL OnInitDialog (void);
   BOOL OnOK (HWND HDlg);
};
```

Listing 1.6:   AboutDlg.cpp

```cpp
////////////////////////////////////////////////////////////////////////
//                                                                    //
// AboutDlg.cpp: Implementation file for About dialog box class       //
//                                                                    //
////////////////////////////////////////////////////////////////////////

#define  STRICT
#include <windows.h>
#include "resource.h"

#include "app.h"
#include "mainwnd.h"
#include "aboutdlg.h"

extern CApp       App;
extern CMainWnd   MainWnd;
extern CAboutDlg AboutDlg;

BOOL CALLBACK DialogProc (HWND HDlg, UINT Msg, WPARAM WParam,
   LPARAM LParam);

////////////////////////////////////////////////////////////////////////
// CAboutDlg public member function:                                  //
////////////////////////////////////////////////////////////////////////

int CAboutDlg::Show (void)
// displays About dialog box
   {
   return DialogBox
```

```cpp
      (App.mHInstance,
      MAKEINTRESOURCE (IDD_ABOUT),
      MainWnd.mHWnd,
      DialogProc);
   }

////////////////////////////////////////////////////////////////////////////
// About dialog box procedure:                                            //
////////////////////////////////////////////////////////////////////////////

BOOL CALLBACK DialogProc
   (HWND   HDlg,
   UINT   Msg,
   WPARAM WParam,
   LPARAM LParam)
   {
   switch (Msg)
      {
      case WM_INITDIALOG:  // dialog box was just created
         return AboutDlg.OnInitDialog ();

      case WM_COMMAND:       // user issued a command
         switch (LOWORD (WParam))
            {
            case IDCANCEL: // user chose Close or pressed Esc
               return AboutDlg.OnCancel (HDlg);

            case IDOK:      // user clicked OK or pressed Enter
               return AboutDlg.OnOK (HDlg);

            default:
               return FALSE;  // default message processing
            }

      case WM_CTLCOLORDLG:     // dialog box about to be painted;
      case WM_CTLCOLORSTATIC: // text about to be painted
         return AboutDlg.OnCtlColor ((HDC)WParam);

      default:              // request default processing for all
         return FALSE;  // other messages
         }
      }

////////////////////////////////////////////////////////////////////////////
// CAboutDlg message handling member functions:                           //
////////////////////////////////////////////////////////////////////////////

BOOL CAboutDlg::OnCancel (HWND HDlg)
// processes WM_COMMAND / IDCANCEL messages
   {
   // close the dialog box:
   EndDialog (HDlg, IDCANCEL);
   return TRUE;
   }
```

```
BOOL CAboutDlg::OnCtlColor (HDC HDc)
// processes WM_CTLCOLORDLG and WM_CTLCOLORSTATIC messages
   {
   // set text background to light gray:
   SetBkColor (HDc, RGB (192,192,192));

   // supply a handle to a light-gray brush:
   return (BOOL)GetStockObject (LTGRAY_BRUSH);
   }

BOOL CAboutDlg::OnInitDialog (void)
// processes WM_INITDIALOG messages
   {
   // return TRUE to set focus to first control:
   return TRUE;
   }

BOOL CAboutDlg::OnOK (HWND HDlg)
// processes WM_COMMAND / IDOK messages
   {
   // close the dialog box:
   EndDialog (HDlg, IDOK);
   return TRUE;
   }
```

The Flow of Program Control

Before the chapter goes into the programming details, this section provides an overview of the flow of control in the Template program and briefly explains the unique architecture of Windows applications.

When the program begins running, the first function to receive control is `WinMain` (rather than `main`, as in a standard C++ program written to run directly under a system such as MS-DOS or UNIX). `WinMain` is defined in Template.cpp, and it is passed four parameters:

```
int APIENTRY  WinMain
   (HINSTANCE  HInstCurrent,
    HINSTANCE  HInstPrevious,
    LPSTR      CmdLine,
    int        CmdShow)
```

`HInstCurrent` contains a handle to the current program instance (running a program creates a new program *instance*); as you will see, you need to pass this handle to certain API functions. `CmdLine` is a pointer to a NULL-terminated string containing the command line—if any—that was passed to the program when it was started (this string does *not* contain the program name, but contains only any flags, file names, or other text included on the command line that was used to run the program). The other two parameters are provided chiefly for compatibility with previous Windows versions: `HInstPrevious` formerly contained the handle of any previous program instance that was still running; in Windows 95, however, it is always set to 0. `CmdShow` contains a value indicating the initial state of the program window that was requested when the program was run (for example, if the program was run through a Windows 95 shortcut, the user may have requested that the window be initially minimized); in Windows 95, however, you do not need to save this value because you can simply pass an appropriate flag to the `ShowWindow` API function to set the window to the requested state, as explained later.

`WinMain` begins by saving the `HInstCurrent` and `CmdLine` parameters in the global application object, so that the parameter values will be available to other parts of the program:

```
// store program informaton in application object:
App.Initialize (HInstCurrent, CmdLine);
```

`WinMain` then proceeds to create the main program window in a two-part process that will be explained later in the chapter. So far, Template resembles a conventional non-Windows program; now, however, the `WinMain` function diverges radically from this model by entering a *message loop*, where control remains for the duration of the program:

```
// main message loop:
MSG Msg;
while (GetMessage (&Msg, NULL, NULL, NULL))
   {
   TranslateMessage (&Msg);
   DispatchMessage (&Msg);
   }
```

Beginning at this point in the program, Template performs all actions in response to a series of *messages*, rather than actively initiating a sequence of tasks as in a conventional procedural program. The remainder of this section will briefly explain this message-based program architecture, which is a central feature of Windows programs.

Whenever an important event occurs that affects the program window (for example, the window has just been created, it needs repainting, or it is about to be destroyed), Windows places a data structure known as a *message* in a queue that it maintains for the program; this queue can store several messages. Placing a message in the queue is known as *posting a message to the window*. When the program calls `GetMessage` at the beginning of the message loop, the first message is extracted from the message queue and the message data is assigned to the fields of the `MSG` structure that is passed to `GetMessage`. If the queue does not currently contain a message, `GetMessage` waits until a message is posted before it returns.

The call to `TranslateMessage` within the message loop generates messages that make it easier for the program to read character keys (that is, `WM_CHAR` messages). Although the call to `TranslateMessage` is not required in the Template program, it is included because it is a traditional part of a message loop and may be required in programs based upon Template.

When the program calls `DispatchMessage` at the end of the message loop, Windows calls the *window procedure* that is associated with the main window. The program specifies the address of the window procedure when it creates the window (as will be described later). In Template, the main window procedure is named `MainWndProc`, and it is defined in the MainWnd.cpp source file. Windows passes the message data (that is, the value of the first four fields of the `MSG` structure) to the window procedure, and the window procedure's job is to perform whatever tasks are required to handle the message.

The following is the basic structure of the `MainWndProc` window procedure:

```
LRESULT CALLBACK MainWndProc
    (HWND HWnd,        // handle of window
     UINT Msg,         // identifier of message
     WPARAM WParam,    // message-specific information
     LPARAM LParam)    // more message-specific information
    {
    switch (Msg)
      {
      case WM_COMMAND:
         // process WM_COMMAND message and return

      case WM_DESTROY:
         // process WM_DESTROY message and return

      case WM_PAINT:
         // process WM_PAINT message and return

      default:
         // default processing for all other messages:
         return DefWindowProc (HWnd, Msg, WParam, LParam);
      }
    }
```

The `Msg` parameter contains a value that identifies the type of message. The message that is posted when the window needs painting or repainting has the identifier `WM_PAINT`. A `WM_COMMAND` message is posted whenever the user chooses a menu command, and a `WM_DESTROY` message is posted whenever the window is about to be destroyed. `MainWndProc` tests `Msg` and branches to a routine to handle the particular message type. In typical fashion, `MainWndProc` provides custom processing for only a few of the many message types; for all other messages, it passes the message information to the `DefWindowProc` API function, which performs minimal default processing. To process the `WM_COMMAND`, `WM-DESTROY`, and `WM_PAINT` messages, `MainWndProc` calls appropriate member functions of the main window class; the processing of each of these messages is described later in the chapter.

When the window procedure returns, control returns from the call to `DispatchMessage` and the message loop in `WinMain` calls `GetMessage` again to obtain the next message. When the program is being terminated, the window receives a special message (`WM_QUIT`) that causes `GetMessage` to return 0 and the message loop to end. After the message loop ends, `WinMain` returns and the program terminates. Note that if `WinMain` encounters an error before it enters the message loop, it should return 0; in Template, `WinMain` returns 0 if either `CMainWnd::RegisterClass` or `CMainWnd::Create` encounters an error. After processing messages, `WinMain` should return the application-defined exit code, which will be described in the section "Terminating the Program."

Figure 1.5 illustrates the processes described in this section.

TIP

Because the window procedure processes messages one at a time, it should return *as quickly as possible* so that the program can handle any additional messages waiting in its queue. Otherwise, the program will respond slowly to the user's commands (remember that all keyboard and mouse actions are processed through messages). If the window procedure needs to perform a lengthy task such as drawing complex graphics, it should start a secondary *thread of execution* to perform this task and then should return. The primary thread can then continue to processes messages while the secondary thread completes the lengthy task. To start a new thread, you can call the API function `CreateThread`.

Creating the Program Window

Creating a window is a two-step process: First, `WinMain` calls the `RegisterClass` member function of the main window class,

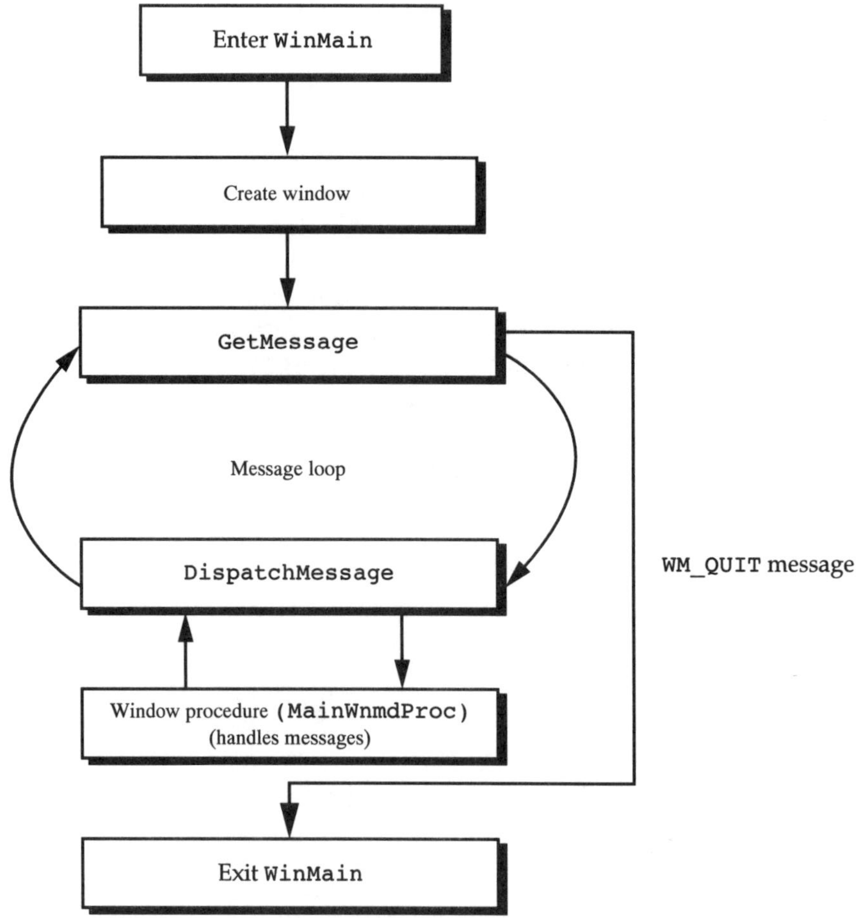

Figure 1.5:   The flow of control in the Template program. `WinMain` is the first function to receive control; when it returns, the program terminates.

```
// register class for main program window:
if (!MainWnd.RegisterClass ())
   return 0;
```

to register (that is, define) a *window class*. Second, it calls the `Create` member function of the main window class,

```
   // create and display main program window:
   if (!MainWnd.Create ())
      return 0;
```

to create the actual window. A window class is a general description of a window. Once the program has registered a window class, it can create one or more windows that belong to this class. Each window acquires all of the features of its window class plus any additional features that are specified when the window is created.

TIP　　Do not confuse a Windows *window class* with a C++ *class*. The Win32 API uses several object-oriented terms (notably, *class, instance,* and *object*), which have different meanings from those they have in the context of the C++ language. (The API was designed at a time when object-oriented concepts were becoming popular, but before C++ was used to write Windows programs. Accordingly, some of the terminology conflicts.)

CMAINWnd::RegisterClass　　CMainWnd::RegisterClass, which is defined in MainWnd.cpp, registers the window class by calling the RegisterClass API function:

```
BOOL CMainWnd::RegisterClass (void)
// registers class for main program window; returns TRUE on
// success or FALSE on error
   {
   WNDCLASS WC;

   // specify class information:
   WC.style = 0;
   WC.lpfnWndProc = MainWndProc;
   WC.cbClsExtra = 0;
   WC.cbWndExtra = 0;
   WC.hInstance = App.mHInstance;
   WC.hIcon = LoadIcon (App.mHInstance,
      MAKEINTRESOURCE (IDI_ICON1));
   WC.hCursor = LoadCursor (NULL, IDC_ARROW);
   WC.hbrBackground = (HBRUSH)GetStockObject (WHITE_BRUSH);
   WC.lpszMenuName = MAKEINTRESOURCE (IDR_MENU1);
   WC.lpszClassName = "DemoClass";

   // register class:
   return (BOOL)::RegisterClass (&WC);
   }
```

The values assigned to the WNDCLASS structure specify the general features of any window belonging to the class. The lpfnWndProc WNDCLASS field is assigned the address of the window procedure, MainWndProc (this is how

`DispatchMessage` knows which procedure to call when it dispatches a message). The `hInstance` field is assigned the program instance handle stored in the application object.

FYI

Because the window procedure is called by the Windows system—rather than by the C++ code in your program—it cannot be a member function of a C++ class. In Template, however, the `MainWndProc` window procedure calls member functions of the main window class to do all the work of processing messages.

`CMainWnd::RegisterClass` calls the API function `LoadIcon` to load the program icon, passing it the identifier that was assigned the icon when it was created in the icon editor (note that it first passes the icon identifier to the Win32 macro `MAKEINTRESOURCE`, which converts the integer identifier to the appropriate data type for the `LoadIcon` function). `LoadIcon` returns a handle to the icon, which is assigned to the `hIcon` `WNDCLASS` field. As a result, this icon is assigned to the main window (it is displayed in the title bar, in the Windows task bar, and in other locations).

`CMainWnd::RegisterClass` calls the API function `LoadCursor` to load the standard arrow mouse pointer (the API documentation uses the term *cursor* to refer to the mouse pointer). `LoadCursor` returns a handle to the pointer, which is assigned to the `hCursor` `WNDCLASS` field. Consequently, the mouse pointer will have the standard arrow shape whenever it is located within the *client area* of the window (the client area is the open portion of the window inside of the borders, as shown in Figure 1.1). If `hCursor` were assigned 0, the pointer would retain whatever shape it had immediately before entering the client area.

Likewise, `CMainWnd::RegisterClass` calls the `GetStockObject` API function to load a standard white brush and obtain a handle to this brush (brushes will be explained in Chapters 2 and 4). As a result of assigning the handle to the `hbrBackground` field, the window background will be erased with solid white whenever the window needs drawing or redrawing (if `hbrBackground` were assigned 0, the window would *not* be automatically erased).

The `lpszMenuName` field of the `WNDCLASS` structure is assigned the identifier that was specified for the menu when it was created in the menu editor (again, the identifier is first converted to the correct data type by the `MAKEINTRESOURCE` macro). Finally, a string containing a class name,

"DemoClass", is assigned to the `lpszClassName` field. This string is used to refer to the class when the main window is created.

CMainWnd::Create   CMainWnd::Create, also defined in MainWnd.cpp, creates the window by calling the `CreateWindow` API function:

```
BOOL CMainWnd::Create (void)
// creates and displays main program window; returns TRUE on
// success or FALSE on error
   {
   // create main program window and save handle:
   mHWnd = CreateWindow
     ("DemoClass",
      "Template",
      WS_OVERLAPPED | WS_SYSMENU | WS_MINIMIZEBOX,
      CW_USEDEFAULT,
      CW_USEDEFAULT,
      WINWIDTH,
      WINHEIGHT,
      NULL,
      NULL,
      App.mHInstance,
      NULL);
   if (!mHWnd)
      return FALSE;

   // display window:
   ShowWindow
     (mHWnd,
      SW_SHOWDEFAULT);

   return TRUE;
   }
```

The first parameter, "DemoClass", specifies the name of the window class. The resulting window will possess all of the general features that were specified when this class was registered. The second parameter, "Template", is the text that is to appear in the program's title bar.

The third parameter specifies the window *styles*. The WS_OVERLAPPED style causes the window to have a title bar and a border. The WS_SYSMENU style gives it a system menu (which is represented by a small version of the program icon), and WS_MINIMIZEBOX adds a minimize box. Note that because the styles do *not* include WS_THICKFRAME (or WS_OVERLAPPED-WINDOW, which incorporates WS_THICKFRAME), the window has only a thin border, which does not allow the user to change the size of the window. To simplify the programming logic, the example programs in this book display fixed-sized windows. The window parts are labeled in Figure 1.1.

`CreateWindow` returns a handle to the newly created window, which `CMainWnd::Create` saves in the mHWnd data member. The handle is saved because it must be passed to several API functions.

After creating the window, `CMainWnd::Create` calls the API function `ShowWindow`. Passing the value `SW_SHOWDEFAULT` causes `ShowWindow` to set the window to the state that was requested when the program was run. That is, the window will be initially minimized, maximized, or displayed in its normal size (the *normal* size is the size specified by the sixth and seventh parameters passed to `CreateWindow`).

Painting the Window

The main window receives a message with the `WM_PAINT` identifier whenever the window needs painting or repainting—for example, when the window is first created, when the user changes the size of the window, or when the user removes an overlapping window. To process the `WM_PAINT` message, the `MainWndProc` window procedure calls the `OnPaint` member function of the main window class:

```
switch (Msg)
   {
   // other case statements...

   case WM_PAINT: // window needs painting or repainting
      return MainWnd.OnPaint ();

   // other case statements...
   }
```

`OnPaint` processes the message as follows:

```
LRESULT CMainWnd::OnPaint (void)
// processes WM_PAINT messages
   {
   HDC HDCPaint;              // client area device-context handle
   PAINTSTRUCT PaintStruct;   // paint information
   RECT Rect;                 // dimensions of client area

   // initiate painting and obtain a device context:
   HDCPaint = BeginPaint (mHWnd, &PaintStruct);

   // get dimensions of client area of main window:
   GetClientRect (mHWnd, &Rect);

   // display text centered within client area:
   DrawText
      (HDCPaint,
      "Greetings...",
      -1,
```

```
    &Rect,
    DT_CENTER | DT_SINGLELINE | DT_VCENTER);

    // terminate painting and release device context:
    EndPaint (mHWnd, &PaintStruct);
    return NULL;
    }
```

Repainting the window starts with a call to `BeginPaint` and finishes with a call to `EndPaint`. `BeginPaint` erases the client area of the window using the white brush that was supplied to the `RegisterClass` API function when the window class was registered. The program now need only redraw the "Greetings . . . " text message that is displayed in the center of the window.

`BeginPaint` also returns a handle to a *device context* that allows the program to draw within the client area of the window. Under Windows, a program does not display text or graphics directly on a device; rather, it draws on an abstract surface known as a device context. Each device context is associated with a physical device, and drawing on the device context results in output appearing on the associated device. (Also, as you will see in Chapter 2, a device context stores a variety of settings that affect the output, such as the color of text and the width of lines.) When you call any text or graphics drawing function, you must pass it the handle of the device context on which you want to display the output. The device context returned by `DrawText` is associated with the screen—specifically, the portion of the screen within the client area of the main window.

To draw the text message, `OnPaint` first obtains the current dimensions of the client area of the window by calling the API function `GetClientRect`. It then displays the text—centered within the client area—by calling the `DrawText` API function.

Finally, `OnPaint` calls `EndPaint`, which releases the device context and terminates the paint job. `OnPaint` returns the value `NULL`; this return value is then returned by the `MainWndProc` window procedure. Usually, a window procedure returns `NULL` to indicate that it has processed the message (there are, however, some messages that require the window procedure to return a different value after processing the message; an example is the `WM_QUERYENDSESSION` message described in Chapter 8).

Processing the Menu Commands

Whenever the user chooses a menu command, the main window receives a `WM_COMMAND` message, with the low-order word of the `WParam` parameter set to the identifier of the command (that is, the identifier that was assigned to the command when the menu was designed in the menu editor; the constants for the identifiers, such as `ID_OPTIONS_ABOUT`, are defined in the resource header file, Resource.h). The routine in the `MainWndProc` window procedure that processes `WM_COMMAND` messages reads the command identifier (using the API macro `LOWORD`) and calls the appropriate member function of the main window class:

```
switch (Msg)
   {
   // other case statements...

   case WM_COMMAND: // user chose a menu command
      switch (LOWORD (WParam))
         {

         .case ID_OPTIONS_ABOUT: // user chose Options/About
            return MainWnd.OnOptionsAbout ();

         case ID_OPTIONS_EXIT:  // user chose Options/Exit
            return MainWnd.OnOptionsExit ();

         default:
            // default processing for other commands:
            return DefWindowProc (HWnd, Msg, WParam, LParam);
         }

  // other case statements...
   }
```

Displaying the Dialog Box

`CMainWnd::OnOptionsAbout` calls the `Show` member function of `CAboutDlg`, the program class that manages the About dialog box:

```
LRESULT CMainWnd::OnOptionsAbout (void)
// processes WMCOMMAND / ID   OPTIONS ABOUT messages
   {
   AboutDlg.Show (); // display About dialog box
   return NULL;
   }
```

`CAboutDlg::Show`, which is defined in AboutDlg.cpp, then displays the dialog box by calling the `DialogBox` API function:

```
int CAboutDlg::Show (void)
// displays About dialog box
   {
   return DialogBox
      (App.mHInstance,
      MAKEINTRESOURCE (IDD_ABOUT),
      MainWnd.mHWnd,
```

```
        DialogProc);
    }
```

The first parameter passed to `DialogBox` is the handle of the current program instance. The second parameter is the identifier (converted by `MAKEINTRESOURCE`) that was assigned to the dialog box when it was designed in the dialog editor, and the third parameter is the handle of the main program window, which becomes the *owner* of the dialog box. `DialogBox` displays the dialog box and waits until the user closes the dialog box before returning control. While the dialog box is displayed, the owning window (the main program window) is disabled; as a result, the user must dismiss the dialog box before choosing another menu command or manipulating the main program window with the mouse. This type of dialog box is termed *modal* (in contrast, while a *modeless* dialog box is displayed, the user can continue to work with the main program window).

FYI   Because the program's message loop never receives control while a modal dialog box is displayed, you may wonder how messages for the dialog box and other windows are extracted and dispatched during this time. To do this, the `DialogBox` API function provides an internal message loop that is active while the dialog box is displayed.

The fourth parameter is the address of the *dialog box procedure* for the dialog box. A dialog box is a type of window; just like the main program window, it receives messages while it is displayed. Accordingly, the program must define a procedure to process these messages. Such a procedure is known as a dialog box procedure and is defined slightly differently from a window procedure that processes messages sent to a main program window. The dialog box procedure for the About dialog box is defined in AboutDlg.cpp as follows:

```
BOOL CALLBACK DialogProc
    (HWND   HDlg,
    UINT    Msg,
    WPARAM WParam,
    LPARAM LParam)
    {
    switch (Msg)
        {
        case WM_INITDIALOG: // dialog box was just created
            return AboutDlg.OnInitDialog ();
```

```
    case WM_COMMAND:        // user issued a command
       switch (LOWORD (WParam))
          {
          case IDCANCEL: // user chose Close or pressed Esc
             return AboutDlg.OnCancel (HDlg);

          case IDOK:       // user clicked OK or pressed Enter
             return AboutDlg.OnOK (HDlg);

          default:
             return FALSE;  // default message processing
          }

    case WM_CTLCOLORDLG:     // dialog box about to be painted;
    case WM_CTLCOLORSTATIC: // text about to be painted
       return AboutDlg.OnCtlColor ((HDC)WParam);

    default:             // request default processing for all
       return FALSE; // other messages
    }
 }
```

The parameters passed to a dialog box procedure are the same as those
passed to a main window procedure (the first parameter, `HDlg`, is the window handle of the dialog box). The primary difference between a main window procedure and a dialog box procedure is the following: If the dialog box
procedure processes a message, it normally returns `TRUE`; if it does not
process a message, it normally returns `FALSE` to obtain default processing
(rather than calling `DefWindowProc`). `DialogProc` provides custom processing for several message types by calling the appropriate member function
of `CAboutDlg`; for all other message types, it simply returns `FALSE` to
request default processing. Note, however, that the first two messages that
will be discussed are exceptions to the general return-value convention.

When the dialog box is first displayed, it receives a `WM_INITDIALOG` message. The `CAboutDlg::OnInitDialog` function processes this message by
returning `TRUE`:

```
BOOL CAboutDlg::OnInitDialog (void)
// processes WMINITDIALOG messages
    {
    // return TRUE to set focus to first control:
    return TRUE;
    }
```

Returning `TRUE` causes Windows to set the *input focus* to the first control in
the dialog box that can receive the focus (for the About dialog box, this is the
OK push button; the control with the input focus is the one that receives messages when the user presses keys on the keyboard). A `WM_INITDIALOG` han-

dler should return FALSE if it has explicitly set the focus to a particular control (by calling the SetFocus API function).

When the dialog box is about to be painted, it receives a WM_CTLCOLORDLG message, and when its text control is about to be painted, it receives a WM_CTL-COLORSTATIC message. In either case, the DialogProc dialog box procedure calls the CAboutDlg member function OnCtlColor to handle the message:

```
BOOL CAboutDlg::OnCtlColor (HDC HDc)
// processes WM_CTLCOLORDLG and WM_CTLCOLORSTATIC messages
   {
   // set text background to light gray:
   SetBkColor (HDc, RGB (192,192,192));

   // supply a handle to a light-gray brush:
   return (BOOL)GetStockObject (LTGRAY_BRUSH);
   }
```

OnCtlColor is passed the handle of the device context that Windows will use to draw the text or the dialog box background. OnCtlColor first calls the SetBkColor API function to set the text background color to light gray. It then returns a handle to a light-gray brush. Windows will use the text background color if it is drawing text, and it will use the light-gray brush if it is painting the dialog box background. As a result, the dialog box will have an aesthetically pleasing light-gray background rather than the default white. (The background color and brushes will be discussed in the following chapters.) Figure 1.6 shows the dialog box as it is displayed by the program.

If the user clicks the OK button or presses Enter, the dialog box receives a WM_COMMAND message with WParam set to the identifier of the OK button, IDOK. In this case, DialogProc calls CAboutDlg::OnOK:

Figure 1.6:   The About dialog box as it appears when displayed at run time

```
BOOL CAboutDlg::OnOK (HWND HDlg)
// processes WM_COMMAND / IDOK messages
   {
   // close the dialog box:
   EndDialog (HDlg, IDOK);
   return TRUE;
   }
```

OnOK calls the API function EndDialog to cause Windows to close the dialog box. The second parameter passed to EndDialog is the value that will be returned to the program by the DialogBox API function after the dialog box is closed; this parameter allows the dialog box procedure to indicate the *way* that the dialog box was closed (OnOK passes the value IDOK to indicate that the user closed the dialog box by clicking the OK button, although the Template program does not actually test the value returned by DialogBox).

If the user clicks the Close button on the dialog box, chooses the Close command on the dialog box's system menu, or presses Esc, the dialog box receives a WM_COMMAND message with WParam set to the value IDCANCEL. In this case, DialogProc calls CAboutDlg::OnCancel:

```
BOOL CAboutDlg::OnCancel (HWND HDlg)
// processes WM_COMMAND / IDCANCEL messages
   {
   // close the dialog box:
   EndDialog (HDlg, IDCANCEL);
   return TRUE;
   }
```

OnCancel also calls EndDialog to close the dialog box, but passes the value IDCANCEL as the second parameter. (If a dialog box contains a Cancel button, it is normally given the identifier IDCANCEL. Clicking the Cancel button thus activates the same routine as does clicking the Close box or choosing the Close system menu command.)

Terminating the Program

When the user clicks the Close box on the Template program window or chooses the Close command on the system menu, the main window receives a WM_CLOSE message. The window procedure, MainWndProc, does *not* provide custom processing for this message; rather, it simply passes it on to the DefWindowProc API function for default processing. DefWindowProc handles the message by calling the API function DestroyWindow to destroy the program window.

When the user chooses the Exit menu command, the main window is sent a WM_COMMAND message with WParam equal to IDM_EXIT (the Exit command

TIP

If you want to warn the user before destroying the program window (and thereby terminating the program), you can provide a routine for processing for the `WM_CLOSE` message. Your routine could call `DestroyWindow` only if the user chooses to proceed with the program termination. For an example, see the `CMainWnd::OnClose` function in the MainWnd.cpp source file of DrawIt version 5, presented in Chapter 8.

identifier). In response, `MainWndProc` calls `CMainWnd::OnOptionsExit`:

```
LRESULT CMainWnd::OnOptionsExit (void)
// processes WM_COMMAND / ID_OPTIONS_EXIT messages
   {
   DestroyWindow (mHWnd);    // destroy main window
   return NULL;
   }
```

`OnOptionsExit` explicitly calls `DestroyWindow` to destroy the main window.

When the window is being destroyed by `DestroyWindow`, it receives a `WM_DESTROY` message; `MainWndProc` calls `CMainWnd::OnDestroy` to handle this message:

```
LRESULT CMainWnd::OnDestroy (void)
// processes WM_DESTROY messages
   {
   PostQuitMessage (0);   // post a WM_QUIT message to
   return NULL;           // cause message loop to exit
   }
```

`OnDestroy` calls the API function `PostQuitMessage`, which posts a `WM_QUIT` message to the main program window. When the `GetMessage` function in the message loop extracts this message, it returns `FALSE`, which causes the message loop to exit and the program to terminate (note that when `GetMessage` extracts any other message, it returns `TRUE`). The value passed to `PostQuitMessage` is copied to the `wParam` field of the `MSG` structure placed in the queue; the `WinMain` function then returns this value:

```
while (GetMessage (&Msg, NULL, NULL, NULL))
   {
   TranslateMessage (&Msg);
   DispatchMessage (&Msg);
   }
return Msg.wParam;
```

<table>
<tr><td>WARNING</td><td>If you fail to provide a <code>WM_DESTROY</code> message handler that calls <code>PostQuitMessage</code>, the main program window will be destroyed but the program will continue running, invisibly consuming Windows resources.</td></tr>
</table>

The value that `WinMain` returns to the system is known as the *application-defined exit code*. Under Windows, the exit code normally has little value. If, however, you are running the program in a debugger (such as the Microsoft Visual C++ integrated debugger), the exit code will be displayed immediately after the program terminates. You might find some diagnostic use for this feature

<table>
<tr><td>TIP</td><td>The function that processes the <code>WM_DESTROY</code> routine can perform any additional required cleanup tasks. Note, however, that by the time the <code>WM_DESTROY</code> message is received it is too late to prevent destruction of the window (and termination of the application). If you want to be able to resume the program after the user chooses an exit command, you should provide a <code>WM_CLOSE</code> message-handling routine, as mentioned previously.</td></tr>
</table>

CHAPTER 2

DRAWING GRAPHICS IN WINDOWS 95

This chapter provides an overview of the six basic steps required to display graphics in a Windows 95 program. The chapter begins with a list of these steps and an example drawing routine that illustrates them. It then introduces the basic elements involved in displaying graphics: device contexts, drawing attributes, graphic objects, and drawing functions. The following chapters will provide much more information on these topics.

THE SIX BASIC STEPS

The following are the six basic steps for drawing graphics in a Windows 95 program (see Figure 2.1):

1. Obtain a device context.
2. Set drawing attributes.
3. Create and select graphic objects.
4. Call drawing functions.
5. Deselect and destroy graphic objects.
6. Release the device context.

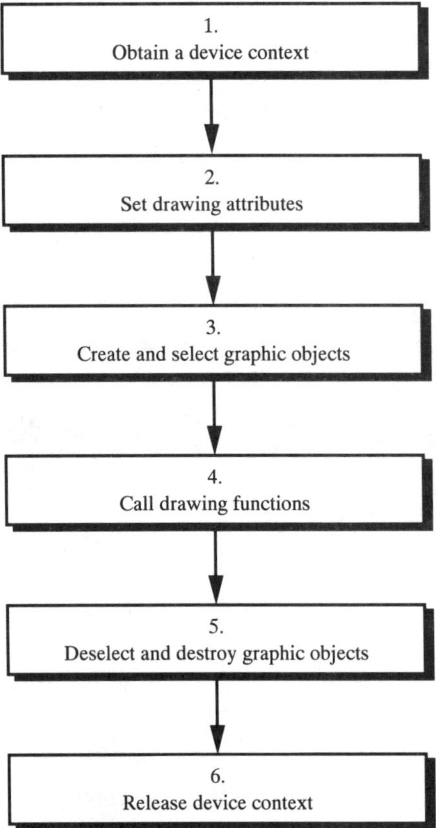

Figure 2.1:   The six basic steps for drawing graphics in Windows 95

In step 1, you obtain a handle to a Windows device context, which is the entity that receives all graphics output and routes it to a physical output device. In step 2, you set attributes such as the mapping mode (the units used by drawing functions) and the mix mode (the way graphics output is combined with the current colors on the display surface). In step 3, you create and select any required *graphic objects*—usually a pen and a brush, which affect the color and pattern used to draw lines and fill closed figures (the word *object* in the expression *graphic object* refers to a Windows data structure, *not* a C++ object). In step 4, you generate the actual graphics output by calling graphics API functions, such as `LineTo` and `Ellipse`. When you call an API drawing function, you pass it the handle of the device context you created in step 1; the figure is drawn with the attributes and graphic objects you selected in steps 2 and 3 (the attributes and graphic objects are stored in the device context). After you have finished drawing the graphics, you relinquish the graphic objects in step 5 and the device context in step 6.

An Example

The following function illustrates the six basic steps for drawing graphics. It is the same as the `OnPaint` function of the Template program presented in Chapter 1 (defined in MainWnd.cpp), except that rather than drawing a text message, it draws a rectangle with a blue, 3-pixel-wide border, which is filled with red hatch lines on a yellow background (see Figure 2.2). This function is designed to paint or repaint the program window in response to `WM_PAINT` messages (as you will see, the method for obtaining and releasing the device context depends upon whether or not you are drawing in response to a `WM_PAINT` message).

```
LRESULT CMainWnd::OnPaint (void)
// processes WM_PAINT messages
    {
    //////////////////////////////////////////
    // (1) Obtain a device context:          //
    //////////////////////////////////////////

PAINTSTRUCT PaintStruct;   // stores paint information
HDC HDCPaint = BeginPaint (mHWnd, &PaintStruct);

    //////////////////////////////////////////
    // (2) Set drawing attributes:           //
    //////////////////////////////////////////

    // set background color:
    SetBkColor (HDCPaint, RGB (255,255,0));
```

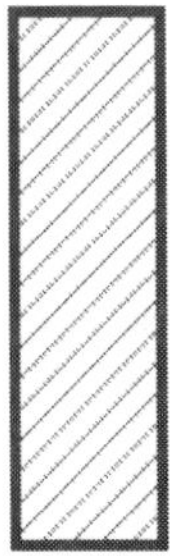

Figure 2.2:   The figure drawn by the example drawing routine

```cpp
/////////////////////////////////////////////
// (3) Create and select graphic objects:    //
/////////////////////////////////////////////

// store pen color in LOGBRUSH structure:
LOGBRUSH LB = {BS_SOLID, RGB (0,0,255), 0};

// create pen:
HPEN HPen = ExtCreatePen
   (PS_GEOMETRIC | PS_SOLID,   // pen style
    3,                         // pen width
    &LB,                       // pen color
    0, 0);                     // not used

// select pen (and save handle to old pen):
HPEN HPenOld = (HPEN)SelectObject (HDCPaint, HPen);

// store brush features in LOGBRUSH structure:
LB.lbStyle = BS_HATCHED;
LB.lbColor = RGB (255,0,0);
LB.lbHatch = HS_BDIAGONAL;

// create brush:
HBRUSH HBrush = CreateBrushIndirect (&LB);
// select brush (and save handle to old brush):
HBRUSH HBrushOld = (HBRUSH)SelectObject (HDCPaint, HBrush);

/////////////////////////////////////////////
// (4) Call drawing functions:               //
/////////////////////////////////////////////

// draw a filled rectangle:
Rectangle (HDCPaint, 35, 35, 75, 175);

/////////////////////////////////////////////
// (5) Deselect and destroy graphic objects: //
/////////////////////////////////////////////

// deselect pen:
SelectObject (HDCPaint, HPenOld);
// destroy pen:
DeleteObject (HPen);

// deselect brush:
SelectObject (HDCPaint, HBrushOld);
// destroy brush:
DeleteObject (HBrush);

/////////////////////////////////////////////
// (6) Release device context:               //
/////////////////////////////////////////////

EndPaint (mHWnd, &PaintStruct);

return NULL;
}
```

The techniques used in this function will be explained in detail in the remainder of the chapter, as well as in the following chapters.

THE DEVICE CONTEXT

This section explains steps 1 and 6 of the drawing process: obtaining and releasing the device context. When you call an API drawing function, such as `Ellipse`, you do *not* specify a physical output device; rather, you pass the function a handle to a *device context*. A device context is a data structure managed by Windows that is *associated with* a physical output device, such as a video display or a printer. When you pass a given device context to a graphics function, the output appears on the associated device.

In addition to maintaining an association with a physical device, a device context also stores a set of drawing attributes and graphic objects (which you can modify, if necessary, in drawing steps 2 and 3). When you pass a particular device context to a drawing function, the function automatically uses the attributes and graphic objects currently assigned to the device context.

Thus, rather than having to specify an output device, a drawing mode, a color, a pattern, and other features each time you call a graphics function, you store all these features in a device context and then simply pass the device context handle to a single drawing function or to an entire set of drawing functions.

Display Device Contexts

To draw graphics or text within a window, a program must obtain a device context that is associated with the appropriate portion of the video display. As explained in Chapter 1, whenever a program window needs painting or repainting, it receives a `WM_PAINT` message. If a program is currently processing a `WM_PAINT` message, it must obtain a device context by calling the `BeginPaint` API function and—when it has completed drawing in the window—it must release this device context by calling the `EndPaint` API function:

```
PAINTSTRUCT PaintStruct;
HDC HDCPaint = BeginPaint (HWnd, &PaintStruct);

// draw in client area of window...

EndPaint (HWnd, &PaintStruct);
```

`HWnd` is the handle of the window that has received the `WM_PAINT` message, and `PaintStruct` is a `PAINTSTRUCT` structure that `BeginPaint` fills with information on the device context (more on this structure shortly). The device context supplied by `BeginPaint` allows the program to draw graphics or text within the client area of the window; if the program attempts to draw outside of the current client area, the output is *clipped* (that is, it is simply discarded with no harm done).

When it is *not* processing a `WM_PAINT` message, the program can obtain a device context by calling the `GetDC` API function. It must release such a device context by calling `ReleaseDC`:

```
HDC HDCClient = GetDC (HWnd);

// draw in client area of window...

ReleaseDC (HWnd, HDCClient);
```

`HWnd` is the handle of the window in which the program wants to draw. The device context supplied by `GetDC`—like that supplied by `BeginPaint`—allows the program to draw within the client area of the window.

TIP
You can call the `GetWindowDC` API function to obtain a *window device context*, which allows you to draw *anywhere* within a window, including the portions outside of the client area. Drawing outside of the client area, however, is seldom required because Windows takes care of drawing all of the window features in the non-client area.

There is an important difference between a device context supplied by `GetDC` and one supplied by `BeginPaint` that has to do with the `WM_PAINT` message mechanism: With a device context from `GetDC`, the program can freely draw at *any* position within the client area that is currently visible. However, with a device context from `BeginPaint`, the program can draw *only within* the portion of the window that requires repainting; all other output is clipped. The following summary of the `WM_PAINT` mechanism explains how this clipping comes about:

1. An event occurs that makes it necessary to paint or repaint all or part of the window. For example, the window has just been created, the user enlarges the window, or the user removes an overlapping window.

2. Windows adds the portion of the window that requires painting to the current Windows *update region*. The update region—which is not necessarily rectangular—consists of all portions of the client area that currently need repainting. Adding a portion of the client area to the update region is known as *invalidating* that area.

3. Whenever the update region is nonempty, and the program has no other pending messages, the window receives a `WM_PAINT` message.

4. The program's `WM_PAINT` routine calls `BeginPaint`, which sets the *clipping region* of the device context equal to the current update region. The clipping region represents the only portion of the client area in which the program can draw; that is, all output that falls *outside* of the clipping region is discarded. (In contrast, a device context supplied by `GetDC` does not have a clipping region; you can therefore display graphics on any visible part of the display surface.) See Chapter 5 for more information on regions and clipping. `BeginPaint` also resets the update region to empty (to prevent further `WM_PAINT` messages from being generated).

The `rcPaint` field of the `PAINTSTRUCT` structure supplied by `BeginPaint` is a `RECT` structure containing the dimensions of the clipping region (technically, `rcPaint` contains the dimensions of the smallest rectangle *bounding* the clipping region, which is not necessarily rectangular). A program can use these dimensions to avoid wasting time attempting to draw outside of the clipping region.

TIP

A program can call the `RectVisible` or `PtVisible` API function to avoid drawing outside of the clipping region. For an example, see the `CMainWnd::OnDraw` function in the MainWnd.cpp file of the DrawIt version 1 program, presented at the end of Chapter 3.

Also, the `BeginPaint` function usually *erases* the clipping region (the former update region). To do this, it uses the brush that was specified when the window class was registered (that is, the brush assigned to the `hbrBackground` field of the `WNDCLASS` structure passed to `RegisterClass`). For example, the Template program given in Chapter 1 assigned a white brush to create a white window background. If no brush was assigned, `BeginPaint` will *not* erase the region.

FYI

`BeginPaint` also hides the current caret—if any—that marks the insertion point within text, and `EndPaint` restores the caret. This allows a program to draw within the window without corrupting the caret area. (The example programs in this book do not display a caret.)

Changing the Contents of the Client Area   The WM_PAINT mechanism works well for generating the initial window display and for "repairing" a static window display whenever an external event erases any part of it. A program, however, may need to change its window display—for example, when the user of a word-processing program types a character or opens a new file. In this case, the program must actively initiate drawing in the client area. There are two general ways it can do this. First, it can simply obtain a client-area device context by calling GetDC and then use this device context to redraw the affected area.

Second, the program can *invalidate* the affected area of the window by calling the InvalidateRect API function:

```
BOOL InvalidateRect (HWND hwnd, CONST RECT *lprc, BOOL fErase);
```

The lprc parameter contains the coordinates of the portion of the client area that is to be invalidated (if you pass NULL, the entire client area is invalidated). You must be sure to include the entire portion of the client area that needs changing, because the program will not be able to draw outside of the specified area. If you assign TRUE to fErase, the invalidated area will be erased (as explained in the previous section). Calling InvalidateRect causes the window to receive a WM_PAINT message; the WM_PAINT routine can then redraw the changed area (this routine presumably has access to the updated data that needs to be displayed). When you call InvalidateRect, the WM_PAINT mechanism proceeds exactly as listed in the previous section, except that in step 2 the program actively invalidates a portion (or all) of its own client area rather than Windows performing this task in response to an external event.

TIP   To invalidate a nonrectangular area, you can call the InvalidateRgn API function.

Using GetDC is ideal for efficiently making small changes to the window contents (for example, adding a new character to the window text) because it avoids the overhead of invoking the entire WM_PAINT mechanism. However, for making substantial changes (for example, displaying a newly opened document), invalidating the window is generally best because it allows you to consolidate the window-painting code within a single routine. The DrawIt program, presented in the following chapters, illustrates both methods.

TIP

After calling `InvalidateRect`, the window will not receive a `WM_PAINT` message until all other pending messages have been processed. If it is important to update the window immediately, you can call the `UpdateWindow` API function *after* calling `InvalidateRect`. `UpdateWindow` directly calls the window procedure, passing it a `WM_PAINT` message and entirely bypassing the message queue (this process is known as *sending* a message rather than *posting* it).

Alternatively, you can call the `RedrawWindow` API function to both invalidate *and* immediately send a `WM_PAINT` message. This function has many options, but is a bit more complex than required for most purposes.

Common and Private Display Device Contexts   The Template program—as well as the other example programs in this book—uses what is known as a *common* device context for drawing in its window. Windows maintains a number of common device contexts in an internal cache. Whenever a program calls `BeginPaint` or `GetDC`, Windows initializes one of these device contexts so that it has a default set of drawing attributes and graphic objects, and then returns its handle. Each time a program obtains a handle to a common device context, it must select all desired nondefault drawing attributes and graphic objects (drawing steps 2 and 3). When the program releases the common device context by calling `EndPaint` or `ReleaseDC`, the device context becomes available to other programs. A program should always release a common device context as soon as it is done using it because such device contexts are shared by other programs and their number is limited.

Alternatively, a program can obtain a *private* display device context, which is *not* shared by other programs. To use a private device context for drawing in a particular window, the program must specify the `CS_OWNDC` class style when it registers the window's class (see the section "Creating the Program Window" in Chapter 1), as in the following example:

```
WNDCLASS WC;

WC.style = CS_OWNDC;

// assign other WNDCLASS fields...

RegisterClass (&WC);
```

When the program creates a window that belongs to a class with the `CS_OWNDC` style, a private device context is automatically created and initialized with a default set of drawing attributes and graphic objects. When the window is destroyed, the private device context is automatically released. Whenever the program calls `GetDC` or `BeginPaint`, Windows returns a handle to the private device context (the returned handle value is always the same), and calling `ReleaseDC` has no effect. Note, however, that even if the display device context is private, the program must still call both `BeginPaint` and `EndPaint` when it handles a `WM_PAINT` message, because these functions perform important tasks *in addition* to obtaining and releasing a device context.

The most important feature of a private device context is that once the program has obtained a handle to it and has set all desired nondefault drawing attributes and graphic objects, these attributes and objects are *retained* until the program explicitly changes them.

TIP

With a private device context, rather than performing drawing steps 1 through 6 each time it needs to draw, a program can perform steps 1, 2, and 3 only *once,* after the window is first created (it can store the device context handle in a global variable). Then, each time it draws, it needs to perform only step 4 (in addition to calling `BeginPaint` and `EndPaint` in a `WM_PAINT` routine). It should not perform step 5 until it has finished using its graphic objects, and it does not need to perform step 6 (Windows automatically releases a private device context when the window is destroyed).

Although creating a private device context consumes more system resources than using a common one, a private device context is well suited for a program that draws frequently. It eliminates the overhead of repeatedly obtaining and releasing the device context and setting its attributes and graphic objects.

FYI

Windows provides a third type of device context known as a *class* device context, which is created by specifying the `CS_CLASSDC` class style. This type of device context, however, is provided only for compatibility with previous Windows versions. The Microsoft documentation advises against using it for a Windows 95 program.

Other Types of Device Contexts

This section briefly discusses the API functions for obtaining and releasing device contexts that are associated with devices other than the video display.

To obtain a device context associated with a printer, plotter, or other output device, you can call the `CreateDC` API function (to specify a particular printer) or you can call the `PrintDlg` API function (to allow the user to choose the printer and print settings in the standard Print dialog box). Alternatively, you can call the `CreateIC` function to quickly obtain a device context associated with a printer or other device that allows you to efficiently obtain *information* on the device but *not* to generate output. To release the device context obtained by any of these means, you call `DeleteDC`. Using these functions is the topic of Chapter 7.

You can call the `CreateEnhMetaFile` API function to obtain a *metafile* device context. In this case, the associated "device" is a Windows enhanced metafile, which stores a drawing in memory or in a disk file by recording the commands that are used to generate the drawing. Enhanced metafiles are discussed in Chapter 8.

Finally, you can call `CreateCompatibleDC` to obtain a *memory* device context. In this case, the associated "device" is a Windows *bitmap*, which stores a drawing by saving the color of each of the pixels that generate the drawing on a raster device. Memory device contexts and bitmaps are not discussed in this book.

Regardless of the type of device context you have obtained, the way that you *use* the device context is consistent. That is, for any type of device context, you use a common method for setting drawing attributes and selecting graphic objects; and when you call a drawing function, the output appears on the device that is associated with the device context (provided that the device supports the particular graphics operation). This device independence is illustrated in the final version of the DrawIt program (presented in Chapter 8). DrawIt defines a *single* function for drawing a specific type of figure. When the program passes this function a display device context, the figure appears in the program window; when it passes it a printer device context, the figure appears on a printed page; and when it passes it a metafile device context, the figure is stored in a metafile on disk.

DRAWING ATTRIBUTES

This section explains step 2 of the Windows 95 drawing process: setting drawing attributes. The drawing attributes affect the way that graphics are drawn. When you first obtain a device context, it has a default set of drawing attributes. If you want to *change* any of the default attributes, you must call the appropriate API function. For example, in a new device context, the default *background color* (that is, the color used for filling the gaps in nonsolid lines and hatched fill patterns) is white. To change the background color, you must call the `SetBkColor` API function. The API drawing functions that are subsequently called will use the newly specified color.

For example, the following code changes the background color to red:

```
SetBkColor (HDc, RGB (255,0,0));
```

In this example, `HDc` is the device context handle that was obtained in step 1 of the drawing process. (The `RGB` macro, used to specify the color, will be discussed in Chapter 3.)

Table 2.1 summarizes the drawing attributes that are discussed in this book. Each attribute will be discussed when the book first presents an API drawing function that is affected by the attribute.

GRAPHIC OBJECTS

This section introduces steps 3 and 5 in the drawing process: creating and selecting Windows graphic objects, and then deselecting and destroying them when the program is done using them. The most common types of graphic objects that you create and select before calling drawing functions are *pens* and *brushes*. The current pen affects the style, color, and width of straight and curved lines as well as the borders of closed figures (such as rectangles and ellipses). The current brush affects the pattern and color used to fill closed figures.

FYI   The types of Windows graphic objects other than pens and brushes are bitmaps, palettes, fonts, paths, and regions. Paths and regions are discussed in Chapter 5. The other types are not discussed in this book.

A newly supplied device context has a default pen, brush, and other graphic objects. The default pen results in solid, black lines that are one pixel wide. The default brush fills the interior of closed figures with solid white.

Table 2.1: Windows 95 drawing attributes

Attribute	Default Value	Function Used to Set [Get]	Chapter(s) where Discussed	Effect of Attribute
Arc direction	`AD_COUNTER CLOCKWISE`	`SetArcDirection` `[GetArcDirection]`	3, 4	Determines the direction in which Windows draws arcs, chords, and pies
Background color	White	`SetBkColor` `[GetBkColor]`	3, 4	Sets the color used to fill the spaces within text, lines drawn with nonsolid pens, or areas filled with hatched brushes
Background mode	`OPAQUE` (spaces are filled)	`SetBkMode` `[GetBkMode]`	3, 4	Determines whether drawing functions paint the spaces within text, nonsolid lines, or hatched areas, using the current background color
Brush origin	Upper-left corner of client area	`SetBrushOrgEx` `[GetBrushOrgEx]`	4	Sets the origin of hatched or patterned brushes
Current position	0, 0	`MoveToEx (also LineTo, PolylineTo, and PolyBezierTo) [GetCurrentPositionEx]`	3	Sets the starting coordinate of the next line drawn with `LineTo`, `PolyLineTo`, and `PolyBezierTo`
Mapping mode	`MM_TEXT`	`SetMapMode` `[GetMapMode]`	6	Affects the units, as well as the directions, of increasing coordinate values, used to specify the size or position of graphics

Table 2.1: (Continued)

Attribute	Default Value	Function Used to Set [Get]	Chapter(s) where Discussed	Effect of Attribute
Mix mode	`R2_COPYPEN`	`SetROP2` `[GetRop2]`	3,4	Determines the way Windows combines pen and brush colors with the existing display colors when drawing lines or filling closed figures
Polygon filling mode	`ALTERNATE`	`SetPolyFillMode` `[GetPolyFillMode]`	4	Affects the way polygons are filled by the `Polygon` and `PolyPolygon` functions
Viewport extents	1, 1	`SetViewportExtEx` `[GetViewportExtEx]`	6	Specifies mapping of device units in `MM_ISOTROPIC` and `MM_ANISOTROPIC` mapping modes
Viewport origin	0, 0	`SetViewportOrgEx` `[GetViewportOrgEx]`	6	Specifies the coordinate system origin in device space
Window extents	1, 1	`SetWindowExtEx` `[GetWindowExtEx]`	6	Specifies mapping of logical units in `MM_ISOTROPIC` and `MM_ANISOTROPIC` mapping modes
Window origin	0, 0	`SetWindowOrgEx` `[GetWindowOrgEx]`	6	Specifies the coordinate system origin in page space

TIP

Although Windows 95 automatically deletes any undeleted graphic objects when the program exits (unlike previous Windows versions), your program should explicitly delete graphic objects as soon as it is done using them, because each extant object consumes space in a local Windows heap that has a limited size.

If you want to use a different pen or brush, you must first either obtain a stock pen or brush or create a custom pen or brush. You then need to call the `SelectObject` API function to select the pen or brush into the device context (these operations constitute step 3 of the drawing process). When you are done drawing, you need to call `SelectObject` again to deselect any custom pen or brush and then call `DeleteObject` to destroy it (drawing step 5). Pens will be fully explained in Chapter 3 and brushes in Chapter 4.

TIP

If you use a particular graphic object frequently, rather than creating and destroying it each time you call drawing functions, you can create it once at the beginning of the program, store its handle in a global variable, and then simply select it each time you obtain a device context (for a private display device context, you need to select it only once). You can then delete the object when the program is done using it. However, keep the previous tip in mind and avoid holding a large number of graphic objects at a given time.

DRAWING FUNCTIONS

Step 4 of the drawing procedure is to call API graphics functions to produce the actual graphics output. Chapter 3 discusses the functions for drawing straight and curved lines, Chapter 4 explains the functions for drawing closed figures such as rectangles and ellipses, and Chapter 6 presents the functions for manipulating specific areas on the display surface (regions and paths).

Note that if your program displays text, you would also call appropriate text-drawing functions during step 4 (such as `DrawText`, which was used in the Template program given in Chapter 1).

DRAWING STRAIGHT LINES AND CURVES

In this chapter, you will learn how to draw lines—both straight (single straight lines or sets of connected straight lines) and curved (arcs or free-form curves). The chapter begins by explaining how to set the drawing attributes that affect the drawing of lines. It then shows how to obtain and select a pen to modify the way that Windows draws lines. Next, it describes the API line-drawing functions. Finally, it presents the first version of the DrawIt vector drawing program, which illustrates the programming techniques given in the chapter and allows you to experiment with the line-drawing features of Windows 95.

SETTING LINE-DRAWING ATTRIBUTES

As explained in Chapter 2, the first step in drawing graphics is to obtain a device context. A newly supplied device has a default set of drawing attributes. The second step is to modify one or more of these attributes, if necessary. The modified attributes will affect all drawing functions that you subsequently call. The following are the attributes that affect the drawing of lines:

- Mix mode
- Background mode
- Background color
- Mapping mode
- Viewport and window origins
- Current position
- Arc direction

Setting the Mix Mode

The *mix mode* determines the way that Windows combines the color of the pen with the current colors on the display surface to generate the colors of the lines that are drawn.

FYI

The mix mode *also* determines the way that Windows combines the color of the brush with the current colors on the display surface to paint the inside of closed figures. Brushes and closed figures are discussed in Chapter 4.

You set the mix mode by calling the API function `SetRop2`,

```
int SetROP2 (HDC hdc, int fnDrawMode);
```

where `hdc` is the handle of the device context and `fnDrawMode` is a code for the mix mode. There are 16 possible mix-mode codes; Table 3.1 lists some of the more common ones (see the documentation on `SetROP2` for a complete list).

With the default mix mode, `R2_COPYPEN`, Windows simply copies the pen color to the display. For example, if the pen is blue, a line will be blue regard-

Table 3.1: Common mix modes

Mix-mode Code Passed to `SetROP2`	*Resulting Color of Lines and Interiors of Closed Figures*
`R2_COPYPEN` (the default)	Color is the same as pen color
`R2_NOT`	Color is the inverse of display color
`R2_NOTCOPYPEN`	Color is the inverse of pen color
`R2_BLACK`	Color is black
`R2_WHITE`	Color is white
`R2_NOT`	Color is the same as display color (nothing is drawn)

less of the current colors on the display surface over which the line is drawn.

With the R2_NOT mix mode, Windows draws lines by *inverting* the current colors on the display (the pen color has no effect). This mode has two advantages:

1. A line will be visible when drawn over almost any background color.
2. You can easily erase a line by simply drawing it a second time (the display colors are inverted back to their original colors).

The DrawIt program, presented at the end of the chapter, uses the R2_NOT mode to draw temporary lines (see the CFigure::GetTempDC function in Figure.cpp). You might also use this mode to generate animation.

FYI

The effect of inverting a color depends upon the video hardware and video mode. Usually, however, inverting a color generates its complementary color. For example, black becomes white, red becomes cyan, green becomes magenta, and blue becomes yellow. Likewise, white becomes black, cyan becomes red, magenta becomes green, and yellow becomes blue. The intensity of the color may also change; for example, *light* blue becomes *dark* yellow.

If you call the API function GetROP2,

```
int GetROP2 (HDC hdc);
```

it will return the current mix-mode code for the specified device context.

You can use the DrawIt program to experiment with any of the 16 different mix modes (choose the Default Attributes... command on the Options menu). DrawIt calls GetROP2 in the CFigure::Draw function of Figure.cpp.

Setting the Background Mode and Color

As you will learn later in the chapter, you can select a pen that draws dotted or dashed lines. The *background mode* controls the way that Windows paints the spaces *between* the dots or dashes. You set the background mode by calling the SetBkMode API function,

```
int SetBkMode (HDC hdc, int iBkMode);
```

where hdc is the handle of the device context and iBkMode is a code for the desired background mode. If you assign iBkMode the value TRANSPARENT, Windows will *not* paint the spaces between dots or dashes. Rather, it will leave the existing display colors in the spaces unaltered (regardless of the current mix mode).

If you assign the value OPAQUE (which is the default), Windows will paint the spaces using the current *background color*.

FYI

In the OPAQUE background mode, Windows paints the spaces within dotted or dashed lines by combining the background color with the current colors on the display surface, using the mix mode that is in effect. For example, with the default R2_COPYPEN mix mode, Windows simply copies the background color to the space areas, and in the R2_NOT mix mode, it inverts the existing display colors (ignoring the background color).

The default background color is white. You can set the background color by calling the SetBkColor API function,

```
COLORREF SetBkColor (HDC hdc, COLORREF crColor);
```

where hdc is the handle of the device context and crColor is the value of the desired background color. The easiest way to assign a color value to crColor (or to any parameter of type COLORREF) is to use the API macro RGB,

```
COLORREF RGB (BYTE bRed, BYTE bGreen, BYTE bBlue);
```

where bRed, bGreen, and bBlue are the relative intensities of the red, green, and blue components of the desired color. You can assign each parameter a value between 0 and 255. For example, the following call would create a bright red background color:

```
SetBkColor (HDc, RGB (255,0,0));
```

Table 3.2 lists the RGB values corresponding to each of the standard colors available under 16-color video modes.

FYI

The background mode and background color also affect the way that Windows paints the spaces between the hatch lines when it fills closed figures using a hatched brush. Brushes and closed figures are discussed in Chapter 4.

Table 3.2:   The red, green, and blue components of the standard colors available under 16-color video modes

Color	RGB *Values*
Dark red	(128, 0, 0)
Light red	(255, 0, 0)
Dark green	(0, 128, 0)
Light green	(0, 255, 0)
Dark blue	(0, 0, 128)
Light blue	(0, 0, 255)
Dark yellow	(128, 128, 0)
Light yellow	(255, 255, 0)
Dark cyan	(0, 128, 128)
Light cyan	(0, 255, 255)
Dark magenta	(128, 0, 128)
Light magenta	(255, 0, 255)
Black	(0, 0, 0)
Dark gray	(128, 128, 128)
Light gray	(192, 192, 192)
White	(255, 255, 255)

Note that Windows always uses a *pure* color for the background color. A pure color is one that is generated directly by the video hardware (the colors in Table 3.2 are the pure colors available in 16-color video modes). The opposite of a pure color is a *dithered* color, which is a simulated color generated in software by combining different-colored pixels in a uniform pattern. If you choose a background color that does not correspond to one of the available pure colors, Windows will use the closest pure color.

TIP

You can call the `ChooseColor` API function to display the standard Color dialog box, which allows the user to *select* a specific color. `ChooseColor` supplies a `COLORREF` value for the selected color, which you can then pass to an API function to set a color (such as for the background, a pen, or a brush). The DrawIt program given at the end of the chapter displays the Color dialog box if you click the Set Custom Color... button in the Default Pen dialog box or the Default Attributes dialog box (choose Default Pen... or Default Attributes... on the Options menu). DrawIt calls `ChooseColor` in the `CAttrDlg::OnSetColor` and `CPenDlg::OnSetColor` functions in Dialog.cpp.

You can obtain the current background mode by calling the `GetBkMode` API function, and you can obtain the current background color by calling the `GetBkColor` function.

The DrawIt program lets you experiment with different background mode and background color values (choose Default Attributes... on the Options menu). DrawIt calls `SetBkMode` and `SetBkColor` in the `CFigure::Draw` function in Figure.cpp.

Setting Other Line-Drawing Attributes

There are several additional drawing attributes that affect the drawing of lines.

First, the *mapping mode* affects the way that Windows interprets the coordinates that you pass to the drawing functions. It determines both the units and the directions of increasing values of coordinates. The default mapping mode is explained in the section "Calling the Line-Drawing Functions," later in the chapter. Chapter 6 discusses the alternative mapping modes.

Second, the *viewport* and *window origins* also affect the way Windows interprets the coordinates you pass to drawing functions. They determine the vertical and horizontal position of an object on the display surface at a particular set of coordinates. The origins are discussed in Chapter 6.

FYI	The mapping mode and origins affect *all* of the drawing functions, not just those discussed in this chapter.

Third, the *current position* is the starting point that Windows uses when drawing lines with `LineTo`, `PolylineTo`, and `PolyBezierTo`. The current position will be explained in the section "Drawing Straight Lines" later in the chapter.

Fourth, the *arc direction* determines the direction in which Windows draws arcs, chords, and pies. It will be explained in the section "Drawing Arcs."

CREATING AND SELECTING PENS

When you first obtain a device context, it has a default pen that causes the line-drawing functions to draw solid black lines that are one pixel wide. You can change the appearance of lines by obtaining and selecting a different pen.

You can obtain one of several standard pens by calling the `GetStockObject` API function,

```
HGDIOBJ GetStockObject (int fnObject);
```

assigning `fnObject` one of the values shown in Table 3.3.

The standard pens supplied by `GetStockObject` draw solid lines that have a width of exactly one pixel (regardless of the mapping mode). Note, however, that if you select a pen with the NULL_PEN style, *no* lines or borders will be drawn (regardless of the current mix mode).

`GetStockObject` returns a pen handle, which the program should store in a variable of type HPEN. For example, the following code obtains a pen for drawing one-pixel-wide white lines and stores the pen handle:

```
HPEN HWhitePen = (HPEN)GetStockObject (WHITE_PEN);
```

Another way to obtain a pen is to create a custom pen by calling the `ExtCreatePen` API function:

```
HPEN ExtCreatePen
    (DWORD dwPenStyle,      // pen type and style
     DWORD dwWidth,         // pen width
     CONST LOGBRUSH *lplb,  // structure containing pen color
     DWORD dwStyleCount,    // must be 0 under Windows 95
     CONST DWORD *lpStyle); // must be 0 under Windows 95
```

The `dwPenStyle` parameter specifies the pen *type* and *style*. That is, you must assign it a value for the pen type combined with a value for the pen style (using the | operator to combine the two values).

The type value must be either PS_COSMETIC to create a *cosmetic* pen or PS_GEOMETRIC to create a *geometric* pen. A cosmetic pen has the following features:

- It draws lines quickly.
- It is always exactly one pixel wide (regardless of the current mapping mode).
- It can be solid, dashed, or dotted (according to the pen style).

A geometric pen has these features:

- It draws lines somewhat more slowly.
- It can be set to any width (and the width will be scaled if you change the mapping mode, as explained in Chapter 6).
- It is always solid (that is, you cannot choose a dotted or dashed style).

Table 3.3: The values that can be passed to `GetStockObject` to obtain different standard pens

Value Passed to `GetStockObject`	Resulting Pen
`BLACK_PEN` (the default pen)	Black pen
`WHITE_PEN`	White pen
`NULL_PEN`	Null pen: pen draws nothing, regardless of mix mode

Figure 3.1 lists the style values that you can assign to the `dwPenStyle` parameter. For each style, it shows a sample of the lines that are drawn and indicates which types of pen (cosmetic, geometric, or both) can be assigned the style.

The `PS_INSIDEFRAME` style affects only a geometric pen with a width greater than one. It creates a solid pen with the following property: If you draw a figure that is bounded by a rectangle (an arc or any of the closed figures described in Chapter 4 except polygons), the line or border will be drawn completely *inside* of the bounding rectangle (with other styles, a wide line will extend partially outside of the bounding rectangle).

Assigning the `NULL_PEN` style creates a null pen—that is, one that draws nothing (just like a pen obtained by passing `PS_NULL` to `GetStockObject`).

The `dwWidth` parameter specifies the pen width. Note that if the pen is cosmetic, this parameter is ignored (the width will always be one pixel).

Style	Sample	**Pen Types**
`PS_SOLID`	————————————	Cosmetic, geometric
`PS_DASH`	— — — — — — —	Cosmetic
`PS_DOT`	-------------------------	Cosmetic
`PS_DASHDOT`	— - — - — - — - — - — -	Cosmetic
`PS_DASHDOTDOT`	— - - — - - — - - — - -	Cosmetic
`PS_NULL`		Cosmetic, geometric
`PS_INSIDEFRAME`	————————————	Geometric

Figure 3.1: The pen style values that can be assigned to the `dwPenStyle` parameter passed to `ExtCreatePen`

Finally, the `lplb` parameter must point to a `LOGBRUSH` structure that is defined as follows:

```
typedef struct tagLOGBRUSH
   {
   UINT      lbStyle;  // must be set to BS_SOLID
   COLORREF  lbColor;  // pen color
   LONG      lbHatch;  // must be 0
   }
LOGBRUSH;
```

You should assign the desired pen color to the `lbColor` field. As explained previously in the chapter, the easiest way to assign a color is to use the `RGB` macro. If the color you assign `lbColor` is not a pure color, Windows will normally use the nearest available pure color. If, however, you create a geometric pen with the `PS_INSIDEFRAME` style and a width greater than one, Windows will use a dithered color if the selected color is not a pure color.

FYI

> Under Windows 95, the `LOGBRUSH` structure you pass to `ExtCreatePen` serves only to specify the color of the pen. You must assign `BS_SOLID` to the `lbStyle` field and 0 to the `lbHatch` field. Under Windows NT, these fields allow you to create pens that draw using hatched or pattern brushes.

As an example, the following code creates a geometric, solid, light-red pen that is 25 pixels wide (under the default mapping mode):

```
LOGBRUSH LogBrush = {BS_SOLID, RGB (255,0,0), 0};
HPEN HRedPen = ExtCreatePen
   (PS_GEOMETRIC | PS_SOLID,
   25,
   &LogBrush,
   0,
   0);
```

To begin using a pen that you have obtained by either of these two methods, you must select it into the device context by calling the `SelectObject` API function,

```
HGDIOBJ SelectObject (HDC hdc, HGDIOBJ hgdiobj);
```

where `hdc` is the handle of the device context and `hgdiobj` is the handle of the pen returned by `GetStockObject` or `ExtCreatePen`. `SelectObject` returns the handle of the *previous* pen selected into the device context; be sure to save this handle.

When you are done using the pen, you should first remove it from the device context by calling `SelectObject` to select the *previous* pen back into the device context, and then delete it by calling the API function `DeleteObject`:

```
BOOL DeleteObject (HGDIOBJ hObject);
```

As an example, the following code uses the red pen that was created by the call to `ExtCreatePen` in the example above:

```
// select red pen and save handle to previous pen:
HPEN HPenOld = (HPEN)SelectObject (HDc, HRedPen);

// call drawing functions...
// (all lines and borders will be drawn with red pen)

// remove pen from device context by selecting previous pen:
SelectObject (HDc, HPenOld);

// destroy red pen:
DeleteObject (HRedPen);
```

FYI   You do not need to deselect and delete a standard pen obtained by calling `GetStockObject`. Doing so, however, is harmless.

The DrawIt program presented at the end of the chapter lets you create a custom pen with any combination of features (choose Default Pen... on the Options menu) and then draw figures using the pen. DrawIt calls `ExtCreatePen`, `SelectObject`, and `DestroyObject` in the `CFigure::Draw` function in Figure.cpp.

FYI   The following are related API functions: `CreatePen`, `CreatePenIndirect`, `GetCurrentObject`, `EnumObjects`, `GetObject`, and `GetObjectType`.

CALLING THE LINE-DRAWING FUNCTIONS

After you have created the device context, set the drawing attributes, and selected the pen, you are ready to start calling the API line-drawing functions.

When you call an API drawing function, you always pass the handle of the device context associated with the device on which you want to display the graphics. You also pass one or more pairs of coordinates. For example, the following call draws a line from the current position to the point at the coordinates (10, 15):

```
LineTo (HDc, 10, 15);
```

When you pass a pair of coordinates, you always pass the horizontal (or x) coordinate followed by the vertical (or y) coordinate. The actual position on the display surface corresponding to a pair of coordinates depends upon the current *mapping mode* and *origins*.

With the default mapping mode (known as MM_TEXT), all coordinates are in pixels (also known as *device units*), x coordinates increase as you move to the right, and y coordinates increase as you move down. With the default *viewport* and *window* origins, the coordinates (0, 0) refer to the upper-left corner of the display surface. If you are drawing graphics in a window, the coordinates (0, 0) are at the upper-left corner of the client area; if you are drawing graphics on the printer, the coordinates (0, 0) are at the upper-left corner of the printable area of the page. Thus, the example call to LineTo given above would draw a line to the point that is 10 pixels from the left border of the client area and 15 pixels from the top border (assuming that HDc is associated with the client area of a window).

Figure 3.2 illustrates the default mapping mode and origins. All of the examples through Chapter 6 use the default mapping mode and origins. Chapter 6 discusses using alternative mapping modes and adjusting the origins.

Finally, coordinate parameters passed to all drawing functions are int values. In a Windows 95 program, the size of an int is 32 bits. The int can therefore store values that range from -2 to +2 gigabytes. The Windows 95 drawing functions, however, allow you to pass coordinate values *only within the range of -32 to +32 kilobytes* (which represents the storage range of a 16-bit integer). Windows will truncate any values you pass that are outside of this range.

Drawing Straight Lines

To draw a single straight line, you first specify the starting point of the line by calling the API function MoveToEx:

```
BOOL MoveToEx (HDC hdc, int X, int Y, LPPOINT lpPoint);
```

MoveToEx moves the current position to the point given by the X and Y parameters. It also assigns the coordinates of the former current position to the POINT structure pointed to by the lpPoint parameter (you can assign 0 to lpPoint if you do not need the former current position).

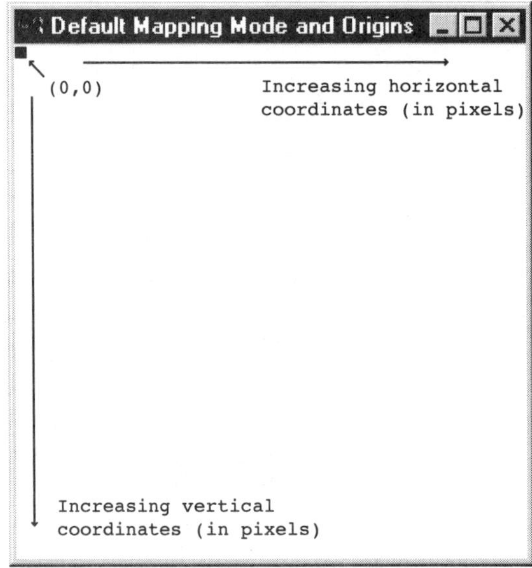

Figure 3.2:   The default mapping mode and origins

You then call the API function `LineTo`:

```
BOOL LineTo (HDC hdc, int nXEnd, int nYEnd);
```

`LineTo` draws a straight line *from* the current position *to* the coordinates given by `nXEnd` and `nYEnd`. For example, the following code draws a line from the point (5, 10) to the point (27, 35):

```
MoveToEx (HDc, 5, 10, 0);
LineTo (HDc, 27, 35);
```

`LineTo` also sets the current position to the end point of the line that it draws. Therefore, to draw several connected lines, you need to call `MoveToEx` only before the *first* call to `LineTo`. For example, the following code draws a set of connected lines forming an M:

```
MoveToEx (HDc, 50, 150, 0);
LineTo (HDc, 50, 50);
LineTo (HDc, 100, 100);
LineTo (HDc, 150, 50);
LineTo (HDc, 150, 150);
```

You can also draw a set of connected lines with a single call to the `Polyline` API function,

```
BOOL Polyline (HDC hdc, CONST POINT *lppt, int cPoints);
```

where `lppt` is an array of `POINT` structures containing the coordinates of a set of points and `cPoints` is the number of points (there must be at least two). `Polyline` draws a line from the first point to the second point, from the second point to the third point, and so on through the following points in the array. `Polyline` neither uses nor sets the current position. For example, the following code uses `Polyline` to draw the same M-shaped figure as that drawn by the calls to `LineTo` in the previous example:

```
POINT Points [5];
Points [0].x = 50;  Points [0].y = 150;
Points [1].x = 50;  Points [1].y = 50;
Points [2].x = 100; Points [2].y = 100;
Points [3].x = 150; Points [3].y = 50;
Points [4].x = 150; Points [4].y = 150;

Polyline (HDc, Points, 5);
```

FYI

Neither `LineTo` nor `Polyline` color the pixel at the end point of a line. Thus, when you use either function to draw a set of connected lines, the end point of each line is drawn only once. The number of times a point is drawn makes a difference in certain mix modes, such as `R2_NOT`.

The DrawIt program uses `MoveToEx` and `LineTo` to draw straight lines (when you choose Line on the Figure menu), and it uses `Polyline` to draw sets of connected lines (when you choose Polyline on the Figure menu). The code for drawing lines is in the `CLine::PureDraw` function, and the code for drawing connected lines is in `CPolyline::PureDraw;`. Both functions are in Figure.cpp.

FYI

The following are related API functions: `GetCurrentPositionEx`, `LineDDA`, `PolyLineTo`, and `PolyPolyline`.

Drawing Arcs

An *arc* is a portion of the border around an ellipse. You can draw an arc by calling the `Arc` API function:

```
BOOL Arc
  (HDC hdc,
   int nLeftRect,   int nTopRect,
   int nRightRect,  int nBottomRect,
   int nXStartArc,  int nYStartArc,
   int nXEndArc,    int nYEndArc);
```

When you call **Arc**, you must specify an ellipse *and* indicate the portion of the ellipse that is to be included in the arc that is drawn. To do this, you pass four sets of coordinates. The parameters `nLeftRect` and `nTopRect` are the coordinates of the upper-left corner of the rectangle that bounds the ellipse, and the parameters `nRightRect` and `nBottomRect` are the coordinates of the lower-right corner. The parameters `nXStartArc` and `nYStartArc` are the coordinates of a point on the starting line for the arc, and the parameters `nXEndArc` and `nYEndArc` are the coordinates of a point on the ending line (see Figure 3.3).

<table>
<tr><td>**FYI**</td><td>For guidelines on specifying *bounding rectangles* when calling API functions, see the section "Calling Functions to Draw Closed Figures" in Chapter 4.</td></tr>
</table>

Arc draws the arc from the point where the starting line intersects the ellipse to the point where the ending line intersects it. By default, **Arc** draws the arc in the counterclockwise direction (as shown in Figure 3.3). You can, however, change the drawing direction by calling the `SetArcDirection` API function:

```
int SetArcDirection (HDC hdc, int ArcDirection);
```

You assign the `ArcDirection` parameter the value `AD_COUNTERCLOCK-WISE` to have Windows draw arcs in the counterclockwise direction (the default) or `AD_CLOCKWISE` to have Windows draw arcs in the clockwise direction.

<table>
<tr><td>**FYI**</td><td>The arc-drawing direction set by `SetArcDirection` also affects the drawing of chords and pies, which are discussed in Chapter 4.</td></tr>
</table>

You can *obtain* the current arc-drawing direction by calling the `GetArcDirection` API function:

```
int GetArcDirection (HDC hdc);
```

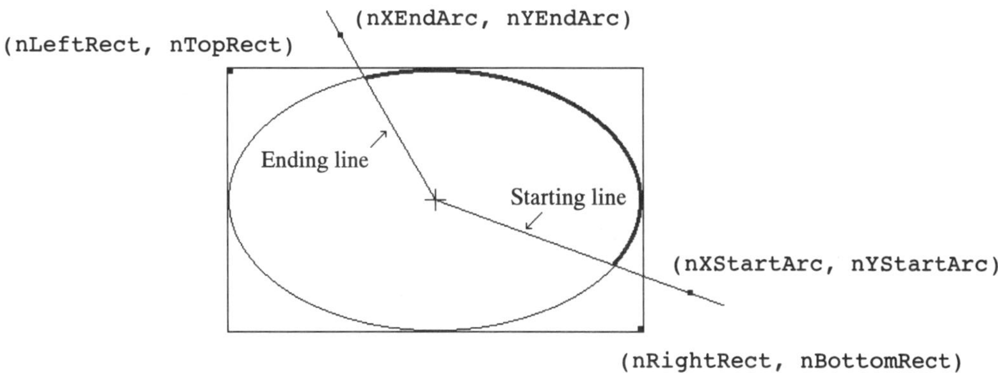

Figure 3.3:   Drawing an arc with the Arc API function

The DrawIt program at the end of the chapter uses the `Arc` function to draw arcs (when you choose Arc on the Figure menu). The code is in the `CArc::PureDraw` function in Figure.cpp.

Drawing Free-Form Curves

You can draw a free-form curved line (that is, a line that is not a portion of an ellipse) by calling the API function `PolyBezier`:

```
BOOL PolyBezier (HDC hdc, CONST POINT *lppt, DWORD cPoints);
```

The `lppt` parameter is an array of `POINT` structures containing the coordinates of starting, ending, and control points, and the `cPoints` parameter is the number of points (that is, the number of elements in the `POINT` array). You can use `PolyBezier` to draw a curved line consisting of a single Bézier curve, or a curved line consisting of set of connected Bézier curves.

To draw a single Bézier curve, `lppt` must contain the coordinates of four points: The first point is the starting point of the curve, the second and third points are the control points that determine the curve's shape, and the fourth point is the ending point. For example, the following code draws a single Bézier curve:

```
POINT Points [4];
Points [0].x = 49;  Points [0].y = 71;
```

```
Points [1].x = 77;  Points [1].y = 139;
Points [2].x = 132; Points [2].y = 60;
Points [3].x = 186; Points [3].y = 108;

PolyBezier (HDc, Points, 4);
```

The resulting curve is shown in Figure 3.4.

To draw two connected Bézier curves, you need to add only *three* points to the `POINT` array. The starting point of the second curve is the same as the ending point of the first curve. The first and second added points are the control points for the second curve, and the third added point is the ending point for the second curve. For example, the following code draws a curved line consisting of two connected Bézier curves (the first curve is the same as the one drawn by the previous example):

```
POINT Points [7];
// first Bezier curve:
Points [0].x = 49;  Points [0].y = 71;
Points [1].x = 77;  Points [1].y = 139;
Points [2].x = 132; Points [2].y = 60;
Points [3].x = 186; Points [3].y = 108;

// second Bezier curve:
Points [4].x = 240; Points [4].y = 157;
Points [5].x = 271; Points [5].y = 93;
Points [6].x = 321; Points [6].y = 130;

PolyBezier (HDc, Points, 7);
```

The resulting curve is shown in Figure 3.5.

You can add additional connected Bézier curves in the same way. In general, the number of elements in the `POINT` array must be three times the number of connected Bézier curves you want to draw, plus one.

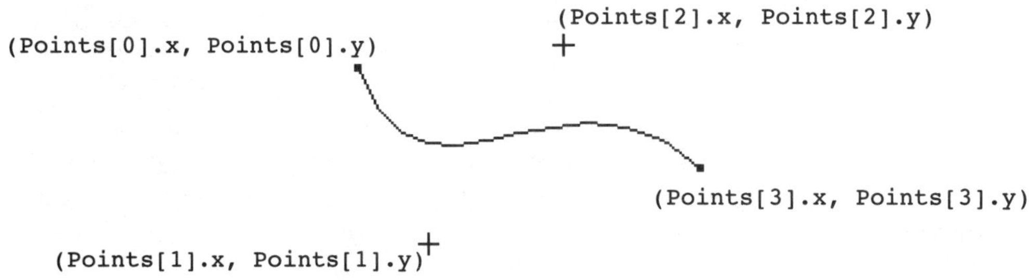

Figure 3.4:   The single Bézier curve drawn by the example call to `PolyBezier`

TIP

To make the transition between two connected Bézier curves smooth, make sure that the second control point of the first curve, the ending point of the first curve (which is also the starting point of the second curve), and the first control point of the second curve all lie within a single line. For example, in Figure 3.5, the connection between the two Bézier curves is smooth because the points (`Points [2].x`, `Points [2].y`), (`Points [3].x`, `Points [3].y`), and (`Points [4].x`, `Points [4].y`) lie in the same line.

The DrawIt program lets you draw single Bézier curves by specifying the starting, ending, and control points (choose Bézier on the Figure menu). The code for drawing the curves is in the `CBezier::PureDraw` function in Figure.cpp.

FYI

The following are related API functions: `PolyBezierTo` and `PolyDraw`.

DRAWIT VERSION 1

This chapter presents the first version of the DrawIt vector drawing program. DrawIt Version 1 lets you set any of the drawing attributes that were discussed in the chapter and allows you to select a custom pen with any combination of features. You can then draw any of the figures that were covered in the chapter and see the results of your choices. The DrawIt code demonstrates most of the programming techniques that were given.

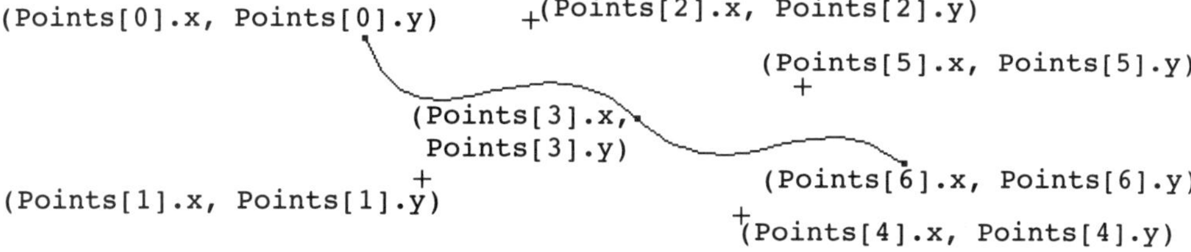

Figure 3.5:   The two connected Bézier curves drawn by the example call to `PolyBezier`

	Keep in mind that DrawIt was designed as a tool to help programmers learn the techniques given in this book. Consequently, the menus and dialog boxes use the Windows API terminology (for example, *geometric pen* and *mix mode*) and the program allows you to choose any combination of settings, even those that have no effect (for example, you can choose a cosmetic pen with a width of 10). If you were designing a vector drawing program for the end user, you would probably use more friendly terminology and prevent the user from making ineffective choices.
TIP	

Using DrawIt Version 1

To start DrawIt Version 1, run the DrawIt.exe executable file contained in the DrawIt1 subfolder of the folder in which you installed the companion disk files. This version of DrawIt lets you:

- Select a combination of drawing attributes.
- Select a pen.
- Draw lines.

The DrawIt program window is shown in Figure 3.6.

To select drawing attributes that affect the drawing of lines, choose Default Attributes... on the Options menu and enter your choices in the Default Attributes dialog box (see Figure 3.7). To use a custom background color, select the <Custom> item in the Color list and then click the Set Custom Color... button to select the desired color.

To select a pen, choose Default Pen... on the Options menu and enter your choices into the Default Pen dialog box (see Figure 3.8).

	When you first run DrawIt, all drawing attributes are set to their default values and the default pen is selected.
TIP	

The pen and attributes you choose will affect all figures you subsequently draw. (DrawIt Version 2, presented in Chapter 4, lets you *change* the pen, brush, and attributes for a figure you have already drawn.)

You can draw different kinds of lines by choosing commands on the Figure menu, as follows:

Figure 3.6:   The DrawIt Version 1 program window

Figure 3.7:   The Default Attributes dialog box displayed by the DrawIt Version 1 program

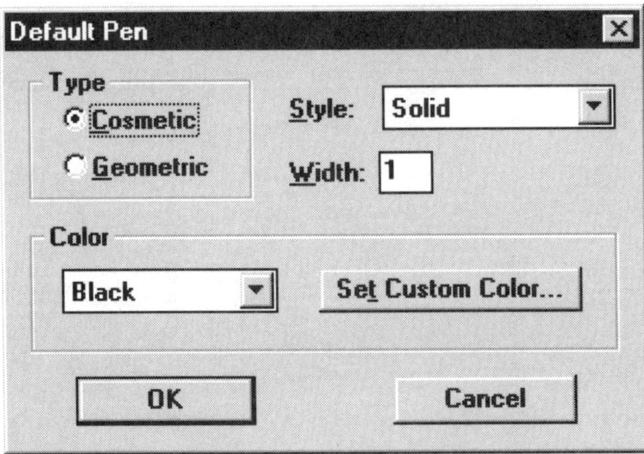

Figure 3.8:   The Default Pen dialog box displayed by the DrawIt Version 1 program

- To draw a straight line, choose Line on the Figure menu, place the cursor at the starting point, and drag to the ending point.

- To draw an arc, choose Arc, place the cursor at one corner of the bounding rectangle, drag to mark the ellipse, click to mark the starting line for the arc, and click to mark the ending line.

- To draw a Bézier curve, choose Bézier, place the cursor at the starting point, drag to the ending point, click on the first control point, and click on the second control point.

- To draw a series of connected lines, choose Polyline, click on each point (and drag if you want to move the point), and double-click on the last point.

You can cancel the drawing of any figure by pressing Esc before the line is complete.

The DrawIt Version 1 Program Classes

The DrawIt program is based upon the Template program presented in Chapter 1. Table 3.4 lists the DrawIt program classes and describes the division of labor among them.

Like the Template.cpp file of the Template program, the DrawIt.cpp file contains the `WinMain` entry function and also defines an instance of each of the global program classes (`CApp, CMainWnd, CDocument, CAttrDlg, CPenDlg,` and `CAboutDlg`). The main window class (`CMainWnd`) dynamically creates an instance of the appropriate figure class (`CArc, CBezier, CLine,` or `CPolyline`) for each figure that is drawn.

Table 3.4:   The program classes defined in DrawIt Version 1

Class	Header and Implementation Files	Purpose
CApp	App.h	Application class: stores information on the program
CMainWnd	MainWnd.h MainWnd.cpp	Main window class: manages the main program window and performs initial processing of all keyboard and menu commands and mouse actions
CFigure	Figure.h Figure.cpp	Abstract base class for all figure classes (CArc, CBezier, CLine, and CPolyline)
CArc	Figure.h Figure.cpp	Stores and draws an arc
CBezier	Figure.h Figure.cpp	Stores and draws a Bézier curve
CLine	Figure.h Figure.cpp	Stores and draws a straight line
CPolyline	Figure.h Figure.cpp	Stores and draws a set of connected line segments
CDocument	Document.h Document.cpp	Document class: stores a linked list containing a figure object for each figure that has been drawn
CAttrDlg	Dialog.h Dialog.cpp	Manages the Default Attributes dialog box for setting drawing attributes
CPenDlg	Dialog.h Dialog.cpp	Manages the Default Pen dialog box for selecting a pen
CAboutDlg	Dialog.h Dialog.cpp	Manages the About dialog box

The DrawIt Version 1 Source Code

The following are the C++ source code listings for DrawIt Version 1. You will find a complete copy of these listings in the DrawIt1 subfolder of the folder in which you installed your companion disk files.

Listing 3.1:   DrawIt.cpp

```cpp
///////////////////////////////////////////////////////////////////////
//                                                                     //
// DrawIt.cpp: Main program object declarations and WinMain            //
//             program entry function.                                 //
//                                                                     //
///////////////////////////////////////////////////////////////////////

#define  STRICT
#include <windows.h>

// header files for main program classes:
#include "app.h"
#include "figure.h"
#include "mainwnd.h"
#include "document.h"
#include "dialog.h"

// main program objects:
CApp       App;
CMainWnd   MainWnd;
CDocument  Document;
CAboutDlg  AboutDlg;
CAttrDlg   AttrDlg;
CPenDlg    PenDlg;

///////////////////////////////////////////////////////////////////////
// program entry function:                                             //
///////////////////////////////////////////////////////////////////////

int APIENTRY  WinMain
   (HINSTANCE HInstCurrent,
    HINSTANCE HInstPrevious,
    LPSTR     CmdLine,
    int       CmdShow)
    {
    MSG Msg;

    // store program informaton in application object:
    App.Initialize (HInstCurrent, CmdLine);

    // register class for main program window:
    if (!MainWnd.RegisterClass ())
       return 0;

    // create and display main program window:
    if (!MainWnd.Create ())
       return 0;

    // main message loop:
    while (GetMessage (&Msg, NULL, NULL, NULL))
       {
```

```
        TranslateMessage (&Msg);
        DispatchMessage (&Msg);
        }

    // return "application-defined exit code":
    return Msg.wParam;
    }
```

Listing 3.2:   App.h

```
////////////////////////////////////////////////////////////////////////////
//                                                                        //
// App.h: Header file for application class.                              //
//                                                                        //
////////////////////////////////////////////////////////////////////////////

class CApp
{
public:
   HINSTANCE mHInstance;   // handle of program instance
   LPSTR     mCmdLine;     // pointer to program command line

   void Initialize (HINSTANCE HInstCurrent, LPSTR CmdLine)
   // saves application values
      {
      mHInstance = HInstCurrent;
      mCmdLine = CmdLine;
      }
};
```

Listing 3.3:   MainWnd.h

```
////////////////////////////////////////////////////////////////////////////
//                                                                        //
// MainWnd.h: Header file for main window class.                          //
//                                                                        //
////////////////////////////////////////////////////////////////////////////

#define WINWIDTH  350 // dimensions of main program window
#define WINHEIGHT 400

class CMainWnd
{
public:
   enum // current drawing mode
      {
      ModeNone,
      ModeDragging,
      ModeMark1,
      ModeMark2
      }
   mMode;
```

```cpp
    CFigure *mCurrentFig; // pointer to current figure object
    HPEN mHPenDotted;      // handle to dotted pen
    HWND mHWnd;            // main window handle

    CMainWnd (void);
    BOOL Create (void);
    BOOL RegisterClass (void);

    // message-handling functions:
    LRESULT OnDestroy (void);
    LRESULT OnFigure (WORD MenuCommandID);
    LRESULT OnHelpAbout (void);
    LRESULT OnKeyDown (int VirtKeyCode);
    LRESULT OnKillFocus (void);
    LRESULT OnOptionsAttributes (void);
    LRESULT OnOptionsPen (void);
    LRESULT OnPaint (void);

protected:
    UINT mCurrentFigID; // ID of menu command for curr. figure
};
```

Listing 3.4:   MainWnd.cpp

```cpp
//////////////////////////////////////////////////////////////////////////
//                                                                        //
// MainWnd.cpp: Implementation file for main window class.                //
//                                                                        //
//////////////////////////////////////////////////////////////////////////

#define STRICT
#include <windows.h>
#include "resource.h"

#include "app.h"
#include "figure.h"
#include "mainwnd.h"
#include "document.h"
#include "dialog.h"

extern CApp       App;
extern CMainWnd   MainWnd;
extern CDocument  Document;
extern CAboutDlg  AboutDlg;
extern CAttrDlg   AttrDlg;
extern CPenDlg    PenDlg;

LRESULT CALLBACK MainWndProc (HWND HWnd, UINT Msg, WPARAM WParam,
    LPARAM LParam);

//////////////////////////////////////////////////////////////////////////
// CMainWnd constructor:                                                  //
//////////////////////////////////////////////////////////////////////////
```

```cpp
CMainWnd::CMainWnd (void)
   {
   mCurrentFig = new CLine;
   mCurrentFigID = ID_FIGURE_LINE;
   mHPenDotted = CreatePen (PS_DOT, 1, RGB (0,0,0));
   mMode = ModeNone;
   }

//////////////////////////////////////////////////////////////////////////////
// CMainWnd public member functions:                                        //
//////////////////////////////////////////////////////////////////////////////

BOOL CMainWnd::Create (void)
// creates and displays main program window; returns TRUE on
// success or FALSE on error
   {
    // create main program window and save handle:
   mHWnd = CreateWindow
      ("DemoClass",
      "DrawIt",
      WS_OVERLAPPED | WS_SYSMENU | WS_MINIMIZEBOX,
      CW_USEDEFAULT,
      CW_USEDEFAULT,
      WINWIDTH,
      WINHEIGHT,
      NULL,
      NULL,
      App.mHInstance,
      NULL);
    if (!mHWnd)
      return FALSE;

   // display window:
   ShowWindow
      (mHWnd,
      SW_SHOWDEFAULT);

   return TRUE;
   }

BOOL CMainWnd::RegisterClass (void)
// registers class for main program window; returns TRUE on
// success or FALSE on error
   {
   WNDCLASS WC;

   // specify class information:
   WC.style = CS_DBLCLKS;
   WC.lpfnWndProc = MainWndProc;
   WC.cbClsExtra = 0;
   WC.cbWndExtra = 0;
   WC.hInstance = App.mHInstance;
   WC.hIcon = LoadIcon (App.mHInstance,
      MAKEINTRESOURCE (IDI_ICON1));
   WC.hCursor = LoadCursor (0, IDC_CROSS);
```

```cpp
  WC.hbrBackground = (HBRUSH)GetStockObject (WHITE_BRUSH);
  WC.lpszMenuName = MAKEINTRESOURCE (IDR_MENU1);
  WC.lpszClassName = "DemoClass";

  // register class:
  return (BOOL)::RegisterClass (&WC);
  }

//////////////////////////////////////////////////////////////////////////
// window procedure for main window:                                      //
//////////////////////////////////////////////////////////////////////////

LRESULT CALLBACK MainWndProc
  (HWND   HWnd,
   UINT   Msg,
   WPARAM WParam,
   LPARAM LParam)
  {
  switch (Msg)
    {
    case WM_COMMAND: // user chose a menu command
       switch (LOWORD (WParam))
          {
          case ID_HELP_ABOUT: // user chose Help/About
             return MainWnd.OnHelpAbout ();

          case ID_FIGURE_ARC:     // user chose command on
          case ID_FIGURE_BEZIER: // Figure menu
          case ID_FIGURE_LINE:
          case ID_FIGURE_POLYLINE:
             return MainWnd.OnFigure (LOWORD (WParam));

          case ID_OPTIONS_ATTRIBUTES: // user chose
                                      // Options/Attributes
             return MainWnd.OnOptionsAttributes ();

          case ID_OPTIONS_PEN: // user chose Options/Pen
             return MainWnd.OnOptionsPen ();

          default:
             // default processing for other commands:
             return DefWindowProc (HWnd, Msg, WParam, LParam);
          }

     case WM_DESTROY:    // DestroyWindow was called
        return MainWnd.OnDestroy ();

     case WM_KEYDOWN:    // user pressed a key
        return MainWnd.OnKeyDown ((int)WParam);

     case WM_KILLFOCUS:  // program window has lost focus
        return MainWnd.OnKillFocus ();
```

```cpp
    case WM_LBUTTONDBLCLK:   // user double-clicked left mouse
                             // button
        return MainWnd.mCurrentFig->OnLButtonDblClk
           (LOWORD (LParam), HIWORD (LParam));

    case WM_LBUTTONDOWN:      // user pressed left button
        return MainWnd.mCurrentFig->OnLButtonDown
           (LOWORD (LParam), HIWORD (LParam));

    case WM_LBUTTONUP:        // user released left button
        return MainWnd.mCurrentFig->OnLButtonUp
           (LOWORD (LParam), HIWORD (LParam));

    case WM_MOUSEMOVE:        // user moved mouse pointer
        return MainWnd.mCurrentFig->OnMouseMove
           (LOWORD (LParam), HIWORD (LParam));

    case WM_PAINT:    // window needs painting or repainting
        return MainWnd.OnPaint ();

    default:
        // default processing for all other messages:
        return DefWindowProc (HWnd, Msg, WParam, LParam);
    }
  }

///////////////////////////////////////////////////////////////////////
// CMainWnd message handling member functions:                       //
///////////////////////////////////////////////////////////////////////

LRESULT CMainWnd::OnDestroy (void)
// processes WM_DESTROY messages
  {
  PostQuitMessage (0);   // post a WM_QUIT message to
  return NULL;           // cause message loop to exit
  }

LRESULT CMainWnd::OnFigure (WORD MenuCommandID)
// processes WM_COMMAND messages from ALL commands on Figure menu
  {
  if (mCurrentFigID == MenuCommandID)
     return NULL;

  // cancel current drawing operation and delete figure object:
  mCurrentFig->Cancel ();
  delete mCurrentFig;

  // create figure object for new figure type:
  switch (MenuCommandID)
     {
     case ID_FIGURE_ARC:
        mCurrentFig = new CArc;
        break;
```

```cpp
        case ID_FIGURE_BEZIER:
            mCurrentFig = new CBezier;
            break;

        case ID_FIGURE_LINE:
            mCurrentFig = new CLine;
            break;

        case ID_FIGURE_POLYLINE:
            mCurrentFig = new CPolyline;
            break;
        }
    // move check mark to command for new figure type:
    CheckMenuItem (GetMenu (mHWnd), mCurrentFigID, MF_UNCHECKED);
    mCurrentFigID = MenuCommandID;
    CheckMenuItem (GetMenu (mHWnd), mCurrentFigID, MF_CHECKED);
    return NULL;
    }

LRESULT CMainWnd::OnHelpAbout (void)
// processes WM_COMMAND / ID_HELP_ABOUT messages
    {
    AboutDlg.Show (); // display About dialog box
    return NULL;
    }

LRESULT CMainWnd::OnKeyDown (int VirtKeyCode)
// processes WM_KEYDOWN messages
    {
    // if user pressed Esc, cancel drawing operation:
    if (VirtKeyCode == VK_ESCAPE)
      mCurrentFig->Cancel ();
    return NULL;
    }

LRESULT CMainWnd::OnKillFocus (void)
// processes WM_KILLFOCUS messages
    {
    mCurrentFig->Cancel (); // cancel drawing operation
    return NULL;
    }

LRESULT CMainWnd::OnOptionsAttributes (void)
// processes WM_COMMAND / ID_OPTIONS_ATTRIBUTES messages
    {
    AttrDlg.Show (); // display Attributes dialog box
    return NULL;
    }

LRESULT CMainWnd::OnOptionsPen (void)
// processes WM_COMMAND / ID_OPTIONS_PEN messages
    {
    PenDlg.Show (); // display Pen dialog box
```

```cpp
   return NULL;
   }

LRESULT CMainWnd::OnPaint (void)
// processes WM_PAINT messages
   {
   HDC HDCPaint;
   PAINTSTRUCT PaintStruct;
   RECT RectBound;

   // cancel current drawing operation (if any):
   mCurrentFig->Cancel ();

   // initiate painting and obtain a device context:
   HDCPaint = BeginPaint (mHWnd, &PaintStruct);

   // draw all figures stored in document:
   FigCell *PCell = Document.mPFirstFig;
   while (PCell)
      {
      RectBound = PCell->PFigure->GetBoundRect ();
      if (RectVisible (HDCPaint, &RectBound))
         PCell->PFigure->Draw (HDCPaint);
      PCell = PCell->PNextFig;
      }

   // terminate painting and release device context:
   EndPaint (mHWnd, &PaintStruct);
   return NULL;
   }
```

Listing 3.5:   Figure.h

```cpp
///////////////////////////////////////////////////////////////////////////
//                                                                       //
// Figure.h: Header file for figure classes.                            //
//                                                                       //
///////////////////////////////////////////////////////////////////////////

class CFigure // abstract base class for all figure classes
{
public:
   // description of pen used to draw figure:
   COLORREF mPenColor;
   DWORD mPenStyle;
   DWORD mPenType;
   DWORD mPenWidth;

   // drawing attributes:
   COLORREF mBkColor;
   int mBkMode;
   int mMixMode;
```

```cpp
   CFigure (void);
   void Cancel (void);
   virtual CFigure *CreateObject (void) = 0;
   virtual void Draw (HDC HDc);
   virtual RECT GetBoundRect (void);
   virtual void PureDraw (HDC HDc) = 0;

   // message-handling functions:
   virtual LRESULT OnLButtonDblClk (WORD XCursor, WORD YCursor)
      {
      return NULL;
      }
   virtual LRESULT OnLButtonDown (WORD XCursor, WORD YCursor) = 0;
   virtual LRESULT OnLButtonUp (WORD XCursor, WORD YCursor) = 0;
   virtual LRESULT OnMouseMove (WORD XCursor, WORD YCursor) = 0;

protected:
   int mX1, mY1, mX2, mY2; // basic figure dimensions

   HDC GetTempDC (void);
   int Max4 (int A, int B, int C, int D)
      {
      return max (max (max (A, B), C), D);
      }
   int Min4 (int A, int B, int C, int D)
      {
      return min (min (min (A, B), C), D);
      }
   void StartDrag (void);
};

class CArc : public CFigure
{
public:
   virtual CFigure *CreateObject (void)
      {
      return new CArc;
      }
   virtual void PureDraw (HDC HDc);

   // message-handling functions:
   virtual LRESULT OnLButtonDown (WORD XCursor, WORD YCursor);
   virtual LRESULT OnLButtonUp (WORD XCursor, WORD YCursor);
   virtual LRESULT OnMouseMove (WORD XCursor, WORD YCursor);

protected:
   int mX3, mY3, mX4, mY4;   // additional arc dimensions
};

class CBezier : public CFigure
{
public:
   virtual CFigure *CreateObject (void)
```

```cpp
      {
      return new CBezier;
      }
   virtual RECT GetBoundRect (void);
   virtual void PureDraw (HDC HDc);

   // message-handling functions:
   virtual LRESULT OnLButtonDown (WORD XCursor, WORD YCursor);
   virtual LRESULT OnLButtonUp (WORD XCursor, WORD YCursor);
   virtual LRESULT OnMouseMove (WORD XCursor, WORD YCursor);

protected:
   int mX3, mY3, mX4, mY4;  // additional bezier curve dimensions
};

class CLine : public CFigure
{
public:
   virtual CFigure *CreateObject (void)
      {
      return new CLine;
      }
   virtual void PureDraw (HDC HDc);

   // message-handling functions:
   virtual LRESULT OnLButtonDown (WORD XCursor, WORD YCursor);
   virtual LRESULT OnLButtonUp (WORD XCursor, WORD YCursor);
   virtual LRESULT OnMouseMove (WORD XCursor, WORD YCursor);
};

#define MAXPOINTS 25 // maximum number of vertices in polyline

class CPolyline : public CFigure
{
public:
   virtual CFigure *CreateObject (void)
      {
      return new CPolyline;
      }
   virtual RECT GetBoundRect (void);
   virtual void PureDraw (HDC HDc);

   // message-handling functions:
   virtual LRESULT OnLButtonDblClk (WORD XCursor, WORD YCursor);
   virtual LRESULT OnLButtonDown (WORD XCursor, WORD YCursor);
   virtual LRESULT OnLButtonUp (WORD XCursor, WORD YCursor);
   virtual LRESULT OnMouseMove (WORD XCursor, WORD YCursor);

protected:
   int mNumPoints;              // number of points stored
   POINT mPoints [MAXPOINTS]; // stores coordinates of vertices
};
```

Listing 3.6:   Figure.cpp

```cpp
////////////////////////////////////////////////////////////////////////
//                                                                    //
// Figure.cpp: Implementaton file for figure classes.                 //
//                                                                    //
////////////////////////////////////////////////////////////////////////

#define STRICT
#include <windows.h>
#include <limits.h>
#include "resource.h"

#include "figure.h"
#include "mainwnd.h"
#include "document.h"

extern CMainWnd  MainWnd;
extern CDocument Document;

////////////////////////////////////////////////////////////////////////
// CFigure:                                                           //
////////////////////////////////////////////////////////////////////////

CFigure::CFigure (void)
   {
   mPenWidth = 1;
   }

void CFigure::Cancel (void)
// cancels a drawing operation
   {
   if (MainWnd.mMode == MainWnd.ModeNone)
      return;

   // erase temporary line(s) and redraw affected area of window:
   RECT Rect = GetBoundRect ();
   InvalidateRect (MainWnd.mHWnd, &Rect, TRUE);

   // end dragging operation:
   if (MainWnd.mMode == MainWnd.ModeDragging)
      {
      ReleaseCapture ();
      ClipCursor (NULL);
      }
   MainWnd.mMode = MainWnd.ModeNone;
   return;
   }

 void CFigure::Draw (HDC HDc)
 // prepares the device context AND draws the current object
    {
    // set drawing attributes:
```

```cpp
   SetBkColor (HDc, mBkColor);
   SetBkMode (HDc, mBkMode);
   SetROP2 (HDc, mMixMode);

   // create and select object's pen:
   LOGBRUSH LogBrush = {BS_SOLID, mPenColor, 0};
   HPEN HPen = ExtCreatePen
      (mPenType | mPenStyle,
      mPenWidth,
      &LogBrush,
      0,
      0);
   HPEN HPenOld = (HPEN)SelectObject (HDc, HPen);

   // call the appropriate drawing function for the object:
   PureDraw (HDc);

   // deselect and destroy pen:
   SelectObject (HDc, HPenOld);
   DeleteObject (HPen);
   return;
   }

RECT CFigure::GetBoundRect (void)
// returns smallest rectangle bounding figure
   {
   RECT Rect =
      {min (mX1, mX2),
       min (mY1, mY2),
       max (mX1, mX2) + 1,
       max (mY1, mY2) + 1};

   // expand rectangle to accommodate wide lines:
   int LineAdd = (mPenWidth-1) / 2 + (mPenWidth-1) % 2;
   InflateRect (&Rect, LineAdd, LineAdd);

   return Rect;
   }

HDC CFigure::GetTempDC (void)
// returns a device-context handle for drawing temporary lines
   {
   HDC HDCClient = GetDC (MainWnd.mHWnd);
   SetROP2 (HDCClient, R2_NOT);
   HPEN HPenOld = (HPEN)SelectObject
      (HDCClient, MainWnd.mHPenDotted);
   SetBkMode (HDCClient, TRANSPARENT);
   SelectObject (HDCClient, GetStockObject (NULL_BRUSH));
   return HDCClient;
   }

void CFigure::StartDrag (void)
// initializes a drag operation for drawing a figure
```

```cpp
   {
   // capture mouse messages:
   SetCapture (MainWnd.mHWnd);

   // confine mouse cursor to client area of window:
   RECT Rect;
   GetClientRect (MainWnd.mHWnd, &Rect);
   ClientToScreen (MainWnd.mHWnd, (LPPOINT)&Rect);
   ClientToScreen (MainWnd.mHWnd, (LPPOINT)&Rect.right);
   ClipCursor (&Rect);
   return;
   }

////////////////////////////////////////////////////////////////////////////
// CArc:                                                                    //
////////////////////////////////////////////////////////////////////////////

void CArc::PureDraw (HDC HDc)
// draws the arc
   {
   Arc (HDc, mX1, mY1, mX2, mY2, mX3, mY3, mX4, mY4);
   return;
   }

LRESULT CArc::OnLButtonDown (WORD XCursor, WORD YCursor)
// processes WM_LBUTTONDOWN messages
   {
   switch (MainWnd.mMode)
      {
      case MainWnd.ModeNone:    // draw bounding ellipse
         StartDrag ();
         mX1 = XCursor; mY1 = YCursor;
         mX2 = XCursor; mY2 = YCursor;
         MainWnd.mMode = MainWnd.ModeDragging;
         break;

      case MainWnd.ModeMark1:  // mark start of arc
         mX3 = XCursor; mY3 = YCursor;
         MainWnd.mMode = MainWnd.ModeMark2;
         break;

      case MainWnd.ModeMark2:  // mark end of arc
         // erase temporary ellipse:
         HDC HDCClient = GetTempDC ();
         Ellipse (HDCClient, mX1, mY1, mX2, mY2);

         // add arc to document:
         mX4 = XCursor; mY4 = YCursor;
         Document.AddFigure (this);
         MainWnd.mCurrentFig = CreateObject ();

         // draw arc:
         Draw (HDCClient);
         ReleaseDC (MainWnd.mHWnd, HDCClient);
```

```cpp
            MainWnd.mMode = MainWnd.ModeNone;
            break;
        }
    return NULL;
    }

LRESULT CArc::OnLButtonUp (WORD XCursor, WORD YCursor)
// processes WM_LBUTTONUP messages
    {
    if (MainWnd.mMode != MainWnd.ModeDragging)
        return NULL;

    // end drag operation:
    ReleaseCapture ();
    ClipCursor (NULL);

    // erase old temporary ellipse / draw new temporary ellipse:
    HDC HDCClient = GetTempDC ();
    Ellipse (HDCClient, mX1, mY1, mX2, mY2);
    Ellipse (HDCClient, mX1, mY1, XCursor, YCursor);
    ReleaseDC (MainWnd.mHWnd, HDCClient);

    // save new coordinates / stop drawing if ellipse is trivial:
    mX2 = XCursor; mY2 = YCursor;
    if (mX1 == mX2 && mY1 == mY2)
        MainWnd.mMode = MainWnd.ModeNone;
    else
        MainWnd.mMode = MainWnd.ModeMark1;
    return NULL;
    }

LRESULT CArc::OnMouseMove (WORD XCursor, WORD YCursor)
// processes WM_MOUSEMOVE messages
    {
    if (MainWnd.mMode != MainWnd.ModeDragging)
        return NULL;

    // erase old temporary ellipse / draw new temporary ellipse:
    HDC HDCClient = GetTempDC ();
    Ellipse (HDCClient, mX1, mY1, mX2, mY2);
    Ellipse (HDCClient, mX1, mY1, XCursor, YCursor);
    ReleaseDC (MainWnd.mHWnd, HDCClient);

    // save new coordinates:
    mX2 = XCursor; mY2 = YCursor;
    return NULL;
    }

////////////////////////////////////////////////////////////////////////
// CBezier:                                                            //
////////////////////////////////////////////////////////////////////////
```

```
RECT CBezier::GetBoundRect (void)
// returns the smallest rectangle bounding the Bezier curve
   {
   RECT Rect =
       {Min4 (mX1, mX2, mX3, mX4),
        Min4 (mY1, mY2, mY3, mY4),
        Max4 (mX1, mX2, mX3, mX4) + 1,
        Max4 (mY1, mY2, mY3, mY4) + 1};

   // expand rectangle to accommodate wide lines:
   int LineAdd = (mPenWidth-1) / 2 + (mPenWidth-1) % 2;
   InflateRect (&Rect, LineAdd, LineAdd);

   return Rect;
   }

void CBezier::PureDraw (HDC HDc)
// draws the Bezier curve
   {
   POINT Points [4] =
       {{mX1, mY1},
        {mX2, mY2},
        {mX3, mY3},
        {mX4, mY4}};
   PolyBezier (HDc, Points, 4);
   return;
   }

LRESULT CBezier::OnLButtonDown (WORD XCursor, WORD YCursor)
// processes WM_LBUTTONDOWN messages
   {
   HDC HDCClient;

   switch (MainWnd.mMode)
      {
      case MainWnd.ModeNone: // draw straight line
         StartDrag ();
         mX1 = XCursor; mY1 = YCursor;
         mX2 = XCursor; mY2 = YCursor;
         mX3 = XCursor; mY3 = YCursor;
         mX4 = XCursor; mY4 = YCursor;
         MainWnd.mMode = MainWnd.ModeDragging;
         break;

      case MainWnd.ModeMark1:  // mark first control point
         // erase straight line / draw temporary bezier:
         HDCClient = GetTempDC ();
         MoveToEx (HDCClient, mX1, mY1, 0);
         LineTo (HDCClient, mX4, mY4);
         mX2 = XCursor; mY2 = YCursor;
         mX3 = XCursor; mY3 = YCursor;
         PureDraw (HDCClient);
         ReleaseDC (MainWnd.mHWnd, HDCClient);
```

```
            MainWnd.mMode = MainWnd.ModeMark2;
            break;

        case MainWnd.ModeMark2:  // mark second control point
            // erase temporary bezier:
            HDCClient = GetTempDC ();
            PureDraw (HDCClient);

            // add bezier to document and draw it:
            mX3 = XCursor; mY3 = YCursor;
            Document.AddFigure (this);
            MainWnd.mCurrentFig = CreateObject ();
            Draw (HDCClient);
            ReleaseDC (MainWnd.mHWnd, HDCClient);

            MainWnd.mMode = MainWnd.ModeNone;
            break;
        }
    return NULL;
    }

LRESULT CBezier::OnLButtonUp (WORD XCursor, WORD YCursor)
// processes WM_LBUTTONUP messages
    {
    if (MainWnd.mMode != MainWnd.ModeDragging)
        return NULL;

    // end drag operation:
    ReleaseCapture ();
    ClipCursor (NULL);

    // erase old temp. straight line / draw new one:
    HDC HDCClient = GetTempDC ();
    MoveToEx (HDCClient, mX1, mY1, 0);
    LineTo   (HDCClient, mX4, mY4);
    MoveToEx (HDCClient, mX1, mY1, 0);
    LineTo   (HDCClient, XCursor, YCursor);
    ReleaseDC (MainWnd.mHWnd, HDCClient);

    // save new coordinates / stop drawing if line is trivial:
    mX4 = XCursor; mY4 = YCursor;
    if (mX1 == mX4 && mY1 == mY4)
        MainWnd.mMode = MainWnd.ModeNone;
    else
        MainWnd.mMode = MainWnd.ModeMark1;
    return NULL;
    }

LRESULT CBezier::OnMouseMove (WORD XCursor, WORD YCursor)
// processes WM_MOUSEMOVE messages
    {
    if (MainWnd.mMode != MainWnd.ModeDragging)
        return NULL;
```

```cpp
   // erase old temporary straight line / draw new one:
   HDC HDCClient = GetTempDC ();
   MoveToEx (HDCClient, mX1, mY1, 0);
   LineTo   (HDCClient, mX4, mY4);
   MoveToEx (HDCClient, mX1, mY1, 0);
   LineTo   (HDCClient, XCursor, YCursor);
   mX4 = XCursor; mY4 = YCursor;
   ReleaseDC (MainWnd.mHWnd, HDCClient);
   return NULL;
   }

/////////////////////////////////////////////////////////////////////////////
// CLine:                                                                   //
/////////////////////////////////////////////////////////////////////////////

void CLine::PureDraw (HDC HDc)
// draws the line
   {
   MoveToEx (HDc, mX1, mY1, 0);
   LineTo (HDc, mX2, mY2);
   return;
   }

LRESULT CLine::OnLButtonDown (WORD XCursor, WORD YCursor)
// processes WM_LBUTTONDOWN messages
   {
   StartDrag ();
   mX1 = XCursor; mY1 = YCursor;
   mX2 = XCursor; mY2 = YCursor;
   MainWnd.mMode = MainWnd.ModeDragging;
   return NULL;
   }

LRESULT CLine::OnLButtonUp (WORD XCursor, WORD YCursor)
// processes WM_LBUTTONUP messages
   {
   if (MainWnd.mMode != MainWnd.ModeDragging)
      return NULL;

   // end drag operation:
   ReleaseCapture ();
   ClipCursor (NULL);

   // erase temporary line:
   HDC HDCClient = GetTempDC ();
   PureDraw (HDCClient);

   // if line is not trivial, add it to document and draw it:
   mX2 = XCursor; mY2 = YCursor;
   if (mX1 != mX2 || mY1 != mY2)
      {
      Document.AddFigure (this);
      MainWnd.mCurrentFig = CreateObject ();
```

```
     Draw (HDCClient);
     }
   ReleaseDC (MainWnd.mHWnd, HDCClient);
   MainWnd.mMode = MainWnd.ModeNone;
   return NULL;
   }

LRESULT CLine::OnMouseMove (WORD XCursor, WORD YCursor)
// processes WM_MOUSEMOVE messages
   {
   if (MainWnd.mMode != MainWnd.ModeDragging)
      return NULL;

   // erase old temporary line / draw new one:
   HDC HDCClient = GetTempDC ();
   PureDraw (HDCClient);
   mX2 = XCursor; mY2 = YCursor;
   PureDraw (HDCClient);
   ReleaseDC (MainWnd.mHWnd, HDCClient);
   return NULL;
   }

//////////////////////////////////////////////////////////////////////////////
// CPolyline:                                                                 //
//////////////////////////////////////////////////////////////////////////////

RECT CPolyline::GetBoundRect (void)
// returns the smallest rectangle bounding all lines
   {
   int NP; // number of points
   RECT Rect = {0,0,0,0};

   NP = mNumPoints;
   // if dragging, must include the new point not yet added:
   if (MainWnd.mMode == MainWnd.ModeDragging)
      ++NP;

   if (NP < 2)  // if less than 2 points, return empty
      return Rect; // rectangle

   // obtain dimensions of bounding rectangle:
   Rect.left = INT_MAX;
   Rect.top = INT_MAX;
   Rect.right = INT_MIN;
   Rect.bottom = INT_MIN;
   for (int i = 0; i < NP; ++i)
      {
      Rect.left   = min (Rect.left,   mPoints [i].x);
      Rect.top    = min (Rect.top,    mPoints [i].y);
      Rect.right  = max (Rect.right,  mPoints [i].x);
      Rect.bottom = max (Rect.bottom, mPoints [i].y);
      }
   ++Rect.right; ++Rect.bottom;
```

```cpp
   // expand rectangle to accommodate wide lines:
   int LineAdd = (mPenWidth-1) / 2 + (mPenWidth-1) % 2;
   InflateRect (&Rect, LineAdd, LineAdd);

   return Rect;
   }


void CPolyline::PureDraw (HDC HDc)
// draws the connected lines:
   {
   Polyline (HDc, mPoints, mNumPoints);
   return;
   }


LRESULT CPolyline::OnLButtonDblClk (WORD XCursor, WORD YCursor)
// processes WM_LBUTTONDBLCLK messages
   {
   // if more than 1 point marked, add polyline figure to
   // document and draw it:
   if (mNumPoints > 1)
      {
      Document.AddFigure (this);
      MainWnd.mCurrentFig = CreateObject ();
      HDC HDCClient = GetDC (MainWnd.mHWnd);
      Draw (HDCClient);
      ReleaseDC (MainWnd.mHWnd, HDCClient);
      }
   MainWnd.mMode = MainWnd.ModeNone;
   return NULL;
   }


LRESULT CPolyline::OnLButtonDown (WORD XCursor, WORD YCursor)
// processes WM_LBUTTONDOWN messages
   {
   // initialize first point:
   if (MainWnd.mMode == MainWnd.ModeNone)
      {
      mNumPoints = 1;
      mPoints [0].x = XCursor;
      mPoints [0].y = YCursor;
      }

   // save coordinates:
   mPoints [mNumPoints].x = XCursor;
   mPoints [mNumPoints].y = YCursor;

   // draw temporary line back to previous point:
   HDC HDCClient = GetTempDC ();
   MoveToEx (HDCClient, mPoints [mNumPoints-1].x,
      mPoints [mNumPoints-1].y, 0);
   LineTo (HDCClient, mPoints [mNumPoints].x,
      mPoints [mNumPoints].y);
   ReleaseDC (MainWnd.mHWnd, HDCClient);
```

```
   StartDrag ();
   MainWnd.mMode = MainWnd.ModeDragging;
   return NULL;
   }

LRESULT CPolyline::OnLButtonUp (WORD XCursor, WORD YCursor)
// processes WM_LBUTTONUP messages
   {
   if (MainWnd.mMode != MainWnd.ModeDragging)
   return NULL;

   // end drag operation:
   ReleaseCapture ();
   ClipCursor (NULL);

   // erase old temporary line / draw new one:
   HDC HDCClient = GetTempDC ();
   MoveToEx (HDCClient, mPoints [mNumPoints-1].x,
      mPoints [mNumPoints-1].y, 0);
   LineTo (HDCClient, mPoints [mNumPoints].x,
      mPoints [mNumPoints].y);
   MoveToEx (HDCClient, mPoints [mNumPoints-1].x,
      mPoints [mNumPoints-1].y, 0);
   LineTo (HDCClient, XCursor, YCursor);
   ReleaseDC (MainWnd.mHWnd, HDCClient);

   mPoints [mNumPoints].x = XCursor;
   mPoints [mNumPoints].y = YCursor;

   // if new point is not on top of previous point, increment
   // number of points:
   if (mPoints [mNumPoints].x != mPoints [mNumPoints-1].x ||
      mPoints [mNumPoints].y != mPoints [mNumPoints-1].y)
      ++mNumPoints;

   // if maximum number of points has been used, end drawing now:
   if (mNumPoints == MAXPOINTS)
      OnLButtonDblClk (XCursor, YCursor);

   MainWnd.mMode = MainWnd.ModeMark1;
   return NULL;
   }

LRESULT CPolyline::OnMouseMove (WORD XCursor, WORD YCursor)
// processes WM_MOUSEMOVE messages
   {
   if (MainWnd.mMode != MainWnd.ModeDragging)
      return NULL;

   // erase old temporary line / draw new one:
   HDC HDCClient = GetTempDC ();
   MoveToEx (HDCClient, mPoints [mNumPoints-1].x,
      mPoints [mNumPoints-1].y, 0);
```

```cpp
LineTo (HDCClient, mPoints [mNumPoints].x,
   mPoints [mNumPoints].y);
MoveToEx (HDCClient, mPoints [mNumPoints-1].x,
   mPoints [mNumPoints-1].y, 0);
LineTo (HDCClient, XCursor, YCursor);
ReleaseDC (MainWnd.mHWnd, HDCClient);

// save new coordinates:
mPoints [mNumPoints].x = XCursor;
mPoints [mNumPoints].y = YCursor;
return NULL;
}
```

Listing 3.7:   Document.h

```cpp
///////////////////////////////////////////////////////////////////////
//                                                                     //
// Document.h: Header file for document class.                         //
//                                                                     //
///////////////////////////////////////////////////////////////////////

struct FigCell          // element of linked list storing figures
{
   FigCell *PNextFig; // pointer to next element in list
   CFigure *PFigure;  // pointer to figure object
};

class CDocument
{
public:
   FigCell *mPFirstFig;  // pointer to start of linked list

   CDocument (void);
   void AddFigure (CFigure *PFigure);
};
```

Listing 3.8:   Document.cpp

```cpp
///////////////////////////////////////////////////////////////////////
//                                                                     //
// Document.cpp: Implementation file for document class.               //
//                                                                     //
///////////////////////////////////////////////////////////////////////

#define STRICT
#include <windows.h>

#include "figure.h"
#include "document.h"
#include "dialog.h"
```

```
extern CAttrDlg AttrDlg;
extern CPenDlg PenDlg;

CDocument::CDocument (void)
   {
   mPFirstFig = 0;
   return;
   }

void CDocument::AddFigure (CFigure *PFigure)
// adds a new figure to end of linked list
   {
   FigCell *PCell;

   // save default pen features:
   PFigure->mPenColor = PenDlg.mPenColor;
   PFigure->mPenStyle = PenDlg.mPenStyle;
   PFigure->mPenType = PenDlg.mPenType;
   PFigure->mPenWidth = PenDlg.mPenWidth;

   // save default drawing attributes:
   PFigure->mBkColor = AttrDlg.mBkColor;
   PFigure->mBkMode = AttrDlg.mBkMode;
   PFigure->mMixMode = AttrDlg.mMixMode;

   // set PCell to new cell at end of list:
   if (mPFirstFig == 0)
      {
      mPFirstFig = new FigCell;
      PCell = mPFirstFig;
      }
   else
      {
      PCell = mPFirstFig;
      while (PCell->PNextFig != 0)
         PCell = PCell->PNextFig;
      PCell->PNextFig = new FigCell;
      PCell = PCell->PNextFig;
      }

   // assign values to new cell:
   PCell->PNextFig = 0;
   PCell->PFigure = PFigure;
   return;
   }
```

Listing 3.9:   Dialog.h

```
//////////////////////////////////////////////////////////////////////
//                                                                    //
// Dialog.h: Header file for the dialog box classes.                  //
//                                                                    //
//////////////////////////////////////////////////////////////////////
```

```
class CAboutDlg
{
public:
   int Show (void);

   // message-handling functions:
   BOOL OnCancel (HWND HDlg);
   BOOL OnCtlColor (HDC HDc);
   BOOL OnInitDialog (void);
   BOOL OnOK (HWND HDlg);
};

class CAttrDlg
{
public:
   // store default drawing attributes:
   COLORREF mBkColor;
   int mBkMode;
   int mMixMode;

   CAttrDlg (void);
   int Show (void);

   // message-handling functions:
   BOOL OnCancel (HWND HDlg);
   BOOL OnCtlColor (HDC HDc);
   BOOL OnInitDialog (HWND HDlg);
   BOOL OnOK (HWND HDlg);
   BOOL OnSetColor (HWND HDlg);

protected:
   // saves custom colors user chooses in Color dialog box:
   DWORD mCustColors [16];
};

class CPenDlg
{
public:
   // store default pen description:
   COLORREF mPenColor;
   DWORD mPenStyle;
   DWORD mPenType;
   DWORD mPenWidth;

   CPenDlg (void);
   int Show (void);

   // message-handling functions:
   BOOL OnCancel (HWND HDlg);
   BOOL OnCtlColor (HDC HDc);
   BOOL OnInitDialog (HWND HDlg);
   BOOL OnOK (HWND HDlg);
   BOOL OnSetColor (HWND HDlg);
```

```
protected:
   // saves custom colors user chooses in Color dialog box:
   DWORD mCustColors [16];
};
```

Listing 3.10:　Dialog.cpp

```cpp
////////////////////////////////////////////////////////////////////////////
//                                                                        //
// Dialog.cpp: Implementation file for the dialog box classes.            //
//                                                                        //
////////////////////////////////////////////////////////////////////////////

#define STRICT
#include <windows.h>
#include "resource.h"

#include "app.h"
#include "figure.h"
#include "mainwnd.h"
#include "dialog.h"

#include <memory.h>

extern CApp       App;
extern CMainWnd   MainWnd;
extern CAboutDlg  AboutDlg;
extern CAttrDlg   AttrDlg;
extern CPenDlg    PenDlg;

BOOL CALLBACK AboutDialogProc (HWND HDlg, UINT Msg,
   WPARAM WParam, LPARAM LParam);
BOOL CALLBACK AttrDialogProc (HWND HDlg, UINT Msg, WPARAM WParam,
   LPARAM LParam);
BOOL CALLBACK PenDialogProc (HWND HDlg, UINT Msg, WPARAM WParam,
   LPARAM LParam);

// global tables for combo box data:

static struct  // stores strings and color values for all
{              // elements to be added to Color combo box
   char *ColorName;
   COLORREF ColorValue;
}
ColorTable [10] =
   {{"Black", RGB (0,0,0)},
    {"Gray",  RGB (192,192,192)},
    {"White", RGB (255,255,255)},
    {"Red",   RGB (255,0,0)},
    {"Green", RGB (0,255,0)},
    {"Blue",  RGB (0,0,255)},
    {"Yellow",  RGB (255,255,0)},
```

```
   {"Cyan",      RGB (0,255,255)},
   {"Magenta",   RGB (255,0,255)},
   {"<Custom>", RGB (0,0,0)}};

static struct // stores strings and IDs for all elements to be
{              // added to Mix Mode combo box
   char *MixModeName;
   int MixModeID;
}
MixModeTable [16] =
   {{"R2_BLACK",        R2_BLACK},
    {"R2_COPYPEN",      R2_COPYPEN},
    {"R2_MASKNOTPEN",   R2_MASKNOTPEN},
    {"R2_MASKPEN",      R2_MASKPEN},
    {"R2_MASKPENNOT",   R2_MASKPENNOT},
    {"R2_MERGENOTPEN",  R2_MERGENOTPEN},
    {"R2_MERGEPEN",     R2_MERGEPEN},
    {"R2_MERGEPENNOT",  R2_MERGEPENNOT},
    {"R2_NOP",          R2_NOP},
    {"R2_NOT",          R2_NOT},
    {"R2_NOTCOPYPEN",   R2_NOTCOPYPEN},
    {"R2_NOTMASKPEN",   R2_NOTMASKPEN},
    {"R2_NOTMERGEPEN",  R2_NOTMERGEPEN},
    {"R2_NOTXORPEN",    R2_NOTXORPEN},
    {"R2_WHITE",        R2_WHITE},
    {"R2_XORPEN",       R2_XORPEN}};

static struct  // stores strings and IDs for all elements to be
{              // added to Style combo box
   char *StyleName;
   DWORD StyleID;
}
StyleTable [7] =
   {{"Solid",        PS_SOLID},
    {"Dash",         PS_DASH},
    {"Dot",          PS_DOT},
    {"Dash-Dot",     PS_DASHDOT},
    {"Dash-Dot-Dot", PS_DASHDOTDOT},
    {"Null",         PS_NULL},
    {"Inside-Frame", PS_INSIDEFRAME}};

//////////////////////////////////////////////////////////////////////////////
// About dialog box:                                                         //
//////////////////////////////////////////////////////////////////////////////

//////////////////////////////////////////////////////////////////////////////
// CAboutDlg public member function:                                         //
//////////////////////////////////////////////////////////////////////////////

int CAboutDlg::Show (void)
// displays About dialog box
   {
   return DialogBox
```

```
      (App.mHInstance,
      MAKEINTRESOURCE (IDD_ABOUT),
      MainWnd.mHWnd,
      AboutDialogProc);
   }

////////////////////////////////////////////////////////////////////////////
// About dialog box procedure:                                              //
////////////////////////////////////////////////////////////////////////////

BOOL CALLBACK AboutDialogProc
   (HWND   HDlg,
    UINT   Msg,
    WPARAM WParam,
    LPARAM LParam)
    {
    switch (Msg)
       {
       case WM_INITDIALOG:   // dialog box was just created
          return AboutDlg.OnInitDialog ();

       case WM_COMMAND:        // user issued a command
          switch (LOWORD (WParam))
             {
             case IDCANCEL: // user chose Close or pressed Esc
                return AboutDlg.OnCancel (HDlg);

             case IDOK:       // user clicked OK or pressed Enter
                return AboutDlg.OnOK (HDlg);

             default:
                return FALSE;  // default message processing
             }

       case WM_CTLCOLORDLG:    // dialog box about to be painted;
       case WM_CTLCOLORSTATIC: // text about to be painted
          return AboutDlg.OnCtlColor ((HDC)WParam);

       default:            // request default processing for all
          return FALSE;  // other messages
       }
    }

////////////////////////////////////////////////////////////////////////////
// CAboutDlg message handling member functions:                             //
////////////////////////////////////////////////////////////////////////////

BOOL CAboutDlg::OnCancel (HWND HDlg)
// processes WM_COMMAND / IDCANCEL messages
   {
   // close the dialog box:
   EndDialog (HDlg, IDCANCEL);
   return TRUE;
   }
```

```cpp
BOOL CAboutDlg::OnCtlColor (HDC HDc)
// processes WM_CTLCOLORDLG and WM_CTLCOLORSTATIC messages
   {
   // set text background to light gray:
   SetBkColor (HDc, RGB (192,192,192));

   // supply a handle to a light-gray brush:
   return (BOOL)GetStockObject (LTGRAY_BRUSH);
   }

BOOL CAboutDlg::OnInitDialog (void)
// processes WM_INITDIALOG messages
   {
   // return TRUE to set focus to first control:
   return TRUE;
   }

BOOL CAboutDlg::OnOK (HWND HDlg)
// processes WM_COMMAND / IDOK messages
   {
   // close the dialog box:
   EndDialog (HDlg, IDOK);
   return TRUE;
   }

/////////////////////////////////////////////////////////////////////////////
// Attributes dialog box:                                                   //
/////////////////////////////////////////////////////////////////////////////

/////////////////////////////////////////////////////////////////////////////
// CAttrDlg public member functions:                                        //
/////////////////////////////////////////////////////////////////////////////

CAttrDlg::CAttrDlg (void)
   {
   mBkColor = RGB (255,255,255);
   mBkMode = OPAQUE;
   mMixMode = R2_COPYPEN;
   memset (mCustColors, 0, sizeof (mCustColors));
   return;
   }

int CAttrDlg::Show (void)
// displays Attributes dialog box
   {
   return DialogBox
      (App.mHInstance,
      MAKEINTRESOURCE (IDD_ATTR),
      MainWnd.mHWnd,
      AttrDialogProc);
   }
```

```
/////////////////////////////////////////////////////////////////////////
// Attributes dialog box procedure:                                      //
/////////////////////////////////////////////////////////////////////////

BOOL CALLBACK AttrDialogProc
   (HWND   HDlg,
    UINT   Msg,
    WPARAM WParam,
    LPARAM LParam)
   {
   switch (Msg)
      {
      case WM_INITDIALOG:  // dialog box was just created
         return AttrDlg.OnInitDialog (HDlg);

      case WM_COMMAND:       // user issued a command
         switch (LOWORD (WParam))
            {
            case IDC_SETCOLOR:  // user clicked Set Custom Color
               return AttrDlg.OnSetColor (HDlg);

            case IDCANCEL: // user chose Close or pressed Esc
               return AttrDlg.OnCancel (HDlg);

            case IDOK:      // user clicked OK or pressed Enter
               return AttrDlg.OnOK (HDlg);

            default:
               return FALSE;  // default message processing
            }

      case WM_CTLCOLORBTN:    // button is about to be painted;
      case WM_CTLCOLORDLG:    // dialog box about to be painted;
      case WM_CTLCOLORSTATIC: // dialog text about to be painted
         return AttrDlg.OnCtlColor ((HDC)WParam);

      default:             // request default processing for all
         return FALSE; // other messages
      }
   }

/////////////////////////////////////////////////////////////////////////
// CAttrDlg message handling member functions:                           //
/////////////////////////////////////////////////////////////////////////

BOOL CAttrDlg::OnCancel (HWND HDlg)
// processes WM_COMMAND / IDCANCEL messages
   {
   // close the dialog box:
   EndDialog (HDlg, IDCANCEL);
   return TRUE;
   }
```

```cpp
BOOL CAttrDlg::OnCtlColor (HDC HDc)
// processes WM_CTLCOLORBTN, WM_CTLCOLORDLG, and
// WM_CTLCOLORSTATIC messages
   {
   // set text background to light gray:
   SetBkColor (HDc, RGB (192,192,192));

   // supply a handle to a light-gray brush:
   return (BOOL)GetStockObject (LTGRAY_BRUSH);
   }

BOOL CAttrDlg::OnInitDialog (HWND HDlg)
// processes WM_INITDIALOG messages
   {
   // initialize Mix Mode combo box and select current value:
   for (int i = 0; i < 16; ++i)
      {
      SendDlgItemMessage (HDlg, IDC_MIXMODE, CB_ADDSTRING,
         0, (LPARAM)(LPCSTR)MixModeTable [i].MixModeName);
      if (MixModeTable [i].MixModeID == mMixMode)
         SendDlgItemMessage (HDlg, IDC_MIXMODE, CB_SETCURSEL,
            (WPARAM)i, 0);
      }

   // check Background Mode radio button:
   CheckDlgButton
      (HDlg,
      mBkMode == TRANSPARENT ? IDC_TRANSPARENT : IDC_OPAQUE,
      1);

   // initialize Color combo box and select current value:
   BOOL Selected = FALSE;
   for (i = 0; i < 10; ++i)
      {
      SendDlgItemMessage (HDlg, IDC_COLOR, CB_ADDSTRING, 0,
         (LPARAM)(LPCSTR)ColorTable [i].ColorName);
      if (!Selected && ColorTable [i].ColorValue == mBkColor)
         {
         SendDlgItemMessage (HDlg, IDC_COLOR, CB_SETCURSEL,
            (WPARAM)i, 0);
         Selected = TRUE;
         }
      }
   if (!Selected)
      {
      ColorTable [9].ColorValue = mBkColor;
      SendDlgItemMessage (HDlg, IDC_COLOR, CB_SETCURSEL,
         (WPARAM)9, 0);
      }

   // return TRUE to set focus to first control:
   return TRUE;
   }
```

```cpp
BOOL CAttrDlg::OnOK (HWND HDlg)
// processes WM_COMMAND / IDOK messages
   {
   // save selection from Mix Mode combo box:
   mMixMode = MixModeTable [SendDlgItemMessage (HDlg,
      IDC_MIXMODE, CB_GETCURSEL, 0, 0)].MixModeID;

   // save Background Mode choice:
   mBkMode = IsDlgButtonChecked (HDlg, IDC_TRANSPARENT) ?
      TRANSPARENT : OPAQUE;

   // save selection from Color combo box:
   mBkColor = ColorTable [SendDlgItemMessage (HDlg,
      IDC_COLOR, CB_GETCURSEL, 0, 0)].ColorValue;

   // close the dialog box:
   EndDialog (HDlg, IDOK);
   return TRUE;
   }

BOOL CAttrDlg::OnSetColor (HWND HDlg)
// processes WM_COMMAND / ID_SETCOLOR messages
   {
   CHOOSECOLOR CC;

   // assign values to structure to control Color dialog box:
   memset (&CC, 0, sizeof (CC));
   CC.lStructSize = sizeof (CC);
   CC.hwndOwner = HDlg;
   CC.rgbResult = ColorTable [9].ColorValue;
   CC.lpCustColors = mCustColors;
   CC.Flags = CC_RGBINIT;

   // display Color common dialog box; save selected color if
   // user clicked OK:
   if (ChooseColor (&CC))
   ColorTable [9].ColorValue = CC.rgbResult;
   return TRUE;
   }

/////////////////////////////////////////////////////////////////////////////
// Pen dialog box:                                                          //
/////////////////////////////////////////////////////////////////////////////

/////////////////////////////////////////////////////////////////////////////
// CPenDlg public member functions:                                         //
/////////////////////////////////////////////////////////////////////////////

CPenDlg::CPenDlg (void)
   {
   mPenColor = RGB (0,0,0);
   mPenStyle = PS_SOLID;
   mPenType = PS_COSMETIC;
   mPenWidth = 1;
```

```cpp
    memset (mCustColors, 0, sizeof (mCustColors));
    return;
    }

int CPenDlg::Show (void)
// displays Pen dialog box
    {
    return DialogBox
        (App.mHInstance,
        MAKEINTRESOURCE (IDD_PEN),
        MainWnd.mHWnd,
        PenDialogProc);
    }

////////////////////////////////////////////////////////////////////////
// Pen dialog box procedure:                                            //
////////////////////////////////////////////////////////////////////////

BOOL CALLBACK PenDialogProc
    (HWND    HDlg,
    UINT    Msg,
    WPARAM WParam,
    LPARAM LParam)
    {
    switch (Msg)
        {
        case WM_INITDIALOG:  // dialog box was just created
            return PenDlg.OnInitDialog (HDlg);

        case WM_COMMAND:      // user issued a command
            switch (LOWORD (WParam))
              {
              case IDC_SETCOLOR: // user clicked Set Custom Color
                return PenDlg.OnSetColor (HDlg);

              case IDCANCEL: // user chose Close or pressed Esc
                 return PenDlg.OnCancel (HDlg);

              case IDOK:      // user clicked OK or pressed Enter
                return PenDlg.OnOK (HDlg);

              default:
                return FALSE; // default message processing
              }

        case WM_CTLCOLORBTN:    // button is about to be painted;
        case WM_CTLCOLORDLG:    // dialog box about to be painted;
        case WM_CTLCOLORSTATIC: // dialog text about to be painted
            return PenDlg.OnCtlColor ((HDC)WParam);

        default:              // request default processing for all
            return FALSE; // other messages
        }
    }
```

```
///////////////////////////////////////////////////////////////////////
// CPenDlg message handling member functions:                          //
///////////////////////////////////////////////////////////////////////

BOOL CPenDlg::OnCancel (HWND HDlg)
// processes WM_COMMAND / IDCANCEL messages
   {
   // close the dialog box:
   EndDialog (HDlg, IDCANCEL);
   return TRUE;
   }

BOOL CPenDlg::OnCtlColor (HDC HDc)
// processes WM_CTLCOLORBTN, WM_CTLCOLORDLG, and
// WM_CTLCOLORSTATIC messages
   {
   // set text background to light gray:
   SetBkColor (HDc, RGB (192,192,192));

   // supply a handle to a light-gray brush:
   return (BOOL)GetStockObject (LTGRAY_BRUSH);
   }

BOOL CPenDlg::OnInitDialog (HWND HDlg)
// processes WM_INITDIALOG messages
   {
   // check Type radio button:
   CheckDlgButton
      (HDlg,
      mPenType == PS_COSMETIC ? IDC_COSMETIC : IDC_GEOMETRIC,
      1);

   // initialize Style combo box and select current value:
   for (int i = 0; i < 7; ++i)
      {
      SendDlgItemMessage (HDlg, IDC_STYLE, CB_ADDSTRING,
         0, (LPARAM)(LPCSTR)StyleTable [i].StyleName);
      if (StyleTable [i].StyleID == mPenStyle)
         SendDlgItemMessage (HDlg, IDC_STYLE, CB_SETCURSEL,
            (WPARAM)i, 0);
      }

   // limit Width edit control to 2 characters and set value:
   SendDlgItemMessage (HDlg, IDC_WIDTH, EM_SETLIMITTEXT,
      (WPARAM)2, 0);
   SetDlgItemInt (HDlg, IDC_WIDTH, mPenWidth, FALSE);

   // initialize Color combo box and select current value:
   BOOL Selected = FALSE;
   for (i = 0; i < 10; ++i)
      {
      SendDlgItemMessage (HDlg, IDC_COLOR, CB_ADDSTRING, 0,
         (LPARAM)(LPCSTR)ColorTable [i].ColorName);
```

```cpp
      if (!Selected && ColorTable [i].ColorValue == mPenColor)
         {
         SendDlgItemMessage (HDlg, IDC_COLOR, CB_SETCURSEL,
            (WPARAM)i, 0);
         Selected = TRUE;
         }
      }
   if (!Selected)
      {
      ColorTable [9].ColorValue = mPenColor;
      SendDlgItemMessage (HDlg, IDC_COLOR, CB_SETCURSEL
         (WPARAM)9, 0);
      }

   // return TRUE to set focus to first control:
   return TRUE;
   }

BOOL CPenDlg::OnOK (HWND HDlg)
// processes WM_COMMAND / IDOK messages
   {
   // save Type choice:
   mPenType = IsDlgButtonChecked (HDlg, IDC_COSMETIC) ?
      PS_COSMETIC : PS_GEOMETRIC;

   // save selection from Style combo box:
   mPenStyle = StyleTable [SendDlgItemMessage (HDlg, IDC_STYLE,
      CB_GETCURSEL, 0, 0)].StyleID;

   // save value from Width edit control:
   BOOL Translated;
   mPenWidth = GetDlgItemInt (HDlg, IDC_WIDTH, &Translated,
      FALSE);

   // save selection from Color combo box:
   mPenColor = ColorTable [SendDlgItemMessage (HDlg,
      IDC_COLOR, CB_GETCURSEL, 0, 0)].ColorValue;

   // close the dialog box:
   EndDialog (HDlg, IDOK);
   return TRUE;
   }

BOOL CPenDlg::OnSetColor (HWND HDlg)
// processes WM_COMMAND / ID_SETCOLOR messages
   {
   CHOOSECOLOR CC;

   // assign values to structure to control Color dialog box:
   memset (&CC, 0, sizeof (CC));
   CC.lStructSize = sizeof (CC);
   CC.hwndOwner = HDlg;
   CC.rgbResult = ColorTable [9].ColorValue;
```

```
CC.lpCustColors = mCustColors;
CC.Flags = CC_RGBINIT;

// display Color common dialog box; save selected color if
// user clicked OK:
if (ChooseColor (&CC))
   ColorTable [9].ColorValue = CC.rgbResult;
return TRUE;
}
```

DRAWING CLOSED FIGURES

In this chapter, you will learn how to draw closed figures with straight sides (rectangles and other polygons) as well as closed figures based upon ellipses (ellipses, chords, and pies). The chapter first explains how to set the drawing attributes that affect the drawing of closed figures. It then shows you how to obtain and select pens and brushes, which affect the way that Windows draws the borders and interiors of closed figures. Next, the chapter describes the API functions used to draw closed figures. It concludes by presenting the second version of the DrawIt program, which adds features for choosing brushes and drawing closed figures.

SETTING ATTRIBUTES FOR CLOSED FIGURES

The following drawing attributes affect the way that Windows draws one or more of the different types of closed figures:

- Mix mode
- Background mode
- Background color

- Mapping mode
- Viewport and window origins
- Arc direction
- Brush origin
- Polygon filling mode

Notice that this list is similar to the list of line-drawing attributes given at the beginning of Chapter 3. However, it is missing the *current position* attribute and has two new attributes: the *brush origin* and the *polygon filling mode*.

A closed figure consists of two parts that are drawn separately: a border and an interior. Windows draws the border using the current pen, and it draws the interior using the current brush.

The *mix mode* determines the way that Windows combines the pen color with the existing colors on the display surface when drawing borders. The mix mode also determines the way that Windows combines the brush color with the existing colors on the display surface when filling interiors. For instructions on setting the mix mode and an explanation of the effects of different mix-mode values, see Chapter 3 (the section entitled "Setting the Mix Mode").

As explained later in the chapter, you can select a *hatched brush* to have Windows paint the interiors of closed figures with hatch lines. The *background mode* and *background color* determine the way that Windows paints the spaces *between* the hatch lines. For instructions on setting the background mode and color, see Chapter 3 (the section entitled "Setting the Background Mode and Color").

The *mapping mode* and the *viewport* and *window origins* affect the way that Windows interprets the coordinates that you pass to all drawing functions, including those for drawing closed figures. For an explanation of the default mapping mode and origins, see Chapter 3 (the section "Calling the Line-Drawing Functions" and Figure 3.2). For an explanation of the alternative mapping modes and the techniques for adjusting the origins, see Chapter 6.

The *arc direction* determines the direction in which Windows draws chords and pies (as well as arcs, which were described in Chapter 3). Drawing chords and pies is discussed later in the chapter.

Finally, there are two drawing attributes that uniquely affect the drawing of closed figures: the *brush origin* and the *polygon filling mode*. The brush origin affects the alignment of hatch lines or patterns used to fill closed figures and is discussed in the next section. The polygon filling mode determines how Windows fills closed areas within polygons drawn with the `Polygon` or `PolyPolygon` function. It is discussed later in the chapter (in the section

"Drawing Rectangles and Polygons").

The DrawIt Version 2 program, presented at the end of the chapter, lets you set both the brush origin and the polygon filling mode in addition to the attributes you can set with DrawIt Version 1 (choose Default Attributes... on the Options menu). The code that sets these attributes is in the `CFigure::Draw` function in Figure.cpp.

CREATING AND SELECTING PENS AND BRUSHES

Windows uses the current *pen* belonging to the device context to draw the borders of all closed figures. For a complete discussion on obtaining and selecting various types of pens, see Chapter 3 (the section "Creating and Selecting Pens").

Windows uses the current *brush* to paint the interiors of closed figures— that is, the area inside of the borders. With the default brush, Windows fills interiors with solid white. You can change the color or pattern used to fill interiors by obtaining and selecting a different pen.

You can obtain one of several standard brushes by calling the `GetStockObject` API function,

```
HGDIOBJ GetStockObject (int fnObject);
```

assigning `fnObject` one of the values shown in Table 4.1

All of the brushes provided by `GetStockObject` (unless you pass `NULL_BRUSH`) are *solid*—that is, they completely fill the interiors of closed figures with the brush color. `GetStockObject` returns a handle for the

Table 4.1: The values that can be passed to `GetStockObject` to obtain different standard brushes

Value Passed to `GetStockObject`	*Resulting Brush*
`WHITE_BRUSH` (the default brush)	Solid white
`BLACK_BRUSH`	Solid black
`DKGRAY_BRUSH`	Solid dark gray
`GRAY_BRUSH`	Solid medium gray
`LTGRAY_BRUSH`	Solid light gray
`NULL_BRUSH`	Null brush: draws nothing, regardless of the mix mode

brush, which you should store in a variable of type HBRUSH. For example, the following code obtains a standard medium-gray brush and saves the handle:

```
HBRUSH HGrayBrush = (HBRUSH)GetStockObject (GRAY_BRUSH);
```

As you can see, the choice of brushes you can procure from GetStockObject is very limited. You can choose from a much greater variety of brush features by calling the CreateBrushIndirect API function to create a custom brush:

```
HBRUSH CreateBrushIndirect (CONST LOGBRUSH *lplb);
```

The lplb parameter is a pointer to a LOGBRUSH structure to which you assign the desired brush features:

```
typedef struct tagLOGBRUSH
    {
    UINT      lbStyle;
    COLORREF  lbColor;
    LONG      lbHatch;
    }
LOGBRUSH;
```

You assign to the lbStyle field the brush *style*. Table 4.2 lists the most common style values (see the LOGBRUSH documentation for a complete list).

TIP	If you want to draw a closed figure that consists of only a border, without filling the interior, you can select a null brush obtained by passing NULL_BRUSH to GetStockObject or by specifying the BS_NULL style when calling CreateBrushIndirect. If you want to draw a closed figure that consists of only the fill color or pattern, without a visible border, you can select a null pen (see Chapter 3) *or*—if you are using a solid brush—you can simply make the pen the same color as the brush.

You assign the desired *fill color* to the lbColor field. As described in Chapter 3 (in the section "Setting the Background Mode and Color"), the easiest way to assign a color value is to use the RGB macro. See Table 3.2 for the RGB values for some common colors.

If you assigned BS_SOLID to the lbStyle field, Windows will use the specified color to fill the entire interior areas of closed figures. If you specify a color value that does *not* correspond to a pure color, Windows will use a dithered color.

Table 4.2: The brush style values that can be assigned to the `lbStyle` field of the `LOGBRUSH` structure passed to `CreateBrushIndirect`

Brush Style Value Assigned to `lbStyle`	Resulting Brush
`BS_SOLID`	Solid: fills the interiors of figures with the brush color
`BS_HATCHED`	Hatched: fills the interiors of figures with hatch lines
`BS_PATTERN`	Pattern: fills the interiors of figures with copies of an 8-by-8-pixel bitmap
`BS_NULL`	Null: does not fill figures (leaves existing display colors unchanged regardless of the current mix mode)

If you assigned `BS_HATCHED` to the `lbStyle` field, Windows will use the specified color for drawing the hatch lines. If you specify a color value that does *not* correspond to a pure color, Windows will use the closest available pure color. Recall that the way Windows paints the spaces *between* the hatch lines depends upon the current background mode and color (see Chapter 3, the section entitled "Setting the Background Mode and Color").

If you assigned `BS_PATTERN` or `BS_NULL` to the `lbStyle` field, the `lbColor` field is ignored.

Finally, the `lbHatch` field specifies the brush *hatch style* or *pattern*. If you assigned `BS_HATCHED` to `lbStyle`, you must assign `lbHatch` a value indicating the desired hatch style. The values you can assign are shown in Figure 4.1.

If you assigned `BS_PATTERN` to the `lbStyle` field, you must assign `lbHatch` the handle of a bitmap containing the desired pattern. Interiors of solid figures will be filled with copies of this bitmap, placed side by side like tiles. The size of this bitmap must be 8 pixels by 8 pixels. You can obtain a bitmap handle by calling the `LoadBitmap` API function to load a bitmap that you have included in the program's resources using a bitmap resource editor, or by using one of several other methods.

If you assigned `BS_SOLID` or `BS_NULL` to the `lbStyle` field, the lbHatch field is ignored.

As an example, the following code creates a brush that fills interiors with light-blue hatch lines:

```
LOGBRUSH LB = {BS_HATCHED, RGB (0,0,255), HS_DIAGCROSS};
HBRUSH HHatchBrush = CreateBrushIndirect (&LB);
```

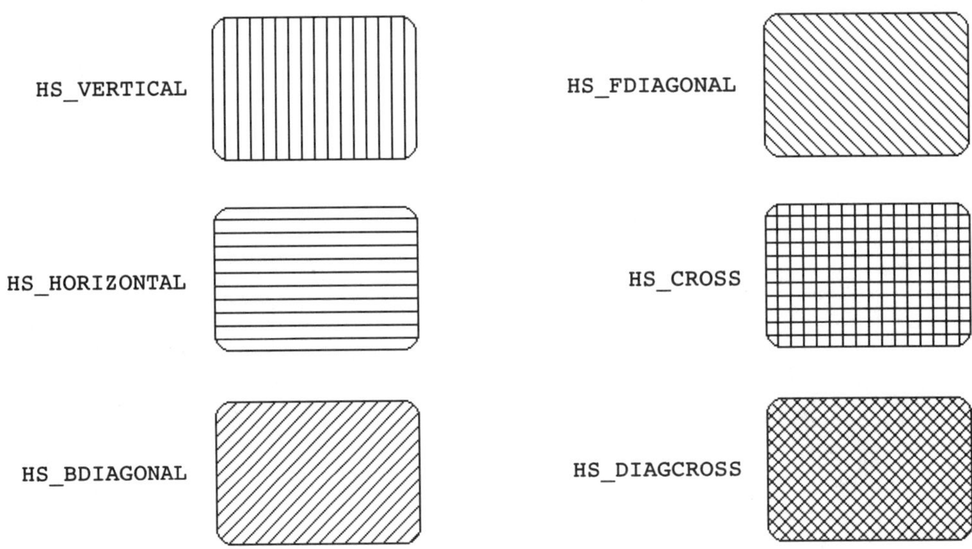

Figure 4.1:   The hatch styles you can assign to the `lbHatch` field of the `LOGBRUSH` structure you pass to `CreateBrushIndirect`. To create a hatched brush, you must also assign `BS_HATCHED` to the `lbStyle` `LOGBRUSH` field.

If you use a hatched or pattern brush, you can *shift* the position of the hatch lines or pattern on the display surface by calling the `SetBrushOrgEx` API function:

```
BOOL SetBrushOrgEx (HDC hdc, int nXOrg, int nYOrg, LPPOINT lppt);
```

`SetBrushOrgEx` modifies the *brush origin* drawing attribute. You might call this function, for example, to align the hatch lines or pattern with the top and left edges of a closed figure you are drawing. The parameter `hdc` is the device-context handle, and `nXOrg` and `nYOrg` are the horizontal and vertical distances by which you want to shift the hatch lines or pattern. You can assign `nXOrg` a value between 0 and 7. Assigning 0 positions the hatch lines or pattern at their default horizontal position, the value 1 shifts them right by one pixel, and so on. Likewise, you can assign `nYOrg` a value between 0 and 7 to specify the number of pixels by which you want to shift the hatch lines or pattern *down*. (An interior that is painted with a hatched or pattern brush is composed of identical 8-by-8-pixel units, placed side by side like tiles. Thus, the maximum amount by which you can shift the hatch lines or pattern in either direction is eight pixels.)

If you pass the address of a `POINT` structure to the `lppt` parameter, `SetBrushOrgEx` will assign it the previous brush origin (you can simply pass 0 if you do not need the previous origin). You can also obtain the current brush origin by calling the `GetBrushOrgEx` API function.

WARNING You must call `SetBrushOrgEx` *before* selecting the brush into the device context (`SetBrushOrgEx` has no effect on a brush that has already been selected into the device context).

To begin using a brush that you have obtained by either of these two methods, you must select it into the device context by calling the `SelectObject` API function,

```
HGDIOBJ SelectObject (HDC hdc, HGDIOBJ hgdiobj);
```

where `hdc` is the handle of the device context and `hgdiobj` is the handle of the brush returned by `GetStockObject` or `CreateBrushIndirect`. `SelectObject` returns the handle of the *previous* brush selected into the device context; be sure to save this handle.

When you are done using the brush, you should first remove it from the device context by calling `SelectObject` to select the *previous* brush back into the device context, and then delete it by calling the API function `DeleteObject`:

```
BOOL DeleteObject (HGDIOBJ hObject);
```

For example, the following code uses the hatched brush that was created by the call to `CreateBrushIndirect` in the example above:

```
// select hatched brush and save handle to previous brush:
HBRUSH HBrushOld = (HBRUSH)SelectObject (HDc, HHatchBrush);

// call drawing functions . . .
// (interiors of all closed figures will be painted with the
// hatched brush)

// remove hatched brush from device context by selecting previous
// brush:
SelectObject (HDc, HBrushOld);

// destroy hatched brush:
DeleteObject (HHatchBrush);
```

<table>
<tr><td>FYI</td><td>You do not need to deselect and delete a standard brush obtained by calling <code>GetStockObject</code>. Doing so, however, is harmless.</td></tr>
</table>

The DrawIt Version 2 program allows you to create a custom brush (choose Default Brush... on the Options menu) and also to set the brush origin (choose Default Attributes... on the Options menu). You can then see the results of your choices by drawing closed figures. The code that manages the brush is in the `CFigure::Draw` function in Figure.cpp.

<table>
<tr><td>FYI</td><td>The following are related API functions: <code>CreateSolidBrush</code>, <code>CreateHatchBrush</code>, <code>CreatePatternBrush</code>, <code>GetSysColorBrush</code>, <code>GetSysColor</code>, <code>CreateDIBPatternBrushPt</code>, <code>GetCurrentObject</code>, <code>EnumObjects</code>, <code>GetObject</code>, and <code>GetObjectType</code></td></tr>
</table>

CALLING FUNCTIONS TO DRAW CLOSED FIGURES

After you have set the drawing attributes and selected the pen and brush, you are ready to draw closed figures by calling the API drawing functions. For general guidelines on calling these functions and for a description of the default mapping mode, see the section entitled "Calling the Line-Drawing Functions" in Chapter 3.

When you call the `Arc` function presented in Chapter 3 or any of the drawing functions given in this chapter except `Polygon`, you must specify a *bounding rectangle*. For example, when you call `Ellipse`, you indicate the size and position of the ellipse by passing the coordinates of the rectangle that bounds the ellipse, as in the following example:

```
Ellipse (HDc, 50, 75, 150, 200);
```

In addition to the general guidelines given in Chapter 3, you should observe the following guidelines when calling an API drawing function that uses a bounding rectangle:

- The first pair of coordinates—(50, 75) in the example—gives the position of the upper-left corner of the bounding rectangle, and the second pair of coordinates gives the position of the lower-right corner of the bounding rectangle (see Figure 4.6, given later in the chapter).

- The figure that Windows draws includes the left and upper borders of the bounding rectangle, but excludes the right and bottom borders. That is, the figure extends from the left border to a position that is one pixel short of the right border, and from the top border to a position that is one pixel short of the bottom border.

- Recall from Chapter 3 that if you select a custom pen with the `PS_INSIDEFRAME` style and a width greater than 1, the border of any figure drawn within a bounding rectangle will be drawn completely *inside* of the bounding rectangle (with other pen styles, a wide line will extend partially outside of the bounding rectangle).

The DrawIt Version 2 program allows you to draw any of the closed figures described in the chapter. The code for drawing these figures is contained in the following functions in the Figure.cpp source file: `CRectangle::-PureDraw`, `CRoundRect::PureDraw`, `CPolygon::PureDraw`, `CEllipse::PureDraw`, `CChord::PureDraw`, and `CPie::PureDraw`.

Drawing Rectangles and Polygons

In this section, you will learn how to draw closed figures with straight sides—namely, rectangles and other polygons.

To draw a rectangle, call the `Rectangle` API function,

```
BOOL Rectangle
   (HDC hdc,
    int nLeftRect,   int nTopRect,
    int nRightRect, int nBottomRect);
```

where `hdc` is the handle of the device context, `nLeftRect` and `nTopRect` are the coordinates of the upper-left corner of the rectangle, and `nRightRect` and `nBottomRect` are the coordinates of the lower-right corner of the rectangle. See Figure 4.2.

You can draw a rectangle with rounded corners by calling the `RoundRect` API function:

```
BOOL RoundRect
   (HDC hdc,
    int nLeftRect,   int nTopRect,
    int nRightRect, int nBottomRect,
    int nWidth, nHeight);
```

The first five parameters passed to `RoundRect` are the same as the parameters passed to `Rectangle`. The last two parameters, `nWidth` and `nHeight`,

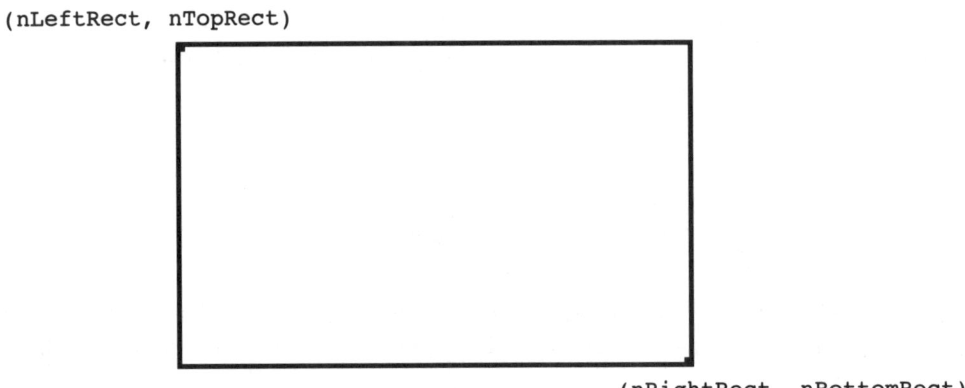

Figure 4.2:   Drawing a rectangle with the `Rectangle` API function

give the width and height of the ellipse used to draw the rounded borders.
See Figure 4.3.

Finally, you can call the `Polygon` API function to draw a polygon, which
consists of two or more vertices connected by straight lines. `Polygon` has the
following form:

```
BOOL Polygon (HDC hdc, CONST POINT *lpPoints, int nCount);
```

The `lpPoints` parameter is an array of `POINT` structures containing the coordinates of the vertices, and nCount is the number of points in the array (there
must be at least two). Unlike the similar `Polyline` function presented in
Chapter 3, `Polygon` automatically connects the last vertex in the array with

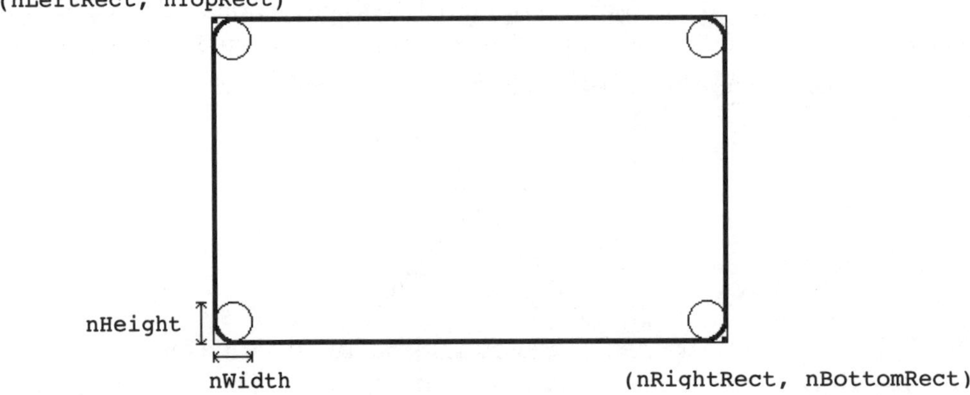

Figure 4.3:   Calling the `RoundRect` API function to draw a rectangle with rounded
corners

the first vertex, if necessary. Thus, unless you specify only two vertices, it always draws a closed figure. For example, the following code draws a triangle (see Figure 4.4):

```
POINT Points [3] =
   {{25, 50},
    {50, 25},
    {75, 50}};
Polygon (HDCPaint, Points, 3);
```

If you draw a complex polygon, in which the borders overlap, you can control which of the interior areas are filled by calling the `SetPolyFillMode` API function,

```
int SetPolyFillMode (HDC hdc, int iPolyFillMode);
```

`SetPolyFillMode` sets the *polygon filling mode*, which is one of the drawing attributes listed at the beginning of the chapter. If you assign `iPolyFillMode` the value `ALTERNATE` (the default), Windows will fill only those interior areas that can be reached from outside the figure by crossing an odd number of borders. If you assign the value `WINDING`, Windows will fill *all* interior areas. The classic example that illustrates the difference is a five-pointed star, as shown in Figure 4.5.

You can obtain the current polygon filling mode by calling the `GetPolyFillMode` API function,

```
int GetPolyFillMode (HDC hdc);
```

where `hdc` is the handle of the device context.

FYI   The following are related API functions: `FrameRect`, `DrawFocusRect`, `FillRect`, `InvertRect`, `DrawAnimatedRects`, `DrawEdge`, `PolyPolygon`, and `ExtFloodFill`

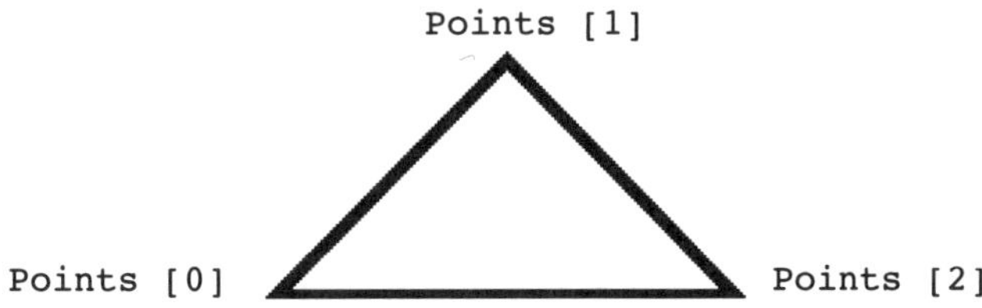

Figure 4.4:   The polygon drawn by the example code using the `Polygon` API function

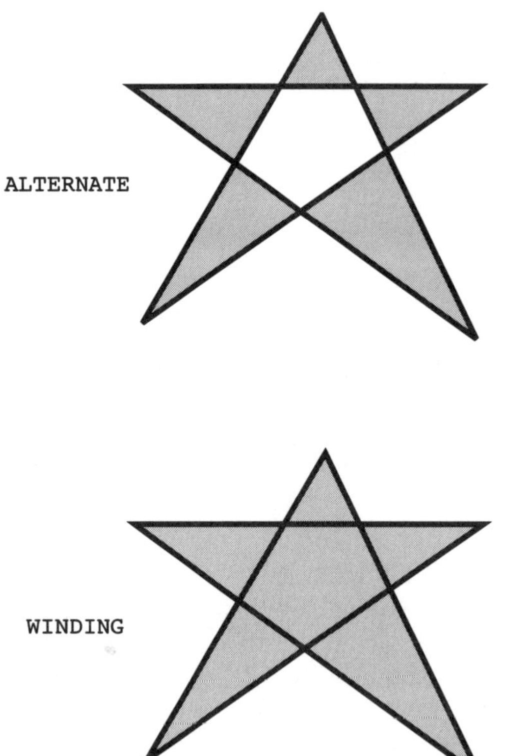

Figure 4.5:   The ALTERNATE versus the WINDING polygon filling mode set by SetPolyFillMode

Drawing Ellipses, Chords, and Pies

In this section, you will learn how to draw ellipses as well as two other closed figures that are based on ellipses: chords and pies.

To draw an ellipse, call the Ellipse API function,

```
BOOL Ellipse
   (HDC hdc,
    int nLeftRect,  int nTopRect,
    int nRightRect, int nBottomRect);
```

where hdc is the handle of the device context, nLeftRect and nTopRect are the coordinates of the upper-left corner of the bounding rectangle, and nRightRect and nBottomRect are the coordinates of the lower-right corner of the bounding rectangle. See Figure 4.6.

```
(nLeftRect, nTopRect)
```

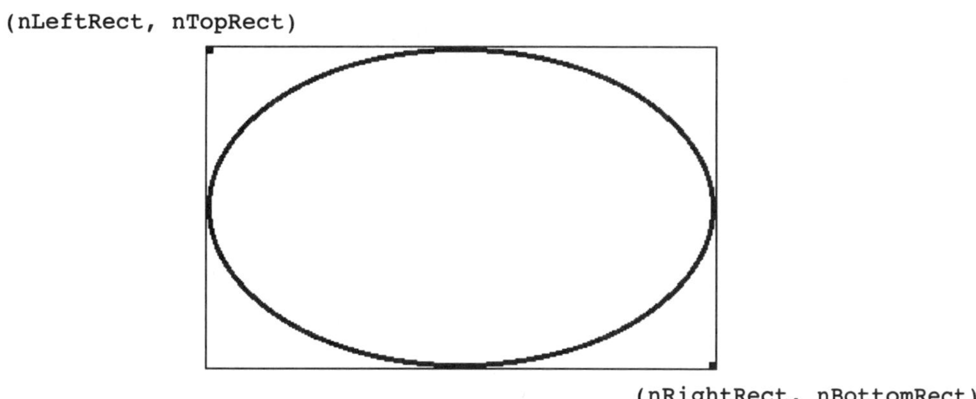

Figure 4.6:   Drawing an ellipse with the `Ellipse` API function

A *chord* is the figure created by the intersection of an ellipse and a line. You can draw a chord by calling the `Chord` API function:

```
BOOL Chord
  (HDC hdc,
    int nLeftRect,   int nTopRect,
    int nRightRect,  int nBottomRect,
    int nXRadial1,   int nYRadial1,
    int nXRadial2,   int nYRadial2);
```

The first two pairs of coordinates specify the bounding rectangle of the ellipse. The parameters `nXRadial1` and `nYRadial1` are the coordinates of a point on the starting line for the chord, and `nXRadial2` and `nYRadial2` are the coordinates of a point on the ending line (see Figure 4.7). `Chord` draws the chord from the point where the starting line intersects the ellipse to the point where the ending line intersects it. By default, `Chord` draws the chord in the counterclockwise direction (as shown in Figure 4.7). You can, however, change the drawing direction by calling the `SetArcDirection` API function, explained in Chapter 3 (in the section "Drawing Arcs").

Similarly, you can draw a pie-shaped figure by calling the `Pie` API function:

```
BOOL Pie
  (HDC hdc,
    int nLeftRect,   int nTopRect,
    int nRightRect,  int nBottomRect,
    int nXRadial1,   int nYRadial1,
    int nXRadial2,   int nYRadial2);
```

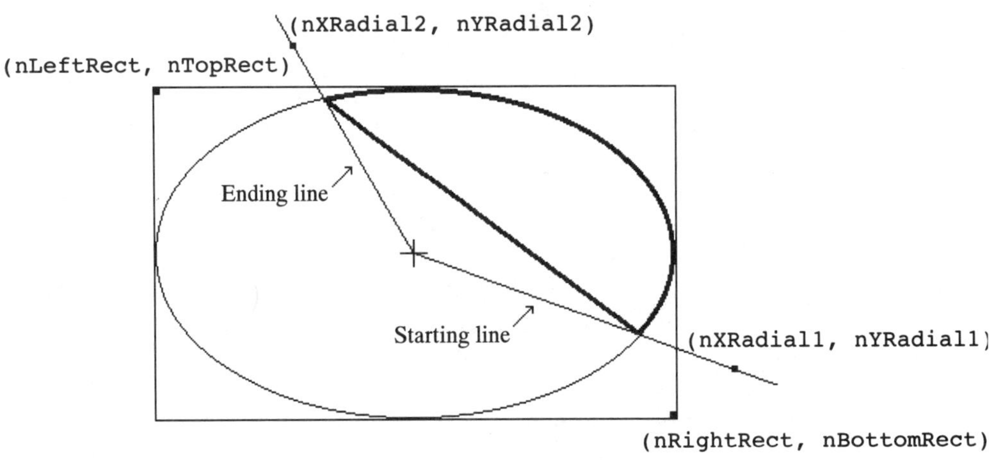

Figure 4.7:   Drawing a chord with the `Chord` API function

The parameters passed to `Pie` work in the same way as do those passed to `Chord`. See Figure 4.8.

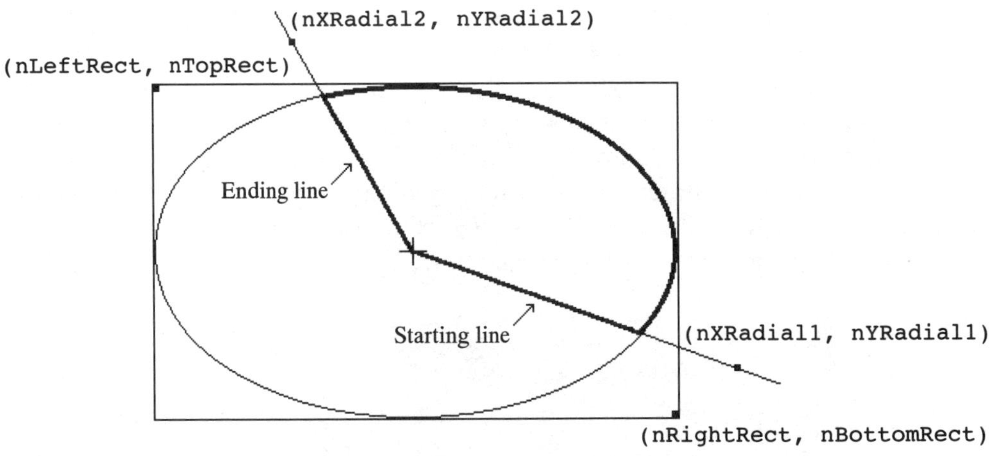

Figure 4.8:   Drawing a pie-shaped figure with the `Pie` API function

DRAWIT VERSION 2

DrawIt Version 2 is based upon DrawIt Version 1 (presented in Chapter 3) and adds features for drawing closed figures. With DrawIt Version 2, you can set the two new drawing attributes that were discussed in this chapter: the brush origin and the polygon filling mode. You can also create a custom brush. You can then see the results of your choices by drawing any of the closed figures that were presented in the chapter: rectangles, rounded rectangles, polygons, ellipses, chords, and pies.

DrawIt Version 2 also allows you to *select* a figure and then move it; change the attributes, pen, or brush used to draw it; or delete it.

Using DrawIt Version 2

To start DrawIt Version 2, run the DrawIt.exe executable file contained in the DrawIt2 subfolder within the folder in which you installed the companion disk files. For instructions on using the program features that are also provided by DrawIt Version 1, see Chapter 3 (the section "Using DrawIt Version 1"). This section explains how to use the *new* program features.

To modify the brush origin or the polygon filling mode, choose Default Attributes... on the Options menu and enter your choices into the Default Attributes dialog box (see Figure 4.9).

To select a custom brush for filling the interiors of the closed figures you draw, choose Default Brush... on the Options menu and enter the desired brush features into the Default Brush Features dialog box (see Figure 4.10). To specify a custom color for the brush, select the <Custom> item in the Color list and then click the Set Custom Color... button to select the desired color.

<table>
<tr><td>FYI</td><td>When you first run DrawIt, all drawing attributes are set to their default values, and the default pen and default brush are selected.</td></tr>
</table>

You can draw the different types of closed figures by choosing commands on the Figure menu, as follows:

- To draw a rectangle, choose Rectangle, place the cursor at one corner of the rectangle, and drag to the other corner.

- To draw a rectangle with rounded corners, choose Rounded

Figure 4.9: The Default Attributes dialog box displayed by the DrawIt Version 2 program

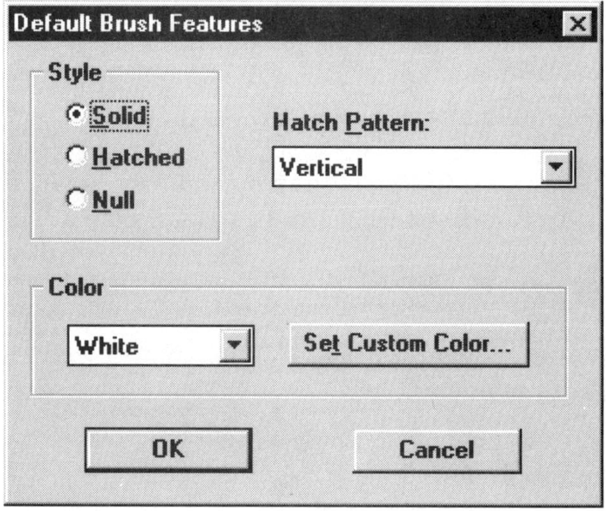

Figure 4.10: The Default Brush Features dialog box displayed by DrawIt Version 2

Rectangle, place the cursor at one corner of the rectangle, and drag to the other corner.

- To draw a polygon, choose Polygon, click on each vertex (and drag if you want to move the vertex), and double-click on the last vertex.

- To draw an ellipse or circle, choose Ellipse, place the cursor at one corner of the bounding rectangle, and drag to the other corner.

- To draw a chord, choose Chord, place the cursor at one corner of the bounding rectangle, drag to mark the ellipse, click to mark the starting line for the chord, and click to mark the ending line.

- To draw a pie-shaped figure, choose Pie, place the cursor at one corner of the bounding rectangle, drag to mark the ellipse, click to mark the starting line for the pie, and click to mark the ending line.

You can cancel the drawing of any figure by pressing Esc before the figure is complete.

You can also move a figure; change a figure's attributes, pen, or brush; or delete it. To perform any of these operations, you must first *select* the figure, as follows:

1. Choose Select on the Figure menu. Notice that the mouse pointer changes from a cross to an arrow, indicating that the program is in selecting rather than drawing mode.

2. Click on the figure you want to select. Alternatively, you can press the Tab or Shift+Tab key to move the selection from figure to figure. DrawIt will draw a dotted rectangle around the selected figure.

To move the selected figure, simply use the mouse to drag it to a new location. Notice that while the pointer is within the selected figure, it becomes a cross with four arrow heads.

To change the drawing attributes, pen, or brush for the selected figure, choose the Figure Attributes…, Figure Pen…, or Figure Brush… command on the Options menu, and enter the new values into the dialog box that is displayed. When a figure is selected, the Options menu commands and the dialog boxes are labeled with the word *Figure* rather than the word *Default*, and the changes you make affect *only the selected figure* (the default settings remain unchanged). Note that the Figure Brush… command is disabled if the figure you select is not a closed figure.

Finally, to delete the selected figure, simply press the Del key.

The DrawIt Version 2 Program Classes

DrawIt Version 2 has the same basic set of classes as DrawIt Version 1 has, plus a new class for each of the closed figures that it draws: `CRectangle`, `CRoundRect`, `CPolygon`, `CEllipse`, `CChord`, and `CPie`. Table 4.3 describes the program classes.

Because DrawIt uses C++ virtual functions and polymorphism, adding support for additional figures was relatively simple. The primary task was to add a new class for each new figure. Only a few changes were required to the code in the main window class (`CMainWnd`) that manages the figures. In DrawIt Version 2, `CFigure` is still the abstract base class for all of the figure classes; however, many of the figure classes are derived *indirectly* from `CFigure`. The hierarchy of the figure classes is shown in Figure 4.11. The sole criterion used in designing this hierarchy was to minimize code duplication.

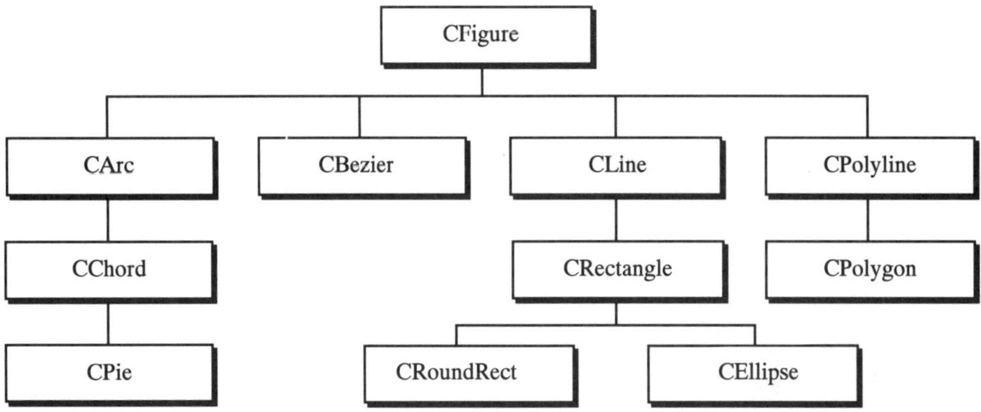

Figure 4.11:   The hierarchy of figure classes in the DrawIt Version 2 program

Class	Header and Implementation Files	Purpose
CApp	App.h	Application class: stores information on the program
CMainWnd	MainWnd.h MainWnd.cpp	Main window class: manages the main program window and performs initial processing of all keyboard and menu commands and mouse actions
CFigure	Figure.h Figure.cpp	Abstract base class for all of the figure classes
CArc	Figure.h Figure.cpp	Stores and draws an arc
CChord	Figure.h Figure.cpp	Stores and draws a chord
CPie	Figure.h Figure.cpp	Stores and draws a pie
CBezier	Figure.h Figure.cpp	Stores and draws a Bézier curve
CLine	Figure.h Figure.cpp	Stores and draws a straight line
CRectangle	Figure.h Figure.cpp	Stores and draws a rectangle
CroundRect	Figure.h Figure.cpp	Stores and draws a rounded rectangle
CEllipse	Figure.h Figure.cpp	Stores and draws an ellipse
CPolyline	Figure.h Figure.cpp	Stores and draws a set of connected line segments
CPolygon	Figure.h Figure.cpp	Stores and draws a polygon
CDocument	Document.h Document.cpp	Document class: stores a linked list containing a figure object for each figure that has been drawn
CAttrDlg	Dialog.h Dialog.cpp	Manages the Default Attributes dialog box for setting drawing attributes
CPenDlg	Dialog.h Dialog.cpp	Manages the Default Pen dialog box for selecting a pen
CBrushDlg	Dialog.h Dialog.cpp	Manages the Default Brush dialog box for selecting a brush
CAboutDlg	Dialog.h Dialog.cpp	Manages the About dialog box

The DrawIt Version 2 Source Code

The following are the C++ source code listings for DrawIt Version 2. You will find a complete copy of these listings in the DrawIt2 subfolder of the folder in which you installed your companion disk files.

Listing 4.1:   DrawIt.cpp

```cpp
///////////////////////////////////////////////////////////////////////////
//                                                                       //
// DrawIt.cpp: Main program object declarations and WinMain              //
//             program entry function.                                   //
//                                                                       //
///////////////////////////////////////////////////////////////////////////

#define STRICT
#include <windows.h>

// header files for main program classes:
#include "app.h"
#include "figure.h"
#include "mainwnd.h"
#include "document.h"
#include "dialog.h"

// main program objects:
CApp       App;
CMainWnd   MainWnd;
CDocument  Document;
CAboutDlg  AboutDlg;
CAttrDlg   AttrDlg;
CBrushDlg  BrushDlg;
CPenDlg    PenDlg;

///////////////////////////////////////////////////////////////////////////
// program entry function:                                               //
///////////////////////////////////////////////////////////////////////////

int APIENTRY WinMain
  (HINSTANCE HInstCurrent,
   HINSTANCE HInstPrevious,
   LPSTR     CmdLine,
   int       CmdShow)
   {
   MSG Msg;

   // store program informaton in application object:
   App.Initialize (HInstCurrent, CmdLine);

   // register class for main program window:
   if (!MainWnd.RegisterClass ())
      return 0;
```

```cpp
   // create and display main program window:
   if (!MainWnd.Create ())
      return 0;

   // main message loop:
   while (GetMessage (&Msg, NULL, NULL, NULL))
      {
      TranslateMessage (&Msg);
      DispatchMessage (&Msg);
      }

   // return "application-defined exit code":
   return Msg.wParam;
   }
```

Listing 4.2:   App.h

```cpp
/////////////////////////////////////////////////////////////////////////
//                                                                     //
// App.h: Header file for application class.                           //
//                                                                     //
/////////////////////////////////////////////////////////////////////////

class CApp
{
public:
   HINSTANCE mHInstance; // handle of program instance
   LPSTR     mCmdLine;   // pointer to program command line

   void Initialize (HINSTANCE HInstCurrent, LPSTR CmdLine)
   // saves application values
      {
      mHInstance = HInstCurrent;
      mCmdLine = CmdLine;
      }
};
```

Listing 4.3:   MainWnd.h

```cpp
/////////////////////////////////////////////////////////////////////////
//                                                                     //
// MainWnd.h: Header file for main window class.                       //
//                                                                     //
/////////////////////////////////////////////////////////////////////////

#define WINWIDTH 350 // dimensions of main program window
#define WINHEIGHT 400

class CMainWnd
{
```

```cpp
public:
   enum // current drawing mode
      {
      ModeNone,
      ModeDragging,
      ModeMark1,
      ModeMark2,
      ModeMoving
      }
   mMode;

   CFigure *mCurrentFig;   // pointer to current figure object
   HPEN mHPenDotted;       // handle to dotted pen
   HWND mHWnd;             // main window handle
   CFigure *mSelectedFig; // currently selected figure (if any)

   CMainWnd (void);
   BOOL Create (void);
   BOOL RegisterClass (void);

   // message-handling functions:
   LRESULT OnDestroy (void);
   LRESULT OnFigure (WORD MenuCommandID);
   LRESULT OnHelpAbout (void);
   LRESULT OnInitMenuPopup (HMENU HMenu, UINT MenuPosition);
   LRESULT OnKeyDown (int VirtKeyCode);
   LRESULT OnKillFocus (void);
   LRESULT OnLButtonDown (WORD XCursor, WORD YCursor);
   LRESULT OnLButtonUp (WORD XCursor, WORD YCursor);
   LRESULT OnMouseMove (WORD XCursor, WORD YCursor);
   LRESULT OnOptionsAttributes (void);
   LRESULT OnOptionsBrush (void);
   LRESULT OnOptionsPen (void);
   LRESULT OnPaint (void);

protected:
   UINT mCurrentFigID;   // ID of menu command for curr. figure
   RECT mRectPrev;       // previous rectangle in moving figure
   BOOL mSelecting;      // Figure / Select menu command chosen
   int mXOrig, mYOrig;   // original point when moving figure
   int mXPrev, mYPrev;   // previous point when moving figure

   void CancelDrag (void);
   void DrawSelection (void);
};
```

Listing 4.4:   MainWnd.cpp

```cpp
///////////////////////////////////////////////////////////////////////
//                                                                     //
// MainWnd.cpp: Implementation file for main window class.             //
//                                                                     //
///////////////////////////////////////////////////////////////////////

#define STRICT
#include <windows.h>
#include "resource.h"

#include "app.h"
#include "figure.h"
#include "mainwnd.h"
#include "document.h"
#include "dialog.h"

extern CApp       App;
extern CMainWnd   MainWnd;
extern CDocument  Document;
extern CAboutDlg  AboutDlg;
extern CAttrDlg   AttrDlg;
extern CBrushDlg  BrushDlg;
extern CPenDlg    PenDlg;

LRESULT CALLBACK MainWndProc (HWND HWnd, UINT Msg, WPARAM WParam,
   LPARAM LParam);

///////////////////////////////////////////////////////////////////////
// CMainWnd constructor:                                               //
///////////////////////////////////////////////////////////////////////

CMainWnd::CMainWnd (void)
   {
   mCurrentFig = new CLine;
   mCurrentFigID = ID_FIGURE_LINE;
   mHPenDotted = CreatePen (PS_DOT, 1, RGB (0,0,0));
   mMode = ModeNone;
   mSelectedFig = 0;
   mSelecting = FALSE;
   }

///////////////////////////////////////////////////////////////////////
// CMainWnd public member functions:                                   //
///////////////////////////////////////////////////////////////////////

void CMainWnd::CancelDrag (void)
// stops a figure move operation; called only if mSelecting is
// TRUE
   {
   if (mMode != ModeMoving)
      return;
```

```cpp
   // end drag operation:
   ReleaseCapture ();
   ClipCursor (NULL);

   // erase temporary bounding rectangle:
   InvalidateRect (mHWnd, &mRectPrev, TRUE);
   RECT Rect = mSelectedFig->GetBoundRect ();
   InvalidateRect (mHWnd, &Rect, TRUE);

   mMode = ModeNone;
   return;
   };

BOOL CMainWnd::Create (void)
// creates and displays main program window; returns TRUE on
// success or FALSE on error
   {
   // create main program window and save handle:
   mHWnd = CreateWindow
      ("DemoClass",
      "DrawIt",
      WS_OVERLAPPED | WS_SYSMENU | WS_MINIMIZEBOX,
      CW_USEDEFAULT,
      CW_USEDEFAULT,
      WINWIDTH,
      WINHEIGHT,
      NULL,
      NULL,
      App.mHInstance,
      NULL);
   if (!mHWnd)
      return FALSE;

   // display window:
   ShowWindow
      (mHWnd,
      SW_SHOWDEFAULT);

   return TRUE;
   }

BOOL CMainWnd::RegisterClass (void)
// registers class for main program window; returns TRUE on
// success or FALSE on error
   {
   WNDCLASS WC;

   // specify class information:
   WC.style = CS_DBLCLKS;
   WC.lpfnWndProc = MainWndProc;
   WC.cbClsExtra = 0;
   WC.cbWndExtra = 0;
   WC.hInstance = App.mHInstance;
```

```cpp
   WC.hIcon = LoadIcon (App.mHInstance,
      MAKEINTRESOURCE (IDI_ICON1));
   WC.hCursor = 0;
   WC.hbrBackground = (HBRUSH)GetStockObject (WHITE_BRUSH);
   WC.lpszMenuName = MAKEINTRESOURCE (IDR_MENU1);
   WC.lpszClassName = "DemoClass";

   // register class:
   return (BOOL)::RegisterClass (&WC);
   }

void CMainWnd::DrawSelection (void)
// obtains device context and draws selection rectangle around
// bounding rectangle of currently selected figure; second call
// erases rectangle
   {
   if (!mSelectedFig)
      return;

   RECT Rect = mSelectedFig->GetBoundRect ();
   HDC HDc = GetDC (mHWnd);
   DrawFocusRect (HDc, &Rect);
   ReleaseDC (mHWnd, HDc);
   return;
   }

////////////////////////////////////////////////////////////////////////////
// window procedure for main window:                                       //
////////////////////////////////////////////////////////////////////////////

LRESULT CALLBACK MainWndProc
   (HWND   HWnd,
   UINT   Msg,
   WPARAM WParam,
   LPARAM LParam)
   {
   switch (Msg)
      {
      case WM_COMMAND: // user chose a menu command
         switch (LOWORD (WParam))
            {
            case ID_HELP_ABOUT: // user chose Help/About
               return MainWnd.OnHelpAbout ();
            case ID_FIGURE_SELECT: // user chose command on
            case ID_FIGURE_ARC:    // Figure menu
            case ID_FIGURE_BEZIER:
            case ID_FIGURE_CHORD:
            case ID_FIGURE_ELLIPSE:
            case ID_FIGURE_LINE:
            case ID_FIGURE_PIE:
            case ID_FIGURE_POLYGON:
            case ID_FIGURE_POLYLINE:
            case ID_FIGURE_RECTANGLE:
```

```cpp
      case ID_FIGURE_ROUNDRECT:
         return MainWnd.OnFigure (LOWORD (WParam));

      case ID_OPTIONS_ATTRIBUTES: // user chose
                                  // Options/Attributes
         return MainWnd.OnOptionsAttributes ();

      case ID_OPTIONS_BRUSH:  // user chose Options/Brush
         return MainWnd.OnOptionsBrush ();

      case ID_OPTIONS_PEN:    // user chose Options/Pen
         return MainWnd.OnOptionsPen ();

      default:
         // default processing for other commands:
         return DefWindowProc (HWnd, Msg, WParam, LParam);
      }

case WM_DESTROY: // DestroyWindow was called
   return MainWnd.OnDestroy ();

case WM_INITMENUPOPUP: // user opened a popup menu
   return MainWnd.OnInitMenuPopup ((HMENU)WParam,
      (UINT)LOWORD(LParam));

case WM_KEYDOWN: // user pressed a key
   return MainWnd.OnKeyDown ((int)WParam);

case WM_KILLFOCUS: // program window has lost focus
   return MainWnd.OnKillFocus ();

case WM_LBUTTONDBLCLK: // user double-clicked left mouse
                       // button
   return MainWnd.mCurrentFig->OnLButtonDblClk
   (LOWORD (LParam), HIWORD (LParam));

case WM_LBUTTONDOWN: // user pressed left button
   return MainWnd.OnLButtonDown
   (LOWORD (LParam), HIWORD (LParam));

case WM_LBUTTONUP:  // user released left button
   return MainWnd.OnLButtonUp
   (LOWORD (LParam), HIWORD (LParam));


case WM_MOUSEMOVE:  // user moved mouse pointer
   return MainWnd.OnMouseMove
   (LOWORD (LParam), HIWORD (LParam));

case WM_PAINT: // window needs painting or repainting
   return MainWnd.OnPaint ();

default:
   // default processing for all other messages:
```

```
            return DefWindowProc (HWnd, Msg, WParam, LParam);
        }
    }

////////////////////////////////////////////////////////////////////////////
// CMainWnd message handling member functions:                             //
////////////////////////////////////////////////////////////////////////////

LRESULT CMainWnd::OnDestroy (void)
// processes WM_DESTROY messages
    {
    PostQuitMessage (0); // post a WM_QUIT message to
    return NULL;         // cause message loop to exit
    }

LRESULT CMainWnd::OnFigure (WORD MenuCommandID)
// processes WM_COMMAND messages from ALL commands on Figure menu
    {
    // exit if user chose same command previously chosen:
    if (mCurrentFigID == MenuCommandID)
       return NULL;

    // move check mark to chosen command:
    CheckMenuItem (GetMenu (mHWnd), mCurrentFigID, MF_UNCHECKED);
    mCurrentFigID = MenuCommandID;
    CheckMenuItem (GetMenu (mHWnd), mCurrentFigID, MF_CHECKED);

    // cancel any drawing or drag operation:
    if (mSelecting)
       CancelDrag ();
    else
       mCurrentFig->Cancel ();

    // cancel current selection, if any:
    DrawSelection ();
    mSelectedFig = 0;

    // if user chose Select command, set flag and exit:
    if (MenuCommandID == ID_FIGURE_SELECT)
       {
       mSelecting = TRUE;
       return NULL;
       }

    // a figure command was chosen; start by setting mSelecting
    // flag to FALSE:
    mSelecting = FALSE;

    // delete figure object:
    delete mCurrentFig;

    // create figure object for new figure type:
    switch (MenuCommandID)
       {
```

```
      case ID_FIGURE_ARC:
         mCurrentFig = new CArc;
         break;

      case ID_FIGURE_BEZIER:
         mCurrentFig = new CBezier;
         break;

      case ID_FIGURE_CHORD:
         mCurrentFig = new CChord;
         break;

      case ID_FIGURE_ELLIPSE:
         mCurrentFig = new CEllipse;
         break;

      case ID_FIGURE_LINE:
         mCurrentFig = new CLine;
         break;

      case ID_FIGURE_PIE:
         mCurrentFig = new CPie;
         break;

      case ID_FIGURE_POLYGON:
         mCurrentFig = new CPolygon;
         break;

      case ID_FIGURE_POLYLINE:
         mCurrentFig = new CPolyline;
         break;

      case ID_FIGURE_RECTANGLE:
         mCurrentFig = new CRectangle;
         break;

      case ID_FIGURE_ROUNDRECT:
         mCurrentFig = new CRoundRect;
         break;
      }
   return NULL;
   }

LRESULT CMainWnd::OnHelpAbout (void)
// processes WM_COMMAND / ID_HELP_ABOUT messages
   {
   AboutDlg.Show (); // display About dialog box
   return NULL;
   }

LRESULT CMainWnd::OnInitMenuPopup (HMENU HMenu,
   UINT MenuPosition)
// processes WM_INITMENUPOPUP messages
```

```
   {
   if (MenuPosition != 1)
      return NULL;

   // modify Options menu commands based upon whether a figure
   // is selected and type of figure selected:
   if (mSelectedFig)
      {
      if (mSelectedFig->IsBrush ())
         ModifyMenu (HMenu, ID_OPTIONS_BRUSH, MF_STRING |
            MF_ENABLED, ID_OPTIONS_BRUSH, "Figure Brush...");
      else
         ModifyMenu (HMenu, ID_OPTIONS_BRUSH,
            MF_STRING | MF_GRAYED, ID_OPTIONS_BRUSH, "Brush...");
      ModifyMenu (HMenu, ID_OPTIONS_PEN, MF_STRING,
         ID_OPTIONS_PEN, "Figure Pen...");
      ModifyMenu (HMenu, ID_OPTIONS_ATTRIBUTES, MF_STRING,
         ID_OPTIONS_ATTRIBUTES, "Figure Attributes...");
      }
   else
      {
      ModifyMenu (HMenu, ID_OPTIONS_BRUSH, MF_STRING |
         MF_ENABLED, ID_OPTIONS_BRUSH, "Default Brush...");
      ModifyMenu (HMenu, ID_OPTIONS_PEN, MF_STRING,
         ID_OPTIONS_PEN, "Default Pen...");
      ModifyMenu (HMenu, ID_OPTIONS_ATTRIBUTES, MF_STRING,
         ID_OPTIONS_ATTRIBUTES, "Default Attributes...");
      }
   return NULL;
   }

LRESULT CMainWnd::OnKeyDown (int VirtKeyCode)
// processes WM_KEYDOWN messages
   {
   // user pressed Esc when not in selecting mode:
   if (VirtKeyCode == VK_ESCAPE && !mSelecting)
      {
      mCurrentFig->Cancel (); // cancel drawing operation
      }

   // user pressed Tab in selecting mode but is NOT dragging a
   // figure:
   else if (VirtKeyCode == VK_TAB && mSelecting &&
         mMode == ModeNone)
      {
      // if figure is currently selected get next/previous one:
      if (mSelectedFig)
         {
         DrawSelection (); // erase old selection rectangle

         // if Shift is pressed, select previous figure:
         if (GetKeyState (VK_SHIFT) < 0)
            mSelectedFig = Document.GetPreviousFig(mSelectedFig);
```

```cpp
        // if Shift not pressed, select next figure:
        else
            mSelectedFig = Document.GetNextFig (mSelectedFig);
        }

    // if no figure selected, select the first one, if any:
    else if (Document.mPFirstFig)
        mSelectedFig = Document.mPFirstFig->PFigure;

    // draw the selection rectangle:
    DrawSelection ();
    }

  // user pressed Delete key, a figure is selected, and user is
  // NOT dragging a figure:
  else if (VirtKeyCode == VK_DELETE && mSelectedFig &&
          mMode == ModeNone)
    {
    // erase the figure from window:
    RECT Rect = mSelectedFig->GetBoundRect ();
    InvalidateRect (mHWnd, &Rect, TRUE);

    // remove figure object from linked list and delete it:
    Document.DeleteFigure (mSelectedFig);
    delete mSelectedFig;
    mSelectedFig = 0;
    }
  return NULL;
  }


LRESULT CMainWnd::OnKillFocus (void)
// processes WM_KILLFOCUS messages
  {
  // cancel any drawing or drag operation:
  if (mSelecting)
    CancelDrag ();
  else
    mCurrentFig->Cancel ();
  return NULL;
  }


LRESULT CMainWnd::OnLButtonDown (WORD XCursor, WORD YCursor)
// processes WM_LBUTTONDOWN messages
  {
  // if Figure/Select command not chosen, have current figure
  // object handle the message:
  if (!mSelecting)
    return mCurrentFig->OnLButtonDown (XCursor, YCursor);

  POINT Point = {XCursor, YCursor};
  RECT Rect;

  // if a selected figure is under the cursor, begin a move
```

```cpp
   // operation:
   if (mSelectedFig)
      {
      Rect = mSelectedFig->GetBoundRect ();
      if (PtInRect (&Rect, Point))
         {
         // save current coordinates:
         mRectPrev = Rect;
         mXOrig = XCursor; mYOrig = YCursor;
         mXPrev = XCursor; mYPrev = YCursor;
         // start drag:
         SetCapture (mHWnd);
         GetClientRect (mHWnd, &Rect);
         ClientToScreen (mHWnd, (LPPOINT)&Rect);
         ClientToScreen (mHWnd, (LPPOINT)&Rect.right);
         ClipCursor (&Rect);

         mMode = ModeMoving;
         return NULL;
         }
      // cancel existing selection:
      DrawSelection ();
      mSelectedFig = 0;
      }

   // no selected figure is under cursor; therefore, select the
   // figure under cursor, if any:

   // perform hit test on all figures stored in document:
   FigCell *PCell = Document.mPFirstFig;
   while (PCell)
      {
      Rect = PCell->PFigure->GetBoundRect ();
      // if figure found under cursor, select it:
      if (PtInRect (&Rect, Point))
         {
         mSelectedFig = PCell->PFigure;
         DrawSelection ();
         return NULL;
         }
      PCell = PCell->PNextFig;
      }
   return NULL;
   }

LRESULT CMainWnd::OnLButtonUp (WORD XCursor, WORD YCursor)
// processes WM_LBUTTONUP messages
   {
   // if Figure/Select command not chosen, have current figure
   // object handle the message:
   if (!mSelecting)
      return mCurrentFig->OnLButtonUp (XCursor, YCursor);
```

```cpp
   // if user was moving a figure, end move operation:
   if (mMode == ModeMoving)
      {
      // end drag:
      ReleaseCapture ();
      ClipCursor (NULL);

      // erase previous temporary rectangle:
      HDC HDc = GetDC (mHWnd);
      DrawFocusRect (HDc, &mRectPrev);
      ReleaseDC (mHWnd, HDc);

      // move the figure and force redrawing of affected areas:
      RECT Rect = mSelectedFig->GetBoundRect ();
      InvalidateRect (mHWnd, &Rect, TRUE);
      mSelectedFig->Move (XCursor-mXOrig, YCursor-mYOrig);
      Rect = mSelectedFig->GetBoundRect ();
      InvalidateRect (mHWnd, &Rect, TRUE);

      // place moved figure on top (i.e., at end of linked list):
      Document.AddFigure (mSelectedFig, FALSE);
      Document.DeleteFigure (mSelectedFig);

      mMode = ModeNone;
   }
   return NULL;
   }

LRESULT CMainWnd::OnMouseMove (WORD XCursor, WORD YCursor)
// processes WM_MOUSEMOVE messages
   {
   // if Figure/Select command not chosen, have current figure
   // object handle the message:
   if (!mSelecting)
   {
      SetCursor (LoadCursor (NULL, IDC_CROSS));
      return mCurrentFig->OnMouseMove (XCursor, YCursor);
      }

   // if user is moving a figure, update selection rectangle and
   // set cursor:
   if (mMode == ModeMoving)
      {
      SetCursor (LoadCursor (NULL, IDC_SIZE));

      HDC HDc = GetDC (mHWnd);
      DrawFocusRect (HDc, &mRectPrev);
      mRectPrev.left   += XCursor - mXPrev;
      mRectPrev.top    += YCursor - mYPrev;
      mRectPrev.right  += XCursor - mXPrev;
      mRectPrev.bottom += YCursor - mYPrev;
      DrawFocusRect (HDc, &mRectPrev);
      mXPrev = XCursor;
```

```
      mYPrev = YCursor;
      ReleaseDC (mHWnd, HDc);

      return NULL;
      }

   // if user is not moving a figure, just set cursor:

   // if a figure is selected, must test for cursor within
   // bounding rectangle:
   if (mSelectedFig)
      {
      RECT Rect = mSelectedFig->GetBoundRect ();
      POINT Point = {XCursor, YCursor};
      if (PtInRect (&Rect, Point))
         {
         SetCursor (LoadCursor (NULL, IDC_SIZE));
         return NULL;
         }
      }

   // in selecting mode, but cursor not within selected figure:
   SetCursor (LoadCursor (NULL, IDC_ARROW));
   return NULL;
   }

LRESULT CMainWnd::OnOptionsAttributes (void)
// processes WM_COMMAND / ID_OPTIONS_ATTRIBUTES messages
   {
   AttrDlg.Show (); // display Attributes dialog box
   return NULL;
   }

LRESULT CMainWnd::OnOptionsBrush (void)
// processes WM_COMMAND / ID_OPTIONS_BRUSH messages
   {
   BrushDlg.Show (); // display Brush dialog box
   return NULL;
   }

LRESULT CMainWnd::OnOptionsPen (void)
// processes WM_COMMAND / ID_OPTIONS_PEN messages
   {
   PenDlg.Show (); // display Pen dialog box
   return NULL;
   }

LRESULT CMainWnd::OnPaint (void)
// processes WM_PAINT messages
   {
   HDC HDCPaint;
   PAINTSTRUCT PaintStruct;
   RECT RectBound;
```

```cpp
// cancel any drawing or drag operation:
if (mSelecting)
   CancelDrag ();
else
   mCurrentFig->Cancel ();

// initiate painting and obtain a device context:
HDCPaint = BeginPaint (mHWnd, &PaintStruct);

// save state of device context:
SaveDC (HDCPaint);

// draw all figures stored in document:
FigCell *PCell = Document.mPFirstFig;
while (PCell)
   {
   RectBound = PCell->PFigure->GetBoundRect ();
   if (RectVisible (HDCPaint, &RectBound))
      PCell->PFigure->Draw (HDCPaint);
   PCell = PCell->PNextFig;
   }

// restore the saved device context:
RestoreDC (HDCPaint, -1);

if (mSelectedFig)
   {
   RectBound = mSelectedFig->GetBoundRect ();
   DrawFocusRect (HDCPaint, &RectBound);
   }

// terminate painting and release device context:
EndPaint (mHWnd, &PaintStruct);
return NULL;
}
```

Listing 4.5:   Figure.h

```cpp
///////////////////////////////////////////////////////////////////////////
//                                                                       //
// Figure.h: Header file for figure classes.                            //
//                                                                       //
///////////////////////////////////////////////////////////////////////////

class CFigure // abstract base class for all figure classes
{
public:
   // description of pen used to draw figure:
   COLORREF mPenColor;
   DWORD mPenStyle;
   DWORD mPenType;
   DWORD mPenWidth;
```

```cpp
   // drawing attributes:
   COLORREF mBkColor;
   int mBkMode;
   int mBrushXOrg;
   int mBrushYOrg;
   int mFillMode;
   int mMixMode;

   CFigure (void);
   void Cancel (void);
   virtual CFigure *CreateObject (void) = 0;
   virtual void DefineBrush (COLORREF BrushColor,
      LONG BrushHatchPattern, DWORD BrushStyle)
      {
      return;
      }
   virtual void Draw (HDC HDc);
   virtual RECT GetBoundRect (void);
   virtual void GetBrushDescription (COLORREF *PBrushColor,
      LONG *PBrushHatchPattern, DWORD *PBrushStyle)
      {
      return;
      }
   virtual BOOL IsBrush (void)
      {
      return FALSE;
      }
   virtual void Move (int DeltaX, int DeltaY);
   virtual void PureDraw (HDC HDc) = 0;

   // message-handling functions:
   virtual LRESULT OnLButtonDblClk (WORD XCursor, WORD YCursor)
      {
      return NULL;
      }
   virtual LRESULT OnLButtonDown (WORD XCursor, WORD YCursor) =0;
   virtual LRESULT OnLButtonUp (WORD XCursor, WORD YCursor) = 0;
   virtual LRESULT OnMouseMove (WORD XCursor, WORD YCursor) = 0;

protected:
   int mX1, mY1, mX2, mY2; // basic figure dimensions

   virtual HBRUSH GetBrush (void)
      {
      return 0;
      }
   HDC GetTempDC (void);
   int Max4 (int A, int B, int C, int D)
      {
      return max (max (max (A, B), C), D);
      }
   int Min4 (int A, int B, int C, int D)
      {
```

```cpp
        return min (min (min (A, B), C), D);
        }
    void StartDrag (void);
};

class CArc : public CFigure
{
public:
    virtual CFigure *CreateObject (void)
        {
        return new CArc;
        }
    virtual RECT GetBoundRect (void);
    virtual void Move (int DeltaX, int DeltaY);
    virtual void PureDraw (HDC HDc);

    // message-handling functions:
    virtual LRESULT OnLButtonDown (WORD XCursor, WORD YCursor);
    virtual LRESULT OnLButtonUp (WORD XCursor, WORD YCursor);
    virtual LRESULT OnMouseMove (WORD XCursor, WORD YCursor);

protected:
    int mX3, mY3, mX4, mY4; // additional arc dimensions
};

class CChord : public CArc
{
public:
    virtual CFigure *CreateObject (void)
        {
        return new CChord;
        }

    virtual void DefineBrush (COLORREF BrushColor,
        LONG BrushHatchPattern, DWORD BrushStyle)
        {
        mBrushColor = BrushColor;
        mBrushHatchPattern = BrushHatchPattern;
        mBrushStyle = BrushStyle;
        }
    virtual void GetBrushDescription (COLORREF *PBrushColor,
        LONG *PBrushHatchPattern, DWORD *PBrushStyle)
        {
        *PBrushColor = mBrushColor;
        *PBrushHatchPattern = mBrushHatchPattern;
        *PBrushStyle = mBrushStyle;
        return;
        }
    virtual BOOL IsBrush (void)
        {
        return TRUE;
        }
    virtual void PureDraw (HDC HDc);
```

```cpp
protected:
    // description of brush used to draw figure:
    COLORREF mBrushColor;
    LONG mBrushHatchPattern;
    DWORD mBrushStyle;

    virtual HBRUSH GetBrush (void);
};

class CPie : public CChord

{
public:
    virtual CFigure *CreateObject (void)
        {
        return new CPie;
        }
    virtual void PureDraw (HDC HDc);
};

class CBezier : public CFigure
{
public:
    virtual CFigure *CreateObject (void)
        {
        return new CBezier;
        }
    virtual RECT GetBoundRect (void);
    virtual void Move (int DeltaX, int DeltaY);
    virtual void PureDraw (HDC HDc);

    // message-handling functions:
    virtual LRESULT OnLButtonDown (WORD XCursor, WORD YCursor);
    virtual LRESULT OnLButtonUp (WORD XCursor, WORD YCursor);
    virtual LRESULT OnMouseMove (WORD XCursor, WORD YCursor);

protected:
    int mX3, mY3, mX4, mY4; // additional bezier curve dimensions
};

class CLine : public CFigure
{
public:
    virtual CFigure *CreateObject (void)
        {
        return new CLine;
        }
    virtual void PureDraw (HDC HDc);

    // message-handling functions:
    virtual LRESULT OnLButtonDown (WORD XCursor, WORD YCursor);
    virtual LRESULT OnLButtonUp (WORD XCursor, WORD YCursor);
    virtual LRESULT OnMouseMove (WORD XCursor, WORD YCursor);
};
```

```cpp
class CRectangle : public CLine
{
public:
   virtual CFigure *CreateObject (void)
      {
      return new CRectangle;
      }
   virtual void DefineBrush (COLORREF BrushColor,
      LONG BrushHatchPattern, DWORD BrushStyle)
      {
      mBrushColor = BrushColor;
      mBrushHatchPattern = BrushHatchPattern;
      mBrushStyle = BrushStyle;
      }
   virtual void GetBrushDescription (COLORREF *PBrushColor,
      LONG *PBrushHatchPattern, DWORD *PBrushStyle)
      {
      *PBrushColor = mBrushColor;
      *PBrushHatchPattern = mBrushHatchPattern;
      *PBrushStyle = mBrushStyle;
      return;
      }
   virtual BOOL IsBrush (void)
      {
      return TRUE;
      }
   virtual void PureDraw (HDC HDc);

protected:
   // description of brush used to draw figure:
   COLORREF mBrushColor;
   LONG mBrushHatchPattern;
   DWORD mBrushStyle;

   virtual HBRUSH GetBrush (void);
};

class CRoundRect : public CRectangle
{
public:
   virtual CFigure *CreateObject (void)
      {
      return new CRoundRect;
      }
   virtual void PureDraw (HDC HDc);
};

class CEllipse : public CRectangle
{
public:
   virtual CFigure *CreateObject (void)
      {
      return new CEllipse;
      }
```

```cpp
   virtual void PureDraw (HDC HDc);
};

#define MAXPOINTS 25 // maximum number of vertices in polyline

class CPolyline : public CFigure
{
public:
   virtual CFigure *CreateObject (void)
      {
      return new CPolyline;
      }
   virtual RECT GetBoundRect (void);
   virtual void Move (int DeltaX, int DeltaY);
   virtual void PureDraw (HDC HDc);

   // message-handling functions:
   virtual LRESULT OnLButtonDblClk (WORD XCursor, WORD YCursor);
   virtual LRESULT OnLButtonDown (WORD XCursor, WORD YCursor);
   virtual LRESULT OnLButtonUp (WORD XCursor, WORD YCursor);
   virtual LRESULT OnMouseMove (WORD XCursor, WORD YCursor);

protected:
   int mNumPoints;              // number of points stored
   POINT mPoints [MAXPOINTS]; // stores coordinates of vertices
};

class CPolygon : public CPolyline
{
public:
   virtual CFigure *CreateObject (void)
      {
      return new CPolygon;
      }
   virtual void DefineBrush (COLORREF BrushColor,
      LONG BrushHatchPattern, DWORD BrushStyle)
      {
      mBrushColor = BrushColor;
      mBrushHatchPattern = BrushHatchPattern;
      mBrushStyle = BrushStyle;
      return;
      }
   virtual void GetBrushDescription (COLORREF *PBrushColor,
      LONG *PBrushHatchPattern, DWORD *PBrushStyle)
      {
      *PBrushColor = mBrushColor;
      *PBrushHatchPattern = mBrushHatchPattern;
      *PBrushStyle = mBrushStyle;
      return;
      }
   virtual BOOL IsBrush (void)
      {
      return TRUE;
      }
```

```
   virtual void PureDraw (HDC HDc);

protected:
   // description of brush used to draw figure:
   COLORREF mBrushColor;
   LONG mBrushHatchPattern;
   DWORD mBrushStyle;

   virtual HBRUSH GetBrush (void);
};
```

Listing 4.6:   Figure.cpp

```cpp
////////////////////////////////////////////////////////////////////////
//                                                                    //
// Figure.cpp: Implementaton file for figure classes.                 //
//                                                                    //
////////////////////////////////////////////////////////////////////////

#define STRICT
#include <windows.h>
#include <limits.h>
#include "resource.h"

#include "figure.h"
#include "mainwnd.h"
#include "document.h"

extern CMainWnd MainWnd;
extern CDocument Document;

////////////////////////////////////////////////////////////////////////
// CFigure:                                                           //
////////////////////////////////////////////////////////////////////////

CFigure::CFigure (void)
   {
   mPenWidth = 1;
   }

void CFigure::Cancel (void)
// cancels a drawing operation
   {
   if (MainWnd.mMode == MainWnd.ModeNone)
      return;

   // erase temporary line(s) and redraw affected area of window:
   RECT Rect = GetBoundRect ();
   InvalidateRect (MainWnd.mHWnd, &Rect, TRUE);

   // end dragging operation:
   if (MainWnd.mMode == MainWnd.ModeDragging)
      {
```

```cpp
      ReleaseCapture ();
      ClipCursor (NULL);
      }
   MainWnd.mMode = MainWnd.ModeNone;
   return;
   }

void CFigure::Draw (HDC HDc)
// prepares the device context AND draws the current object
   {
   // set drawing attributes:
   SetBkColor (HDc, mBkColor);
   SetBkMode (HDc, mBkMode);
   SetBrushOrgEx (HDc, mBrushXOrg, mBrushYOrg, NULL);
   SetPolyFillMode (HDc, mFillMode);
   SetROP2 (HDc, mMixMode);

   // create and select object's pen:
   LOGBRUSH LogBrush = {BS_SOLID, mPenColor, 0};
   HPEN HPen = ExtCreatePen
      (mPenType | mPenStyle,
      mPenWidth,
      &LogBrush,
      0,
      0);
   HPEN HPenOld = (HPEN)SelectObject (HDc, HPen);

   // get and select object's brush, if any:
   HBRUSH HBrush = GetBrush ();
   HBRUSH HBrushOld;
   if (HBrush)
      HBrushOld = (HBRUSH)SelectObject (HDc, HBrush);

   // call the appropriate drawing function for the object:
   PureDraw (HDc);

   // deselect and destroy brush, if any:
   if (HBrush)
      {
      SelectObject (HDc, HBrushOld);
      DeleteObject (HBrush);
      }

   // deselect and destroy pen:
   SelectObject (HDc, HPenOld);
   DeleteObject (HPen);
   return;
   }

RECT CFigure::GetBoundRect (void)
// returns rectangle bounding figure
   {
   RECT Rect =
```

```
            {min (mX1, mX2)-3,
             min (mY1, mY2)-3,
             max (mX1, mX2) + 3,
             max (mY1, mY2) + 3};

    // expand rectangle to accommodate wide lines:
    int LineAdd = (mPenWidth-1) / 2 + (mPenWidth-1) % 2;
    InflateRect (&Rect, LineAdd, LineAdd);

    return Rect;
    }

HDC CFigure::GetTempDC (void)
// returns a device-context handle for drawing temporary lines
    {
    HDC HDCClient = GetDC (MainWnd.mHWnd);
    SetROP2 (HDCClient, R2_NOT);
    HPEN HPenOld = (HPEN)SelectObject
        (HDCClient, MainWnd.mHPenDotted);
    SetBkMode (HDCClient, TRANSPARENT);
    SelectObject (HDCClient, GetStockObject (NULL_BRUSH));
    return HDCClient;
    }

void CFigure::Move (int DeltaX, int DeltaY)
// moves the figure by the specified offsets
    {
    mX1 += DeltaX;
    mY1 += DeltaY;
    mX2 += DeltaX;
    mY2 += DeltaY;
    return;
    }

void CFigure::StartDrag (void)
// initializes a drag operation for drawing a figure
    {
    // capture mouse messages:
    SetCapture (MainWnd.mHWnd);

    // confine mouse cursor to client area of window:
    RECT Rect;
    GetClientRect (MainWnd.mHWnd, &Rect);
    ClientToScreen (MainWnd.mHWnd, (LPPOINT)&Rect);
    ClientToScreen (MainWnd.mHWnd, (LPPOINT)&Rect.right);
    ClipCursor (&Rect);
    return;
    }

////////////////////////////////////////////////////////////////////////
// CArc:                                                                //
////////////////////////////////////////////////////////////////////////

#include <math.h>
#define PI 3.14159265
```

```cpp
RECT CArc::GetBoundRect (void)
// returns rectangle bounding arc
    {
    // store dimensions of rectangle bounding the full ellipse:
    RECT Rect =
        {min (mX1, mX2) - 3,
         min (mY1, mY2) - 3,
         max (mX1, mX2) + 3,
         max (mY1, mY2) + 3};

    // if user has completed drawing the figure, calculate the
    // rectangle that bounds only those quadrants of the ellipse
    // that contain the figure:
    if (MainWnd.mMode == MainWnd.ModeNone)
        {
        BOOL ContainsEnd, ContainsStart;
        BOOL Started = FALSE;

        // calculate midpoint of ellipse:
        int XMid = (Rect.left + Rect.right) / 2;
        int YMid = (Rect.top + Rect.bottom) / 2;

        // store information on the four ellipse quadrants:
        struct
            {
            double StartAngle; // starting angle of quadrant
            double EndAngle;   // ending angle of quadrant
            RECT Rect;         // dimensions of quadrant
            }
        Quadrants [4] =
            {{-PI,     -PI/2.0, {Rect.left,YMid,XMid,Rect.bottom}},
             {-PI/2.0, 0.0,     {XMid,YMid,Rect.right,Rect.bottom}},
             {0.0,     PI/2.0,  {XMid,Rect.top,Rect.right,YMid}},
             {PI/2.0,  PI,      {Rect.left,Rect.top,XMid,YMid}}};

        // calculate angles of starting and ending lines of arc:
        double ThetaStart = atan2 (YMid - mY3, mX3 - XMid);
        double ThetaEnd   = atan2 (YMid - mY4, mX4 - XMid);

        // initialize bounding rectangle to null:
        Rect.left = Rect.top = Rect.right = Rect.bottom = 0;

        // find the ellipse quadrant that contains starting line:
        for (int Q = 0; Q <= 3; ++Q)
            {
            ContainsStart = ThetaStart>=Quadrants [Q].StartAngle &&
                ThetaStart < Quadrants [Q].EndAngle;
            if (ContainsStart)
                break;
            }

        // add ellipse quadrants to bounding rectangle until the
        // ending line is encountered:
```

```cpp
   for (int i = 1; i <= 3; ++i)
      {
      UnionRect (&Rect, &Rect, &Quadrants [Q].Rect);
      ContainsEnd = ThetaEnd >= Quadrants [Q].StartAngle &&
         ThetaEnd < Quadrants [Q].EndAngle;
      if (ContainsEnd && !(i == 1 && ThetaEnd <= ThetaStart))
         break;
      Q = (Q + 1) % 4;
      }
   }

// expand rectangle to accommodate wide lines:
int LineAdd = (mPenWidth-1) / 2 + (mPenWidth-1) % 2;
InflateRect (&Rect, LineAdd, LineAdd);

return Rect;
}

void CArc::Move (int DeltaX, int DeltaY)
// moves the arc by the specified offsets
   {
   mX1 += DeltaX;
   mY1 += DeltaY;
   mX2 += DeltaX;
   mY2 += DeltaY;
   mX3 += DeltaX;
   mY3 += DeltaY;
   mX4 += DeltaX;
   mY4 += DeltaY;
   return;
   }

void CArc::PureDraw (HDC HDc)
// draws the arc
   {
   Arc (HDc, mX1, mY1, mX2, mY2, mX3, mY3, mX4, mY4);
   return;
   }

LRESULT CArc::OnLButtonDown (WORD XCursor, WORD YCursor)
// processes WM_LBUTTONDOWN messages
   {
   switch (MainWnd.mMode)
      {
      case MainWnd.ModeNone: // draw bounding ellipse
         StartDrag ();
         mX1 = XCursor; mY1 = YCursor;
         mX2 = XCursor; mY2 = YCursor;
         MainWnd.mMode = MainWnd.ModeDragging;
         break;

      case MainWnd.ModeMark1: // mark start of arc
         mX3 = XCursor; mY3 = YCursor;
```

```cpp
            MainWnd.mMode = MainWnd.ModeMark2;
            break;

        case MainWnd.ModeMark2: // mark end of arc
            // erase temporary ellipse:
            HDC HDCClient = GetTempDC ();
            Ellipse (HDCClient, mX1, mY1, mX2, mY2);

            // add arc to document:
            mX4 = XCursor; mY4 = YCursor;
            Document.AddFigure (this, TRUE);
            MainWnd.mCurrentFig = CreateObject ();

            // draw arc:
            Draw (HDCClient);
            ReleaseDC (MainWnd.mHWnd, HDCClient);

            MainWnd.mMode = MainWnd.ModeNone;
            break;
        }
   return NULL;
   }

LRESULT CArc::OnLButtonUp (WORD XCursor, WORD YCursor)
// processes WM_LBUTTONUP messages
   {
   if (MainWnd.mMode != MainWnd.ModeDragging)
      return NULL;

   // end drag operation:
   ReleaseCapture ();
   ClipCursor (NULL);

   // erase old temporary ellipse / draw new temporary ellipse:
   HDC HDCClient = GetTempDC ();
   Ellipse (HDCClient, mX1, mY1, mX2, mY2);
   Ellipse (HDCClient, mX1, mY1, XCursor, YCursor);
   ReleaseDC (MainWnd.mHWnd, HDCClient);

   // save new coordinates / stop drawing if ellipse is trivial:
   mX2 = XCursor; mY2 = YCursor;
   if (mX1 == mX2 && mY1 == mY2)
      MainWnd.mMode = MainWnd.ModeNone;
   else
      MainWnd.mMode = MainWnd.ModeMark1;
   return NULL;
   }

LRESULT CArc::OnMouseMove (WORD XCursor, WORD YCursor)
// processes WM_MOUSEMOVE messages
   {
   if (MainWnd.mMode != MainWnd.ModeDragging)
      return NULL;
```

```
    // erase old temporary ellipse / draw new temporary ellipse:
    HDC HDCClient = GetTempDC ();
    Ellipse (HDCClient, mX1, mY1, mX2, mY2);
    Ellipse (HDCClient, mX1, mY1, XCursor, YCursor);
    ReleaseDC (MainWnd.mHWnd, HDCClient);

    // save new coordinates:
    mX2 = XCursor; mY2 = YCursor;
    return NULL;
    }

////////////////////////////////////////////////////////////////////////////
// CChord:                                                                  //
////////////////////////////////////////////////////////////////////////////

HBRUSH CChord::GetBrush (void)
// returns a handle to a brush for the chord
    {
    LOGBRUSH LB =
        {mBrushStyle,
        mBrushColor,
        mBrushHatchPattern};
    return CreateBrushIndirect (&LB);
    }

void CChord::PureDraw (HDC HDc)
// draws the chord
    {
    Chord (HDc, mX1, mY1, mX2, mY2, mX3, mY3, mX4, mY4);
    return;
    }

////////////////////////////////////////////////////////////////////////////
// CPie:                                                                    //
////////////////////////////////////////////////////////////////////////////

void CPie::PureDraw (HDC HDc)
// draws the pie
    {
    Pie (HDc, mX1, mY1, mX2, mY2, mX3, mY3, mX4, mY4);
    return;
    }

////////////////////////////////////////////////////////////////////////////
// CBezier:                                                                 //
////////////////////////////////////////////////////////////////////////////

RECT CBezier::GetBoundRect (void)
// returns rectangle bounding the Bezier curve
    {
    RECT Rect =
      {Min4 (mX1, mX2, mX3, mX4) — 3,
       Min4 (mY1, mY2, mY3, mY4) — 3,
       Max4 (mX1, mX2, mX3, mX4) + 3,
       Max4 (mY1, mY2, mY3, mY4) + 3};
```

```cpp
   // expand rectangle to accommodate wide lines:
   int LineAdd = (mPenWidth-1) / 2 + (mPenWidth-1) % 2;
   InflateRect (&Rect, LineAdd, LineAdd);
   return Rect;
   }

void CBezier::Move (int DeltaX, int DeltaY)
// moves the bezier curve by the specified offsets
   {
   mX1 += DeltaX;
   mY1 += DeltaY;
   mX2 += DeltaX;
   mY2 += DeltaY;
   mX3 += DeltaX;
   mY3 += DeltaY;
   mX4 += DeltaX;
   mY4 += DeltaY;
   return;
   }

void CBezier::PureDraw (HDC HDc)
// draws the Bezier curve
   {
   POINT Points [4] =
     {{mX1, mY1},
      {mX2, mY2},
      {mX3, mY3},
      {mX4, mY4}};
   PolyBezier (HDc, Points, 4);
   return;
   }

LRESULT CBezier::OnLButtonDown (WORD XCursor, WORD YCursor)
// processes WM_LBUTTONDOWN messages
   {
   HDC HDCClient;

   switch (MainWnd.mMode)
      {
      case MainWnd.ModeNone: // draw straight line
         StartDrag ();
         mX1 = XCursor; mY1 = YCursor;
         mX2 = XCursor; mY2 = YCursor;
         mX3 = XCursor; mY3 = YCursor;
         mX4 = XCursor; mY4 = YCursor;
         MainWnd.mMode = MainWnd.ModeDragging;
         break;

      case MainWnd.ModeMark1: // mark first control point
         // erase straight line / draw temporary bezier:
         HDCClient = GetTempDC ();
         MoveToEx (HDCClient, mX1, mY1, 0);
         LineTo (HDCClient, mX4, mY4);
```

```cpp
            mX2 = XCursor; mY2 = YCursor;
            mX3 = XCursor; mY3 = YCursor;
            PureDraw (HDCClient);
            ReleaseDC (MainWnd.mHWnd, HDCClient);

            MainWnd.mMode = MainWnd.ModeMark2;
            break;

    case MainWnd.ModeMark2: // mark second control point
            // erase temporary bezier:
            HDCClient = GetTempDC ();
            PureDraw (HDCClient);

            // add bezier to document and draw it:
            mX3 = XCursor; mY3 = YCursor;
            Document.AddFigure (this, TRUE);
            MainWnd.mCurrentFig = CreateObject ();
            Draw (HDCClient);
            ReleaseDC (MainWnd.mHWnd, HDCClient);

            MainWnd.mMode = MainWnd.ModeNone;
            break;
        }
    return NULL;
    }


LRESULT CBezier::OnLButtonUp (WORD XCursor, WORD YCursor)
// processes WM_LBUTTONUP messages
    {
    if (MainWnd.mMode != MainWnd.ModeDragging)
        return NULL;

    // end drag operation:
    ReleaseCapture ();
    ClipCursor (NULL);

    // erase old temp. straight line / draw new one:
    HDC HDCClient = GetTempDC ();
    MoveToEx (HDCClient, mX1, mY1, 0);
    LineTo   (HDCClient, mX4, mY4);
    MoveToEx (HDCClient, mX1, mY1, 0);
    LineTo   (HDCClient, XCursor, YCursor);
    ReleaseDC (MainWnd.mHWnd, HDCClient);

    // save new coordinates / stop drawing if line is trivial:
    mX4 = XCursor; mY4 = YCursor;
    if (mX1 == mX4 && mY1 == mY4)
        MainWnd.mMode = MainWnd.ModeNone;
    else
        MainWnd.mMode = MainWnd.ModeMark1;
    return NULL;
    }
```

```
LRESULT CBezier::OnMouseMove (WORD XCursor, WORD YCursor)
// processes WM_MOUSEMOVE messages
   {
   if (MainWnd.mMode != MainWnd.ModeDragging)
      return NULL;

   // erase old temporary straight line / draw new one:
   HDC HDCClient = GetTempDC ();
   MoveToEx (HDCClient, mX1, mY1, 0);
   LineTo   (HDCClient, mX4, mY4);
   MoveToEx (HDCClient, mX1, mY1, 0);
   LineTo   (HDCClient, XCursor, YCursor);
   mX4 = XCursor; mY4 = YCursor;
   ReleaseDC (MainWnd.mHWnd, HDCClient);
   return NULL;
   }

/////////////////////////////////////////////////////////////////////////////
// CLine:                                                                    //
/////////////////////////////////////////////////////////////////////////////

void CLine::PureDraw (HDC HDc)
// draws the line
   {
   MoveToEx (HDc, mX1, mY1, 0);
   LineTo (HDc, mX2, mY2);
   return;
   }

LRESULT CLine::OnLButtonDown (WORD XCursor, WORD YCursor)
// processes WM_LBUTTONDOWN messages
   {
   StartDrag ();
   mX1 = XCursor; mY1 = YCursor;
   mX2 = XCursor; mY2 = YCursor;
   MainWnd.mMode = MainWnd.ModeDragging;
   return NULL;
   }

LRESULT CLine::OnLButtonUp (WORD XCursor, WORD YCursor)
// processes WM_LBUTTONUP messages
   {
   if (MainWnd.mMode != MainWnd.ModeDragging)
      return NULL;

   // end drag operation:
   ReleaseCapture ();
   ClipCursor (NULL);

   // erase temporary line:
   HDC HDCClient = GetTempDC ();
   PureDraw (HDCClient);

   // if line is not trivial, add it to document and draw it:
   mX2 = XCursor; mY2 = YCursor;
```

```cpp
    if (mX1 != mX2 || mY1 != mY2)
        {
        Document.AddFigure (this, TRUE);
        MainWnd.mCurrentFig = CreateObject ();
        Draw (HDCClient);
        }
    ReleaseDC (MainWnd.mHWnd, HDCClient);
    MainWnd.mMode = MainWnd.ModeNone;
    return NULL;
    }

LRESULT CLine::OnMouseMove (WORD XCursor, WORD YCursor)
// processes WM_MOUSEMOVE messages
    {
    if (MainWnd.mMode != MainWnd.ModeDragging)
        return NULL;

    // erase old temporary line / draw new one:
    HDC HDCClient = GetTempDC ();
    PureDraw (HDCClient);
    mX2 = XCursor; mY2 = YCursor;
    PureDraw (HDCClient);
    ReleaseDC (MainWnd.mHWnd, HDCClient);
    return NULL;
    }

///////////////////////////////////////////////////////////////////////////
// CRectangle:                                                             //
///////////////////////////////////////////////////////////////////////////

HBRUSH CRectangle::GetBrush (void)
// returns a handle to a brush for the rectangle
    {
    LOGBRUSH LB =
        {mBrushStyle,
        mBrushColor,
        mBrushHatchPattern};
    return CreateBrushIndirect (&LB);
    }

void CRectangle::PureDraw (HDC HDc)
// draws the rectangle
    {
    Rectangle (HDc, mX1, mY1, mX2, mY2);
    return;
    }

///////////////////////////////////////////////////////////////////////////
// CRoundRect:                                                             //
///////////////////////////////////////////////////////////////////////////

void CRoundRect::PureDraw (HDC HDc)
// draws the rounded rectangle
    {
```

```cpp
   int RoundDiameter = (mX2 - mX1 + mY2 - mY2) / 6;
   RoundRect (HDc, mX1, mY1, mX2, mY2, RoundDiameter,
      RoundDiameter);
   return;
   }

//////////////////////////////////////////////////////////////////////////
// CEllipse:                                                              //
//////////////////////////////////////////////////////////////////////////

void CEllipse::PureDraw (HDC HDc)
// draws the ellipse
   {
   Ellipse (HDc, mX1, mY1, mX2, mY2);
   return;
   }

//////////////////////////////////////////////////////////////////////////
// CPolyline:                                                             //
//////////////////////////////////////////////////////////////////////////

RECT CPolyline::GetBoundRect (void)
// returns rectangle bounding all lines
   {
   int NP = mNumPoints;
   RECT Rect = {0,0,0,0};

   // if dragging, must include the new point not yet added:
   if (MainWnd.mMode == MainWnd.ModeDragging)
      ++NP;

   if (NP < 2)     // if less than 2 points, return empty
      return Rect; // rectangle

   // obtain dimensions of bounding rectangle:
   Rect.left   = INT_MAX;
   Rect.top    = INT_MAX;
   Rect.right  = INT_MIN;
   Rect.bottom = INT_MIN;
   for (int i = 0; i < NP; ++i)
      {
      Rect.left   = min (Rect.left,   mPoints [i].x);
      Rect.top    = min (Rect.top,    mPoints [i].y);
      Rect.right  = max (Rect.right,  mPoints [i].x);
      Rect.bottom = max (Rect.bottom, mPoints [i].y);
      }
   Rect.left   -= 3; Rect.top     -= 3;
   Rect.right  += 3; Rect.bottom  += 3;

   // expand rectangle to accommodate wide lines:
   int LineAdd = (mPenWidth-1) / 2 + (mPenWidth-1) % 2;
   InflateRect (&Rect, LineAdd, LineAdd);

   return Rect;
   }
```

```
void CPolyline::Move (int DeltaX, int DeltaY)
// moves the polyline by the specified offsets
    {
    for (int i = 0; i < mNumPoints; ++i)
        {
        mPoints [i].x += DeltaX;
        mPoints [i].y += DeltaY;
        }
    return;
    }


void CPolyline::PureDraw (HDC HDc)
// draws the connected lines:
    {
    Polyline (HDc, mPoints, mNumPoints);
    return;
    }

LRESULT CPolyline::OnLButtonDblClk (WORD XCursor, WORD YCursor)
// processes WM_LBUTTONDBLCLK messages
    {
    // if more than 1 point marked, add polyline figure to
    // document and draw it:
    if (mNumPoints > 1)
        {
        Document.AddFigure (this, TRUE);
        MainWnd.mCurrentFig = CreateObject ();
        HDC HDCClient = GetDC (MainWnd.mHWnd);
        Draw (HDCClient);
        ReleaseDC (MainWnd.mHWnd, HDCClient);
        }
    MainWnd.mMode = MainWnd.ModeNone;
    return NULL;
    }

LRESULT CPolyline::OnLButtonDown (WORD XCursor, WORD YCursor)
// processes WM_LBUTTONDOWN messages
    {
    // initialize first point:
    if (MainWnd.mMode == MainWnd.ModeNone)
        {
        mNumPoints = 1;
        mPoints [0].x = XCursor;
        mPoints [0].y = YCursor;
        }

    // save coordinates:
    mPoints [mNumPoints].x = XCursor;
    mPoints [mNumPoints].y = YCursor;

    // draw temporary line back to previous point:
    HDC HDCClient = GetTempDC ();
    MoveToEx (HDCClient, mPoints [mNumPoints-1].x,
```

```cpp
         mPoints [mNumPoints-1].y, 0);
   LineTo (HDCClient, mPoints [mNumPoints].x,
      mPoints [mNumPoints].y);
   ReleaseDC (MainWnd.mHWnd, HDCClient);

   StartDrag ();
   MainWnd.mMode = MainWnd.ModeDragging;
   return NULL;
   }

LRESULT CPolyline::OnLButtonUp (WORD XCursor, WORD YCursor)
// processes WM_LBUTTONUP messages
   {
   if (MainWnd.mMode != MainWnd.ModeDragging)
      return NULL;

   // end drag operation:
   ReleaseCapture ();
   ClipCursor (NULL);

   // erase old temporary line / draw new one:
   HDC HDCClient = GetTempDC ();
   MoveToEx (HDCClient, mPoints [mNumPoints-1].x,
      mPoints [mNumPoints-1].y, 0);
   LineTo (HDCClient, mPoints [mNumPoints].x,
      mPoints [mNumPoints].y);
   MoveToEx (HDCClient, mPoints [mNumPoints-1].x,
      mPoints [mNumPoints-1].y, 0);
   LineTo (HDCClient, XCursor, YCursor);
   ReleaseDC (MainWnd.mHWnd, HDCClient);

   mPoints [mNumPoints].x = XCursor;
   mPoints [mNumPoints].y = YCursor;

   // if new point is not on top of previous point, increment
   // number of points:
   if (mPoints [mNumPoints].x != mPoints [mNumPoints-1].x
      mPoints [mNumPoints].y != mPoints [mNumPoints-1].y)
      ++mNumPoints;

   // if maximum number of points has been used, end drawing now:
   if (mNumPoints == MAXPOINTS)
      OnLButtonDblClk (XCursor, YCursor);

   MainWnd.mMode = MainWnd.ModeMark1;
   return NULL;
   }

LRESULT CPolyline::OnMouseMove (WORD XCursor, WORD YCursor)
// processes WM_MOUSEMOVE messages
   {
   if (MainWnd.mMode != MainWnd.ModeDragging)
      return NULL;
```

```
   // erase old temporary line / draw new one:
   HDC HDCClient = GetTempDC ();
   MoveToEx (HDCClient, mPoints [mNumPoints-1].x,
      mPoints [mNumPoints-1].y, 0);
   LineTo (HDCClient, mPoints [mNumPoints].x,
      mPoints [mNumPoints].y);
   MoveToEx (HDCClient, mPoints [mNumPoints-1].x,
      mPoints [mNumPoints-1].y, 0);
   LineTo (HDCClient, XCursor, YCursor);
   ReleaseDC (MainWnd.mHWnd, HDCClient);

   // save new coordinates:
   mPoints [mNumPoints].x = XCursor;
   mPoints [mNumPoints].y = YCursor;
   return NULL;
   }

//////////////////////////////////////////////////////////////////////
// CPolygon:                                                         //
//////////////////////////////////////////////////////////////////////

HBRUSH CPolygon::GetBrush (void)
// returns a handle to a brush for the polygon
   {
   LOGBRUSH LB =
      {mBrushStyle,
      mBrushColor,
      mBrushHatchPattern};
   return CreateBrushIndirect (&LB);
   }

void CPolygon::PureDraw (HDC HDc)
// draws the polygon:
   {
   Polygon (HDc, mPoints, mNumPoints);
   return;
   }
```

Listing 4.7:   Document.h

```
//////////////////////////////////////////////////////////////////////
//                                                                   //
// Document.h: Header file for document class.                       //
//                                                                   //
//////////////////////////////////////////////////////////////////////

struct FigCell          // element of linked list storing figures
{
   FigCell *PNextFig; // pointer to next element in list
   CFigure *PFigure;  // pointer to figure object
};
```

```cpp
class CDocument
{
public:
   FigCell *mPFirstFig; // pointer to start of linked list

   CDocument (void);
   void AddFigure (CFigure *PFigure, BOOL StoreDefaults);
   void DeleteFigure (CFigure *PFigure);
   CFigure *GetNextFig (CFigure *PFigure);
   CFigure *GetPreviousFig (CFigure *PFigure);
};
```

Listing 4.8:   Document.cpp

```cpp
///////////////////////////////////////////////////////////////////////
//                                                                     //
// Document.cpp: Implementation file for document class.               //
//                                                                     //
///////////////////////////////////////////////////////////////////////

#define STRICT
#include <windows.h>

#include "figure.h"
#include "document.h"
#include "dialog.h"

extern CAttrDlg  AttrDlg;
extern CBrushDlg BrushDlg;
extern CPenDlg   PenDlg;

CDocument::CDocument (void)
   {
   mPFirstFig = 0;
   return;
   }

void CDocument::AddFigure (CFigure *PFigure, BOOL StoreDefaults)
// adds a new figure to end of linked list; if StoreDefaults is
// TRUE, stores the default attributes & drawing tools in object
   {
   FigCell *PCell;

   if (StoreDefaults)
      {
      // save default brush features:
      PFigure->DefineBrush (BrushDlg.mBrushColor,
         BrushDlg.mBrushHatchPattern, BrushDlg.mBrushStyle);

      // save default pen features:
      PFigure->mPenColor = PenDlg.mPenColor;
```

```cpp
    PFigure->mPenStyle = PenDlg.mPenStyle;
    PFigure->mPenType = PenDlg.mPenType;
    PFigure->mPenWidth = PenDlg.mPenWidth;

    // save default drawing attributes:
    PFigure->mBkColor = AttrDlg.mBkColor;
    PFigure->mBkMode = AttrDlg.mBkMode;
    PFigure->mBrushXOrg = AttrDlg.mBrushXOrg;
    PFigure->mBrushYOrg = AttrDlg.mBrushYOrg;
    PFigure->mFillMode = AttrDlg.mFillMode;
    PFigure->mMixMode = AttrDlg.mMixMode;
    }

// set PCell to new cell at end of list:
if (mPFirstFig == 0)
    {
    mPFirstFig = new FigCell;
    PCell = mPFirstFig;
    }
else
    {
    PCell = mPFirstFig;
    while (PCell->PNextFig != 0)
        PCell = PCell->PNextFig;
    PCell->PNextFig = new FigCell;
    PCell = PCell->PNextFig;
    }

// assign values to new cell:
PCell->PNextFig = 0;
PCell->PFigure = PFigure;
return;
}

void CDocument::DeleteFigure (CFigure *PFigure)
// deletes the linked-list cell that points to the figure object
// pointed to by PFigure; does not delete the figure object
// itself; assumes that the list DOES CONTAIN this cell
    {
    FigCell *PCell;

    // test first cell in list:
    if (mPFirstFig->PFigure == PFigure)
        {
        PCell = mPFirstFig;
        mPFirstFig = mPFirstFig->PNextFig;
        delete PCell;
        return;
        }

    // test remaining cells in list:
    FigCell *PPrevCell = mPFirstFig;
    PCell = mPFirstFig->PNextFig;
    while (PCell)
```

```cpp
      {
      if (PCell->PFigure == PFigure)
         {
         PPrevCell->PNextFig = PCell->PNextFig;
         delete PCell;
         return;
         }
      PPrevCell = PCell;
      PCell = PCell->PNextFig;
      }
 }

CFigure *CDocument::GetNextFig (CFigure *PFigure)
// returns a pointer to the CFigure object that immediately
// FOLLOWS the object pointed to by PFigure in the linked list;
// if there is only 1 object in the list, it returns a pointer to
// that object
   {
   FigCell *PCell = mPFirstFig;

   while (PCell)
      {
      if (PCell->PFigure == PFigure)
         break;
      PCell = PCell->PNextFig;
      }
   if (PCell->PNextFig == 0)
      return mPFirstFig->PFigure;
   else
      return PCell->PNextFig->PFigure;
   }

CFigure *CDocument::GetPreviousFig (CFigure *PFigure)
// returns a pointer to the CFigure object that immediately
// PRECEDES the object pointed to by PFigure in the linked list;
// if there is only 1 object in the list, it returns a pointer to
// that object
   {
   FigCell *PCell = mPFirstFig;
   FigCell *PPrevFig;

   // get pointer to last cell in list:
   while (PCell)
      {
      if (PCell->PNextFig == 0)
         PPrevFig = PCell;
      PCell = PCell->PNextFig;
      }

   // search list from beginning for match:
   PCell = mPFirstFig;
   while (PCell)
      {
```

```cpp
    if (PCell->PFigure == PFigure)
        return PPrevFig->PFigure;
    PPrevFig = PCell;
    PCell = PCell->PNextFig;
    }
return 0;
}
```

Listing 4.9:   Dialog.h

```cpp
/////////////////////////////////////////////////////////////////////////////
//                                                                         //
// Dialog.h: Header file for the dialog box classes.                       //
//                                                                         //
/////////////////////////////////////////////////////////////////////////////

class CAboutDlg
{
public:
   int Show (void);

   // message-handling functions:
   BOOL OnCancel (HWND HDlg);
   BOOL OnCtlColor (HDC HDc);
   BOOL OnInitDialog (void);
   BOOL OnOK (HWND HDlg);
};

class CAttrDlg
{
public:
   // store default drawing attributes:
   COLORREF mBkColor;
   int mBkMode;
   int mBrushXOrg;
   int mBrushYOrg;
   int mFillMode;
   int mMixMode;

   CAttrDlg (void);
   int Show (void);

   // message-handling functions:
   BOOL OnCancel (HWND HDlg);
   BOOL OnCtlColor (HDC HDc);
   BOOL OnInitDialog (HWND HDlg);
   BOOL OnOK (HWND HDlg);
   BOOL OnSetColor (HWND HDlg);

protected:
   // store temporary drawing attributes:
```

```cpp
   COLORREF mTBkColor;
   int mTBkMode;
   int mTBrushXOrg;
   int mTBrushYOrg;
   int mTFillMode;
   int mTMixMode;

   // saves custom colors user chooses in Color dialog box:
   DWORD mCustColors [16];
};

class CBrushDlg
{
public:
   // store default brush description:
   COLORREF mBrushColor;
   DWORD mBrushStyle;
   LONG mBrushHatchPattern;

   CBrushDlg (void);
   int Show (void);

   // message-handling functions:
   BOOL OnCancel (HWND HDlg);
   BOOL OnCtlColor (HDC HDc);
   BOOL OnInitDialog (HWND HDlg);
   BOOL OnOK (HWND HDlg);
   BOOL OnSetColor (HWND HDlg);

protected:
   // store temporary brush description:
   COLORREF mTBrushColor;
   DWORD mTBrushStyle;
   LONG mTBrushHatchPattern;

   // saves custom colors user chooses in Color dialog box:
   DWORD mCustColors [16];
};

class CPenDlg
{
public:
   // store default pen description:
   COLORREF mPenColor;
   DWORD mPenStyle;
   DWORD mPenType;
   DWORD mPenWidth;
   CPenDlg (void);
   int Show (void);

   // message-handling functions:
   BOOL OnCancel (HWND HDlg);
   BOOL OnCtlColor (HDC HDc);
   BOOL OnInitDialog (HWND HDlg);
```

```cpp
    BOOL OnOK (HWND HDlg);
    BOOL OnSetColor (HWND HDlg);

protected:
    // store temporary pen description:
    COLORREF mTPenColor;
    DWORD mTPenStyle;
    DWORD mTPenType;
    DWORD mTPenWidth;

    // saves custom colors user chooses in Color dialog box:
    DWORD mCustColors [16];
};
```

Listing 4.10:   Dialog.cpp

```cpp
////////////////////////////////////////////////////////////////////////////
//                                                                        //
// Dialog.cpp: Implementation file for the dialog box classes.            //
//                                                                        //
////////////////////////////////////////////////////////////////////////////

#define STRICT
#include <windows.h>
#include "resource.h"

#include "app.h"
#include "figure.h"
#include "mainwnd.h"
#include "dialog.h"

#include <memory.h>

extern CApp        App;
extern CMainWnd   MainWnd;
extern CAboutDlg  AboutDlg;
extern CAttrDlg   AttrDlg;
extern CBrushDlg  BrushDlg;
extern CPenDlg    PenDlg;

BOOL CALLBACK AboutDialogProc (HWND HDlg, UINT Msg,
    WPARAM WParam, LPARAM LParam);
BOOL CALLBACK AttrDialogProc (HWND HDlg, UINT Msg, WPARAM WParam,
    LPARAM LParam);
BOOL CALLBACK BrushDialogProc (HWND HDlg, UINT Msg,
    WPARAM WParam, LPARAM LParam);
BOOL CALLBACK PenDialogProc (HWND HDlg, UINT Msg, WPARAM WParam,
    LPARAM LParam);

////////////////////////////////////////////////////////////////////////////
// global tables for combo box data:                                      //
////////////////////////////////////////////////////////////////////////////
```

```
static struct // stores strings and color values for all
{              // elements to be added to Color combo box
   char *ColorName;
   COLORREF ColorValue;
}
ColorTable [10] =
  {{"Black",    RGB (0,0,0)},
   {"Gray",     RGB (192,192,192)},
   {"White",    RGB (255,255,255)},
   {"Red",      RGB (255,0,0)},
   {"Green",    RGB (0,255,0)},
   {"Blue",     RGB (0,0,255)},
   {"Yellow",   RGB (255,255,0)},
   {"Cyan",     RGB (0,255,255)},
   {"Magenta",  RGB (255,0,255)},
   {"<Custom>", RGB (0,0,0)}};

static struct // stores strings and IDs for all elements to be
{              // added to Hatch Pattern combo box
   char *HatchName;
   LONG HatchID;
}
HatchTable [6] =
  {{"Vertical",            HS_VERTICAL},
   {"Horizontal",          HS_HORIZONTAL},
   {"Up Diagonal",         HS_BDIAGONAL},
   {"Down Diagonal",       HS_FDIAGONAL},
   {"Crosshatch",          HS_CROSS},
   {"Diagonal crosshatch", HS_DIAGCROSS}};

static struct // stores strings and IDs for all elements to be
{              // added to Mix Mode combo box
   char *MixModeName;
   int MixModeID;
}
MixModeTable [16] =
  {{"R2_BLACK",        R2_BLACK},
   {"R2_COPYPEN",      R2_COPYPEN},
   {"R2_MASKNOTPEN",   R2_MASKNOTPEN},
   {"R2_MASKPEN",      R2_MASKPEN},
   {"R2_MASKPENNOT",   R2_MASKPENNOT},
   {"R2_MERGENOTPEN",  R2_MERGENOTPEN},
   {"R2_MERGEPEN",     R2_MERGEPEN},
   {"R2_MERGEPENNOT",  R2_MERGEPENNOT},
   {"R2_NOP",          R2_NOP},
   {"R2_NOT",          R2_NOT},
   {"R2_NOTCOPYPEN",   R2_NOTCOPYPEN},
   {"R2_NOTMASKPEN",   R2_NOTMASKPEN},
   {"R2_NOTMERGEPEN",  R2_NOTMERGEPEN},
   {"R2_NOTXORPEN",    R2_NOTXORPEN},
   {"R2_WHITE",        R2_WHITE},
   {"R2_XORPEN",       R2_XORPEN}};
```

```
static struct // stores strings and IDs for all elements to be
{             // added to Style combo box
   char *StyleName;
   DWORD StyleID;
}
StyleTable [7] =
  {{"Solid",         PS_SOLID},
   {"Dash",          PS_DASH},
   {"Dot",           PS_DOT},
   {"Dash-Dot",      PS_DASHDOT},
   {"Dash-Dot-Dot",  PS_DASHDOTDOT},
   {"Null",          PS_NULL},
   {"Inside-Frame",  PS_INSIDEFRAME}};

///////////////////////////////////////////////////////////////////////////////
// About dialog box:                                                         //
///////////////////////////////////////////////////////////////////////////////

///////////////////////////////////////////////////////////////////////////////
// CAboutDlg public member function:                                         //
///////////////////////////////////////////////////////////////////////////////

int CAboutDlg::Show (void)
// displays About dialog box
   {
   return DialogBox
      (App.mHInstance,
      MAKEINTRESOURCE (IDD_ABOUT),
      MainWnd.mHWnd,
      AboutDialogProc);
   }

///////////////////////////////////////////////////////////////////////////////
// About dialog box procedure:                                               //
///////////////////////////////////////////////////////////////////////////////

BOOL CALLBACK AboutDialogProc
   (HWND    HDlg,
    UINT    Msg,
    WPARAM  WParam,
    LPARAM  LParam)
   {
   switch (Msg)
      {
      case WM_INITDIALOG: // dialog box was just created
         return AboutDlg.OnInitDialog ();

      case WM_COMMAND:  // user issued a command
         switch (LOWORD (WParam))
            {
            case IDCANCEL: // user chose Close or pressed Esc
               return AboutDlg.OnCancel (HDlg);

            case IDOK:  // user clicked OK or pressed Enter
               return AboutDlg.OnOK (HDlg);
```

```cpp
        default:
            return FALSE; // default message processing
        }

    case WM_CTLCOLORDLG:    // dialog box about to be painted;
    case WM_CTLCOLORSTATIC: // text about to be painted
        return AboutDlg.OnCtlColor ((HDC)WParam);

    default:            // request default processing for all
        return FALSE; // other messages
        }
 }

///////////////////////////////////////////////////////////////////////////
// CAboutDlg message handling member functions:                          //
///////////////////////////////////////////////////////////////////////////

BOOL CAboutDlg::OnCancel (HWND HDlg)
// processes WM_COMMAND / IDCANCEL messages
    {
    // close the dialog box:
    EndDialog (HDlg, IDCANCEL);
    return TRUE;
    }

BOOL CAboutDlg::OnCtlColor (HDC HDc)
// processes WM_CTLCOLORDLG and WM_CTLCOLORSTATIC messages
    {
    // set text background to light gray:
    SetBkColor (HDc, RGB (192,192,192));

    // supply a handle to a light-gray brush:
    return (BOOL)GetStockObject (LTGRAY_BRUSH);
    }

BOOL CAboutDlg::OnInitDialog (void)
// processes WM_INITDIALOG messages
    {
    // return TRUE to set focus to first control:
    return TRUE;
    }

BOOL CAboutDlg::OnOK (HWND HDlg)
// processes WM_COMMAND / IDOK messages
    {
    // close the dialog box:
    EndDialog (HDlg, IDOK);
    return TRUE;
    }

///////////////////////////////////////////////////////////////////////////
// Attributes dialog box:                                                //
///////////////////////////////////////////////////////////////////////////
```

```cpp
/////////////////////////////////////////////////////////////////////////
// CAttrDlg public member functions:                                    //
/////////////////////////////////////////////////////////////////////////

CAttrDlg::CAttrDlg (void)
   {
   mBkColor = RGB (255,255,255);
   mBkMode = OPAQUE;
   mBrushXOrg = 0;
   mBrushYOrg = 0;
   mFillMode = ALTERNATE;
   mMixMode = R2_COPYPEN;
   memset (mCustColors, 0, sizeof (mCustColors));
   return;
   }

int CAttrDlg::Show (void)
// displays Attributes dialog box
   {
   return DialogBox
      (App.mHInstance,
       MAKEINTRESOURCE (IDD_ATTR),
       MainWnd.mHWnd,
       AttrDialogProc);
   }

/////////////////////////////////////////////////////////////////////////
// Attributes dialog box procedure:                                     //
/////////////////////////////////////////////////////////////////////////

BOOL CALLBACK AttrDialogProc
   (HWND   HDlg,
    UINT   Msg,
    WPARAM WParam,
    LPARAM LParam)
   {
   switch (Msg)
      {
      case WM_INITDIALOG: // dialog box was just created
         return AttrDlg.OnInitDialog (HDlg);

      case WM_COMMAND:  // user issued a command
         switch (LOWORD (WParam))
            {
            case IDC_SETCOLOR: // user clicked Set Custom Color
               return AttrDlg.OnSetColor (HDlg);

            case IDCANCEL: // user chose Close or pressed Esc
               return AttrDlg.OnCancel (HDlg);

            case IDOK:  // user clicked OK or pressed Enter
               return AttrDlg.OnOK (HDlg);
```

```
            default:
                return FALSE; // default message processing
            }

        case WM_CTLCOLORBTN:     // button is about to be painted;
        case WM_CTLCOLORDLG:     // dialog box about to be painted;
        case WM_CTLCOLORSTATIC: // dialog text about to be painted
            return AttrDlg.OnCtlColor ((HDC)WParam);

    default:                     // request default processing for all
            return FALSE; // other messages
        }
 }

//////////////////////////////////////////////////////////////////////////////
// CAttrDlg message handling member functions:                              //
//////////////////////////////////////////////////////////////////////////////

BOOL CAttrDlg::OnCancel (HWND HDlg)
// processes WM_COMMAND / IDCANCEL messages
    {
    // close the dialog box:
    EndDialog (HDlg, IDCANCEL);
    return TRUE;
    }

BOOL CAttrDlg::OnCtlColor (HDC HDc)
// processes WM_CTLCOLORBTN, WM_CTLCOLORDLG, and
// WM_CTLCOLORSTATIC messages
    {
    // set text background to light gray:
    SetBkColor (HDc, RGB (192,192,192));

    // supply a handle to a light-gray brush:
    return (BOOL)GetStockObject (LTGRAY_BRUSH);
    }

BOOL CAttrDlg::OnInitDialog (HWND HDlg)
// processes WM_INITDIALOG messages
    {
    // obtain current attributes from selected figure or defaults:
    if (MainWnd.mSelectedFig) // figure is selected
        {
        mTBkColor = MainWnd.mSelectedFig->mBkColor;
        mTBkMode = MainWnd.mSelectedFig->mBkMode;
        mTBrushXOrg = MainWnd.mSelectedFig->mBrushXOrg;
        mTBrushYOrg = MainWnd.mSelectedFig->mBrushYOrg;
        mTFillMode = MainWnd.mSelectedFig->mFillMode;
        mTMixMode = MainWnd.mSelectedFig->mMixMode;
        SetWindowText (HDlg, "Figure Attributes");
        }
    else        // no figure selected
        {
```

```cpp
   mTBkColor = mBkColor;
   mTBkMode = mBkMode;
   mTBrushXOrg = mBrushXOrg;
   mTBrushYOrg = mBrushYOrg;
   mTFillMode = mFillMode;
   mTMixMode = mMixMode;
   }
// initialize Mix Mode combo box and select current value:
for (int i = 0; i < 16; ++i)
   {
   SendDlgItemMessage (HDlg, IDC_MIXMODE, CB_ADDSTRING,
      0, (LPARAM)(LPCSTR)MixModeTable [i].MixModeName);
   if (MixModeTable [i].MixModeID == mTMixMode)
      SendDlgItemMessage (HDlg, IDC_MIXMODE, CB_SETCURSEL,
      (WPARAM)i, 0);
   }

// check Background Mode radio button:
CheckDlgButton
   (HDlg,
   mTBkMode == TRANSPARENT ? IDC_TRANSPARENT : IDC_OPAQUE,
   1);

// initialize Color combo box and select current value:
BOOL Selected = FALSE;
for (i = 0; i < 10; ++i)
   {
   SendDlgItemMessage (HDlg, IDC_COLOR, CB_ADDSTRING, 0,
      (LPARAM)(LPCSTR)ColorTable [i].ColorName);
   if (!Selected && ColorTable [i].ColorValue == mTBkColor)
      {
      SendDlgItemMessage (HDlg, IDC_COLOR, CB_SETCURSEL,
         (WPARAM)i, 0);
      Selected = TRUE;
      }
   }
if (!Selected)
   {
   ColorTable [9].ColorValue = mTBkColor;
   SendDlgItemMessage (HDlg, IDC_COLOR, CB_SETCURSEL,
      (WPARAM)9, 0);
   }

// check Polygon Fill Mode radio button:
CheckDlgButton
   (HDlg,
mTFillMode == ALTERNATE ? IDC_ALTERNATE : IDC_WINDING,
   1);

// set values of Brush Origin edit controls:
SetDlgItemInt (HDlg, IDC_XORG, mTBrushXOrg, TRUE);
SetDlgItemInt (HDlg, IDC_YORG, mTBrushYOrg, TRUE);
```

```cpp
   // return TRUE to set focus to first control:
   return TRUE;
   }

BOOL CAttrDlg::OnOK (HWND HDlg)
// processes WM_COMMAND / IDOK messages
   {
   // save selection from Mix Mode combo box:
   mTMixMode = MixModeTable [SendDlgItemMessage (HDlg,
      IDC_MIXMODE, CB_GETCURSEL, 0, 0)].MixModeID;

   // save Background Mode choice:
   mTBkMode = IsDlgButtonChecked (HDlg, IDC_TRANSPARENT) ?
      TRANSPARENT : OPAQUE;

   // save selection from Color combo box:
   mTBkColor = ColorTable [SendDlgItemMessage (HDlg,
      IDC_COLOR, CB_GETCURSEL, 0, 0)].ColorValue;

   // save Polygon Fill Mode choice:
   mTFillMode = IsDlgButtonChecked (HDlg, IDC_ALTERNATE) ?
      ALTERNATE : WINDING;

   // save Brush Origin values:
   BOOL Translated;
   mTBrushXOrg = GetDlgItemInt(HDlg, IDC_XORG, &Translated,TRUE);
   mTBrushYOrg = GetDlgItemInt(HDlg, IDC_YORG, &Translated,TRUE);

   // store values in figure or in default data members:
   if (MainWnd.mSelectedFig) // figure is selected
      {
      MainWnd.mSelectedFig->mBkColor = mTBkColor;
      MainWnd.mSelectedFig->mBkMode = mTBkMode;
      MainWnd.mSelectedFig->mBrushXOrg = mTBrushXOrg;
      MainWnd.mSelectedFig->mBrushYOrg = mTBrushYOrg;
      MainWnd.mSelectedFig->mFillMode = mTFillMode;
      MainWnd.mSelectedFig->mMixMode = mTMixMode;

      // force redrawing of figure:
      RECT Rect = MainWnd.mSelectedFig->GetBoundRect ();
      InvalidateRect (MainWnd.mHWnd, &Rect, TRUE);
      }
   else       // no figure selected
      {
      mBkColor = mTBkColor;
      mBkMode = mTBkMode;
      mBrushXOrg = mTBrushXOrg;
      mBrushYOrg = mTBrushYOrg;
      mFillMode = mTFillMode;
      mMixMode = mTMixMode;
      }

   // close the dialog box:
```

```cpp
    EndDialog (HDlg, IDOK);
    return TRUE;
    }

BOOL CAttrDlg::OnSetColor (HWND HDlg)
// processes WM_COMMAND / ID_SETCOLOR messages
    {
    CHOOSECOLOR CC;

    // assign values to structure to control Color dialog box:
    memset (&CC, 0, sizeof (CC));
    CC.lStructSize = sizeof (CC);
    CC.hwndOwner = HDlg;
    CC.rgbResult = ColorTable [9].ColorValue;
    CC.lpCustColors = mCustColors;
    CC.Flags = CC_RGBINIT;

    // display Color common dialog box; save selected color if
    // user clicked OK:
    if (ChooseColor (&CC))
        ColorTable [9].ColorValue = CC.rgbResult;
    return TRUE;
    }
//////////////////////////////////////////////////////////////////////
//Brush dialog box:                                                  //
//////////////////////////////////////////////////////////////////////

//////////////////////////////////////////////////////////////////////
// CBrushDlg public member functions:                                //
//////////////////////////////////////////////////////////////////////

CBrushDlg::CBrushDlg (void)
    {
    mBrushColor = RGB (255,255,255);
    mBrushHatchPattern = HS_VERTICAL;
    mBrushStyle = BS_SOLID;
    memset (mCustColors, 0, sizeof (mCustColors));
    return;
    }

 int CBrushDlg::Show (void)
 // displays Brush dialog box
    {
    return DialogBox
        (App.mHInstance,
        MAKEINTRESOURCE (IDD_BRUSH),
        MainWnd.mHWnd,
        BrushDialogProc);
    }

 //////////////////////////////////////////////////////////////////////
 // Brush dialog box procedure:                                       //
 //////////////////////////////////////////////////////////////////////
```

```
BOOL CALLBACK BrushDialogProc
   (HWND   HDlg,
    UINT   Msg,
    WPARAM WParam,
    LPARAM LParam)
    {
    switch (Msg)
       {
       case WM_INITDIALOG: // dialog box was just created
          return BrushDlg.OnInitDialog (HDlg);

       case WM_COMMAND:  // user issued a command
          switch (LOWORD (WParam))
          {
          case IDC_SETCOLOR: // user clicked Set Custom Color
             return BrushDlg.OnSetColor (HDlg);

          case IDCANCEL: // user chose Close or pressed Esc
             return BrushDlg.OnCancel (HDlg);

          case IDOK:  // user clicked OK or pressed Enter
             return BrushDlg.OnOK (HDlg);

          default:
             return FALSE; // default message processing
          }

       case WM_CTLCOLORBTN:    // button is about to be painted;
       case WM_CTLCOLORDLG:    // dialog box about to be painted;
       case WM_CTLCOLORSTATIC: // dialog text about to be painted
          return BrushDlg.OnCtlColor ((HDC)WParam);

       default:           // request default processing for all
          return FALSE; // other messages
       }
    }

//////////////////////////////////////////////////////////////////////////
// CBrushDlg message handling member functions:                         //
//////////////////////////////////////////////////////////////////////////

BOOL CBrushDlg::OnCancel (HWND HDlg)
// processes WM_COMMAND / IDCANCEL messages
   {
   // close the dialog box:
   EndDialog (HDlg, IDCANCEL);
   return TRUE;
   }


BOOL CBrushDlg::OnCtlColor (HDC HDc)
// processes WM_CTLCOLORBTN, WM_CTLCOLORDLG, and
// WM_CTLCOLORSTATIC messages
   {
```

```cpp
    // set text background to light gray:
    SetBkColor (HDc, RGB (192,192,192));

    // supply a handle to a light-gray brush:
    return (BOOL)GetStockObject (LTGRAY_BRUSH);
    }

BOOL CBrushDlg::OnInitDialog (HWND HDlg)
// processes WM_INITDIALOG messages
    {
    // obtain current brush description:
    if (MainWnd.mSelectedFig) // figure is selected
        {
        MainWnd.mSelectedFig->GetBrushDescription
            (&mTBrushColor,
            &mTBrushHatchPattern,
            &mTBrushStyle);
        SetWindowText (HDlg, "Figure Brush");
        }
    else        // no figure selected
        {
        mTBrushColor = mBrushColor;
        mTBrushHatchPattern = mBrushHatchPattern;
        mTBrushStyle = mBrushStyle;
        }

    // check Style radio button:
    switch (mTBrushStyle)
        {
        case BS_SOLID:
            CheckDlgButton (HDlg, IDC_SOLID, 1);
            break;

        case BS_HATCHED:
            CheckDlgButton (HDlg, IDC_HATCHED, 1);
            break;

        case BS_NULL:
            CheckDlgButton (HDlg, IDC_NULL, 1);
            break;
        }

    // initialize Hatch Pattern combo box / select current value:
    for (int i = 0; i < 6; ++i)
        {
        SendDlgItemMessage (HDlg, IDC_HATCHPATTERN, CB_ADDSTRING,
            0, (LPARAM)(LPCSTR)HatchTable [i].HatchName);
        if (HatchTable [i].HatchID == mTBrushHatchPattern)
            SendDlgItemMessage (HDlg, IDC_HATCHPATTERN,
            CB_SETCURSEL, (WPARAM)i, 0);
        }

    // initialize Color combo box and select current value:
```

```cpp
   BOOL Selected = FALSE;
   for (i = 0; i < 10; ++i)
      {
      SendDlgItemMessage (HDlg, IDC_COLOR, CB_ADDSTRING, 0,
         (LPARAM)(LPCSTR)ColorTable [i].ColorName);
      if (!Selected && ColorTable [i].ColorValue == mTBrushColor)
         {
         SendDlgItemMessage (HDlg, IDC_COLOR, CB_SETCURSEL,
            (WPARAM)i, 0);
         Selected = TRUE;
         }
      }
   if (!Selected)
      {
      ColorTable [9].ColorValue = mTBrushColor;
      SendDlgItemMessage (HDlg, IDC_COLOR, CB_SETCURSEL,
         (WPARAM)9, 0);
      }

   // return TRUE to set focus to first control:
   return TRUE;
   }

BOOL CBrushDlg::OnOK (HWND HDlg)
// processes WM_COMMAND / IDOK messages
   {
   // save Style choice:
   if (IsDlgButtonChecked (HDlg, IDC_SOLID))
      mTBrushStyle = BS_SOLID;
   else if (IsDlgButtonChecked (HDlg, IDC_HATCHED))
      mTBrushStyle = BS_HATCHED;
   else
      mTBrushStyle = BS_NULL;

   // save selection from Hatch Pattern combo box:
   mTBrushHatchPattern = HatchTable [SendDlgItemMessage
      (HDlg, IDC_HATCHPATTERN, CB_GETCURSEL, 0, 0)].HatchID;

   // save selection from Color combo box:
   mTBrushColor = ColorTable [SendDlgItemMessage (HDlg,
      IDC_COLOR, CB_GETCURSEL, 0, 0)].ColorValue;

   // store values in figure or in default data members:
   if (MainWnd.mSelectedFig) // figure is selected
      {
      MainWnd.mSelectedFig->DefineBrush
         (mTBrushColor,
         mTBrushHatchPattern,
         mTBrushStyle);

      // force redrawing of figure:
      RECT Rect = MainWnd.mSelectedFig->GetBoundRect ();
      InvalidateRect (MainWnd.mHWnd, &Rect, TRUE);
```

```
        }
    else        // no figure selected
        {
      mBrushColor = mTBrushColor;
      mBrushHatchPattern = mTBrushHatchPattern;
      mBrushStyle = mTBrushStyle;
        }

    // close the dialog box:
    EndDialog (HDlg, IDOK);
    return TRUE;
        }

BOOL CBrushDlg::OnSetColor (HWND HDlg)
// processes WM_COMMAND / ID_SETCOLOR messages
    {
    CHOOSECOLOR CC;

    // assign values to structure to control Color dialog box:
    memset (&CC, 0, sizeof (CC));
    CC.lStructSize = sizeof (CC);
    CC.hwndOwner = HDlg;
    CC.rgbResult = ColorTable [9].ColorValue;
    CC.lpCustColors = mCustColors;
    CC.Flags = CC_RGBINIT;

    // display Color common dialog box; save selected color if
    // user clicked OK:
    if (ChooseColor (&CC))
        ColorTable [9].ColorValue = CC.rgbResult;
    return TRUE;
        }

///////////////////////////////////////////////////////////////////////////
// Pen dialog box:                                                        //
///////////////////////////////////////////////////////////////////////////

///////////////////////////////////////////////////////////////////////////
// CPenDlg public member functions:                                       //
///////////////////////////////////////////////////////////////////////////

CPenDlg::CPenDlg (void)
    {
    mPenColor = RGB (0,0,0);
    mPenStyle = PS_SOLID;
    mPenType = PS_COSMETIC;
    mPenWidth = 1;
    memset (mCustColors, 0, sizeof (mCustColors));
    return;
        }

  int CPenDlg::Show (void)
  // displays Pen dialog box
    {
    return DialogBox
```

```cpp
          (App.mHInstance,
          MAKEINTRESOURCE (IDD_PEN),
          MainWnd.mHWnd,
          PenDialogProc);
   }

//////////////////////////////////////////////////////////////////////////////
// Pen dialog box procedure:                                                 //
//////////////////////////////////////////////////////////////////////////////

BOOL CALLBACK PenDialogProc
   (HWND   HDlg,
    UINT   Msg,
    WPARAM WParam,
    LPARAM LParam)
   {
   switch (Msg)
      {
      case WM_INITDIALOG: // dialog box was just created
         return PenDlg.OnInitDialog (HDlg);

      case WM_COMMAND:  // user issued a command
         switch (LOWORD (WParam))
         {
         case IDC_SETCOLOR: // user clicked Set Custom Color
            return PenDlg.OnSetColor (HDlg);

         case IDCANCEL: // user chose Close or pressed Esc
            return PenDlg.OnCancel (HDlg);

         case IDOK:  // user clicked OK or pressed Enter
            return PenDlg.OnOK (HDlg);

         default:
            return FALSE; // default message processing
         }

      case WM_CTLCOLORBTN:    // button is about to be painted;
      case WM_CTLCOLORDLG:    // dialog box about to be painted;
      case WM_CTLCOLORSTATIC: // dialog text about to be painted
         return PenDlg.OnCtlColor ((HDC)WParam);

      default:           // request default processing for all
         return FALSE; // other messages
      }
   }

//////////////////////////////////////////////////////////////////////////////
// CPenDlg message handling member functions:                                //
//////////////////////////////////////////////////////////////////////////////

BOOL CPenDlg::OnCancel (HWND HDlg)
// processes WM_COMMAND / IDCANCEL messages
   {
   // close the dialog box:
```

```cpp
  EndDialog (HDlg, IDCANCEL);
  return TRUE;
  }

BOOL CPenDlg::OnCtlColor (HDC HDc)
// processes WM_CTLCOLORBTN, WM_CTLCOLORDLG, and
// WM_CTLCOLORSTATIC messages
  {
  // set text background to light gray:
  SetBkColor (HDc, RGB (192,192,192));

  // supply a handle to a light-gray brush:
  return (BOOL)GetStockObject (LTGRAY_BRUSH);
  }

BOOL CPenDlg::OnInitDialog (HWND HDlg)
// processes WM_INITDIALOG messages
  {
  // obtain current pen description:
  if (MainWnd.mSelectedFig) // figure is selected
     {
     mTPenColor = MainWnd.mSelectedFig->mPenColor;
     mTPenStyle = MainWnd.mSelectedFig->mPenStyle;
     mTPenType = MainWnd.mSelectedFig->mPenType;
     mTPenWidth = MainWnd.mSelectedFig->mPenWidth;
     SetWindowText (HDlg, "Figure Pen");
     }
  else        // no figure selected
     {
     mTPenColor = mPenColor;
     mTPenStyle = mPenStyle;
     mTPenType = mPenType;
     mTPenWidth = mPenWidth;
     }

  // check Type radio button:
  CheckDlgButton
     (HDlg,
     mTPenType == PS_COSMETIC ? IDC_COSMETIC : IDC_GEOMETRIC,
     1);

  // initialize Style combo box and select current value:
  for (int i = 0; i < 7; ++i)
     {
     SendDlgItemMessage (HDlg, IDC_STYLE, CB_ADDSTRING,
        0, (LPARAM)(LPCSTR)StyleTable [i].StyleName);
     if (StyleTable [i].StyleID == mTPenStyle)
        SendDlgItemMessage (HDlg, IDC_STYLE, CB_SETCURSEL,
        (WPARAM)i, 0);
     }

  // limit Width edit control to 2 characters and set value:
  SendDlgItemMessage (HDlg, IDC_WIDTH, EM_SETLIMITTEXT,
     (WPARAM)2, 0);
  SetDlgItemInt (HDlg, IDC_WIDTH, mTPenWidth, FALSE);
```

```cpp
    // initialize Color combo box and select current value:
    BOOL Selected = FALSE;
    for (i = 0; i < 10; ++i)
        {
        SendDlgItemMessage (HDlg, IDC_COLOR, CB_ADDSTRING, 0,
            (LPARAM)(LPCSTR)ColorTable [i].ColorName);
        if (!Selected && ColorTable [i].ColorValue == mTPenColor)
            {
            SendDlgItemMessage (HDlg, IDC_COLOR, CB_SETCURSEL,
                (WPARAM)i, 0);
            Selected = TRUE;
            }
        }
    if (!Selected)
        {
        ColorTable [9].ColorValue = mTPenColor;
        SendDlgItemMessage (HDlg, IDC_COLOR, CB_SETCURSEL,
            (WPARAM)9, 0);
        }

    // return TRUE to set focus to first control:
    return TRUE;
    }

BOOL CPenDlg::OnOK (HWND HDlg)
// processes WM_COMMAND / IDOK messages
    {
    // save Type choice:
    mTPenType = IsDlgButtonChecked (HDlg, IDC_COSMETIC) ?
        PS_COSMETIC : PS_GEOMETRIC;

    // save selection from Style combo box:
    mTPenStyle = StyleTable [SendDlgItemMessage (HDlg, IDC_STYLE,
        CB_GETCURSEL, 0, 0)].StyleID;

    // save value from Width edit control:
    BOOL Translated;
    mTPenWidth = GetDlgItemInt (HDlg, IDC_WIDTH, &Translated,
        FALSE);

    // save selection from Color combo box:
    mTPenColor = ColorTable [SendDlgItemMessage (HDlg,
        IDC_COLOR, CB_GETCURSEL, 0, 0)].ColorValue;

    // store values in figure or in default data members:
    if (MainWnd.mSelectedFig) // figure is selected
        {
        MainWnd.mSelectedFig->mPenColor = mTPenColor;
        MainWnd.mSelectedFig->mPenStyle = mTPenStyle;
        MainWnd.mSelectedFig->mPenType = mTPenType;
        MainWnd.mSelectedFig->mPenWidth = mTPenWidth;

        // force redrawing of figure:
        RECT Rect = MainWnd.mSelectedFig->GetBoundRect ();
```

```cpp
        InvalidateRect (MainWnd.mHWnd, &Rect, TRUE);
        }
    else                            // no figure selected
        {
      mPenColor = mTPenColor;
      mPenStyle = mTPenStyle;
      mPenType = mTPenType;
      mPenWidth = mTPenWidth;
        }

    // close the dialog box:
    EndDialog (HDlg, IDOK);
    return TRUE;
    }

BOOL CPenDlg::OnSetColor (HWND HDlg)
// processes WM_COMMAND / ID_SETCOLOR messages
    {
    CHOOSECOLOR CC;

    // assign values to structure to control Color dialog box:
    memset (&CC, 0, sizeof (CC));
    CC.lStructSize = sizeof (CC);
    CC.hwndOwner = HDlg;
    CC.rgbResult = ColorTable [9].ColorValue;
    CC.lpCustColors = mCustColors;
    CC.Flags = CC_RGBINIT;

    // display Color common dialog box; save selected color if
    // user clicked OK:
    if (ChooseColor (&CC))
       ColorTable [9].ColorValue = CC.rgbResult;
    return TRUE;
    }
```

CHAPTER **5**

USING REGIONS, PATHS, AND CLIPPING

In the previous chapters, you learned how to draw *individual* lines and closed figures. In this chapter, you will learn how to manage complex areas on a display surface consisting of *several* lines or closed figures. The techniques presented here will help you to create more complex graphic images and will allow you to generate a variety of graphic effects.

The chapter describes two types of graphic objects that store and manage complex areas: *regions* and *paths*. It then shows how to use regions or paths to *clip* graphics output—that is, to restrict it to a well-defined area on the display surface.

USING REGIONS

A *region* is a Windows graphic object that stores a description of an area on a display surface. This area can consist of one or more rectangles, other polygons, or ellipses, which may be combined using various logical operators. Once you have created a region, you can perform a variety of operations on the region itself or on the corresponding area of the display surface. The following are some of these operations:

- You can fill, draw a border around, or invert the area on a display surface that is defined by the region.
- You can perform hit testing; that is, you can quickly find out whether a given point, such as the current position of the mouse cursor, is within the region area.
- You can "move" the region—that is, offset the coordinate values that the region stores.
- You can use the region to clip graphics output.

The Region program, presented later in the chapter, demonstrates many of the region techniques that will be described.

Creating Regions

In general, you create a region by first creating two or more simple regions and then combining them in various ways to define a more complex area.

To create a region that consists of a simple rectangle, you can call the `CreateRectRgn` API function,

```
HRGN CreateRectRgn
   (int nLeftRect,  int nTopRect,
    int nRightRect, int nBottomRect);
```

where `nLeftRect` and `nTopRect` are the coordinates of the upper-left corner of the rectangular area, and `nRightRect` and `nBottomRect` are the coordinates of the lower-right corner of the area.

To create a region consisting of a rectangle with rounded corners, call the `CreateRoundRectRgn` API function:

```
HRGN CreateRoundRectRgn
   (int nLeftRect,     int nTopRect,
    int nRightRect,    int nBottomRect,
    int nWidthEllipse, int nHeightEllipse);
```

The first four parameters give the coordinates of the rectangle, and the last two parameters (`nWidthEllipse` and `nHeightEllipse`) give the width and height of the ellipse used to draw the rounded corners (see Figure 4.3).

To create a polygonal region, call the `CreatePolygonRgn` API function,

```
HRGN CreatePolygonRgn
   (CONST POINT *lppt,
    int cPoints,
    int fnPolyFillMode);
```

where `lppt` is an array of `POINT` structures containing the coordinates of the vertices and `cPoints` is the number of vertices. For information on drawing polygons, see the section "Drawing Rectangles and Polygons" in Chapter 4. The parameter `fnPolyFillMode` specifies the polygon filling mode and can be assigned either `ALTERNATE` (the default) or `WINDING`. `CreatePolygonRgn` uses the polygon filling mode to determine which of the areas enclosed by a complex polygon are to be included in the region. For an explanation of the polygon filling mode, see Chapter 4, the section "Drawing Rectangles and Polygons," and Figure 4.5.

Finally, you can create a simple elliptical region by calling the `CreateEllipticRgn` API function:

```
HRGN CreateEllipticRgn
    (int nLeftRect,  int nTopRect,
     int nRightRect, int nBottomRect);
```

The parameters give the coordinates of the rectangle bounding the ellipse (see Figure 4.6).

`CreateRectRgn`, `CreateRoundRectRgn`, `CreatePolygonRgn`, and `CreateEllipticRgn` all return a *handle* to the region. The program should save this handle in a variable of type `HRGN` so that it can perform operations with the region.

Once you have created one or more regions, you can combine them to create a more complex region by calling the `CombineRgn` API function:

```
int CombineRgn
   (HRGN hrgnDest,
    HRGN hrgnSrc1,
    HRGN hrgnSrc2,
    int  fnCombineMode);
```

The parameters `hrgnSrc1` and `hrgnSrc2` are the handles of the two source regions that you want to combine. The parameter `hrgnDest` is the handle of the destination region, which will be assigned the result of combining the two source regions (the original region referenced by `hrgnDest` will be discarded). Note that you can assign the same region handle to `hrgnDest` *and* to `hrgnSrc1` or `hrgnSrc2`. The `fnCombineMode` parameter indicates the way that the two regions are to be combined; the different values you can assign `fnCombineMode` are illustrated in Figure 5.1.

As an example, the following code creates two elliptical regions and then combines them into a single complex region:

```
// create two simple elliptical regions:
HRGN HRegion = CreateEllipticRgn (23, 50, 161, 152);
HRGN HRegionTemp = CreateEllipticRgn (46, 25, 138, 177);

// combine them to create a complex region:
// assign a value to CombineMode...
CombineRgn (HRegion, mHRegion, HRegionTemp, CombineMode);
```

In this example, the original region with the handle `HRegion` is replaced with the combined region. Figure 5.1 shows the combined region generated by passing each possible value to the `fnCombineMode` parameter.

Using `CombineRgn` to create complex regions and then drawing those regions (as described in the next section) allows you to easily draw figures that would be difficult to draw using individual calls to drawing functions.

As with a pen or brush, when you are done using a region, you should pass its handle to the `DeleteObject` API function to release the system resources that the region consumes:

```
BOOL DeleteObject (HGDIOBJ hObject);
```

FYI

The following are related API functions: `CreateRectRgnIndirect`, `CreatePolyPolygonRgn`, `CreateEllipticRgnIndirect`, `ExtCreateRgn`, and `GetRegionData`.

Drawing Regions

Once you have created a region, you can draw within the display surface area that is described by the region. The Windows API provides several functions for drawing within a region area: `PaintRgn`, `FillRgn`, `InvertRgn`, and `FrameRgn`. When you call one of these functions, you must pass the handle of a device context to specify the device surface on which you want to draw, and you must pass the handle of a region to specify the *area* on that surface on which you want to draw.

You can fill the entire region area using the brush that is currently selected into the device context by calling the `PaintRgn` API function:

```
BOOL PaintRgn (HDC hdc, HRGN hrgn);
```

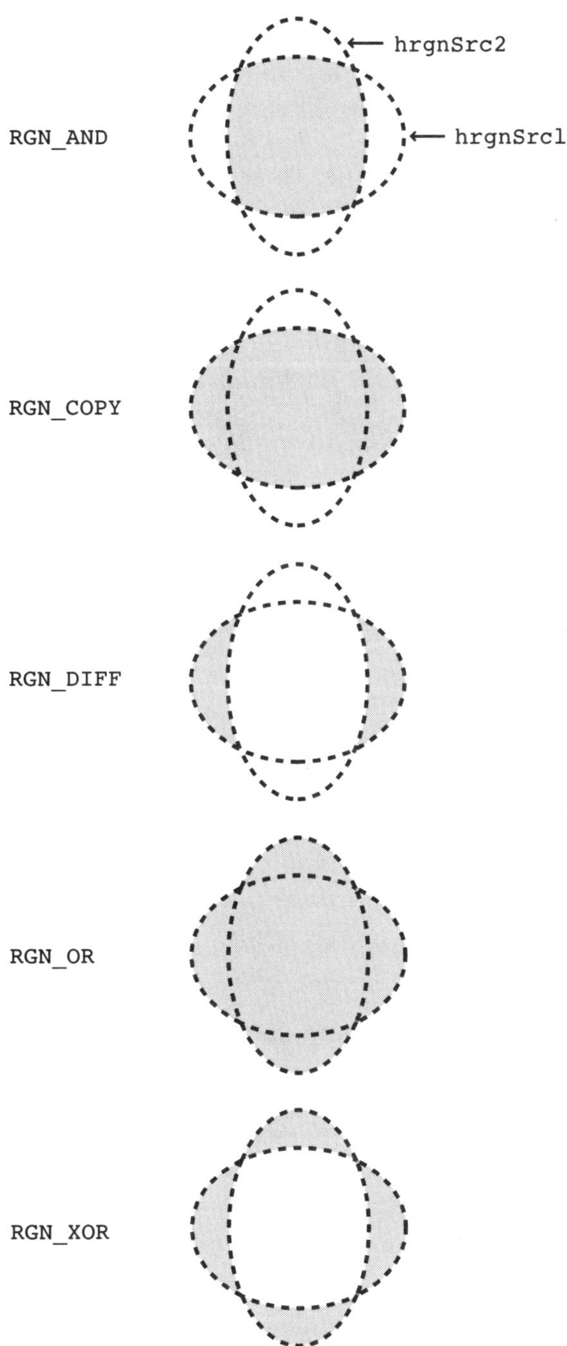

Figure 5.1:   The results of passing the different possible `fnCombineMode` values to the `CombineRgn` function to combine two elliptical regions

Alternatively, you can fill the region area using a specified brush by calling the `FillRgn` API function,

```
BOOL FillRgn (HDC hdc, HRGN hrgn, HBRUSH hbr);
```

where `hbr` is the handle of the brush you want to use. The advantage of using `FillRgn` rather than `PaintRgn` is that you do not have to select and deselect the brush from the device context.

FYI   When you use `FillRgn` or `PaintRgn` to fill a complex region, the specific interior areas that are filled depend upon the current polygon filling mode, which is set through the `SetPolyFillMode` function described in Chapter 4 ("Drawing Rectangles and Polygons" and Figure 4.5).

To invert the colors within the region area, call the `InvertRgn` API function:

```
BOOL InvertRgn (HDC hdc, HRGN hrgn);
```

See the FYI note on inverting colors in Chapter 3 (in the section "Setting the Mix Mode").

Finally, you can draw a border around the region area using a specified brush (yes, a brush, *not* a pen) by calling the `FrameRgn` API function,

```
BOOL FrameRgn
    (HDC hdc,
     HRGN hrgn,
     HBRUSH hbr,
     int nWidth,
     int nHeight);
```

where `hrgn` is the handle of the brush, `nWidth` is the border width, and `nHeight` is the border height. Horizontal portions of the border will be made `nHeight` pixels high, vertical portions will be made `nWidth` pixels wide, and oblique portions will be given an intermediate thickness. If you make `nWidth` greater than `nHeight`, the border will look like a line drawn with a calligraphy pen. For example, Figure 5.2 shows a border drawn around a region by calling `FrameRgn` and assigning 10 to `nWidth` and 2 to `nHeight`.

Performing Other Region Operations

You can test whether two regions are the same by calling the `EqualRgn` API function,

Figure 5.2:   A border drawn around a region by calling `FrameRgn` and assigning 10 to the border width (`nWidth`) and 2 to the border height (`nHeight`)

```
BOOL EqualRgn (HRGN hSrcRgn1, HRGN hSrcRgn2);
```

which returns TRUE if the two regions are identical, or FALSE otherwise.
   The `GetRgnBox` API function,

```
int GetRgnBox (HRGN hrgn, LPRECT lprc);
```

provides the coordinates of the smallest rectangle that bounds a region. It assigns these coordinates to the RECT structure pointed to by the `lprc` parameter.
   You can *move* a region by calling the `OffsetRgn` API function,

```
int OffsetRgn
   (HRGN hrgn,
    int nXOffset,
    int nYOffset);
```

where `nXOffset` is the amount by which the region is to be moved in the horizontal direction, and `nYOffset` is the amount by which it is to be moved in the vertical direction. `OffsetRgn` will appropriately adjust the region description stored in the `hrgn` region. This function might be useful if you are animating a complex figure.
   You can also call the `PtInRegion` or `RectInRegion` API function to perform *hit testing*. `PtInRegion`,

```
BOOL PtInRegion (HRGN hrgn, int X, int Y);
```

returns TRUE if the specified *point* is within the region area, and `RectInRegion`,

```
BOOL RectInRegion (HRGN hrgn, CONST RECT *lprc);
```

returns TRUE if the specified *rectangle* is partially or completely within the region area.

Finally, you can call the `SelectObject,` `SelectClipRgn,` or `ExtSelectClipRgn` API function to create a clipping region that is equal to a specified region. For information, see the section "Using Clipping Regions," later in the chapter.

The Region Program

This section presents the Region program, which demonstrates several of the region techniques given in the chapter. To run Region, execute the Region.exe file in the Region subfolder of the folder in which you installed the companion disk files.

Region combines two elliptical regions to create a single complex region and fills the region area within the window using a red pen (see Figure 5.3). If you click within the region area, the Region program inverts the color within the filled area.

Table 5.1 lists the region operations that are used in the Region program and gives the location of each operation in the source code.

The Region Program Source Code   The following are the source code listings for the Region program. A copy of these files is included in the Region subfolder of the folder in which you installed the companion disk files.

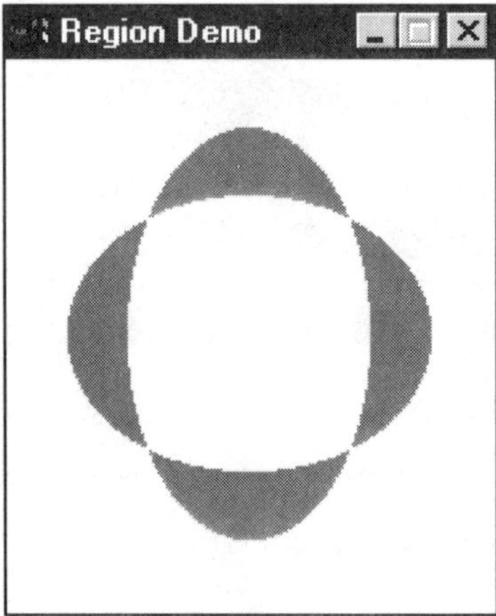

Figure 5.3:   The Region program window

Table 5.1: Region operations performed by the Region program

Region Operation Performed by the Region Program	Location of Operation in Source Code
Creates two simple elliptical regions by calling `CreateEllipticRgn` and combines these regions by calling `CombineRgn`	`CMainWnd::Create` function in MainWnd.cpp, which `WinMain` calls to create the program window
Creates a red brush and calls `FillRgn` to fill the region area; also calls `InvertRgn` if the region needs to be inverted	`CMainWnd::OnPaint` in MainWnd.cpp, which receives control whenever the window needs painting or repainting
When the user clicks within the program window, calls `PtInRegion` to determine whether the pointer is within the region area; if so, calls `InvertRgn` to invert the region area	`CMainWnd::OnLButtonDown` function in MainWnd.cpp, which receives control when the user clicks within the client area of the program window
Destroys the region by calling `DeleteObject` before the program exits	`CMainWnd::OnDestroy` function in MainWnd.cpp, which receives control when the program window is destroyed

Listing 5.1: Region.cpp

```
////////////////////////////////////////////////////////////////////////////
//                                                                        //
// Region.cpp:    Main program object declarations and WinMain            //
//                program entry function.                                 //
//                                                                        //
////////////////////////////////////////////////////////////////////////////

#define STRICT
#include <windows.h>

// header files for main program classes:
#include "app.h"
#include "mainwnd.h"

// main program objects:
CApp      App;
CMainWnd  MainWnd;

////////////////////////////////////////////////////////////////////////////
// program entry function:                                                //
////////////////////////////////////////////////////////////////////////////

int APIENTRY WinMain
  (HINSTANCE HInstCurrent,
```

```
HINSTANCE HInstPrevious,
LPSTR     CmdLine,
int       CmdShow)
{
// store program informaton in application object:
App.Initialize (HInstCurrent, CmdLine);

// register class for main program window:
if (!MainWnd.RegisterClass ())
   return 0;

// create and display main program window:
if (!MainWnd.Create ())
   return 0;

// main message loop:
MSG Msg;
while (GetMessage (&Msg, NULL, NULL, NULL))
   {
   TranslateMessage (&Msg);
   DispatchMessage (&Msg);
   }

// return "application-defined exit code":
return Msg.wParam;
}
```

Listing 5.2:   App.h

```
/////////////////////////////////////////////////////////////////////////
//                                                                     //
// App.h: Header file for application class.                           //
//                                                                     //
/////////////////////////////////////////////////////////////////////////

class CApp
{
public:
   HINSTANCE  mHInstance;   // handle of program instance
   LPSTR      mCmdLine;     // pointer to program command line

   void Initialize (HINSTANCE HInstCurrent, LPSTR CmdLine)
   // saves application values
      {
      mHInstance = HInstCurrent;
      mCmdLine = CmdLine;
      }
};
```

Listing 5.3:   MainWnd.h

```
/////////////////////////////////////////////////////////////////////////
//                                                                       //
// MainWnd.h: Header file for main window class.                         //
//                                                                       //
/////////////////////////////////////////////////////////////////////////

// dimensions of main program window:
#define WINWIDTH  186
#define WINHEIGHT 224

class CMainWnd
{
public:
   HRGN mHRegion;  // handle to region
   HWND mHWnd;      // main window handle
   BOOL mInverted; // flag indicating region is inverted

   BOOL Create (void);
   BOOL RegisterClass (void);

   // message-handling functions:
   LRESULT OnDestroy (void);
   LRESULT OnLButtonDown (WORD XCursor, WORD YCursor);
   LRESULT OnPaint (void);
};
```

Listing 5.4:   MainWnd.cpp

```
/////////////////////////////////////////////////////////////////////////
//                                                                       //
// MainWnd.cpp: Implementation file for main window class.               //
//                                                                       //
/////////////////////////////////////////////////////////////////////////

#define STRICT
#include <windows.h>

#include "app.h"
#include "mainwnd.h"

extern CApp      App;
extern CMainWnd  MainWnd;

LRESULT CALLBACK MainWndProc (HWND HWnd, UINT Msg, WPARAM WParam,
   LPARAM LParam);

/////////////////////////////////////////////////////////////////////////
// CMainWnd public member functions:                                     //
/////////////////////////////////////////////////////////////////////////
```

```
BOOL CMainWnd::Create (void)
// creates and displays main program window; returns TRUE on
// success or FALSE on error
   {
    // create main program window and save handle:
   mHWnd = CreateWindow
      ("DemoClass",
       "Region Demo",
       WS_OVERLAPPED | WS_SYSMENU | WS_MINIMIZEBOX,
       CW_USEDEFAULT,
       CW_USEDEFAULT,
       WINWIDTH,
       WINHEIGHT,
       NULL,
       NULL,
       App.mHInstance,
       NULL);
   if (!mHWnd)
      return FALSE;

   // display window:
   ShowWindow
      (mHWnd,
       SW_SHOWDEFAULT);

   // create the region:

   // get dimensions of client area of main window:
   RECT Rect;
   GetClientRect (mHWnd, &Rect);

   // create two elliptical regions:
   mHRegion = CreateEllipticRgn
      (Rect.right / 8,
       Rect.bottom / 4,
       (Rect.right * 7) / 8,
       (Rect.bottom * 3) / 4);
   HRGN HRegionTemp = CreateEllipticRgn
      (Rect.right / 4,
       Rect.bottom / 8,
       (Rect.right * 3) / 4,
       (Rect.bottom * 7) / 8);

   // combine the two regions
   CombineRgn (mHRegion, mHRegion, HRegionTemp, RGN_XOR);

   // initialize mInverted flag:
   mInverted = FALSE;
   return TRUE;
   }

BOOL CMainWnd::RegisterClass (void)
// registers class for main program window; returns TRUE on
```

```cpp
// success or FALSE on error
   {
   WNDCLASS WC;

   // specify class information:
   WC.style = 0;
   WC.lpfnWndProc = MainWndProc;
   WC.cbClsExtra = 0;
   WC.cbWndExtra = 0;
   WC.hInstance = App.mHInstance;
   WC.hIcon = 0;
   WC.hCursor = LoadCursor (NULL, IDC_ARROW);
   WC.hbrBackground = (HBRUSH)GetStockObject (WHITE_BRUSH);
   WC.lpszMenuName = 0;
   WC.lpszClassName = “DemoClass”;

   // register class:
   return (BOOL)::RegisterClass (&WC);
   }

///////////////////////////////////////////////////////////////////////////
// window procedure for main window:                                      //
///////////////////////////////////////////////////////////////////////////

LRESULT CALLBACK MainWndProc
   (HWND   HWnd,
    UINT   Msg,
    WPARAM WParam,
    LPARAM LParam)
   {
   switch (Msg)
      {
      case WM_DESTROY: // DestroyWindow was called
         return MainWnd.OnDestroy ();

      case WM_LBUTTONDOWN: // user pressed left button
         return MainWnd.OnLButtonDown
            (LOWORD (LParam), HIWORD (LParam));

      case WM_PAINT: // window needs painting or repainting
         return MainWnd.OnPaint ();

      default:
         // default processing for all other messages:
         return DefWindowProc (HWnd, Msg, WParam, LParam);
      }
   }

///////////////////////////////////////////////////////////////////////////
// CMainWnd message handling member functions:                            //
///////////////////////////////////////////////////////////////////////////

LRESULT CMainWnd::OnDestroy (void)
```

```cpp
// processes WM_DESTROY messages
   {
   // delete region
   DeleteObject (mHRegion);
   PostQuitMessage (0);  // post a WM_QUIT message to
   return NULL;          // cause message loop to exit
   }

LRESULT CMainWnd::OnLButtonDown (WORD XCursor, WORD YCursor)
// processes WM_LBUTTONDOWN messages
   {
   // hit test
   if (PtInRegion (mHRegion, XCursor, YCursor))
      {
      // pointer is within region; therefore, invert it
      HDC HDc = GetDC (mHWnd);
      InvertRgn (HDc, mHRegion);
      ReleaseDC (mHWnd, HDc);
      mInverted = !mInverted;
      }
   return NULL;
   }

LRESULT CMainWnd::OnPaint (void)
// processes WM_PAINT messages
   {
   HDC HDCPaint;               // client area device-context handle
   PAINTSTRUCT PaintStruct; // paint information

   // initiate painting and obtain a device context:
   HDCPaint = BeginPaint (mHWnd, &PaintStruct);

   // create a red brush:
   LOGBRUSH LB = {BS_SOLID, RGB (255,0,0), 0};
   HBRUSH HRedBrush = CreateBrushIndirect (&LB);

   // fill the region using brush:
   FillRgn (HDCPaint, mHRegion, HRedBrush);

   // if user has inverted region, re-invert it:
   if (mInverted)
      InvertRgn (HDCPaint, mHRegion);

   // delete the red brush:
   DeleteObject (HRedBrush);

   // terminate painting and release device context:
   EndPaint (mHWnd, &PaintStruct);
   return NULL;
   }
```

USING PATHS

A *path* is another type of Windows graphic object that stores a description of an area on a display surface. The area described by a path can consist of one or more lines, polygons, Bézier curves, or blocks of text. The following are among the operations you can perform on a path that you have created:

- You can draw a border around the area described by the path, you can fill the area, or you can do both.
- You can convert the path to a region, so that you can take advantage of any of the region features discussed previously in the chapter.
- You can use the path to clip graphics output.

Creating Paths

You create a path by recording a series of calls to drawing functions. To do this, perform the following three steps:

1. Call the `BeginPath` API function,

   ```
   BOOL BeginPath (HDC hdc);
   ```

   passing it the handle of a device context. Calling `BeginPath` is said to *open a path bracket*.

2. Call one or more drawing functions, passing the handle of the device context that you specified in step 1. When you call each function, the figure that would normally be drawn on the display surface is added to the path. *No output will appear on the device.*

The following are the drawing functions that you can call to define a path:

`ExtTextOut`	`Polyline`
`LineTo`	`PolylineTo`
`MoveToEx`	`PolyPolygon`
`PolyBezier`	`PolyPolyline`
`PolyBezierTo`	`TextOut`
`Polygon`	

3. When you are done adding figures to the path, call the `EndPath` API function:

   ```
   BOOL EndPath (HDC hdc);
   ```

   Calling `EndPath` is said to *close the path bracket*.

For example, the following code creates a path consisting of a block of text:

```
BeginPath (HDCPaint);
TextOut (HDCPaint, 25, 25, "fade", 4);
EndPath (HDCPaint);
```

(This code is from the WM_PAINT routine of the Clip program, which will be presented at the end of the chapter. HDCPaint is the device context handle returned by BeginPaint.)

Notice that when you create a path, Windows does *not* supply a handle to the path. Rather, the path is automatically selected into the specified device context. To draw the path or perform other operations, you need specify only the handle of this device context. When you create a path, any previous path selected into the device context is discarded.

FYI   The following are related API functions: CloseFigure, AbortPath, and GetPath.

Drawing Paths

You can draw a border around the area defined by a path, using the current pen, by calling the StrokePath API function,

```
BOOL StrokePath (HDC hdc);
```

where hdc is the handle of the device context for which you defined the path.

You can fill the interior areas of a path, using the current brush and polygon filling mode, by calling the FillPath API function:

```
BOOL FillPath (HDC hdc);
```

Finally, you can simultaneously draw a border around a path *and* fill the path by calling the StrokeAndFillPath API function:

```
BOOL StrokeAndFillPath (HDC hdc);
```

FYI   When you call StrokePath, FillPath, or StrokeAndFillPath (or PathToRegion or SelectClipPath, discussed in the next section), the path is deleted. Consequently, if you were to call StrokePath and then call FillPath, FillPath would do nothing. Calling these two functions is therefore *not* equivalent to calling StrokeAndFillPath.

FYI	The following are related API functions: `GetPath` and `PolyDraw`.

Other Path Operations

You can convert a path to a region by calling the `PathToRegion` API function,

```
HRGN PathToRegion (HDC hdc);
```

where `hdc` is the handle of the device context for which you defined the path. `PathToRegion` removes the path from the device context, creates a region that defines the same area as the path, and returns a handle to this region. You can then use the region in any of the ways that were described previously in the chapter.

Also, you can call the `SelectClipPath` API function to create a clipping region that is equal to a path. For instructions, see the next section.

FYI	The following are related API functions: `WidenPath` and `FlattenPath`.

USING CLIPPING REGIONS

The term *clipping region* refers to a region that has been selected into a device context. A clipping region defines the portion of a display surface in which you can draw graphics. Not every device context has a clipping region. If a device context does not have a clipping region, you can display graphics anywhere on the display surface. If, however, a device context does have a clipping region, graphics output can be displayed only within this region. All graphics output that falls outside of the clipping region will be clipped—that is, made invisible.

In Windows programs, clipping regions are used to confine graphics output to the part of the window that needs repainting and also to achieve unique graphic effects (such as the fading text displayed by the Clip program given at the end of the chapter).

As you saw in Chapter 2 (in the section "Display Device Contexts"), a device context supplied by the `BeginPaint` API function has an initial clipping region that is set to the area of the window that needs repainting. In contrast, a device context supplied by `GetDC` and other API functions has no clipping region. In the following sections, you will learn how to explicitly define and manage clipping regions for any device context.

In Chapter 2, you learned how to invalidate a rectangular portion of a program window by calling the `InvalidateRect` API function. Now that you understand regions, you might find a use for the `InvalidateRgn` API function, which invalidates the portion of a window corresponding to a region.

Defining a Clipping Region

To define a clipping region, you must first create either a region or a path using the techniques explained in the previous sections of the chapter.

If you have created a region, you can define a clipping region by *selecting the region into a device context*. You can select a region by calling the `ExtSelectClipRgn` API function:

```
int ExtSelectClipRgn (HDC hdc, HRGN hrgn, int fnMode);
```

The parameter `hdc` is the handle of the device context to which you want to assign the clipping region; `hrgn` is the handle of the region that you created previously; and `fnMode` specifies how the region is to be combined with any existing clipping region already selected into the device context. The values that you can assign `fnMode` are the same as those that you can pass to the `CombineRgn` function, discussed previously. For a list of the values and an illustration of their results, see Figure 5.1.

You can also select a region by calling either the `SelectObject` or the `SelectClipRgn` API function, although both of these functions create a clipping region that is a simple copy of the specified region (this is the same as passing `RGN_COPY` to `ExtSelectClipRgn`) and do not let you choose other combination modes.

If you have created a path, you can first convert the path to a region by calling `PathToRegion` and then select the region by calling `ExtSelectClipRgn`. As a shortcut, however, you can convert the path that you have created for a device context to a region *and* select the region into this same device context by calling the `SelectClipPath` API function:

```
BOOL SelectClipPath (HDC hdc, int iMode);
```

The `hdc` parameter is the handle of the device context for which you have defined the path. The clipping region will be selected into this same device context. The parameter `iMode` specifies how the path area is to be combined with any existing clipping region already selected into the device context; you can assign to it the same set of values that you can assign to the `iMode` parameter passed to `ExtSelectClipRgn` (see Figure 5.1).

Managing a Clipping Region

The Windows API provides several functions that allow you to determine the location of a clipping region: `PtVisible`, `RectVisible`, and `GetClipBox`. Calling one of these functions can help you avoid a futile but time-consuming attempt to draw outside of the clipping region.

The `PtVisible` function,

```
BOOL PtVisible
   (HDC hdc,
    int X, int Y);
```

returns `TRUE` if the point at the coordinates given by `X` and `Y` is within the clipping region of the device context `hdc`.

The `RectVisible` function,

```
BOOL RectVisible
   (HDC hdc,
    CONST RECT *lprc);
```

returns `TRUE` if the rectangle specified by the `lprec` parameter is partially or completely within the clipping region. (The DrawIt program calls this function from the `CMainWnd::OnPaint` function in the MainWnd.cpp file, to avoid attempting to draw figures that fall completely outside of the clipping region.)

FYI   Stated more precisely, `PtVisible` and `RectVisible` return `TRUE` if the point or rectangle is within the *visible* portion of the clipping region. The clipping region may not be completely visible; part of it may extend beyond the boundaries of the display surface or, for a window, may be covered by an overlapping window. Also, if the device context does not have a clipping region, these functions will return `TRUE` if the point or rectangle is within the visible portion of the display surface.

Finally, `GetClipBox`,

```
int GetClipBox
   (HDC hdc,
    LPRECT lprc);
```

supplies the coordinates of the smallest rectangle that bounds the visible portion of the clipping region (or, if the device context has no clipping region, the entire visible portion of the display surface). It assigns these coordinates to the RECT structure pointed to by the `lprc` parameter.

TIP　　Recall from Chapter 2 that the coordinates of the smallest rectangle bounding the clipping region are also returned by the `BeginPaint` function, which you call at the beginning of a `WM_PAINT` routine.

You can also *modify* a clipping region by calling the `IntersectClipRect`, `ExcludeClipRect`, or `OffsetClipRgn` API function. `IntersectClipRect`,

```
int IntersectClipRect
   (HDC hdc,
    int nLeftRect,   int nTopRect,
    int nRightRect, int nBottomRect);
```

sets the clipping region to the *intersection* of the current clipping region and the specified rectangle.

The `ExcludeClipRect` function,

```
int ExcludeClipRect
   (HDC hdc,
    int nLeftRect,   int nTopRect,
    int nRightRect, int nBottomRect);
```

sets the clipping region to the current clipping region minus the specified rectangle.

Finally, `OffsetClipRgn`,

```
int OffsetClipRgn
   (HDC hdc,
    int nXOffset,
    int nYOffset);
```

moves the current clipping region by the specified horizontal (`nXOffset`) and vertical offsets (`nYOffset`).

FYI　　The following are related API functions: `GetDCEx`, `ExcludeUpdateRgn`, `GetClipRgn`, `SetMetaRgn`, and `GetMetaRgn`.

The Clip Program

The Clip program shows how you can use a path and a clipping region to generate a unique graphic effect—text that gradually fades from dark to light (see Figure 5.4). To run Clip, execute the Clip.exe file in the Clip subfolder of the folder in which you installed the companion disk.

The text is displayed by the `CMainWnd::OnPaint` function in MainWnd.cpp, which processes `WM_PAINT` messages. After calling `BeginPaint`, `OnPaint` creates and selects a large text font. It then creates a path, as follows:

```
// create path (path bracket):
BeginPath (HDCPaint);
TextOut (HDCPaint, 25, 25, "fade", 4);
EndPath (HDCPaint);
```

This path consists of the area occupied by the characters in the string "fade". `OnPaint` then calls `SelectClipPath` to create a clipping region that is equal to the area defined by the path:

```
// create clipping region from path:
SelectClipPath (HDCPaint, RGN_COPY);
```

Once the clipping region has been established, `OnPaint` draws a series of rectangles across the area occupied by the text (using the `FillRect` API function). Each rectangle has a height of two pixels and a width equal to the

Figure 5.4:   The Clip program window

width of the text. The first rectangle is drawn using a relatively dark gray brush, and each successive rectangle is drawn using a brush with a lighter shade of gray. The resulting fill color is visible only within the clipping region—that is, within the text characters.

The Clip Program Source Code   This section contains the source code listings for the Clip program. You will find a complete copy of these files in the Clip subfolder within the folder in which you installed the companion disk files.

Listing 5.5:   Clip.cpp

```cpp
///////////////////////////////////////////////////////////////////////////////
//                                                                           //
// Clip.cpp:     Main program object declarations and WinMain                //
//               program entry function.                                     //
//                                                                           //
///////////////////////////////////////////////////////////////////////////////

#define STRICT
#include <windows.h>

// header files for main program classes:
#include "app.h"
#include "mainwnd.h"

// main program objects:
CApp       App;
CMainWnd   MainWnd;

///////////////////////////////////////////////////////////////////////////////
// program entry function:                                                   //
///////////////////////////////////////////////////////////////////////////////

int APIENTRY WinMain
   (HINSTANCE HInstCurrent,
    HINSTANCE HInstPrevious,
    LPSTR     CmdLine,
    int       CmdShow)
    {
    // store program informaton in application object:
    App.Initialize (HInstCurrent, CmdLine);

    // register class for main program window:
    if (!MainWnd.RegisterClass ())
       return 0;

    // create and display main program window:
    if (!MainWnd.Create ())
       return 0;
```

```cpp
   // main message loop:
   MSG Msg;
   while (GetMessage (&Msg, NULL, NULL, NULL))
      {
      TranslateMessage (&Msg);
      DispatchMessage (&Msg);
      }

   // return "application-defined exit code":
   return Msg.wParam;
   }
```

Listing 5.6:   App.h

```cpp
////////////////////////////////////////////////////////////////////////////
//                                                                        //
// App.h: Header file for application class.                              //
//                                                                        //
////////////////////////////////////////////////////////////////////////////

class CApp
{
public:
   HINSTANCE mHInstance; // handle of program instance
   LPSTR     mCmdLine;   // pointer to program command line

   void Initialize (HINSTANCE HInstCurrent, LPSTR CmdLine)
   // saves application values
      {
      mHInstance = HInstCurrent;
      mCmdLine = CmdLine;
      }
};
```

Listing 5.7:   MainWnd.h

```cpp
////////////////////////////////////////////////////////////////////////////
//                                                                        //
// MainWnd.h: Header file for main window class.                          //
//                                                                        //
////////////////////////////////////////////////////////////////////////////

// dimensions of main program window:
#define WINWIDTH  235
#define WINHEIGHT 224

class CMainWnd
{
public:
```

```
    HWND mHWnd;   // main window handle

    BOOL Create (void);
    BOOL RegisterClass (void);

    // message-handling functions:
    LRESULT OnDestroy (void);
    LRESULT OnPaint (void);
};
```

Listing 5.8:   MainWnd.cpp

```cpp
////////////////////////////////////////////////////////////////////////
//                                                                    //
// MainWnd.cpp: Implementation file for main window class.            //
//                                                                    //
////////////////////////////////////////////////////////////////////////

#define STRICT
#include <windows.h>
#include <string.h>

#include "app.h"
#include "mainwnd.h"

extern CApp      App;
extern CMainWnd  MainWnd;

LRESULT CALLBACK MainWndProc (HWND HWnd, UINT Msg, WPARAM WParam,
    LPARAM LParam);

////////////////////////////////////////////////////////////////////////
// CMainWnd public member functions:                                  //
////////////////////////////////////////////////////////////////////////

BOOL CMainWnd::Create (void)
// creates and displays main program window; returns TRUE on
// success or FALSE on error
   {
    // create main program window and save handle:
    mHWnd = CreateWindow
       ("DemoClass",
        "Clipping Demo",
        WS_OVERLAPPED | WS_SYSMENU | WS_MINIMIZEBOX,
        CW_USEDEFAULT,
        CW_USEDEFAULT,
        WINWIDTH,
        WINHEIGHT,
        NULL,
        NULL,
        App.mHInstance,
```

```
      NULL);
   if (!mHWnd)
      return FALSE;

   // display window:
   ShowWindow
      (mHWnd,
       SW_SHOWDEFAULT);

   return TRUE;
   }

BOOL CMainWnd::RegisterClass (void)
// registers class for main program window; returns TRUE on
// success or FALSE on error
   {
   WNDCLASS WC;

   // specify class information:
   WC.style = 0;
   WC.lpfnWndProc = MainWndProc;
   WC.cbClsExtra = 0;
   WC.cbWndExtra = 0;
   WC.hInstance = App.mHInstance;
   WC.hIcon = 0;
   WC.hCursor = LoadCursor (NULL, IDC_ARROW);
   WC.hbrBackground = (HBRUSH)GetStockObject (WHITE_BRUSH);
   WC.lpszMenuName = 0;
   WC.lpszClassName = "DemoClass";

   // register class:
   return (BOOL)::RegisterClass (&WC);
   }

//////////////////////////////////////////////////////////////////////////////
// window procedure for main window:                                        //
//////////////////////////////////////////////////////////////////////////////

LRESULT CALLBACK MainWndProc
   (HWND   HWnd,
    UINT   Msg,
    WPARAM WParam,
    LPARAM LParam)
   {
   switch (Msg)
      {
      case WM_DESTROY: // DestroyWindow was called
         return MainWnd.OnDestroy ();

      case WM_PAINT: // window needs painting or repainting
         return MainWnd.OnPaint ();

      default:
```

```cpp
        // default processing for all other messages:
        return DefWindowProc (HWnd, Msg, WParam, LParam);
    }
  }

////////////////////////////////////////////////////////////////////////////
// CMainWnd message handling member functions:                            //
////////////////////////////////////////////////////////////////////////////

LRESULT CMainWnd::OnDestroy (void)
// processes WM_DESTROY messages
  {
  PostQuitMessage (0); // post a WM_QUIT message to
  return NULL;         // cause message loop to exit
  }

LRESULT CMainWnd::OnPaint (void)
// processes WM_PAINT messages
  {
  HDC HDCPaint;               // client area device-context handle
  PAINTSTRUCT PaintStruct;    // paint information

  // initiate painting and obtain a device context:
  HDCPaint = BeginPaint (mHWnd, &PaintStruct);

  // create and select font:
  LOGFONT LF;
  memset (&LF, 0, sizeof (LOGFONT));
  LF.lfHeight = WINHEIGHT / 2;
  strcpy (LF.lfFaceName, "Times New Roman");
  HFONT HFont = CreateFontIndirect (&LF);
  HFONT HOldFont = (HFONT)SelectObject (HDCPaint, HFont);

  // prevent painting text background:
  SetBkMode (HDCPaint, TRANSPARENT);

  // create path (path bracket):
  BeginPath (HDCPaint);
  TextOut (HDCPaint, 25, 25, "fade", 4);
  EndPath (HDCPaint);

  // create clipping region from path:
  SelectClipPath (HDCPaint, RGN_COPY);

  // get size of text:
  SIZE Size;
  GetTextExtentPoint32 (HDCPaint, "fade", 4, &Size);

  // draw a series of gray rectangles across text; shade of
  // gray gets increasing lighter
  HBRUSH HGrayBrush;
  RECT Rect = {25, 0, 25 + Size.cx, 0};
  int ColorVal = 25;
  for (int i = 25; i <= 23 + Size.cy; i += 2)
```

```
      {
      // create gray brush:
      HGrayBrush = CreateSolidBrush
          (RGB (ColorVal, ColorVal, ColorVal));
      ColorVal += 5;

      // fill next rectangular area:
      Rect.top = i;
      Rect.bottom = i + 2;
      FillRect (HDCPaint, &Rect, HGrayBrush);

      // delete gray brush:
      DeleteObject (HGrayBrush);
      }

  // deselect and delete font:
  SelectObject (HDCPaint, HOldFont);
  DeleteObject (HFont);

  // terminate painting and release device context:
  EndPaint (mHWnd, &PaintStruct);
  return NULL;
  }
```

CHAPTER 6

TRANSFORMING GRAPHICS

This chapter deals with ways to modify, or *transform*, the size, orientation, position, or shape of the graphic figures that you display. In Windows programs, there are two general ways to transform graphics. First, your program can have Windows automatically transform the measurement and position values you pass to graphics functions by changing the *mapping mode* or the *origins* for the device context. Second, your program can manipulate the measurement and coordinate values itself to generate virtually any type of transformation. This chapter discusses both of these approaches.

The chapter begins by describing the differences between physical and logical units and coordinates, and by explaining several other general concepts. It then discusses changing the mapping mode and adjusting the origins. Next, it describes the different types of transformations that you can generate. The chapter concludes by presenting the third version of the DrawIt program, which adds the ability to *scale* the figures that you draw.

PHYSICAL VERSUS LOGICAL UNITS AND COORDINATES

On a typical raster device such as a monitor or printer, a measurement is specified in pixels, which are known as *device units*. Also, the position of a graphic element is specified in *device coordinates*. The horizontal (or *x*) device coordinate gives the distance of the element in pixels from the left edge of the display surface, and the vertical (or *y*) device coordinate gives the distance of the element in pixels from the top of the display surface. To state this in other terms, the *origin* (the point (0,0)) of the device coordinate system is at the upper-left corner of the display surface, horizontal coordinates are in pixels and increase as you move right, and vertical coordinates are in pixels and increase as you move down (see Figure 6.1).

FYI The position of the origin of the device coordinate system depends upon the specific device context. For example, with a client-area device context, it is at the upper-left corner of the client area of the program window; with a window device context, it is at the upper-left corner of the window border; and with a printer device context, it is at the upper-left corner of the printable area of the page.

In contrast, the measurement and position values that you pass to Windows graphics functions are given in *logical units* and *logical coordinates*. For example, the pen width measurement you pass to `ExtCreatePen` is in logical units, and the coordinates you pass to `Rectangle` are logical coordinates.

FYI Although all of the API graphics functions discussed in this book use logical units and coordinates, some API functions and Windows messages use device units or coordinates---for example, `WM_LBUTTONDOWN`, `WM_MOUSEMOVE`, `WM_SIZE`, `GetClientRect`, `MoveWindow`, and `ScrollWindow`. The documentation on each message or function should indicate the type of units or coordinates used.

So far in this book, the distinction between logical units and coordinates and device units and coordinates has been unimportant, because all of the program examples have used the default mapping mode and origins. Under

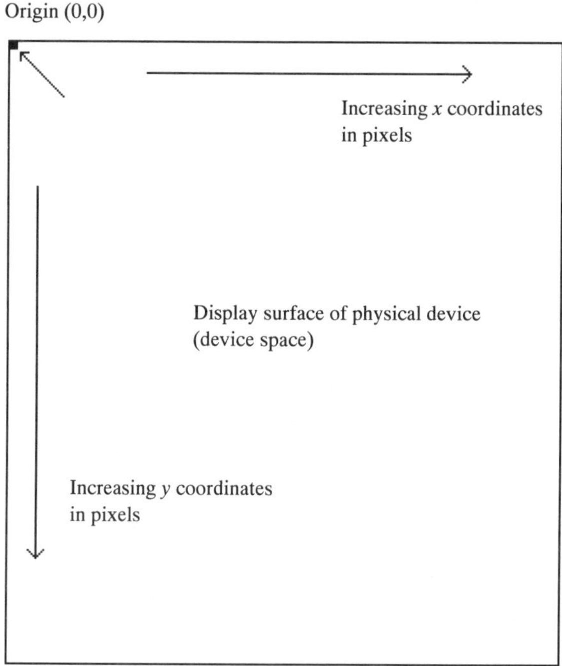

Figure 6.1:   The device coordinate system

the default mapping mode and origins, which were described in Chapter 3 (in the section "Calling the Line-Drawing Functions"), logical units and coordinates are the same as device units and coordinates. That is, you pass all graphics functions the actual device units and device coordinates.

If, however, you choose an alternative mapping mode or adjust the origins—using the techniques given in this chapter—you change the way Windows interprets the measurement and position values you pass to graphics functions. That is, logical units and coordinates are no longer the same as physical units and coordinates. When you subsequently call an API graphics function, Windows *converts* the measurement and position values that you pass into device units or coordinates for the specific output device, so that each graphic element will be given the correct size and position on the physical device.

FYI   As you will see later in the chapter, merely changing an origin alters the meaning of the *coordinates* you pass to graphics functions but not the *measurements* (such as the width of a pen).

To define a few additional terms, logical units and coordinates are said to constitute *page space,* and physical units and coordinates are said to constitute *device space.* If you have changed the mapping mode or origins, when you call a graphics function, Windows must *transform* the values that you supply from page space to device space.

TIP	You can convert device coordinates into logical coordinates by calling the API function `DPtoLP`, and you can convert logical coordinates into device coordinates by calling `LPtoDP`.

SETTING THE MAPPING MODE

The mapping mode is a drawing attribute that specifies the logical units used by graphics API functions, as well as the directions of increasing logical coordinate values.

FYI	For a general discussion on setting drawing attributes, see Chapter 2, the section "Drawing Attributes."

To change the mapping mode for a device context, you call the `SetMapMode` API function,

```
int SetMapMode (HDC hdc, int fnMapMode);
```

where `hdc` is the handle of the device context and `fnMapMode` is a code for the new mapping mode. You can assign `fnMapMode` any of the values shown in Table 6.1.

The first six modes shown in Table 6.1 are *predefined*; that is, they establish a specific unit and specific directions of increasing coordinate values. In contrast, the last two mapping modes, `MM_ANISOTROPIC` and `MM_ISOTROPIC`, let you choose your own units and directions of increasing coordinate values; these two modes will be discussed in the next section.

Figure 6.2 illustrates the default mapping mode (`MM_TEXT`), and Figure 6.3 illustrates the five alternative predefined mapping modes (`MM_LOENGLISH`, `MM_HIENGLISH`, `MM_TWIPS`, `MM_LOMETRIC`, and `MM_HIMETRIC`). Note that with the alternative predefined mapping modes, a visible point must normally have a 0 or negative y coordinate (a positive y coordinate value would place a point above the display surface, causing it to be clipped). As you will see later in the chapter, however, by adjusting the window or view-

Table 6.1: Values that can be assigned to the `fnMapMode` parameter passed to `SetMapMode` to set the mapping mode

Mapping Mode Value	Logical Unit	Direction of Increasing x Coordinates	Direction of Increasing y Coordinates
`MM_TEXT` (the default)	Pixel (device unit)	Right	Down
`MM_LOENGLISH`	0.01 inch	Right	Up
`MM_HIENGLISH`	0.001 inch	Right	Up
`MM_TWIPS`	1/1440 inch (1/20 of a printer's point)	Right	Up
`MM_LOMETRIC`	0.1 millimeter	Right	Up
`MM_HIMETRIC`	0.01 millimeter	Right	Up
`MM_ANISOTROPIC`	You set (x unit == y unit)	You set	You set
`MM_ISOTROPIC`	You set (x unit != y unit)	You set	You set

port origin, you can move the origin so that positive y coordinates fall within the device surface.

Consider, for example, that you call `SetMapMode` and pass it the value `MM_LOMETRIC`. If you then call `ExtCreatePen` to create a geometric pen and pass a pen width value of 25, the pen will be made 2.5 mm wide (25 x .1 mm). Likewise, if you call `LineTo` as follows,

```
LineTo (HDc, 100, -200);
```

the line will be drawn to the point that is 10 mm to the right of the left border of the device surface and 20 mm down from the top border (assuming that you have not changed the origins). The graphics functions must convert the `MM_LOMETRIC` values that you supply into the appropriate numbers of pixels for the particular display device. Or, to use different terminology, the function must transform the values from page space to device space.

FYI

Because you specify the thickness of a geometric pen in logical units, its thickness is scaled according to the mapping mode. A cosmetic pen, however, is *not* scaled; its thickness is always exactly one pixel.

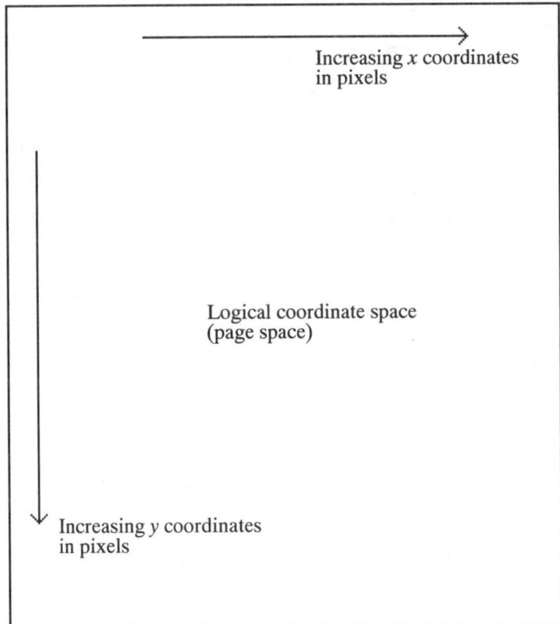

Figure 6.2:   Logical coordinate space (i.e., page space) in the MM_TEXT mapping mode

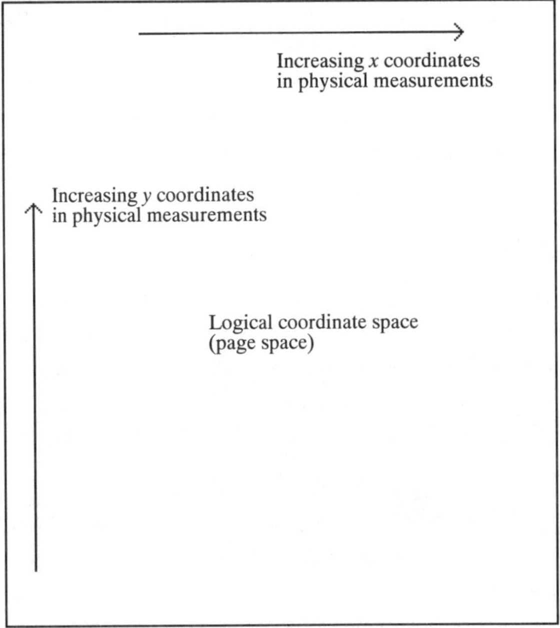

Figure 6.3:   Logical coordinate space (i.e., page space) in the alternative predefined mapping modes (MM_LOENGLISH, MM_HIENGLISH, MM_TWIPS, MM_LOMETRIC, and MM_HIMETRIC)

When using the default MM_TEXT mapping mode, the positions, sizes, and proportions of the graphics you display can vary from device to device, according to the device resolution and the proportions of the pixels. For example, if you display a figure on the screen under the VGA graphics mode, the figure will become much smaller if you then print it on a 300-pixel-per-inch laser printer. For another example, a circle that is round under the VGA graphics mode will become oval under the EGA graphics mode (because the pixel proportions are different).

The primary advantage of using one of the alternative mapping modes (MM_LOENGLISH, MM_HIENGLISH, MM_TWIPS, MM_LOMETRIC, and MM_HIMETRIC—and also MM_ANISOTROPIC and MM_ISOTROPIC provided that you set the extents properly) is that your program can easily work with device-independent units, such as millimeters or inches. Under one of these mapping modes, a figure will retain its position, size, and proportions regardless of the output device.

FYI   The following is a related API function: GetMapMode.

Using the MM_ANISOTROPIC and MM_ISOTROPIC Mapping Modes

When you call a graphics function under one the alternative predefined mapping modes (MM_LOENGLISH, MM_HIENGLISH, MM_TWIPS, MM_LOMETRIC, or MM_HIMETRIC), Windows calculates the number of device units per logical unit for the specific output device. Consider, for example, that you set the MM_LOENGLISH mapping mode and are printing on a 300-pixel-per-inch laser printer. In this case, Windows will calculate a ratio of three device units (pixels) per logical unit, as follows:

```
.01 inch / logical_unit * 300 device_units / inch = 3
device_units / logical_unit
```

If you passed a measurement or coordinate value of 100 to a graphics function, Windows would transform it to 300 device units (it would then send the value 300 to the device driver).

In contrast, when you choose the MM_ANISOTROPIC or MM_ISOTROPIC mapping mode, *you must specify the ratio between logical units and device units*. Windows will *not* calculate the ratio for you. Hence, these modes provide greater flexibility but less convenience.

After calling SetMapMode to choose the MM_ANISOTROPIC mapping mode, you must set the ratio between logical units and device units by calling both the SetWindowExtEx and the SetViewportExtEx API functions:

```
BOOL SetWindowExtEx
   (HDC hdc,           // handle of device context
    int nXExtent,      // x window extent
    int nYExtent,      // y window extent
    LPSIZE lpSize);    // receives former extents

BOOL SetViewportExtEx
   (HDC hdc,           // handle of device context
    int nXExtent,      // x viewport extent
    int nYExtent,      // y viewport extent
    LPSIZE lpSize);    // receives former extents
```

The `nXExtent` and `nYExtent` parameters passed to `SetWindowExtEx` specify the number of horizontal and vertical *logical* units, and the `nXExtent` and `nYExtent` parameters passed to `SetViewportExtEx` specify the number of horizontal and vertical *device* units. The values set by each of these functions mean nothing in themselves; however, the *ratio* of the values is the ratio between logical and device units that Windows will use when you call graphics functions. (You can assign to the `lpSize` parameter the address of a `SIZE` structure, to which Windows will assign the previous extents, or you can assign it 0 if you do not need the previous extents.)

For example, the following function calls,

```
SetMapMode (HDc, MM_ANISOTROPIC);
SetWindowExtEx (HDc, 5, 7, 0);
SetViewportExtEx (HDc, 2, -3, 0);
```

establish a 5-to-2 ratio of horizontal logical to device units and a ratio of 7 vertical logical to –3 device units. If you made these calls and subsequently called a graphics function, Windows would transform each 5 horizontal logical units into 2 horizontal device units and would transform each 7 vertical logical units into –3 vertical device units (the minus sign, which is optional, makes *y* coordinates increase as you move up).

If you call `SetMapMode` to set the `MM_ISOTROPIC` mapping mode, you must also call `SetWindowExtEx` and `SetViewportExtEx` to set the ratios of logical to device units. However, after you call these functions, Windows will automatically *adjust* the ratios to make sure that a horizontal unit has the same physical size on the display surface as a vertical unit. As a result, under the `MM_ISOTROPIC` mapping mode, a figure will have the proportions that you specify when calling a drawing function, regardless of the device on which it is displayed. For example, if you call `Ellipse` and specify a bounding rectangle with equal sides,

```
Ellipse (HDc, 10, 10, 150, 150);
```

the resulting figure will always be circular. (Because of the way Windows performs this adjustment, you should call `SetWindowExtEx` *before* you call `SetViewportExtEx`.)

Note that the DrawIt Version 4 program presented in Chapter 7 uses the `MM_ANISOTROPIC` mapping mode to scale drawings when they are printed. The code that sets the mapping mode and extents is in the `CDocument::OnFilePrint` function in the file Document.cpp.

FYI

The following are related API functions: `GetWindowExtEx`, `GetViewportExtEx`, `ScaleWindowExtEx`, and `ScaleViewportExtEx`.

SETTING THE ORIGINS

The *window origin* and the *viewport origin* are additional drawing attributes that affect the way Windows transforms logical coordinates to physical coordinates. Modifying one of these origins changes the relative position of figures on the display surface (this type of transformation is known as *translation*).

You can modify either the window origin or the viewport origin (although you can modify both, it is unlikely that this would serve a useful purpose). The primary difference between these two origins is that the window origin is specified in logical coordinates whereas the viewport origin is specified in device coordinates.

When Windows transforms logical coordinates into device coordinates, *it maps the window origin onto the viewport origin.* The default window origin is at the logical coordinates (0,0), and the default viewport origin is at the device coordinates (0,0). This means, for example, that if you pass the logical coordinates (0,0) to `LineTo`,

```
LineTo (HDc, 0, 0);
```

Windows will draw the line to the point at the device coordinates (0,0)—that is, to the upper-left corner of the device surface.

You can change the window origin by calling the `SetWindowOrgEx` API function,

```
BOOL SetWindowOrgEx
  (HDC hdc,
   int X, int Y,
   LPPOINT lpPoint);
```

where X and Y are the logical coordinates of the new window origin. (You can pass `lpPoint` the address of a `POINT` structure, which will be assigned the former coordinates of the window origin, or you can pass 0 if you do not need the former origin.) If, for example, you set the window origin to the logical coordinates (10,10),

```
SetWindowOrgEx (HDc, 10, 10, 0);
```

the following call would draw a line to the device coordinates (0,0) (the upper-left corner of the device surface):

```
LineTo (HDc, 10, 10);
```

In other words, all figures would be shifted 10 logical units in the horizontal direction and 10 logical units in the vertical direction (the *direction* of each shift depends upon the mapping mode). This example assumes that the viewport origin has its default value.

Alternatively, you can change the viewport origin by calling the similar `SetViewportOrgEx` API function,

```
BOOL SetWindowOrgEx
    (HDC hdc,
     int X, int Y,
     LPPOINT lpPoint);
```

where X and Y are the device coordinates of the new viewport origin. If, for example, you set the viewport origin to the device coordinates (10, 10),

```
SetViewportOrgEx (HDc, 10, 10, 0);
```

the following call would draw a line to the device coordinates (10, 10) (10 pixels down from and to the right of the upper-left corner of the device surface):

```
LineTo (HDc, 0, 0);
```

In other words, all figures would be shifted 10 pixels right and 10 pixels down on the display surface (this example assumes that the window origin has its default value).

The following are some reasons that you might want to adjust the window or viewport origin in your program:

- You could adjust an origin to *scroll* the contents of the window in response to scroll bar actions or keyboard commands. You would need to erase the window contents, change the origin, and then redraw the contents (passing the same coordinates that were used before scrolling).

- You could adjust an origin before printing each page of a multiple-page document. The drawing routine would not change the coordinates that it passes to drawing functions as it prints various pages; however, changing the origin would shift the part of the document that gets printed. (Printing graphics is discussed in the next chapter.)

- You could adjust an origin so that the logical coordinates (0, 0) would fall at the center of the client area of the window—or at some other convenient location—rather than at the upper-left corner of the client area.

FYI

The following are related API functions: `GetWindowOrgEx`, `GetViewportOrgEx`, `OffsetWindowOrgEx`, and `OffsetViewportOrgEx`.

GENERATING TRANSFORMATIONS

Suppose that you have drawn—or have stored the coordinates for—a graphic figure that has a given size, orientation, position, and shape. Your program might subsequently need to transform the figure, that is, change its size, orientation, position, or shape. For example, a typical drawing program would allow the user to move, scale, and perhaps perform other transformations on a figure that has been drawn.

There are five general ways that you can transform a graphics figure: You can *scale*, *reflect*, *translate*, *rotate*, or *shear* it. These transformations are shown in Figure 6.4.

You can have Windows automatically perform several of these transformations by adjusting the mapping mode or origins. To draw the transformed version of a figure, you would simply change the mapping mode or origins and then call the appropriate drawing function, passing the same coordinates that you used to draw the untransformed version of the figure. Windows would perform all necessary calculations internally.

Specifically, you could *scale* a figure by switching to a mapping mode that uses different logical units. You could *reflect* a figure horizontally or vertically by switching to a mapping mode in which the direction of increasing horizontal or vertical coordinates was changed. Finally, you could *translate* a figure by changing the window or viewport origin.

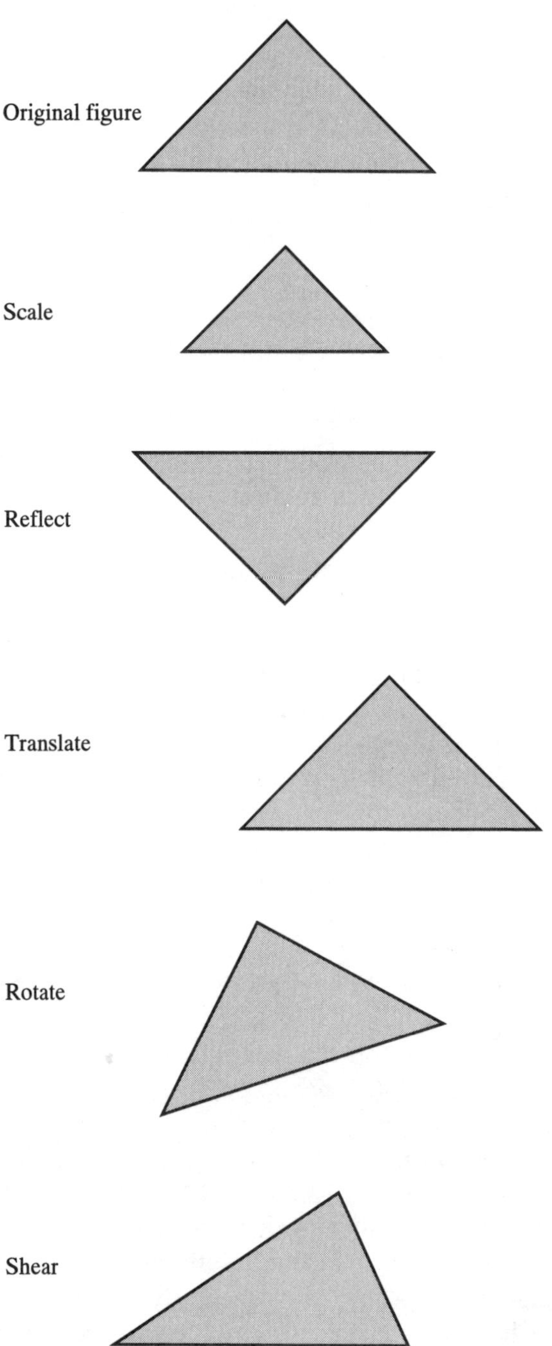

Figure 6.4:   The five general types of graphics transformation

Alternatively, a program can generate virtually any kind of graphics transformation on a figure by explicitly changing the figure's coordinate was that it stores and passes to drawing functions.

For example, the DrawIt Version 2 program, presented in Chapter 4, *translates* a graphic figure whenever the user selects the figure and drags it with the mouse. To do this, the program simply adjusts the coordinate values that are stored in the figure's C++ object by the amount that the user has dragged the figure.

As another example, the DrawIt Version 3 program, presented at the end of this chapter, *scales* a figure when the user selects the figure and then drags the scaling box (the scaling box is the small square displayed in the lower-right corner of the selection rectangle drawn around the figure). See the section "Scaling in DrawIt Version 3," later in this chapter.

Finally, techniques for *rotating* figures are discussed in the next section.

FYI
Under Windows NT, and perhaps future versions of the Windows operating system, you can have the API functions automatically scale, reflect, translate, rotate, or shear graphics by calling the `SetGraphicsMode` and `SetWorldTransform` API functions. These transformations are performed *prior* to the page-space to device-space transformations that are discussed in this chapter. The transformation performed via `SetGraphicsMode` and `SetWorldTransform` is known as the *world-space to page-space transformation.*

Rotating Figures

You can *rotate* a single point—move it in an orbital path—by a specified angle about a specified center by calling the following function:

```
void Rotate (int *X, int *Y, int XCenter, int YCenter,
   double Theta)
   {
   double XNew, YNew;

   // calculate rotated coordinates as floating-point values:
   XNew = ((double)*X - (double)XCenter) * cos (Theta) -
         ((double)YCenter - (double)*Y) * sin (Theta);
   YNew = ((double)*X - (double)XCenter) * sin (Theta) +
         ((double)YCenter - (double)*Y) * cos (Theta);

   // convert floating point values to integers, ROUNDING to
```

```
   // nearest integer:
   *X = (int)(XNew + (double)XCenter + 0.5);
   *Y = (int)((double)YCenter - YNew + 0.5);
   }
```

X and Y are the *addresses* of the variables containing the original coordinates of the point, XCenter and YCenter are the coordinates of the desired center of rotation, and Theta is the angle by which the point is to be rotated, in radians. Rotate calculates the rotated coordinates and assigns them to the variables pointed to by X and Y.

Rotate first calculates the rotated coordinates as floating-point values. The two equations used to calculate the rotated coordinates are derived from a sketch, using standard trigonometric identities. Rotate then rounds the floating-point values to the nearest integers.

You can use Rotate to rotate the various figures that have been discussed in the book. It is easy to rotate a figure that is *not* drawn by specifying a bounding rectangle (a straight line, Bézier curve, polyline, or polygon). Simply rotate each of the pairs of coordinates that are used to draw the figure, and then call the usual API drawing function.

Rotating a figure that is drawn by specifying a bounding rectangle (a rectangle, rounded rectangle, ellipse, arc, chord, or pie) is much harder. Rotating the coordinates of the upper-left and lower-right corners of the bounding rectangle simply creates another bounding rectangle in which the sides are still vertical and horizontal. To rotate one of these figures, you can use the following general method:

1. Store the coordinates of a series of points along the *unrotated* curve or figure in an array of POINT structures. For a rectangle, you need to store only the four pairs of coordinates for the corners. For an ellipse or a figure based upon an ellipse, you need to calculate a series of points along the figure or curve. The points must be sufficiently close to generate a smooth curve (the tighter the curve, the closer the points must be). For complete instructions on using the equation of an ellipse to calculate a series of points along the ellipse, see Chapter 8 in my book *Windows Animation Programming With C++*, published by AP PROFESSIONAL (this chapter also discusses generating three-dimensional rotation).

2. Pass each point in the POINT array to the Rotate function to adjust the coordinates of the point so that it is rotated by the required angle around a specified center.

3. Draw the figure using the "connect-the-dots" method. That is, for a closed figure, pass the POINT array to the Polygon API function,

first selecting a non-null brush if you want to fill the figure (see Chapter 4). For an arc or other open figure, you can pass the POINT array to the `Polyline` API function (see Chapter 3).

DRAWIT VERSION 3

DrawIt Version 3 adds the ability to *scale*—that is, to change the size and pro-portions of—any of the figures that you have drawn. To run the program, execute the file DrawIt.exe contained in the DrawIt3 subfolder of the folder in which you installed the companion disk files.

To scale a figure in DrawIt, do the following:

1. Choose Select on the Figure menu. Then select the figure either by clicking on it or by pressing Tab or Shift+Tab to move the selection to the figure.

2. Drag the *scaling box* (the small square displayed in the lower-right corner of the selection rectangle drawn around the figure) until the figure has the desired size and proportions. Notice that when the pointer is over the scaling box, it becomes a two-headed arrow. See Figure 6.5.

For instructions on using the other features of DrawIt, see the section "Using DrawIt Version 1" in Chapter 3 and the section "Using DrawIt Version 2" in Chapter 4.

Scaling in DrawIt Version 3

The program classes for the DrawIt Version 3 program are the same as those for DrawIt Version 2, as described in Chapter 4. The code for DrawIt Version

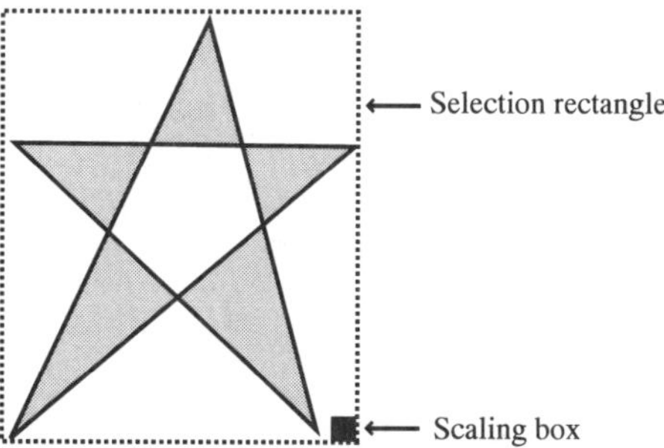

Figure 6.5:   A selected figure in DrawIt Version 3

3, however, adds support for the scaling of figures. DrawIt uses different scaling techniques according to the type of figure.

Scaling Rectangles and Ellipses

Scaling rectangles, rounded rectangles, and ellipses is easy. Because the scaling box is located in the lower-right corner of the selection rectangle, dragging it changes the position of the lower-right corner of the bounding rectangle of the figure, leaving the position of the upper-left corner of the bounding rectangle unchanged. When the user scales a rectangle or ellipse, DrawIt simply adjusts the coordinates of the lower-right corner of the bounding rectangle, which are stored in the figure's object, according to the distance and direction that the user has dragged the scaling box. It then erases the old figure and draws the new one.

The code for scaling rectangles, rounded rectangles, and ellipses is in the `CFigure::Scale` function in the Figure.cpp file.

Scaling Arcs, Chords, and Pies

DrawIt scales an arc, chord, or pie by adjusting the coordinates of the lower-right corner of the bounding rectangle in the same way that it scales a rectangle or ellipse. In addition, it must adjust the point on the starting line and the point on the ending line that are passed to the drawing function (see the section "Drawing Arcs" in Chapter 3 and Figure 3.3). If DrawIt simply moved these points by the x and y distances that the user dragged the scaling box, the figure would acquire a different shape (the arc, chord, or pie would include a relatively larger or smaller portion of the ellipse). To preserve the original shape of the figure, DrawIt uses trigonometric C++ library functions to calculate the positions of new starting and ending points. These points are calculated so that the *angles* (with respect to the horizontal) of the starting and ending lines are the same as in the original unscaled figure.

The code for scaling arcs, chords, and pies is in the `CArc::Scale` function in the Figure.cpp file.

Scaling Straight Lines

DrawIt scales a straight line by adjusting the x coordinate of the rightmost end and the y coordinate of the lower end according to the amount and direction that the user has dragged the scaling box.

If, however, the line is *vertical*, DrawIt does *not* adjust the x coordinate of an end, even if the user dragged the scaling box to the right, for the following reason: A figure is scaled by changing its horizontal and vertical dimensions. Although a vertical line has a line thickness, it does not have a horizontal dimension to scale! In practical terms, the program would not know which end to move horizontally, and if it did move one end, the line would be rotated rather than scaled.

For analogous reasons, DrawIt does not adjust the y coordinates of a horizontal line, even if the user drags the scaling box down.

The code for scaling lines is in the `CFigure::Scale` function in the Figure.cpp file.

Scaling Bézier Curves, Polylines, and Polygons   All of the figures discussed so far are defined by two points (plus the starting and ending points for arcs, chords, and pies). Bézier curves, polylines, and polygons, however, are defined by more than two points. Scaling one of these figures is therefore more complex.

When a Bézier curve, polyline, or polygon is scaled horizontally, DrawIt must adjust the x coordinate of all of the points except the leftmost one, and it must adjust the points in a way that preserves the original proportions of the figure. To do this, DrawIt uses the following general technique:

1. It leaves the leftmost point at its current position.
2. It moves the rightmost point by the amount that the user has dragged the scaling box.
3. It calculates the ratio of the *new* width of the figure to the *old* width of the figure. This ratio represents the horizontal scaling factor.
4. It moves each of the intermediate points horizontally using the horizontal scaling factor. That is, for each point, the *old* distance from the left of the figure to the point is multiplied by the horizontal scaling factor to derive the *new* distance to the point.

When a Bézier curve, polyline, or polygon is scaled vertically, DrawIt uses an analogous technique to adjust the y coordinate of all points except the topmost one.

The code for scaling Bézier curves is in the `CBezier::Scale` function, and the code for scaling polylines and polygons is in the `CPolyLine::Scale` function. Both functions are in the Figure.cpp file.

The DrawIt Version 3 Source Code

This section presents the source code listings for the DrawIt Version 3 program. The DrawIt3 subfolder of your companion disk folder contains a complete copy of these files.

Listing 6.1:   DrawIt.cpp

```cpp
//////////////////////////////////////////////////////////////////////////
//                                                                      //
// DrawIt.cpp: Main program object declarations and WinMain             //
//             program entry function.                                  //
//                                                                      //
//////////////////////////////////////////////////////////////////////////

#define STRICT
#include <windows.h>

// header files for main program classes:
#include "app.h"
#include "figure.h"
#include "mainwnd.h"
#include "document.h"
#include "dialog.h"

// main program objects:
CApp       App;
CMainWnd   MainWnd;
CDocument  Document;
CAboutDlg  AboutDlg;
CAttrDlg   AttrDlg;
CBrushDlg  BrushDlg;
CPenDlg    PenDlg;

//////////////////////////////////////////////////////////////////////////
// program entry function:                                              //
//////////////////////////////////////////////////////////////////////////

int APIENTRY WinMain
   (HINSTANCE HInstCurrent,
    HINSTANCE HInstPrevious,
    LPSTR     CmdLine,
    int       CmdShow)
    {
   MSG Msg;

   // store program informaton in application object:
   App.Initialize (HInstCurrent, CmdLine);

   // register class for main program window:
   if (!MainWnd.RegisterClass ())
      return 0;

   // create and display main program window:
   if (!MainWnd.Create ())
      return 0;

   // main message loop:
   while (GetMessage (&Msg, NULL, NULL, NULL))
      {
```

```
      TranslateMessage (&Msg);
      DispatchMessage (&Msg);
      }

   // return "application-defined exit code":
   return Msg.wParam;
   }
```

Listing 6.2:　App.h

```
/////////////////////////////////////////////////////////////////////////
//                                                                     //
// App.h: Header file for application class.                           //
//                                                                     //
/////////////////////////////////////////////////////////////////////////

class CApp
{
public:
   HINSTANCE mHInstance; // handle of program instance
   LPSTR     mCmdLine;   // pointer to program command line

   void Initialize (HINSTANCE HInstCurrent, LPSTR CmdLine)
   // saves application values
      {
      mHInstance = HInstCurrent;
      mCmdLine = CmdLine;
      }
};
```

Listing 6.3:　MainWnd.h

```
/////////////////////////////////////////////////////////////////////////
//                                                                     //
// MainWnd.h: Header file for main window class.                       //
//                                                                     //
/////////////////////////////////////////////////////////////////////////

#define WINWIDTH   350 // dimensions of main program window
#define WINHEIGHT  400
#define SIZEHANDLE 10  // size of scaling handle

class CMainWnd
{
public:
   enum // current drawing mode
      {
      ModeNone,
      ModeDragging,
```

```cpp
      ModeMark1,
      ModeMark2,
      ModeMoving,
      ModeScaling
      }
   mMode;

   CFigure *mCurrentFig;   // pointer to current figure object
   HPEN mHPenDotted;       // handle to dotted pen
   HWND mHWnd;             // main window handle
   CFigure *mSelectedFig;  // currently selected figure (if any)
   BOOL mSelecting;        // Figure / Select menu command chosen

   CMainWnd (void);
   BOOL Create (void);
   BOOL RegisterClass (void);

   // message-handling functions:
   LRESULT OnDestroy (void);
   LRESULT OnFigure (WORD MenuCommandID);
   LRESULT OnHelpAbout (void);
   LRESULT OnInitMenuPopup (HMENU HMenu, UINT MenuPosition);
   LRESULT OnKeyDown (int VirtKeyCode);
   LRESULT OnKillFocus (void);
   LRESULT OnLButtonDown (WORD XCursor, WORD YCursor);
   LRESULT OnLButtonUp (WORD XCursor, WORD YCursor);
   LRESULT OnMouseMove (WORD XCursor, WORD YCursor);
   LRESULT OnOptionsAttributes (void);
   LRESULT OnOptionsBrush (void);
   LRESULT OnOptionsPen (void);
   LRESULT OnPaint (void);

protected:
   UINT mCurrentFigID; // ID of menu command for curr. figure
   RECT mRectPrev;     // previous rectangle in moving figure
   int mXOrig, mYOrig; // original point when moving figure
   int mXPrev, mYPrev; // previous point when moving figure
   void CancelDrag (void);
   void DrawSelection (void);
   void DrawSelectRect (HDC HDc, RECT *PRect);
};
```

Listing 6.4:   MainWnd.cpp

```cpp
///////////////////////////////////////////////////////////////////////////
//                                                                       //
// MainWnd.cpp: Implementation file for main window class.               //
//                                                                       //
///////////////////////////////////////////////////////////////////////////

#define STRICT
```

```c
#include <windows.h>
#include "resource.h"

#include "app.h"
#include "figure.h"
#include "mainwnd.h"
#include "document.h"
#include "dialog.h"

extern CApp       App;
extern CMainWnd   MainWnd;
extern CDocument  Document;
extern CAboutDlg  AboutDlg;
extern CAttrDlg   AttrDlg;
extern CBrushDlg  BrushDlg;
extern CPenDlg    PenDlg;

LRESULT CALLBACK MainWndProc (HWND HWnd, UINT Msg, WPARAM WParam,
    LPARAM LParam);

///////////////////////////////////////////////////////////////////////////
// CMainWnd constructor:                                                   //
///////////////////////////////////////////////////////////////////////////

CMainWnd::CMainWnd (void)
    {
    mCurrentFig = new CLine;
    mCurrentFigID = ID_FIGURE_LINE;
    mHPenDotted = CreatePen (PS_DOT, 1, RGB (0,0,0));
    mMode = ModeNone;
    mSelectedFig = 0;
    mSelecting = FALSE;
    }

///////////////////////////////////////////////////////////////////////////
// CMainWnd public member functions:                                       //
///////////////////////////////////////////////////////////////////////////

void CMainWnd::CancelDrag (void)
// stops a figure move operation; called only if mSelecting is
// TRUE
    {
    if (mMode != ModeMoving)
        return;

    // end drag operation:
    ReleaseCapture ();
    ClipCursor (NULL);

    // erase temporary bounding rectangle:
    InvalidateRect (mHWnd, &mRectPrev, TRUE);
    RECT Rect = mSelectedFig->GetBoundRect ();
    InvalidateRect (mHWnd, &Rect, TRUE);
```

```cpp
    mMode = ModeNone;
    return;
    };

BOOL CMainWnd::Create (void)
// creates and displays main program window; returns TRUE on
// success or FALSE on error
    {
     // create main program window and save handle:
    mHWnd = CreateWindow
        ("DemoClass",
         "DrawIt",
         WS_OVERLAPPED | WS_SYSMENU | WS_MINIMIZEBOX,
         CW_USEDEFAULT,
         CW_USEDEFAULT,
         WINWIDTH,
         WINHEIGHT,
         NULL,
         NULL,
         App.mHInstance,
         NULL);
    if (!mHWnd)
        return FALSE;

    // display window:
    ShowWindow
        (mHWnd,
         SW_SHOWDEFAULT);

    return TRUE;
    }

BOOL CMainWnd::RegisterClass (void)
// registers class for main program window; returns TRUE on
// success or FALSE on error
    {
    WNDCLASS WC;

    // specify class information:
    WC.style = CS_DBLCLKS;
    WC.lpfnWndProc = MainWndProc;
    WC.cbClsExtra = 0;
    WC.cbWndExtra = 0;
    WC.hInstance = App.mHInstance;
    WC.hIcon = LoadIcon (App.mHInstance,
        MAKEINTRESOURCE (IDI_ICON1));
    WC.hCursor = 0;
    WC.hbrBackground = (HBRUSH)GetStockObject (WHITE_BRUSH);
    WC.lpszMenuName = MAKEINTRESOURCE (IDR_MENU1);
    WC.lpszClassName = "DemoClass";

    // register class:
    return (BOOL)::RegisterClass (&WC);
    }
```

```cpp
void CMainWnd::DrawSelection (void)
// obtains device context and draws selection rectangle around
// bounding rectangle of currently selected figure; second call
// erases rectangle
   {
   if (!mSelectedFig)
      return;
   RECT Rect = mSelectedFig->GetBoundRect ();
   HDC HDc = GetDC (mHWnd);
   DrawSelectRect (HDc, &Rect);
   ReleaseDC (mHWnd, HDc);
   return;
   }

void CMainWnd::DrawSelectRect (HDC HDc, RECT *PRect)
// draws the selection rectangle and scaling handle
   {
   // draw selection rectangle:
   DrawFocusRect (HDc, PRect);
   // draw sizing handle:
   SetROP2 (HDc, R2_NOT);
   Rectangle
      (HDc,
       PRect->right - SIZEHANDLE,
       PRect->bottom - SIZEHANDLE,
       PRect->right,
       PRect->bottom);
   return;
   }

///////////////////////////////////////////////////////////////////////////
// window procedure for main window:                                      //
///////////////////////////////////////////////////////////////////////////

LRESULT CALLBACK MainWndProc
   (HWND   HWnd,
    UINT   Msg,
    WPARAM WParam,
    LPARAM LParam)
   {
   switch (Msg)
      {
      case WM_COMMAND: // user chose a menu command
         switch (LOWORD (WParam))
            {
            case ID_HELP_ABOUT: // user chose Help/About
               return MainWnd.OnHelpAbout ();

            case ID_FIGURE_SELECT: // user chose command on
            case ID_FIGURE_ARC:    // Figure menu
            case ID_FIGURE_BEZIER:
            case ID_FIGURE_CHORD:
            case ID_FIGURE_ELLIPSE:
            case ID_FIGURE_LINE:
```

```cpp
      case ID_FIGURE_PIE:
      case ID_FIGURE_POLYGON:
      case ID_FIGURE_POLYLINE:
      case ID_FIGURE_RECTANGLE:
      case ID_FIGURE_ROUNDRECT:
         return MainWnd.OnFigure (LOWORD (WParam));

      case ID_OPTIONS_ATTRIBUTES: // user chose
                                  // Options/Attributes
         return MainWnd.OnOptionsAttributes ();

      case ID_OPTIONS_BRUSH: // user chose Options/Brush
         return MainWnd.OnOptionsBrush ();

      case ID_OPTIONS_PEN: // user chose Options/Pen
         return MainWnd.OnOptionsPen ();

      default:
         // default processing for other commands:
         return DefWindowProc (HWnd, Msg, WParam, LParam);
      }

case WM_DESTROY: // DestroyWindow was called
   return MainWnd.OnDestroy ();

case WM_INITMENUPOPUP: // user opened a popup menu
   return MainWnd.OnInitMenuPopup ((HMENU)WParam,
      (UINT)LOWORD(LParam));

case WM_KEYDOWN: // user pressed a key
   return MainWnd.OnKeyDown ((int)WParam);

case WM_KILLFOCUS: // program window has lost focus
   return MainWnd.OnKillFocus ();

case WM_LBUTTONDBLCLK: // user double-clicked left mouse
                       // button
   return MainWnd.mCurrentFig->OnLButtonDblClk
      (LOWORD (LParam), HIWORD (LParam));

case WM_LBUTTONDOWN: // user pressed left button
   return MainWnd.OnLButtonDown
      (LOWORD (LParam), HIWORD (LParam));

case WM_LBUTTONUP:  // user released left button
   return MainWnd.OnLButtonUp
      (LOWORD (LParam), HIWORD (LParam));

case WM_MOUSEMOVE:  // user moved mouse pointer
   return MainWnd.OnMouseMove
      (LOWORD (LParam), HIWORD (LParam));

case WM_PAINT: // window needs painting or repainting
   return MainWnd.OnPaint ();
```

```
      default:
         // default processing for all other messages:
         return DefWindowProc (HWnd, Msg, WParam, LParam);
      }
   }

//////////////////////////////////////////////////////////////////////////////
// CMainWnd message handling member functions:                              //
//////////////////////////////////////////////////////////////////////////////

LRESULT CMainWnd::OnDestroy (void)
// processes WM_DESTROY messages
   {
   PostQuitMessage (0); // post a WM_QUIT message to
   return NULL;         // cause message loop to exit
   }

LRESULT CMainWnd::OnFigure (WORD MenuCommandID)
// processes WM_COMMAND messages from ALL commands on Figure menu
   {
   // exit if user chose same command previously chosen:
   if (mCurrentFigID == MenuCommandID)
      return NULL;

   // move check mark to chosen command:
   CheckMenuItem (GetMenu (mHWnd), mCurrentFigID, MF_UNCHECKED);
   mCurrentFigID = MenuCommandID;
   CheckMenuItem (GetMenu (mHWnd), mCurrentFigID, MF_CHECKED);

   // cancel any drawing or drag operation:
   if (mSelecting)
      CancelDrag ();
   else
      mCurrentFig->Cancel ();

   // cancel current selection, if any:
   DrawSelection ();
   mSelectedFig = 0;

   // if user chose Select command, set flag and exit:
   if (MenuCommandID == ID_FIGURE_SELECT)
      {
      mSelecting = TRUE;
      return NULL;
      }

   // a figure command was chosen; start by setting mSelecting
   // flag to FALSE:
   mSelecting = FALSE;

   // delete figure object:
   delete mCurrentFig;
```

```cpp
   // create figure object for new figure type:
   switch (MenuCommandID)
      {
      case ID_FIGURE_ARC:
         mCurrentFig = new CArc;
         break;

      case ID_FIGURE_BEZIER:
         mCurrentFig = new CBezier;
         break;

      case ID_FIGURE_CHORD:
         mCurrentFig = new CChord;
         break;

      case ID_FIGURE_ELLIPSE:
         mCurrentFig = new CEllipse;
         break;

      case ID_FIGURE_LINE:
         mCurrentFig = new CLine;
         break;

      case ID_FIGURE_PIE:
         mCurrentFig = new CPie;
         break;

      case ID_FIGURE_POLYGON:
         mCurrentFig = new CPolygon;
         break;

      case ID_FIGURE_POLYLINE:
         mCurrentFig = new CPolyline;
         break;

      case ID_FIGURE_RECTANGLE:
         mCurrentFig = new CRectangle;
         break;

      case ID_FIGURE_ROUNDRECT:
         mCurrentFig = new CRoundRect;
         break;
      }
   return NULL;
   }

LRESULT CMainWnd::OnHelpAbout (void)
// processes WM_COMMAND / ID_HELP_ABOUT messages
   {
   AboutDlg.Show (); // display About dialog box
   return NULL;
   }
```

```
LRESULT CMainWnd::OnInitMenuPopup (HMENU HMenu,
   UINT MenuPosition)
// processes WM_INITMENUPOPUP messages
   {
   if (MenuPosition != 1)
      return NULL;

   // modify Options menu commands based upon whether a figure
   // is selected and type of figure selected:
   if (mSelectedFig)
      {
      if (mSelectedFig->IsBrush ())
         ModifyMenu (HMenu, ID_OPTIONS_BRUSH, MF_STRING |
            MF_ENABLED, ID_OPTIONS_BRUSH, "Figure Brush...");
      else
         ModifyMenu (HMenu, ID_OPTIONS_BRUSH,
            MF_STRING | MF_GRAYED, ID_OPTIONS_BRUSH, "Brush...");
      ModifyMenu (HMenu, ID_OPTIONS_PEN, MF_STRING,
         ID_OPTIONS_PEN, "Figure Pen...");
      ModifyMenu (HMenu, ID_OPTIONS_ATTRIBUTES, MF_STRING,
         ID_OPTIONS_ATTRIBUTES, "Figure Attributes...");
      }
   else
      {
      ModifyMenu (HMenu, ID_OPTIONS_BRUSH, MF_STRING |
         MF_ENABLED, ID_OPTIONS_BRUSH, "Default Brush...");
      ModifyMenu (HMenu, ID_OPTIONS_PEN, MF_STRING,
         ID_OPTIONS_PEN, "Default Pen...");
      ModifyMenu (HMenu, ID_OPTIONS_ATTRIBUTES, MF_STRING,
         ID_OPTIONS_ATTRIBUTES, "Default Attributes...");
      }
   return NULL;
   }


LRESULT CMainWnd::OnKeyDown (int VirtKeyCode)
// processes WM_KEYDOWN messages
   {
   // user pressed Esc when not in selecting mode:
   if (VirtKeyCode == VK_ESCAPE && !mSelecting)
      {
      mCurrentFig->Cancel (); // cancel drawing operation
      }

   // user pressed Tab in selecting mode but is NOT dragging a
   // figure:
   else if (VirtKeyCode == VK_TAB && mSelecting &&
           mMode == ModeNone)
      {
      // if figure is currently selected get next/previous one:
      if (mSelectedFig)
         {
         DrawSelection (); // erase old selection rectangle
```

```cpp
            // if Shift is pressed, select previous figure:
            if (GetKeyState (VK_SHIFT) < 0)
               mSelectedFig = Document.GetPreviousFig(mSelectedFig);

            // if Shift not pressed, select next figure:
            else
                mSelectedFig = Document.GetNextFig (mSelectedFig);
            }

        // if no figure selected, select the first one, if any:
        else if (Document.mPFirstFig)
            mSelectedFig = Document.mPFirstFig->PFigure;

        // draw the selection rectangle:
        DrawSelection ();
        }

    // user pressed Delete key, a figure is selected, and user is
    // NOT dragging a figure:
    else if (VirtKeyCode == VK_DELETE && mSelectedFig &&
            mMode == ModeNone)
        {
        // erase the figure from window:
        RECT Rect = mSelectedFig->GetBoundRect ();
        InvalidateRect (mHWnd, &Rect, TRUE);

        // remove figure object from linked list and delete it:
        Document.DeleteFigure (mSelectedFig);
        delete mSelectedFig;
        mSelectedFig = 0;
        }
    return NULL;
    }


LRESULT CMainWnd::OnKillFocus (void)
// processes WM_KILLFOCUS messages
    {
    // cancel any drawing or drag operation:
    if (mSelecting)
        CancelDrag ();
    else
        mCurrentFig->Cancel ();
    return NULL;
    }


LRESULT CMainWnd::OnLButtonDown (WORD XCursor, WORD YCursor)
// processes WM_LBUTTONDOWN messages
    {
    // if Figure/Select command not chosen, have current figure
    // object handle the message:
    if (!mSelecting)
        return mCurrentFig->OnLButtonDown (XCursor, YCursor);
```

```cpp
POINT Point = {XCursor, YCursor};
RECT RectBound;

// if a selected figure is under the cursor, begin a move
// or scale operation:
if (mSelectedFig)
    {
    RectBound = mSelectedFig->GetBoundRect ();
    if (PtInRect (&RectBound, Point))
        {
        // save current coordinates:
        mRectPrev = RectBound;
        mXOrig = XCursor; mYOrig = YCursor;
        mXPrev = XCursor; mYPrev = YCursor;

        // start drag:
        SetCapture (mHWnd);
        RECT RectClip;
        GetClientRect (mHWnd, &RectClip);

        // if cursor in scaling handle, start scaling;
        // otherwise, start moving:
        RECT RectHandle =
            {RectBound.right - SIZEHANDLE,
            RectBound.bottom - SIZEHANDLE,
            RectBound.right,
            RectBound.bottom};
        if (PtInRect (&RectHandle, Point))
            {
            // adjust clipping rectangle to keep user from
            // dragging scaling handle to left or above figure:
            RectClip.left = RectBound.left + XCursor -
                RectHandle.left;
            RectClip.top = RectBound.top + YCursor -
                RectHandle.top;
            mMode = ModeScaling;
            }
        else
            mMode = ModeMoving;

        // clip cursor:
        ClientToScreen (mHWnd, (LPPOINT)&RectClip);
        ClientToScreen (mHWnd, (LPPOINT)&RectClip.right);
        ClipCursor (&RectClip);

        return NULL;
        }
    // cancel existing selection:
    DrawSelection ();
    mSelectedFig = 0;
    }

// no selected figure is under cursor; therefore, select the
// figure under cursor, if any:
```

```cpp
    // perform hit test on all figures stored in document:
    FigCell *PCell = Document.mPFirstFig;
    while (PCell)
        {
        RectBound = PCell->PFigure->GetBoundRect ();
        // if figure found under cursor, select it:
        if (PtInRect (&RectBound, Point))
            {
            mSelectedFig = PCell->PFigure;
            DrawSelection ();
            return NULL;
            }
        PCell = PCell->PNextFig;
        }
    return NULL;
    }

LRESULT CMainWnd::OnLButtonUp (WORD XCursor, WORD YCursor)
// processes WM_LBUTTONUP messages
    {
    // if Figure/Select command not chosen, have current figure
    // object handle the message:
    if (!mSelecting)
        return mCurrentFig->OnLButtonUp (XCursor, YCursor);

    // if user was moving or scaling a figure, end operation:
    if (mMode == ModeMoving || mMode == ModeScaling)
        {
        // end drag:
        ReleaseCapture ();
        ClipCursor (NULL);

        // erase previous temporary rectangle:
        HDC HDc = GetDC (mHWnd);
        DrawSelectRect (HDc, &mRectPrev);
        ReleaseDC (mHWnd, HDc);

        // move or scale the figure and force redrawing of affected
        // areas:
        RECT Rect = mSelectedFig->GetBoundRect ();
        InvalidateRect (mHWnd, &Rect, TRUE);
        if (mMode == ModeMoving)
            {
            mSelectedFig->Move (XCursor - mXOrig, YCursor - mYOrig);
            // place moved figure on top (i.e., at end of list):
            Document.AddFigure (mSelectedFig, FALSE);
            Document.DeleteFigure (mSelectedFig);
            }
        else
            mSelectedFig->Scale(XCursor - mXOrig, YCursor - mYOrig);
        Rect = mSelectedFig->GetBoundRect ();
        InvalidateRect (mHWnd, &Rect, TRUE);
```

```cpp
      mMode = ModeNone;
      }
   return NULL;
   }


LRESULT CMainWnd::OnMouseMove (WORD XCursor, WORD YCursor)
// processes WM_MOUSEMOVE messages
   {
   // if Figure/Select command not chosen, have current figure
   // object handle the message:
   if (!mSelecting)
      {
      SetCursor (LoadCursor (NULL, IDC_CROSS));
      return mCurrentFig->OnMouseMove (XCursor, YCursor);
      }

   // if user is moving or scaling a figure, update selection
   // rectangle and set cursor:
   if (mMode == ModeMoving || mMode == ModeScaling)
      {
      HDC HDc = GetDC (mHWnd);
      DrawSelectRect (HDc, &mRectPrev);
      mRectPrev.right += XCursor - mXPrev;
      mRectPrev.bottom += YCursor - mYPrev;

      if (mMode == ModeMoving)
         {
         mRectPrev.left += XCursor - mXPrev;
         mRectPrev.top += YCursor - mYPrev;
         SetCursor (LoadCursor (NULL, IDC_SIZE));
         }
      else
         SetCursor (LoadCursor (NULL, IDC_SIZENWSE));

      DrawSelectRect (HDc, &mRectPrev);
      mXPrev = XCursor;
      mYPrev = YCursor;
      ReleaseDC (mHWnd, HDc);

      return NULL;
      }

   // user is not moving or scaling a figure, just set cursor:

   // if a figure is selected, must test for cursor within
   // bounding rectangle or scaling box:
   if (mSelectedFig)
      {
      // test for cursor in bounding rectangle:
      RECT Rect = mSelectedFig->GetBoundRect ();
      POINT Point = {XCursor, YCursor};
      if (PtInRect (&Rect, Point))
         {
```

```cpp
      // test for cursor in scaling handle:
      Rect.left = Rect.right - SIZEHANDLE;
      Rect.top = Rect.bottom - SIZEHANDLE;
      if (PtInRect (&Rect, Point))
          SetCursor (LoadCursor (NULL, IDC_SIZENWSE));
      else
          SetCursor (LoadCursor (NULL, IDC_SIZE));
      return NULL;
      }
   }

   // in selecting mode, but cursor not within selected figure:
   SetCursor (LoadCursor (NULL, IDC_ARROW));
   return NULL;
   }

LRESULT CMainWnd::OnOptionsAttributes (void)
// processes WM_COMMAND / ID_OPTIONS_ATTRIBUTES messages
   {
   AttrDlg.Show (); // display Attributes dialog box
   return NULL;
   }

LRESULT CMainWnd::OnOptionsBrush (void)
// processes WM_COMMAND / ID_OPTIONS_BRUSH messages
   {
   BrushDlg.Show (); // display Brush dialog box
   return NULL;
   }

LRESULT CMainWnd::OnOptionsPen (void)
// processes WM_COMMAND / ID_OPTIONS_PEN messages
   {
   PenDlg.Show (); // display Pen dialog box
   return NULL;
   }

LRESULT CMainWnd::OnPaint (void)
// processes WM_PAINT messages
   {
   HDC HDCPaint;
   PAINTSTRUCT PaintStruct;
   RECT RectBound;

   // cancel any drawing or drag operation:
   if (mSelecting)
      CancelDrag ();
   else
      mCurrentFig->Cancel ();

   // initiate painting and obtain a device context:
   HDCPaint = BeginPaint (mHWnd, &PaintStruct);
```

```
   // save state of device context:
   SaveDC (HDCPaint);

   // draw all figures stored in document:
   FigCell *PCell = Document.mPFirstFig;
   while (PCell)
      {
      RectBound = PCell->PFigure->GetBoundRect ();
      if (RectVisible (HDCPaint, &RectBound))
         PCell->PFigure->Draw (HDCPaint);
      PCell = PCell->PNextFig;
      }

   // restore the saved device context:
   RestoreDC (HDCPaint, -1);

   if (mSelectedFig)
      {
      RectBound = mSelectedFig->GetBoundRect ();
      DrawSelectRect (HDCPaint, &RectBound);
      }

   // terminate painting and release device context:
   EndPaint (mHWnd, &PaintStruct);
   return NULL;
   }
```

Listing 6.5:   Figure.h

```
/////////////////////////////////////////////////////////////////////////////
//                                                                         //
// Figure.h: Header file for figure classes.                              //
//                                                                         //
/////////////////////////////////////////////////////////////////////////////

class CFigure // abstract base class for all figure classes
{
public:
   // description of pen used to draw figure:
   COLORREF mPenColor;
   DWORD mPenStyle;
   DWORD mPenType;
   DWORD mPenWidth;

   // drawing attributes:
   COLORREF mBkColor;
   int mBkMode;
   int mBrushXOrg;
   int mBrushYOrg;
   int mFillMode;
   int mMixMode;
```

```cpp
   CFigure (void);
   void Cancel (void);
   virtual CFigure *CreateObject (void) = 0;
   virtual void DefineBrush (COLORREF BrushColor,
      LONG BrushHatchPattern, DWORD BrushStyle)
      {
      return;
      }
   virtual void Draw (HDC HDc);
   virtual RECT GetBoundRect (void);
   virtual void GetBrushDescription (COLORREF *PBrushColor,
      LONG *PBrushHatchPattern, DWORD *PBrushStyle)
      {
      return;
      }
   virtual BOOL IsBrush (void)
      {
      return FALSE;
      }
   virtual void Move (int DeltaX, int DeltaY);
   virtual void PureDraw (HDC HDc) = 0;
   virtual void Scale (int DeltaX, int DeltaY);

   // message-handling functions:
   virtual LRESULT OnLButtonDblClk (WORD XCursor, WORD YCursor)
      {
      return NULL;
      }
   virtual LRESULT OnLButtonDown (WORD XCursor, WORD YCursor) =0;
   virtual LRESULT OnLButtonUp (WORD XCursor, WORD YCursor) = 0;
   virtual LRESULT OnMouseMove (WORD XCursor, WORD YCursor) = 0;

protected:
   int mX1, mY1, mX2, mY2; // basic figure dimensions

   virtual HBRUSH GetBrush (void)
      {
      return 0;
      }
   HDC GetTempDC (void);
   int Max4 (int A, int B, int C, int D)
      {
      return max (max (max (A, B), C), D);
      }
   int Min4 (int A, int B, int C, int D)
      {
      return min (min (min (A, B), C), D);
      }
   void StartDrag (void);
};

class CArc : public CFigure
{
```

```cpp
public:
   virtual CFigure *CreateObject (void)
      {
      return new CArc;
      }
   virtual RECT GetBoundRect (void);
   virtual void Move (int DeltaX, int DeltaY);
   virtual void PureDraw (HDC HDc);
   virtual void Scale (int DeltaX, int DeltaY);

   // message-handling functions:
   virtual LRESULT OnLButtonDown (WORD XCursor, WORD YCursor);
   virtual LRESULT OnLButtonUp (WORD XCursor, WORD YCursor);
   virtual LRESULT OnMouseMove (WORD XCursor, WORD YCursor);

protected:
   int mX3, mY3, mX4, mY4; // additional arc dimensions
};

class CChord : public CArc
{
public:
   virtual CFigure *CreateObject (void)
      {
      return new CChord;
      }
   virtual void DefineBrush (COLORREF BrushColor,
      LONG BrushHatchPattern, DWORD BrushStyle)
      {
      mBrushColor = BrushColor;
      mBrushHatchPattern = BrushHatchPattern;
      mBrushStyle = BrushStyle;
      }
   virtual void GetBrushDescription (COLORREF *PBrushColor,
      LONG *PBrushHatchPattern, DWORD *PBrushStyle)
      {
      *PBrushColor = mBrushColor;
      *PBrushHatchPattern = mBrushHatchPattern;
      *PBrushStyle = mBrushStyle;
      return;
      }
   virtual BOOL IsBrush (void)
      {
      return TRUE;
      }
   virtual void PureDraw (HDC HDc);

protected:
   // description of brush used to draw figure:
   COLORREF mBrushColor;
   LONG mBrushHatchPattern;
   DWORD mBrushStyle;
```

```cpp
      virtual HBRUSH GetBrush (void);
};

class CPie : public CChord
{
public:
    virtual CFigure *CreateObject (void)
        {
        return new CPie;
        }
    virtual void PureDraw (HDC HDc);
};

class CBezier : public CFigure
{
public:
    virtual CFigure *CreateObject (void)
        {
        return new CBezier;
        }
    virtual RECT GetBoundRect (void);
    virtual void Move (int DeltaX, int DeltaY);
    virtual void PureDraw (HDC HDc);
    virtual void Scale (int DeltaX, int DeltaY);

    // message-handling functions:
    virtual LRESULT OnLButtonDown (WORD XCursor, WORD YCursor);
    virtual LRESULT OnLButtonUp (WORD XCursor, WORD YCursor);
    virtual LRESULT OnMouseMove (WORD XCursor, WORD YCursor);

protected:
    int mX3, mY3, mX4, mY4; // additional bezier curve dimensions
};

class CLine : public CFigure
{
public:
    virtual CFigure *CreateObject (void)
        {
        return new CLine;
        }
    virtual void PureDraw (HDC HDc);

    // message-handling functions:
    virtual LRESULT OnLButtonDown (WORD XCursor, WORD YCursor);
    virtual LRESULT OnLButtonUp (WORD XCursor, WORD YCursor);
    virtual LRESULT OnMouseMove (WORD XCursor, WORD YCursor);
};

class CRectangle : public CLine
{
public:
    virtual CFigure *CreateObject (void)
        {
```

```cpp
   return new CRectangle;
   }
virtual void DefineBrush (COLORREF BrushColor,
   LONG BrushHatchPattern, DWORD BrushStyle)
   {
   mBrushColor = BrushColor;
   mBrushHatchPattern = BrushHatchPattern;
   mBrushStyle = BrushStyle;
   }
virtual void GetBrushDescription (COLORREF *PBrushColor,
   LONG *PBrushHatchPattern, DWORD *PBrushStyle)
   {
   *PBrushColor = mBrushColor;
   *PBrushHatchPattern = mBrushHatchPattern;
   *PBrushStyle = mBrushStyle;
   return;
   }
virtual BOOL IsBrush (void)
   {
   return TRUE;
   }
virtual void PureDraw (HDC HDc);

protected:
   // description of brush used to draw figure:
   COLORREF mBrushColor;
   LONG mBrushHatchPattern;
   DWORD mBrushStyle;

   virtual HBRUSH GetBrush (void);
};

class CRoundRect : public CRectangle
{
public:
   virtual CFigure *CreateObject (void)
      {
      return new CRoundRect;
      }
   virtual void PureDraw (HDC HDc);
};

class CEllipse : public CRectangle
{
public:
   virtual CFigure *CreateObject (void)
      {
      return new CEllipse;
      }
   virtual void PureDraw (HDC HDc);
};

#define MAXPOINTS 25 // maximum number of vertices in polyline
```

```cpp
class CPolyline : public CFigure
{
public:
   virtual CFigure *CreateObject (void)
      {
      return new CPolyline;
      }
   virtual RECT GetBoundRect (void);
   virtual void Move (int DeltaX, int DeltaY);
   virtual void PureDraw (HDC HDc);
   virtual void Scale (int DeltaX, int DeltaY);

   // message-handling functions:
   virtual LRESULT OnLButtonDblClk (WORD XCursor, WORD YCursor);
   virtual LRESULT OnLButtonDown (WORD XCursor, WORD YCursor);
   virtual LRESULT OnLButtonUp (WORD XCursor, WORD YCursor);
   virtual LRESULT OnMouseMove (WORD XCursor, WORD YCursor);

protected:
   int mNumPoints;               // number of points stored
   POINT mPoints [MAXPOINTS]; // stores coordinates of vertices
};

class CPolygon : public CPolyline
{
public:
   virtual CFigure *CreateObject (void)
      {
      return new CPolygon;
      }
   virtual void DefineBrush (COLORREF BrushColor,
      LONG BrushHatchPattern, DWORD BrushStyle)
      {
      mBrushColor = BrushColor;
      mBrushHatchPattern = BrushHatchPattern;
      mBrushStyle = BrushStyle;
      }
   virtual void GetBrushDescription (COLORREF *PBrushColor,
      LONG *PBrushHatchPattern, DWORD *PBrushStyle)
      {
      *PBrushColor = mBrushColor;
      *PBrushHatchPattern = mBrushHatchPattern;
      *PBrushStyle = mBrushStyle;
      return;
      }
   virtual BOOL IsBrush (void)
      {
      return TRUE;
      }
   virtual void PureDraw (HDC HDc);

protected:
   // description of brush used to draw figure:
```

```cpp
   COLORREF mBrushColor;
   LONG mBrushHatchPattern;
   DWORD mBrushStyle;
   virtual HBRUSH GetBrush (void);
};
```

Listing 6.6:   Figure.cpp

```cpp
//////////////////////////////////////////////////////////////////////////
//                                                                        //
// Figure.cpp: Implementaton file for figure classes.                     //
//                                                                        //
//////////////////////////////////////////////////////////////////////////

#define STRICT
#include <windows.h>
#include <limits.h>
#include <math.h>

#include "resource.h"

#include "figure.h"
#include "mainwnd.h"
#include "document.h"

extern CMainWnd  MainWnd;
extern CDocument Document;

#define PI 3.14159265

//////////////////////////////////////////////////////////////////////////
// CFigure:                                                               //
//////////////////////////////////////////////////////////////////////////

CFigure::CFigure (void)
   {
   mPenWidth = 1;
   }

   void CFigure::Cancel (void)
   // cancels a drawing operation
   {
   if (MainWnd.mMode == MainWnd.ModeNone)
      return;

   // erase temporary line(s) and redraw affected area of window:
   RECT Rect = GetBoundRect ();
   InvalidateRect (MainWnd.mHWnd, &Rect, TRUE);

   // end dragging operation:
   if (MainWnd.mMode == MainWnd.ModeDragging)
```

```cpp
      {
      ReleaseCapture ();
      ClipCursor (NULL);
      }
   MainWnd.mMode = MainWnd.ModeNone;
   return;
   }

void CFigure::Draw (HDC HDc)
// prepares the device context AND draws the current object
   {
   // set drawing attributes:
   SetBkColor (HDc, mBkColor);
   SetBkMode (HDc, mBkMode);
   SetBrushOrgEx (HDc, mBrushXOrg, mBrushYOrg, NULL);
   SetPolyFillMode (HDc, mFillMode);
   SetROP2 (HDc, mMixMode);

   // create and select object's pen:
   LOGBRUSH LogBrush = {BS_SOLID, mPenColor, 0};
   HPEN HPen = ExtCreatePen
      (mPenType | mPenStyle,
      mPenWidth,
      &LogBrush,
      0,
      0);
   HPEN HPenOld = (HPEN)SelectObject (HDc, HPen);

   // get and select object's brush, if any:
   HBRUSH HBrush = GetBrush ();
   HBRUSH HBrushOld;
   if (HBrush)
      HBrushOld = (HBRUSH)SelectObject (HDc, HBrush);

   // call the appropriate drawing function for the object:
   PureDraw (HDc);

   // deselect and destroy brush, if any:
   if (HBrush)
      {
      SelectObject (HDc, HBrushOld);
      DeleteObject (HBrush);
      }

   // deselect and destroy pen:
   SelectObject (HDc, HPenOld);
   DeleteObject (HPen);
   return;
   }

RECT CFigure::GetBoundRect (void)
// returns rectangle bounding figure
   {
```

```cpp
   RECT Rect =
      {min (mX1, mX2),
       min (mY1, mY2),
       max (mX1, mX2),
       max (mY1, mY2)};

   // expand rectangle to accommodate wide lines and margin:
   int LineAdd = (mPenWidth-1) / 2 + (mPenWidth-1) % 2 + 3;
   InflateRect (&Rect, LineAdd, LineAdd);

   // make rectangle at least as large as scaling handle:
   Rect.right = max (Rect.right, Rect.left + SIZEHANDLE);
   Rect.bottom = max (Rect.bottom, Rect.top + SIZEHANDLE);

   return Rect;
   }

HDC CFigure::GetTempDC (void)
// returns a device-context handle for drawing temporary lines
   {
   HDC HDCClient = GetDC (MainWnd.mHWnd);
   SetROP2 (HDCClient, R2_NOT);
   HPEN HPenOld = (HPEN)SelectObject
      (HDCClient, MainWnd.mHPenDotted);
   SetBkMode (HDCClient, TRANSPARENT);
   SelectObject (HDCClient, GetStockObject (NULL_BRUSH));
   return HDCClient;
   }

   void CFigure::Move (int DeltaX, int DeltaY)
   // moves the figure by the specified offsets
   {
   mX1 += DeltaX;
   mY1 += DeltaY;
   mX2 += DeltaX;
   mY2 += DeltaY;
   return;
   }

void CFigure::Scale (int DeltaX, int DeltaY)
// scales the figure by the specified offsets
   {
   if (mX1 < mX2)
      mX2 += DeltaX;
   else if (mX2 < mX1)
      mX1 += DeltaX;

   if (mY1 < mY2)
      mY2 += DeltaY;
   else if (mY2 < mY1)
      mY1 += DeltaY;

   return;
   }
```

```cpp
void CFigure::StartDrag (void)
// initializes a drag operation for drawing a figure
   {
   // capture mouse messages:
   SetCapture (MainWnd.mHWnd);

   // confine mouse cursor to client area of window:
   RECT Rect;
   GetClientRect (MainWnd.mHWnd, &Rect);
   ClientToScreen (MainWnd.mHWnd, (LPPOINT)&Rect);
   ClientToScreen (MainWnd.mHWnd, (LPPOINT)&Rect.right);
   ClipCursor (&Rect);
   return;
   }

////////////////////////////////////////////////////////////////////////////
// CArc:                                                                    //
////////////////////////////////////////////////////////////////////////////

RECT CArc::GetBoundRect (void)
// returns rectangle bounding arc
   {
   // store dimensions of rectangle bounding the full ellipse:
   RECT Rect =
       {min (mX1, mX2),
        min (mY1, mY2),
        max (mX1, mX2),
        max (mY1, mY2)};

   // if user has completed drawing the figure, calculate the
   // rectangle that bounds only those quadrants of the ellipse
   // that contain the figure:
   if (MainWnd.mSelecting || MainWnd.mMode == MainWnd.ModeNone)
       {
       BOOL ContainsEnd, ContainsStart;
       BOOL Started = FALSE;

       // calculate midpoint of ellipse:
       int XMid = (Rect.left + Rect.right) / 2;
       int YMid = (Rect.top + Rect.bottom) / 2;

       // store information on the four ellipse quadrants:
       struct
           {
           double StartAngle; // starting angle of quadrant
           double EndAngle;   // ending angle of quadrant
           RECT Rect;         // dimensions of quadrant
           }
       Quadrants [4] =
           {{-PI,     -PI/2.0, {Rect.left,YMid,XMid,Rect.bottom}},
            {-PI/2.0, 0.0,     {XMid,YMid,Rect.right,Rect.bottom}},
            {0.0,     PI/2.0,  {XMid,Rect.top,Rect.right,YMid}},
            {PI/2.0,  PI,      {Rect.left,Rect.top,XMid,YMid}}};
```

```cpp
   // calculate angles of starting and ending lines of arc:
   double ThetaStart = atan2 (YMid — mY3, mX3 — XMid);
   double ThetaEnd   = atan2 (YMid — mY4, mX4 — XMid);

   // initialize bounding rectangle to null:
   Rect.left = Rect.top = Rect.right = Rect.bottom = 0;

   // find the ellipse quadrant that contains starting line:
   for (int Q = 0; Q <= 3; ++Q)
      {
      ContainsStart = ThetaStart>=Quadrants [Q].StartAngle &&
         ThetaStart < Quadrants [Q].EndAngle;
      if (ContainsStart)
         break;
      }

   // add ellipse quadrants to bounding rectangle until the
   // ending line is encountered:
   for (int i = 1; i <= 3; ++i)
      {
      UnionRect (&Rect, &Rect, &Quadrants [Q].Rect);
      ContainsEnd = ThetaEnd >= Quadrants [Q].StartAngle &&
         ThetaEnd < Quadrants [Q].EndAngle;
      if (ContainsEnd && !(i == 1 && ThetaEnd <= ThetaStart))
         break;
      Q = (Q + 1) % 4;
      }
   }

// expand rectangle to accommodate wide lines and margin:
int LineAdd = (mPenWidth-1) / 2 + (mPenWidth-1) % 2 + 3;
InflateRect (&Rect, LineAdd, LineAdd);

return Rect;
}

void CArc::Move (int DeltaX, int DeltaY)
// moves the arc by the specified offsets
{
mX1 += DeltaX;
mY1 += DeltaY;
mX2 += DeltaX;
mY2 += DeltaY;
mX3 += DeltaX;
mY3 += DeltaY;
mX4 += DeltaX;
mY4 += DeltaY;
return;
}

void CArc::PureDraw (HDC HDc)
// draws the arc
   {
```

```cpp
    Arc (HDc, mX1, mY1, mX2, mY2, mX3, mY3, mX4, mY4);
    return;
    }

void CArc::Scale (int DeltaX, int DeltaY)
// scales the arc by the specified offsets
    {
    int *PXMin, *PXMax, *PYMin, *PYMax;

    // get pointers to max and min coordinates of bounding rect:
    if (mX2 > mX1)
        {
        PXMin = &mX1;
        PXMax = &mX2;
        }
    else
        {
        PXMin = &mX2;
        PXMax = &mX1;
        }
    if (mY2 > mY1)
        {
        PYMin = &mY1;
        PYMax = &mY2;
        }
    else
        {
        PYMin = &mY2;
        PYMax = &mY1;
        }

    // calculate the angles of the starting and ending lines:
    int XMid = (*PXMin + *PXMax) / 2;
    int YMid = (*PYMin + *PYMax) / 2;
    double ThetaStart = atan2 (YMid - mY3, mX3 - XMid);
    double ThetaEnd   = atan2 (YMid - mY4, mX4 - XMid);

    // assign new values to coordinates of bounding rectangle,
    // preserving the size of scaling rectangle:
    RECT Rect = GetBoundRect ();
    if (Rect.left < *PXMin && Rect.right > *PXMax)
        {
        *PXMax += DeltaX;
        }
    else if (Rect.left < *PXMin)
        {
        *PXMax += 2 * DeltaX;
        }
    else
        {
        *PXMin -= DeltaX;
        *PXMax += DeltaX;
        }
    if (Rect.top < *PYMin && Rect.bottom > *PYMax)
```

```cpp
      {
      *PYMax += DeltaY;
      }
   else if (Rect.top < *PYMin)
      {
      *PYMax += 2 * DeltaY;
      }
   else
      {
      *PYMin -= DeltaY;
      *PYMax += DeltaY;
      }

   // assign new starting and ending points so that the starting
   // and ending lines have the SAME angles as before scaling:
   XMid = (*PXMin + *PXMax) / 2;
   YMid = (*PYMin + *PYMax) / 2;

   mX3 = XMid + (int)(100.0 * cos (ThetaStart));
   mY3 = YMid - (int)(100.0 * sin (ThetaStart));

   mX4 = XMid + (int)(100.0 * cos (ThetaEnd));
   mY4 = YMid - (int)(100.0 * sin (ThetaEnd));
   return;
   }

LRESULT CArc::OnLButtonDown (WORD XCursor, WORD YCursor)
// processes WM_LBUTTONDOWN messages
   {
   switch (MainWnd.mMode)
      {
      case MainWnd.ModeNone: // draw bounding ellipse
         StartDrag ();
         mX1 = XCursor; mY1 = YCursor;
         mX2 = XCursor; mY2 = YCursor;
         MainWnd.mMode = MainWnd.ModeDragging;
         break;

      case MainWnd.ModeMark1: // mark start of arc
         mX3 = XCursor; mY3 = YCursor;
         MainWnd.mMode = MainWnd.ModeMark2;
         break;


      case MainWnd.ModeMark2: // mark end of arc
         // erase temporary ellipse:
         HDC HDCClient = GetTempDC ();
         Ellipse (HDCClient, mX1, mY1, mX2, mY2);

         // add arc to document:
         mX4 = XCursor; mY4 = YCursor;
         Document.AddFigure (this, TRUE);
         MainWnd.mCurrentFig = CreateObject ();
```

```cpp
        // draw arc:
        Draw (HDCClient);
        ReleaseDC (MainWnd.mHWnd, HDCClient);

        MainWnd.mMode = MainWnd.ModeNone;
        break;
      }
   return NULL;
   }

LRESULT CArc::OnLButtonUp (WORD XCursor, WORD YCursor)
// processes WM_LBUTTONUP messages
   {
   if (MainWnd.mMode != MainWnd.ModeDragging)
      return NULL;

   // end drag operation:
   ReleaseCapture ();
   ClipCursor (NULL);

   // erase old temporary ellipse / draw new temporary ellipse:
   HDC HDCClient = GetTempDC ();
   Ellipse (HDCClient, mX1, mY1, mX2, mY2);
   Ellipse (HDCClient, mX1, mY1, XCursor, YCursor);
   ReleaseDC (MainWnd.mHWnd, HDCClient);

   // save new coordinates / stop drawing if ellipse is trivial:
   mX2 = XCursor; mY2 = YCursor;
   if (mX1 == mX2 && mY1 == mY2)
      MainWnd.mMode = MainWnd.ModeNone;
   else
      MainWnd.mMode = MainWnd.ModeMark1;
   return NULL;
   }

LRESULT CArc::OnMouseMove (WORD XCursor, WORD YCursor)
// processes WM_MOUSEMOVE messages
   {
   if (MainWnd.mMode != MainWnd.ModeDragging)
      return NULL;

   // erase old temporary ellipse / draw new temporary ellipse:
   HDC HDCClient = GetTempDC ();
   Ellipse (HDCClient, mX1, mY1, mX2, mY2);
   Ellipse (HDCClient, mX1, mY1, XCursor, YCursor);
   ReleaseDC (MainWnd.mHWnd, HDCClient);

   // save new coordinates:
   mX2 = XCursor; mY2 = YCursor;
   return NULL;
   }
```

```cpp
///////////////////////////////////////////////////////////////////////
// CChord:                                                             //
///////////////////////////////////////////////////////////////////////

HBRUSH CChord::GetBrush (void)
// returns a handle to a brush for the chord
   {
   LOGBRUSH LB =
      {mBrushStyle,
       mBrushColor,
       mBrushHatchPattern};
   return CreateBrushIndirect (&LB);
   }

void CChord::PureDraw (HDC HDc)
// draws the chord
   {
   Chord (HDc, mX1, mY1, mX2, mY2, mX3, mY3, mX4, mY4);
   return;
   }

///////////////////////////////////////////////////////////////////////
// CPie:                                                               //
///////////////////////////////////////////////////////////////////////

void CPie::PureDraw (HDC HDc)
// draws the pie
   {
   Pie (HDc, mX1, mY1, mX2, mY2, mX3, mY3, mX4, mY4);
   return;
   }

///////////////////////////////////////////////////////////////////////
// CBezier:                                                            //
///////////////////////////////////////////////////////////////////////

RECT CBezier::GetBoundRect (void)
// returns rectangle bounding the Bezier curve
   {
   RECT Rect =
      {Min4 (mX1, mX2, mX3, mX4),
       Min4 (mY1, mY2, mY3, mY4),
       Max4 (mX1, mX2, mX3, mX4),
       Max4 (mY1, mY2, mY3, mY4)};

   // expand rectangle to accommodate wide lines and margin:
   int LineAdd = (mPenWidth-1) / 2 + (mPenWidth-1) % 2 + 3;
   InflateRect (&Rect, LineAdd, LineAdd);
   return Rect;
   }

void CBezier::Move (int DeltaX, int DeltaY)
// moves the bezier curve by the specified offsets
   {
```

```cpp
   mX1 += DeltaX;
   mY1 += DeltaY;
   mX2 += DeltaX;
   mY2 += DeltaY;
   mX3 += DeltaX;
   mY3 += DeltaY;
   mX4 += DeltaX;
   mY4 += DeltaY;
   return;
   }

void CBezier::PureDraw (HDC HDc)
// draws the Bezier curve
   {
   POINT Points [4] =
      {{mX1, mY1},
       {mX2, mY2},
       {mX3, mY3},
       {mX4, mY4}};
   PolyBezier (HDc, Points, 4);
   return;
   }

void CBezier::Scale (int DeltaX, int DeltaY)
// scales the bezier curve by the specified offsets
   {
   // get minimum and maximum coordinates:
   int XMin = Min4 (mX1, mX2, mX3, mX4);
   int XMax = Max4 (mX1, mX2, mX3, mX4);
   int YMin = Min4 (mY1, mY2, mY3, mY4);
   int YMax = Max4 (mY1, mY2, mY3, mY4);

   // calculate scaling factors:
   double XScaleFact = (double)(XMax - XMin + DeltaX) /
                       (double)(XMax - XMin);
   double YScaleFact = (double)(YMax - YMin + DeltaY) /
                       (double)(YMax - YMin);

   // use scaling factors to calculate new positions of points:
   mX1 = (int)(XMin + XScaleFact * (mX1 - XMin));
   mX2 = (int)(XMin + XScaleFact * (mX2 - XMin));
   mX3 = (int)(XMin + XScaleFact * (mX3 - XMin));
   mX4 = (int)(XMin + XScaleFact * (mX4 - XMin));

   mY1 = (int)(YMin + YScaleFact * (mY1 - YMin));
   mY2 = (int)(YMin + YScaleFact * (mY2 - YMin));
   mY3 = (int)(YMin + YScaleFact * (mY3 - YMin));
   mY4 = (int)(YMin + YScaleFact * (mY4 - YMin));
   return;
   }

LRESULT CBezier::OnLButtonDown (WORD XCursor, WORD YCursor)
// processes WM_LBUTTONDOWN messages
   {
```

```cpp
    HDC HDCClient;

    switch (MainWnd.mMode)
        {
        case MainWnd.ModeNone: // draw straight line
            StartDrag ();
            mX1 = XCursor; mY1 = YCursor;
            mX2 = XCursor; mY2 = YCursor;
            mX3 = XCursor; mY3 = YCursor;
            mX4 = XCursor; mY4 = YCursor;
            MainWnd.mMode = MainWnd.ModeDragging;
            break;

        case MainWnd.ModeMark1:  // mark first control point
            // erase straight line / draw temporary bezier:
            HDCClient = GetTempDC ();
            MoveToEx (HDCClient, mX1, mY1, 0);
            LineTo (HDCClient, mX4, mY4);
            mX2 = XCursor; mY2 = YCursor;
            mX3 = XCursor; mY3 = YCursor;
            PureDraw (HDCClient);
            ReleaseDC (MainWnd.mHWnd, HDCClient);

            MainWnd.mMode = MainWnd.ModeMark2;
            break;

        case MainWnd.ModeMark2: // mark second control point
            // erase temporary bezier:
            HDCClient = GetTempDC ();
            PureDraw (HDCClient);

            // add bezier to document and draw it:
            mX3 = XCursor; mY3 = YCursor;
            Document.AddFigure (this, TRUE);
            MainWnd.mCurrentFig = CreateObject ();
            Draw (HDCClient);
            ReleaseDC (MainWnd.mHWnd, HDCClient);

            MainWnd.mMode = MainWnd.ModeNone;
            break;
        }
    return NULL;
    }

LRESULT CBezier::OnLButtonUp (WORD XCursor, WORD YCursor)
// processes WM_LBUTTONUP messages
    {
    if (MainWnd.mMode != MainWnd.ModeDragging)
        return NULL;

    // end drag operation:
    ReleaseCapture ();
    ClipCursor (NULL);
```

```cpp
    // erase old temp. straight line / draw new one:
    HDC HDCClient = GetTempDC ();
    MoveToEx (HDCClient, mX1, mY1, 0);
    LineTo   (HDCClient, mX4, mY4);
    MoveToEx (HDCClient, mX1, mY1, 0);
    LineTo   (HDCClient, XCursor, YCursor);
    ReleaseDC (MainWnd.mHWnd, HDCClient);

    // save new coordinates / stop drawing if line is trivial:
    mX4 = XCursor; mY4 = YCursor;
    if (mX1 == mX4 && mY1 == mY4)
        MainWnd.mMode = MainWnd.ModeNone;
    else
        MainWnd.mMode = MainWnd.ModeMark1;
    return NULL;
    }

LRESULT CBezier::OnMouseMove (WORD XCursor, WORD YCursor)
// processes WM_MOUSEMOVE messages
    {
    if (MainWnd.mMode != MainWnd.ModeDragging)
        return NULL;

    // erase old temporary straight line / draw new one:
    HDC HDCClient = GetTempDC ();
    MoveToEx (HDCClient, mX1, mY1, 0);
    LineTo   (HDCClient, mX4, mY4);
    MoveToEx (HDCClient, mX1, mY1, 0);
    LineTo   (HDCClient, XCursor, YCursor);
    mX4 = XCursor; mY4 = YCursor;
    ReleaseDC (MainWnd.mHWnd, HDCClient);
    return NULL;
    }

////////////////////////////////////////////////////////////////////////////
// CLine:                                                                  //
////////////////////////////////////////////////////////////////////////////

void CLine::PureDraw (HDC HDc)
// draws the line
    {
    MoveToEx (HDc, mX1, mY1, 0);
    LineTo (HDc, mX2, mY2);
    return;
    }

LRESULT CLine::OnLButtonDown (WORD XCursor, WORD YCursor)
// processes WM_LBUTTONDOWN messages
    {
    StartDrag ();
    mX1 = XCursor; mY1 = YCursor;
    mX2 = XCursor; mY2 = YCursor;
    MainWnd.mMode = MainWnd.ModeDragging;
```

```
   return NULL;
   }

LRESULT CLine::OnLButtonUp (WORD XCursor, WORD YCursor)
// processes WM_LBUTTONUP messages
   {
   if (MainWnd.mMode != MainWnd.ModeDragging)
      return NULL;

   // end drag operation:
   ReleaseCapture ();
   ClipCursor (NULL);

   // erase temporary line:
   HDC HDCClient = GetTempDC ();
   PureDraw (HDCClient);

   // if line is not trivial, add it to document and draw it:
   mX2 = XCursor; mY2 = YCursor;
   if (mX1 != mX2 || mY1 != mY2)
       {
       Document.AddFigure (this, TRUE);
       MainWnd.mCurrentFig = CreateObject ();
       Draw (HDCClient);
       }
   ReleaseDC (MainWnd.mHWnd, HDCClient);
   MainWnd.mMode = MainWnd.ModeNone;
   return NULL;
   }

LRESULT CLine::OnMouseMove (WORD XCursor, WORD YCursor)
// processes WM_MOUSEMOVE messages
   {
   if (MainWnd.mMode != MainWnd.ModeDragging)
      return NULL;

   // erase old temporary line / draw new one:
   HDC HDCClient = GetTempDC ();
   PureDraw (HDCClient);
   mX2 = XCursor; mY2 = YCursor;
   PureDraw (HDCClient);
   ReleaseDC (MainWnd.mHWnd, HDCClient);
   return NULL;
   }

//////////////////////////////////////////////////////////////////////////////
// CRectangle:                                                               //
//////////////////////////////////////////////////////////////////////////////

void CRectangle::PureDraw (HDC HDc)
// draws the rectangle
   {
   Rectangle (HDc, mX1, mY1, mX2, mY2);
```

```cpp
   return;
   }

HBRUSH CRectangle::GetBrush (void)
// returns a handle to a brush for the rectangle
   {
   LOGBRUSH LB =
      {mBrushStyle,
       mBrushColor,
       mBrushHatchPattern};
   return CreateBrushIndirect (&LB);
   }

//////////////////////////////////////////////////////////////////////////
// CRoundRect:                                                            //
//////////////////////////////////////////////////////////////////////////

void CRoundRect::PureDraw (HDC HDc)
// draws the rounded rectangle
   {
   int RoundDiameter = (mX2 - mX1 + mY2 - mY2) / 6;
   RoundRect (HDc, mX1, mY1, mX2, mY2, RoundDiameter,
      RoundDiameter);
   return;
   }

//////////////////////////////////////////////////////////////////////////
// CEllipse:                                                              //
//////////////////////////////////////////////////////////////////////////

void CEllipse::PureDraw (HDC HDc)
// draws the ellipse
   {
   Ellipse (HDc, mX1, mY1, mX2, mY2);
   return;
   }

//////////////////////////////////////////////////////////////////////////
// CPolyline:                                                             //
//////////////////////////////////////////////////////////////////////////

RECT CPolyline::GetBoundRect (void)
// returns rectangle bounding all lines
   {
   int NP = mNumPoints;
   RECT Rect = {0,0,0,0};

   // if dragging, must include the new point not yet added:
   if (MainWnd.mMode == MainWnd.ModeDragging)
      ++NP;

   if (NP < 2)      // if less than 2 points, return empty
      return Rect; // rectangle
```

```cpp
   // obtain dimensions of bounding rectangle:
   Rect.left = INT_MAX;
   Rect.top = INT_MAX;
   Rect.right = INT_MIN;
   Rect.bottom = INT_MIN;
   for (int i = 0; i < NP; ++i)
      {
      Rect.left   = min (Rect.left,   mPoints [i].x);
      Rect.top    = min (Rect.top,    mPoints [i].y);
      Rect.right  = max (Rect.right,  mPoints [i].x);
      Rect.bottom = max (Rect.bottom, mPoints [i].y);
      }

   // expand rectangle to accommodate wide lines and margin:
   int LineAdd = (mPenWidth-1) / 2 + (mPenWidth-1) % 2 + 3;
   InflateRect (&Rect, LineAdd, LineAdd);

   return Rect;
   }

void CPolyline::Move (int DeltaX, int DeltaY)
// moves the polyline by the specified offsets
   {
   for (int i = 0; i < mNumPoints; ++i)
      {
      mPoints [i].x += DeltaX;
      mPoints [i].y += DeltaY;
      }
   return;
   }

void CPolyline::PureDraw (HDC HDc)
// draws the connected lines:
   {
   Polyline (HDc, mPoints, mNumPoints);
   return;
   }

void CPolyline::Scale (int DeltaX, int DeltaY)
// scales the polyline by the specified offsets
   {
   // calculate the maximum and minimum X and Y coordinates:
   int XMax = INT_MIN;
   int XMin = INT_MAX;
   int YMax = INT_MIN;
   int YMin = INT_MAX;
   for (int i = 0; i < mNumPoints; ++i)
      {
      XMin = min (XMin, mPoints [i].x);
      XMax = max (XMax, mPoints [i].x);
      YMin = min (YMin, mPoints [i].y);
      YMax = max (YMax, mPoints [i].y);
      }
```

```cpp
   // calculate the X and Y scaling factors:
   double XScaleFact = (double)(XMax - XMin + DeltaX) /
                       (double)(XMax - XMin);
   double YScaleFact = (double)(YMax - YMin + DeltaY) /
                       (double)(YMax - YMin);

   // use the scaling factors to adjust all the points:
   for (i = 0; i < mNumPoints; ++i)
      {
      mPoints [i].x = (int)(XMin + XScaleFact *
         (mPoints [i].x—XMin));
      mPoints [i].y = (int)(YMin + YScaleFact *
         (mPoints [i].y—YMin));
      }
   return;
   }

LRESULT CPolyline::OnLButtonDblClk (WORD XCursor, WORD YCursor)
// processes WM_LBUTTONDBLCLK messages
   {
   // if more than 1 point marked, add polyline figure to
   // document and draw it:
   if (mNumPoints > 1)
      {
      Document.AddFigure (this, TRUE);
      MainWnd.mCurrentFig = CreateObject ();
      HDC HDCClient = GetDC (MainWnd.mHWnd);
      Draw (HDCClient);
      ReleaseDC (MainWnd.mHWnd, HDCClient);
      }
   MainWnd.mMode = MainWnd.ModeNone;
   return NULL;
   }

LRESULT CPolyline::OnLButtonDown (WORD XCursor, WORD YCursor)
// processes WM_LBUTTONDOWN messages
   {
   // initialize first point:
   if (MainWnd.mMode == MainWnd.ModeNone)
      {
      mNumPoints = 1;
      mPoints [0].x = XCursor;
      mPoints [0].y = YCursor;
      }

   // save coordinates:
   mPoints [mNumPoints].x = XCursor;
   mPoints [mNumPoints].y = YCursor;

   // draw temporary line back to previous point:
   HDC HDCClient = GetTempDC ();
   MoveToEx (HDCClient, mPoints [mNumPoints-1].x,
      mPoints [mNumPoints-1].y, 0);
```

```cpp
LineTo    (HDCClient, mPoints [mNumPoints].x,
   mPoints [mNumPoints].y);
ReleaseDC (MainWnd.mHWnd, HDCClient);

StartDrag ();
MainWnd.mMode = MainWnd.ModeDragging;
return NULL;
}

LRESULT CPolyline::OnLButtonUp (WORD XCursor, WORD YCursor)
// processes WM_LBUTTONUP messages
   {
   if (MainWnd.mMode != MainWnd.ModeDragging)
      return NULL;

   // end drag operation:
   ReleaseCapture ();
   ClipCursor (NULL);

   // erase old temporary line / draw new one:
   HDC HDCClient = GetTempDC ();
   MoveToEx (HDCClient, mPoints [mNumPoints-1].x,
      mPoints [mNumPoints-1].y, 0);
   LineTo    (HDCClient, mPoints [mNumPoints].x,
      mPoints [mNumPoints].y);
   MoveToEx (HDCClient, mPoints [mNumPoints-1].x,
      mPoints [mNumPoints-1].y, 0);
   LineTo    (HDCClient, XCursor, YCursor);
   ReleaseDC (MainWnd.mHWnd, HDCClient);

   mPoints [mNumPoints].x = XCursor;
   mPoints [mNumPoints].y = YCursor;

   // if new point is not on top of previous point, increment
   // number of points:
   if (mPoints [mNumPoints].x != mPoints [mNumPoints-1].x
       mPoints [mNumPoints].y != mPoints [mNumPoints-1].y)
      ++mNumPoints;

   // if maximum number of points has been used, end drawing now:
   if (mNumPoints == MAXPOINTS)
      OnLButtonDblClk (XCursor, YCursor);

   MainWnd.mMode = MainWnd.ModeMark1;
   return NULL;
   }

LRESULT CPolyline::OnMouseMove (WORD XCursor, WORD YCursor)
// processes WM_MOUSEMOVE messages
   {
   if (MainWnd.mMode != MainWnd.ModeDragging)
      return NULL;
```

```
   // erase old temporary line / draw new one:
   HDC HDCClient = GetTempDC ();
   MoveToEx (HDCClient, mPoints [mNumPoints-1].x,
      mPoints [mNumPoints-1].y, 0);
   LineTo    (HDCClient, mPoints [mNumPoints].x,
      mPoints [mNumPoints].y);
   MoveToEx (HDCClient, mPoints [mNumPoints-1].x,
      mPoints [mNumPoints-1].y, 0);
   LineTo    (HDCClient, XCursor, YCursor);
   ReleaseDC (MainWnd.mHWnd, HDCClient);

   // save new coordinates:
   mPoints [mNumPoints].x = XCursor;
   mPoints [mNumPoints].y = YCursor;
   return NULL;
   }

/////////////////////////////////////////////////////////////////////////////
// CPolygon:                                                                 //
/////////////////////////////////////////////////////////////////////////////

HBRUSH CPolygon::GetBrush (void)
// returns a handle to a brush for the polygon
   {
   LOGBRUSH LB =
      {mBrushStyle,
      mBrushColor,
      mBrushHatchPattern};
   return CreateBrushIndirect (&LB);
   }

void CPolygon::PureDraw (HDC HDc)
// draws the polygon:
   {
   Polygon (HDc, mPoints, mNumPoints);
   return;
   }
```

Listing 6.7:   Document.h

```
/////////////////////////////////////////////////////////////////////////////
//                                                                         //
// Document.h: Header file for document class.                             //
//                                                                         //
/////////////////////////////////////////////////////////////////////////////

struct FigCell        // element of linked list storing figures
{
   FigCell *PNextFig; // pointer to next element in list
   CFigure *PFigure;  // pointer to figure object
};
```

```
class CDocument
{
public:
   FigCell *mPFirstFig; // pointer to start of linked list

   CDocument (void);
   void AddFigure (CFigure *PFigure, BOOL StoreDefaults);
   void DeleteFigure (CFigure *PFigure);
   CFigure *GetNextFig (CFigure *PFigure);
   CFigure *GetPreviousFig (CFigure *PFigure);
};
```

Listing 6.8:　　Document.cpp

```
///////////////////////////////////////////////////////////////////////////
//                                                                       //
// Document.cpp: Implementation file for document class.                 //
//                                                                       //
///////////////////////////////////////////////////////////////////////////

#define STRICT
#include <windows.h>

#include "figure.h"
#include "document.h"
#include "dialog.h"

extern CAttrDlg  AttrDlg;
extern CBrushDlg BrushDlg;
extern CPenDlg   PenDlg;

CDocument::CDocument (void)
   {
   mPFirstFig = 0;
   return;
   }

void CDocument::AddFigure (CFigure *PFigure, BOOL StoreDefaults)
// adds a new figure to end of linked list; if StoreDefaults is
// TRUE, stores the default attributes & drawing tools in object
   {
   FigCell *PCell;
   if (StoreDefaults)
      {

      // save default brush features:
      PFigure->DefineBrush (BrushDlg.mBrushColor,
         BrushDlg.mBrushHatchPattern, BrushDlg.mBrushStyle);

      // save default pen features:
      PFigure->mPenColor = PenDlg.mPenColor;
```

```cpp
   PFigure->mPenStyle = PenDlg.mPenStyle;
   PFigure->mPenType = PenDlg.mPenType;
   PFigure->mPenWidth = PenDlg.mPenWidth;

   // save default drawing attributes:
   PFigure->mBkColor = AttrDlg.mBkColor;
   PFigure->mBkMode = AttrDlg.mBkMode;
   PFigure->mBrushXOrg = AttrDlg.mBrushXOrg;
   PFigure->mBrushYOrg = AttrDlg.mBrushYOrg;
   PFigure->mFillMode = AttrDlg.mFillMode;
   PFigure->mMixMode = AttrDlg.mMixMode;
   }

// set PCell to new cell at end of list:
if (mPFirstFig == 0)
   {
   mPFirstFig = new FigCell;
   PCell = mPFirstFig;
   }
else
   {
   PCell = mPFirstFig;
   while (PCell->PNextFig != 0)
      PCell = PCell->PNextFig;
   PCell->PNextFig = new FigCell;
   PCell = PCell->PNextFig;
   }

// assign values to new cell:
PCell->PNextFig = 0;
PCell->PFigure = PFigure;
return;
}

void CDocument::DeleteFigure (CFigure *PFigure)
// deletes the linked-list cell that points to the figure object
// pointed to by PFigure; does not delete the figure object
// itself; assumes that the list DOES CONTAIN this cell
   {
   FigCell *PCell;

   // test first cell in list:
   if (mPFirstFig->PFigure == PFigure)
      {
      PCell = mPFirstFig;
      mPFirstFig = mPFirstFig->PNextFig;
      delete PCell;
      return;
      }

   // test remaining cells in list:
   FigCell *PPrevCell = mPFirstFig;
   PCell = mPFirstFig->PNextFig;
```

```cpp
   while (PCell)
      {
      if (PCell->PFigure == PFigure)
         {
         PPrevCell->PNextFig = PCell->PNextFig;
         delete PCell;
         return;
         }
      PPrevCell = PCell;
      PCell = PCell->PNextFig;
      }
   }

CFigure *CDocument::GetNextFig (CFigure *PFigure)
// returns a pointer to the CFigure object that immediately
// FOLLOWS the object pointed to by PFigure in the linked list;
// if there is only 1 object in the list, it returns a pointer to
// that object
   {
   FigCell *PCell = mPFirstFig;
   while (PCell)
      {
      if (PCell->PFigure == PFigure)
         break;
      PCell = PCell->PNextFig;
      }
   if (PCell->PNextFig == 0)
      return mPFirstFig->PFigure;
   else
      return PCell->PNextFig->PFigure;
   }

CFigure *CDocument::GetPreviousFig (CFigure *PFigure)
// returns a pointer to the CFigure object that immediately
// PRECEDES the object pointed to by PFigure in the linked list;
// if there is only 1 object in the list, it returns a pointer to
// that object
   {
   FigCell *PCell = mPFirstFig;
   FigCell *PPrevFig;

   // get pointer to last cell in list:
   while (PCell)
      {
      if (PCell->PNextFig == 0)
         PPrevFig = PCell;
      PCell = PCell->PNextFig;
      }

   // search list from beginning for match:
   PCell = mPFirstFig;
   while (PCell)
      {
```

```
        if (PCell->PFigure == PFigure)
            return PPrevFig->PFigure;
        PPrevFig = PCell;
        PCell = PCell->PNextFig;
        }
    return 0;
    }
```

Listing 6.9:   Dialog.h

```cpp
//////////////////////////////////////////////////////////////////////////
//                                                                        //
// Dialog.h: Header file for the dialog box classes.                      //
//                                                                        //
//////////////////////////////////////////////////////////////////////////

class CAboutDlg
{
public:
    int Show (void);

    // message-handling functions:
    BOOL OnCancel (HWND HDlg);
    BOOL OnCtlColor (HDC HDc);
    BOOL OnInitDialog (void);
    BOOL OnOK (HWND HDlg);
};

class CAttrDlg
{
public:
    // store default drawing attributes:
    COLORREF mBkColor;
    int mBkMode;
    int mBrushXOrg;
    int mBrushYOrg;
    int mFillMode;
    int mMixMode;

    CAttrDlg (void);
    int Show (void);

    // message-handling functions:
    BOOL OnCancel (HWND HDlg);
    BOOL OnCtlColor (HDC HDc);
    BOOL OnInitDialog (HWND HDlg);
    BOOL OnOK (HWND HDlg);
    BOOL OnSetColor (HWND HDlg);

protected:
    // store temporary drawing attributes:
    COLORREF mTBkColor;
```

```cpp
   int mTBkMode;
   int mTBrushXOrg;
   int mTBrushYOrg;
   int mTFillMode;
   int mTMixMode;

   // saves custom colors user chooses in Color dialog box:
   DWORD mCustColors [16];
};

class CBrushDlg
{
public:
   // store default brush description:
   COLORREF mBrushColor;
   DWORD mBrushStyle;
   LONG mBrushHatchPattern;

   CBrushDlg (void);
   int Show (void);

   // message-handling functions:
   BOOL OnCancel (HWND HDlg);
   BOOL OnCtlColor (HDC HDc);
   BOOL OnInitDialog (HWND HDlg);
   BOOL OnOK (HWND HDlg);
   BOOL OnSetColor (HWND HDlg);

protected:
   // store temporary brush description:
   COLORREF mTBrushColor;
   DWORD mTBrushStyle;
   LONG mTBrushHatchPattern;

   // saves custom colors user chooses in Color dialog box:
   DWORD mCustColors [16];
};

class CPenDlg
{
public:
   // store default pen description:
   COLORREF mPenColor;
   DWORD mPenStyle;
   DWORD mPenType;
   DWORD mPenWidth;

   CPenDlg (void);
   int Show (void);

   // message-handling functions:
   BOOL OnCancel (HWND HDlg);
   BOOL OnCtlColor (HDC HDc);
   BOOL OnInitDialog (HWND HDlg);
```

```
   BOOL OnOK (HWND HDlg);
   BOOL OnSetColor (HWND HDlg);

protected:
   // store temporary pen description:
   COLORREF mTPenColor;
   DWORD mTPenStyle;
   DWORD mTPenType;
   DWORD mTPenWidth;

   // saves custom colors user chooses in Color dialog box:
   DWORD mCustColors [16];
};
```

Listing 6.10:   Dialog.cpp

```cpp
////////////////////////////////////////////////////////////////////////
//                                                                    //
// Dialog.cpp: Implementation file for the dialog box classes.        //
//                                                                    //
////////////////////////////////////////////////////////////////////////

#define STRICT
#include <windows.h>
#include "resource.h"

#include "app.h"
#include "figure.h"
#include "mainwnd.h"
#include "dialog.h"

#include <memory.h>

extern CApp       App;
extern CMainWnd   MainWnd;
extern CAboutDlg  AboutDlg;
extern CAttrDlg   AttrDlg;
extern CBrushDlg  BrushDlg;
extern CPenDlg    PenDlg;

BOOL CALLBACK AboutDialogProc (HWND HDlg, UINT Msg,
   WPARAM WParam, LPARAM LParam);
BOOL CALLBACK AttrDialogProc (HWND HDlg, UINT Msg, WPARAM WParam,
   LPARAM LParam);
BOOL CALLBACK BrushDialogProc (HWND HDlg, UINT Msg,
   WPARAM WParam, LPARAM LParam);
BOOL CALLBACK PenDialogProc (HWND HDlg, UINT Msg, WPARAM WParam,
   LPARAM LParam);

////////////////////////////////////////////////////////////////////////
// global tables for combo box data:                                  //
////////////////////////////////////////////////////////////////////////
```

```c
static struct // stores strings and color values for all
{              // elements to be added to Color combo box
   char *ColorName;
   COLORREF ColorValue;
}

ColorTable [10] =
   {{"Black",    RGB (0,0,0)},
    {"Gray",     RGB (192,192,192)},
    {"White",    RGB (255,255,255)},
    {"Red",      RGB (255,0,0)},
    {"Green",    RGB (0,255,0)},
    {"Blue",     RGB (0,0,255)},
    {"Yellow",   RGB (255,255,0)},
    {"Cyan",     RGB (0,255,255)},
    {"Magenta",  RGB (255,0,255)},
    {"<Custom>", RGB (0,0,0)}}};

static struct // stores strings and IDs for all elements to be
{              // added to Hatch Pattern combo box
   char *HatchName;
   LONG HatchID;
}

HatchTable [6] =
   {{"Vertical",             HS_VERTICAL},
    {"Horizontal",           HS_HORIZONTAL},
    {"Up Diagonal",          HS_BDIAGONAL},
    {"Down Diagonal",        HS_FDIAGONAL},
    {"Crosshatch",           HS_CROSS},
    {"Diagonal crosshatch",  HS_DIAGCROSS}};

static struct // stores strings and IDs for all elements to be
{              // added to Mix Mode combo box
   char *MixModeName;
   int MixModeID;
}
MixModeTable [16] =
   {{"R2_BLACK",        R2_BLACK},
    {"R2_COPYPEN",      R2_COPYPEN},
    {"R2_MASKNOTPEN",   R2_MASKNOTPEN},
    {"R2_MASKPEN",      R2_MASKPEN},
    {"R2_MASKPENNOT",   R2_MASKPENNOT},
    {"R2_MERGENOTPEN",  R2_MERGENOTPEN},
    {"R2_MERGEPEN",     R2_MERGEPEN},
    {"R2_MERGEPENNOT",  R2_MERGEPENNOT},
    {"R2_NOP",          R2_NOP},
    {"R2_NOT",          R2_NOT},
    {"R2_NOTCOPYPEN",   R2_NOTCOPYPEN},
    {"R2_NOTMASKPEN",   R2_NOTMASKPEN},
    {"R2_NOTMERGEPEN",  R2_NOTMERGEPEN},
    {"R2_NOTXORPEN",    R2_NOTXORPEN},
    {"R2_WHITE",        R2_WHITE},
    {"R2_XORPEN",       R2_XORPEN}};
```

```cpp
static struct // stores strings and IDs for all elements to be
{              // added to Style combo box
   char *StyleName;
   DWORD StyleID;
}

StyleTable [7] =
   {{"Solid",         PS_SOLID},
    {"Dash",          PS_DASH},
    {"Dot",           PS_DOT},
    {"Dash-Dot",      PS_DASHDOT},
    {"Dash-Dot-Dot",  PS_DASHDOTDOT},
    {"Null",          PS_NULL},
    {"Inside-Frame",  PS_INSIDEFRAME}};

////////////////////////////////////////////////////////////////////////
// About dialog box:                                                   //
////////////////////////////////////////////////////////////////////////

////////////////////////////////////////////////////////////////////////
// CAboutDlg public member function:                                   //
////////////////////////////////////////////////////////////////////////

int CAboutDlg::Show (void)
// displays About dialog box
   {
   return DialogBox
      (App.mHInstance,
       MAKEINTRESOURCE (IDD_ABOUT),
       MainWnd.mHWnd,
       AboutDialogProc);
   }

////////////////////////////////////////////////////////////////////////
// About dialog box procedure:                                         //
////////////////////////////////////////////////////////////////////////

BOOL CALLBACK AboutDialogProc
   (HWND   HDlg,
    UINT   Msg,
    WPARAM WParam,
    LPARAM LParam)
   {
   switch (Msg)
     {
     case WM_INITDIALOG: // dialog box was just created
        return AboutDlg.OnInitDialog ();

     case WM_COMMAND:     // user issued a command
        switch (LOWORD (WParam))
          {
          case IDCANCEL:   // user chose Close or pressed Esc
             return AboutDlg.OnCancel (HDlg);
```

```cpp
            case IDOK:          // user clicked OK or pressed Enter
                return AboutDlg.OnOK (HDlg);

            default:
                return FALSE; // default message processing
            }

        case WM_CTLCOLORDLG:     // dialog box about to be painted;
        case WM_CTLCOLORSTATIC: // text about to be painted
            return AboutDlg.OnCtlColor ((HDC)WParam);

        default:          // request default processing for all
            return FALSE; // other messages
        }
    }

/////////////////////////////////////////////////////////////////////////////
// CAboutDlg message handling member functions:                              //
/////////////////////////////////////////////////////////////////////////////

BOOL CAboutDlg::OnCancel (HWND HDlg)
// processes WM_COMMAND / IDCANCEL messages
    {
    // close the dialog box:
    EndDialog (HDlg, IDCANCEL);
    return TRUE;
    }

BOOL CAboutDlg::OnCtlColor (HDC HDc)
// processes WM_CTLCOLORDLG and WM_CTLCOLORSTATIC messages
    {
    // set text background to light gray:
    SetBkColor (HDc, RGB (192,192,192));

    // supply a handle to a light-gray brush:
    return (BOOL)GetStockObject (LTGRAY_BRUSH);
    }

BOOL CAboutDlg::OnInitDialog (void)
// processes WM_INITDIALOG messages
    {
    // return TRUE to set focus to first control:
    return TRUE;
    }

BOOL CAboutDlg::OnOK (HWND HDlg)
// processes WM_COMMAND / IDOK messages
    {
    // close the dialog box:
    EndDialog (HDlg, IDOK);
    return TRUE;
    }
```

```cpp
////////////////////////////////////////////////////////////////////////////
// Attributes dialog box:                                                 //
////////////////////////////////////////////////////////////////////////////

////////////////////////////////////////////////////////////////////////////
// CAttrDlg public member functions:                                      //
////////////////////////////////////////////////////////////////////////////

CAttrDlg::CAttrDlg (void)
   {
   mBkColor = RGB (255,255,255);
   mBkMode = OPAQUE;
   mBrushXOrg = 0;
   mBrushYOrg = 0;
   mFillMode = ALTERNATE;
   mMixMode = R2_COPYPEN;
   memset (mCustColors, 0, sizeof (mCustColors));
   return;
   }

int CAttrDlg::Show (void)
// displays Attributes dialog box
   {
   return DialogBox
      (App.mHInstance,
      MAKEINTRESOURCE (IDD_ATTR),
      MainWnd.mHWnd,
      AttrDialogProc);
   }

////////////////////////////////////////////////////////////////////////////
// Attributes dialog box procedure:                                       //
////////////////////////////////////////////////////////////////////////////

BOOL CALLBACK AttrDialogProc
   (HWND     HDlg,
   UINT     Msg,
   WPARAM   WParam,
   LPARAM   LParam)
   {
   switch (Msg)
      {
      case WM_INITDIALOG:   // dialog box was just created
         return AttrDlg.OnInitDialog (HDlg);

      case WM_COMMAND:      // user issued a command
         switch (LOWORD (WParam))
            {
            case IDC_SETCOLOR: // user clicked Set Custom Color
               return AttrDlg.OnSetColor (HDlg);

            case IDCANCEL:     // user chose Close or pressed Esc
               return AttrDlg.OnCancel (HDlg);
```

```
                case IDOK:            // user clicked OK or pressed Enter
                    return AttrDlg.OnOK (HDlg);

                default:
                    return FALSE;  // default message processing
                }

        case WM_CTLCOLORBTN:     // button is about to be painted;
        case WM_CTLCOLORDLG:     // dialog box about to be painted;
        case WM_CTLCOLORSTATIC: // dialog text about to be painted
            return AttrDlg.OnCtlColor ((HDC)WParam);

        default:            // request default processing for all
            return FALSE; // other messages
        }
    }

////////////////////////////////////////////////////////////////////////////
// CAttrDlg message handling member functions:                            //
////////////////////////////////////////////////////////////////////////////

BOOL CAttrDlg::OnCancel (HWND HDlg)
// processes WM_COMMAND / IDCANCEL messages
    {
    // close the dialog box:
    EndDialog (HDlg, IDCANCEL);
    return TRUE;
    }

BOOL CAttrDlg::OnCtlColor (HDC HDc)
// processes WM_CTLCOLORBTN, WM_CTLCOLORDLG, and
// WM_CTLCOLORSTATIC messages
    {
    // set text background to light gray:
    SetBkColor (HDc, RGB (192,192,192));

    // supply a handle to a light-gray brush:
    return (BOOL)GetStockObject (LTGRAY_BRUSH);
    }

BOOL CAttrDlg::OnInitDialog (HWND HDlg)
// processes WM_INITDIALOG messages
    {
    // obtain current attributes from selected figure or defaults:
    if (MainWnd.mSelectedFig) // figure is selected
        {
        mTBkColor = MainWnd.mSelectedFig->mBkColor;
        mTBkMode = MainWnd.mSelectedFig->mBkMode;
        mTBrushXOrg = MainWnd.mSelectedFig->mBrushXOrg;
        mTBrushYOrg = MainWnd.mSelectedFig->mBrushYOrg;
        mTFillMode = MainWnd.mSelectedFig->mFillMode;
        mTMixMode = MainWnd.mSelectedFig->mMixMode;
        SetWindowText (HDlg, "Figure Attributes");
```

```cpp
      }
  else                       // no figure selected
      {
      mTBkColor = mBkColor;
      mTBkMode = mBkMode;
      mTBrushXOrg = mBrushXOrg;
      mTBrushYOrg = mBrushYOrg;
      mTFillMode = mFillMode;
      mTMixMode = mMixMode;
      }

  // initialize Mix Mode combo box and select current value:
  for (int i = 0; i < 16; ++i)
      {
      SendDlgItemMessage (HDlg, IDC_MIXMODE, CB_ADDSTRING,
          0, (LPARAM)(LPCSTR)MixModeTable [i].MixModeName);
      if (MixModeTable [i].MixModeID == mTMixMode)
          SendDlgItemMessage (HDlg, IDC_MIXMODE, CB_SETCURSEL,
              (WPARAM)i, 0);
      }

  // check Background Mode radio button:
  CheckDlgButton
      (HDlg,
      mTBkMode == TRANSPARENT ? IDC_TRANSPARENT : IDC_OPAQUE,
      1);

  // initialize Color combo box and select current value:
  BOOL Selected = FALSE;
  for (i = 0; i < 10; ++i)
      {
      SendDlgItemMessage (HDlg, IDC_COLOR, CB_ADDSTRING, 0,
          (LPARAM)(LPCSTR)ColorTable [i].ColorName);
      if (!Selected && ColorTable [i].ColorValue == mTBkColor)
          {
          SendDlgItemMessage (HDlg, IDC_COLOR, CB_SETCURSEL,
              (WPARAM)i, 0);
          Selected = TRUE;
          }
      }
  if (!Selected)
      {
      ColorTable [9].ColorValue = mTBkColor;
      SendDlgItemMessage (HDlg, IDC_COLOR, CB_SETCURSEL,
          (WPARAM)9, 0);
      }

  // check Polygon Fill Mode radio button:
  CheckDlgButton
      (HDlg,
      mTFillMode == ALTERNATE ? IDC_ALTERNATE : IDC_WINDING,
      1);
```

```
   // set values of Brush Origin edit controls:
   SetDlgItemInt (HDlg, IDC_XORG, mTBrushXOrg, TRUE);
   SetDlgItemInt (HDlg, IDC_YORG, mTBrushYOrg, TRUE);

   // return TRUE to set focus to first control:
   return TRUE;
   }

BOOL CAttrDlg::OnOK (HWND HDlg)
// processes WM_COMMAND / IDOK messages
   {
   // save selection from Mix Mode combo box:
   mTMixMode = MixModeTable [SendDlgItemMessage (HDlg,
      IDC_MIXMODE, CB_GETCURSEL, 0, 0)].MixModeID;

   // save Background Mode choice:
   mTBkMode = IsDlgButtonChecked (HDlg, IDC_TRANSPARENT) ?
      TRANSPARENT : OPAQUE;

   // save selection from Color combo box:
   mTBkColor = ColorTable [SendDlgItemMessage (HDlg,
      IDC_COLOR, CB_GETCURSEL, 0, 0)].ColorValue;

   // save Polygon Fill Mode choice:
   mTFillMode = IsDlgButtonChecked (HDlg, IDC_ALTERNATE) ?
      ALTERNATE : WINDING;

   // save Brush Origin values:
   BOOL Translated;
   mTBrushXOrg = GetDlgItemInt(HDlg, IDC_XORG, &Translated,TRUE);
   mTBrushYOrg = GetDlgItemInt(HDlg, IDC_YORG, &Translated,TRUE);

   // store values in figure or in default data members:
   if (MainWnd.mSelectedFig) // figure is selected
      {
      MainWnd.mSelectedFig->mBkColor = mTBkColor;
      MainWnd.mSelectedFig->mBkMode = mTBkMode;
      MainWnd.mSelectedFig->mBrushXOrg = mTBrushXOrg;
      MainWnd.mSelectedFig->mBrushYOrg = mTBrushYOrg;
      MainWnd.mSelectedFig->mFillMode = mTFillMode;
      MainWnd.mSelectedFig->mMixMode = mTMixMode;

      // force redrawing of figure:
      RECT Rect = MainWnd.mSelectedFig->GetBoundRect ();
      InvalidateRect (MainWnd.mHWnd, &Rect, TRUE);
      }
   else                         // no figure selected
      {
      mBkColor = mTBkColor;
      mBkMode = mTBkMode;
      mBrushXOrg = mTBrushXOrg;
      mBrushYOrg = mTBrushYOrg;
      mFillMode = mTFillMode;
```

```cpp
       mMixMode = mTMixMode;
       }

    // close the dialog box:
    EndDialog (HDlg, IDOK);
    return TRUE;
    }

BOOL CAttrDlg::OnSetColor (HWND HDlg)
// processes WM_COMMAND / ID_SETCOLOR messages
    {
    CHOOSECOLOR CC;

    // assign values to structure to control Color dialog box:
    memset (&CC, 0, sizeof (CC));
    CC.lStructSize = sizeof (CC);
    CC.hwndOwner = HDlg;
    CC.rgbResult = ColorTable [9].ColorValue;
    CC.lpCustColors = mCustColors;
    CC.Flags = CC_RGBINIT;

    // display Color common dialog box; save selected color if
    // user clicked OK:
    if (ChooseColor (&CC))
       ColorTable [9].ColorValue = CC.rgbResult;
    return TRUE;
    }

//////////////////////////////////////////////////////////////////////////////
// Brush dialog box:                                                         //
//////////////////////////////////////////////////////////////////////////////

//////////////////////////////////////////////////////////////////////////////
// CBrushDlg public member functions:                                        //
//////////////////////////////////////////////////////////////////////////////

CBrushDlg::CBrushDlg (void)
    {
    mBrushColor = RGB (255,255,255);
    mBrushHatchPattern = HS_VERTICAL;
    mBrushStyle = BS_SOLID;
    memset (mCustColors, 0, sizeof (mCustColors));
    return;
    }

int CBrushDlg::Show (void)
// displays Brush dialog box
    {
    return DialogBox
       (App.mHInstance,
       MAKEINTRESOURCE (IDD_BRUSH),
       MainWnd.mHWnd,
       BrushDialogProc);
    }
```

```cpp
////////////////////////////////////////////////////////////////////////////
// Brush dialog box procedure:                                            //
////////////////////////////////////////////////////////////////////////////

BOOL CALLBACK BrushDialogProc
   (HWND   HDlg,
    UINT   Msg,
    WPARAM WParam,
    LPARAM LParam)
   {
   switch (Msg)
     {
     case WM_INITDIALOG: // dialog box was just created
        return BrushDlg.OnInitDialog (HDlg);

     case WM_COMMAND:     // user issued a command
        switch (LOWORD (WParam))
           {
           case IDC_SETCOLOR: // user clicked Set Custom Color
              return BrushDlg.OnSetColor (HDlg);

           case IDCANCEL: // user chose Close or pressed Esc
              return BrushDlg.OnCancel (HDlg);

           case IDOK:  // user clicked OK or pressed Enter
              return BrushDlg.OnOK (HDlg);

           default:
              return FALSE; // default message processing
           }

     case WM_CTLCOLORBTN:    // button is about to be painted;
     case WM_CTLCOLORDLG:    // dialog box about to be painted;
     case WM_CTLCOLORSTATIC: // dialog text about to be painted
        return BrushDlg.OnCtlColor ((HDC)WParam);

     default:          // request default processing for all
        return FALSE; // other messages
     }
   }

////////////////////////////////////////////////////////////////////////////
// CBrushDlg message handling member functions:                           //
////////////////////////////////////////////////////////////////////////////

BOOL CBrushDlg::OnCancel (HWND HDlg)
// processes WM_COMMAND / IDCANCEL messages
   {
   // close the dialog box:
   EndDialog (HDlg, IDCANCEL);
   return TRUE;
   }
```

```
BOOL CBrushDlg::OnCtlColor (HDC HDc)
// processes WM_CTLCOLORBTN, WM_CTLCOLORDLG, and
// WM_CTLCOLORSTATIC messages
   {
   // set text background to light gray:
   SetBkColor (HDc, RGB (192,192,192));

   // supply a handle to a light-gray brush:
   return (BOOL)GetStockObject (LTGRAY_BRUSH);
   }

BOOL CBrushDlg::OnInitDialog (HWND HDlg)
// processes WM_INITDIALOG messages
   {
   // obtain current brush description:
   if (MainWnd.mSelectedFig) // figure is selected
      {
      MainWnd.mSelectedFig->GetBrushDescription
         (&mTBrushColor,
          &mTBrushHatchPattern,
          &mTBrushStyle);
      SetWindowText (HDlg, "Figure Brush");
      }
   else                       // no figure selected
      {
      mTBrushColor = mBrushColor;
      mTBrushHatchPattern = mBrushHatchPattern;
      mTBrushStyle = mBrushStyle;
      }

   // check Style radio button:
   switch (mTBrushStyle)
      {
      case BS_SOLID:
         CheckDlgButton (HDlg, IDC_SOLID, 1);
         break;

      case BS_HATCHED:
         CheckDlgButton (HDlg, IDC_HATCHED, 1);
         break;

      case BS_NULL:
         CheckDlgButton (HDlg, IDC_NULL, 1);
         break;
      }

   // initialize Hatch Pattern combo box / select current value:
   for (int i = 0; i < 6; ++i)
      {
      SendDlgItemMessage (HDlg, IDC_HATCHPATTERN, CB_ADDSTRING,
         0, (LPARAM)(LPCSTR)HatchTable [i].HatchName);
      if (HatchTable [i].HatchID == mTBrushHatchPattern)
         SendDlgItemMessage (HDlg, IDC_HATCHPATTERN,
```

```cpp
            CB_SETCURSEL, (WPARAM)i, 0);
      }

   // initialize Color combo box and select current value:
   BOOL Selected = FALSE;
   for (i = 0; i < 10; ++i)
      {
      SendDlgItemMessage (HDlg, IDC_COLOR, CB_ADDSTRING, 0,
         (LPARAM)(LPCSTR)ColorTable [i].ColorName);
      if (!Selected && ColorTable [i].ColorValue == mTBrushColor)
         {
         SendDlgItemMessage (HDlg, IDC_COLOR, CB_SETCURSEL,
            (WPARAM)i, 0);
         Selected = TRUE;
         }
      }
   if (!Selected)
      {
      ColorTable [9].ColorValue = mTBrushColor;
      SendDlgItemMessage (HDlg, IDC_COLOR, CB_SETCURSEL,
         (WPARAM)9, 0);
      }

   // return TRUE to set focus to first control:
   return TRUE;
   }

BOOL CBrushDlg::OnOK (HWND HDlg)
// processes WM_COMMAND / IDOK messages
   {
   // save Style choice:
   if (IsDlgButtonChecked (HDlg, IDC_SOLID))
      mTBrushStyle = BS_SOLID;
   else if (IsDlgButtonChecked (HDlg, IDC_HATCHED))
      mTBrushStyle = BS_HATCHED;
   else
      mTBrushStyle = BS_NULL;

   // save selection from Hatch Pattern combo box:
   mTBrushHatchPattern = HatchTable [SendDlgItemMessage
      (HDlg, IDC_HATCHPATTERN, CB_GETCURSEL, 0, 0)].HatchID;

   // save selection from Color combo box:
   mTBrushColor = ColorTable [SendDlgItemMessage (HDlg,
      IDC_COLOR, CB_GETCURSEL, 0, 0)].ColorValue;

   // store values in figure or in default data members:
   if (MainWnd.mSelectedFig) // figure is selected
      {
      MainWnd.mSelectedFig->DefineBrush
         (mTBrushColor,
         mTBrushHatchPattern,
         mTBrushStyle);
```

```cpp
                    // force redrawing of figure:
                    RECT Rect = MainWnd.mSelectedFig->GetBoundRect ();
                    InvalidateRect (MainWnd.mHWnd, &Rect, TRUE);
                    }
            else                             // no figure selected
                    {
                    mBrushColor = mTBrushColor;
                    mBrushHatchPattern = mTBrushHatchPattern;
                    mBrushStyle = mTBrushStyle;
                    }

            // close the dialog box:
            EndDialog (HDlg, IDOK);
            return TRUE;
            }

BOOL CBrushDlg::OnSetColor (HWND HDlg)
// processes WM_COMMAND / ID_SETCOLOR messages
            {
            CHOOSECOLOR CC;

            // assign values to structure to control Color dialog box:
            memset (&CC, 0, sizeof (CC));
            CC.lStructSize = sizeof (CC);
            CC.hwndOwner = HDlg;
            CC.rgbResult = ColorTable [9].ColorValue;
            CC.lpCustColors = mCustColors;
            CC.Flags = CC_RGBINIT;

            // display Color common dialog box; save selected color if
            // user clicked OK:
            if (ChooseColor (&CC))
                ColorTable [9].ColorValue = CC.rgbResult;
            return TRUE;
            }

//////////////////////////////////////////////////////////////////////////////
// Pen dialog box:                                                           //
//////////////////////////////////////////////////////////////////////////////

//////////////////////////////////////////////////////////////////////////////
// CPenDlg public member functions:                                          //
//////////////////////////////////////////////////////////////////////////////

CPenDlg::CPenDlg (void)
            {
            mPenColor = RGB (0,0,0);
            mPenStyle = PS_SOLID;
            mPenType = PS_COSMETIC;
            mPenWidth = 1;
            memset (mCustColors, 0, sizeof (mCustColors));
            return;
            }
```

```cpp
int CPenDlg::Show (void)
// displays Pen dialog box
    {
    return DialogBox
        (App.mHInstance,
        MAKEINTRESOURCE (IDD_PEN),
        MainWnd.mHWnd,
        PenDialogProc);
    }

/////////////////////////////////////////////////////////////////////////////
// Pen dialog box procedure:                                               //
/////////////////////////////////////////////////////////////////////////////

BOOL CALLBACK PenDialogProc
    (HWND    HDlg,
     UINT    Msg,
     WPARAM WParam,
     LPARAM LParam)
    {
    switch (Msg)
      {
      case WM_INITDIALOG: // dialog box was just created
          return PenDlg.OnInitDialog (HDlg);

      case WM_COMMAND:  // user issued a command
          switch (LOWORD (WParam))
             {
             case IDC_SETCOLOR: // user clicked Set Custom Color
                return PenDlg.OnSetColor (HDlg);

             case IDCANCEL: // user chose Close or pressed Esc
                return PenDlg.OnCancel (HDlg);

             case IDOK:  // user clicked OK or pressed Enter
                return PenDlg.OnOK (HDlg);

             default:
                return FALSE; // default message processing
             }

      case WM_CTLCOLORBTN:    // button is about to be painted;
      case WM_CTLCOLORDLG:     // dialog box about to be painted;
      case WM_CTLCOLORSTATIC: // dialog text about to be painted
          return PenDlg.OnCtlColor ((HDC)WParam);

      default:          // request default processing for all
          return FALSE; // other messages
      }
    }

/////////////////////////////////////////////////////////////////////////////
// CPenDlg message handling member functions:                              //
/////////////////////////////////////////////////////////////////////////////
```

```cpp
BOOL CPenDlg::OnCancel (HWND HDlg)
// processes WM_COMMAND / IDCANCEL messages
   {
   // close the dialog box:
   EndDialog (HDlg, IDCANCEL);
   return TRUE;
   }

BOOL CPenDlg::OnCtlColor (HDC HDc)
// processes WM_CTLCOLORBTN, WM_CTLCOLORDLG, and
// WM_CTLCOLORSTATIC messages
   {
   // set text background to light gray:
   SetBkColor (HDc, RGB (192,192,192));
   // supply a handle to a light-gray brush:
   return (BOOL)GetStockObject (LTGRAY_BRUSH);
   }

BOOL CPenDlg::OnInitDialog (HWND HDlg)
// processes WM_INITDIALOG messages
   {
   // obtain current pen description:
   if (MainWnd.mSelectedFig) // figure is selected
      {
      mTPenColor = MainWnd.mSelectedFig->mPenColor;
      mTPenStyle = MainWnd.mSelectedFig->mPenStyle;
      mTPenType = MainWnd.mSelectedFig->mPenType;
      mTPenWidth = MainWnd.mSelectedFig->mPenWidth;
      SetWindowText (HDlg, "Figure Pen");
      }
   else                     // no figure selected
      {
      mTPenColor = mPenColor;
      mTPenStyle = mPenStyle;
      mTPenType = mPenType;
      mTPenWidth = mPenWidth;
      }

   // check Type radio button:
   CheckDlgButton
      (HDlg,
      mTPenType == PS_COSMETIC ? IDC_COSMETIC : IDC_GEOMETRIC,
      1);

   // initialize Style combo box and select current value:
   for (int i = 0; i < 7; ++i)
      {
      SendDlgItemMessage (HDlg, IDC_STYLE, CB_ADDSTRING,
         0, (LPARAM)(LPCSTR)StyleTable [i].StyleName);
      if (StyleTable [i].StyleID == mTPenStyle)
         SendDlgItemMessage (HDlg, IDC_STYLE, CB_SETCURSEL,
            (WPARAM)i, 0);
      }
```

```cpp
    // limit Width edit control to 2 characters and set value:
    SendDlgItemMessage (HDlg, IDC_WIDTH, EM_SETLIMITTEXT,
        (WPARAM)2, 0);
    SetDlgItemInt (HDlg, IDC_WIDTH, mTPenWidth, FALSE);

    // initialize Color combo box and select current value:
    BOOL Selected = FALSE;
    for (i = 0; i < 10; ++i)
        {
        SendDlgItemMessage (HDlg, IDC_COLOR, CB_ADDSTRING, 0,
            (LPARAM)(LPCSTR)ColorTable [i].ColorName);
        if (!Selected && ColorTable [i].ColorValue == mTPenColor)
            {
            SendDlgItemMessage (HDlg, IDC_COLOR, CB_SETCURSEL,
                (WPARAM)i, 0);
            Selected = TRUE;
            }
        }
    if (!Selected)
        {
        ColorTable [9].ColorValue = mTPenColor;
        SendDlgItemMessage (HDlg, IDC_COLOR, CB_SETCURSEL,
            (WPARAM)9, 0);
        }

    // return TRUE to set focus to first control:
    return TRUE;
    }

BOOL CPenDlg::OnOK (HWND HDlg)
// processes WM_COMMAND / IDOK messages
    {
    // save Type choice:
    mTPenType = IsDlgButtonChecked (HDlg, IDC_COSMETIC) ?
        PS_COSMETIC : PS_GEOMETRIC;

    // save selection from Style combo box:
    mTPenStyle = StyleTable [SendDlgItemMessage (HDlg, IDC_STYLE,
        CB_GETCURSEL, 0, 0)].StyleID;

    // save value from Width edit control:
    BOOL Translated;
    mTPenWidth = GetDlgItemInt (HDlg, IDC_WIDTH, &Translated,
        FALSE);

    // save selection from Color combo box:
    mTPenColor = ColorTable [SendDlgItemMessage (HDlg,
        IDC_COLOR, CB_GETCURSEL, 0, 0)].ColorValue;

    // store values in figure or in default data members:
    if (MainWnd.mSelectedFig) // figure is selected
        {
        MainWnd.mSelectedFig->mPenColor = mTPenColor;
```

```cpp
    MainWnd.mSelectedFig->mPenStyle = mTPenStyle;
    MainWnd.mSelectedFig->mPenType = mTPenType;
    MainWnd.mSelectedFig->mPenWidth = mTPenWidth;

    // force redrawing of figure:
    RECT Rect = MainWnd.mSelectedFig->GetBoundRect ();
    InvalidateRect (MainWnd.mHWnd, &Rect, TRUE);
    }
  else                        // no figure selected
    {
    mPenColor = mTPenColor;
    mPenStyle = mTPenStyle;
    mPenType = mTPenType;
    mPenWidth = mTPenWidth;
    }

  // close the dialog box:
  EndDialog (HDlg, IDOK);
  return TRUE;
  }

BOOL CPenDlg::OnSetColor (HWND HDlg)
// processes WM_COMMAND / ID_SETCOLOR messages
  {
  CHOOSECOLOR CC;

  // assign values to structure to control Color dialog box:
  memset (&CC, 0, sizeof (CC));
  CC.lStructSize = sizeof (CC);
  CC.hwndOwner = HDlg;
  CC.rgbResult = ColorTable [9].ColorValue;
  CC.lpCustColors = mCustColors;
  CC.Flags = CC_RGBINIT;

  // display Color common dialog box; save selected color if
  // user clicked OK:
  if (ChooseColor (&CC))
     ColorTable [9].ColorValue = CC.rgbResult;
  return TRUE;
  }
```

CHAPTER 7

PRINTING GRAPHICS

To print graphics, you use the same basic method that you use to display graphics in a window or on another device. That is, you perform the six steps for drawing graphics that were explained in Chapter 2, following the instructions given in Chapters 3 through 6. For printing graphics, however, you must perform several additional steps that are required to initiate and manage the print job and to divide the output among separate pages. This chapter covers these additional steps and focuses on the techniques that are unique to printing. The chapter also presents the DrawIt Version 4 program, which allows you to print the graphics that you have drawn in the window.

THE NINE BASIC STEPS FOR PRINTING GRAPHICS

The following are the nine basic steps for printing graphics. Note that these steps include the six general steps for displaying graphics on any device, which were given in Chapter 2, *plus* the additional steps that are required to display graphics on a printer. See Figure 7.1.

1. Obtain a printer device context.
2. Set up the abort function, display the Cancel dialog box, and disable the main window.
3. Call `StartDoc` to start the print job.
4. Call `StartPage` to start a page.
5. Prepare the device context and call the drawing functions.
6. Call `EndPage` to end the page. If there is another page, go back to step 4.
7. Call `EndDoc` to end the print job.
8. Enable the main window and remove the Cancel dialog box.
9. Delete the printer device context.

The remainder of the chapter explains each of these steps. The code examples are taken from the DrawIt Version 4 program.

THE PRINTER DEVICE CONTEXT

This section covers steps 1 and 9 of the process for printing graphics: obtaining and deleting the printer device context.

You can obtain a printer device context by calling the `CreateDC` API function:

```
HDC CreateDC
   (LPCTSTR lpszDriver, // assign 0
    LPCTSTR lpszDevice, // printer device name
    LPCTSTR lpszOutput, // assign 0
    CONST DEVMODE *lpInitData); // assign 0 or pointer to DEVMODE
```

You assign the `lpszDevice` parameter a string containing the name of the printer on which you want to print—for example, "HP LaserJet Series II" or "Generic/Text Only." Under Windows 95, you assign 0 to the first and third parameters (`lpszDriver` and `lpszOutput`; these parameters were used by previous versions of Windows). To use the default printer settings selected by the user, you should also assign 0 to the last parameter, `lpInitData`. `CreateDC` returns a handle to the printer device context, which your program should save in a parameter of type `HDC`.

TIP　　To change one or more print settings, such as the paper orientation, paper size, or number of copies, you can assign the `lpInitData` parameter the address of a `DEVMODE` structure containing the desired settings. To prepare the `DEVMODE` structure, you can call the `DocumentProperties` API function.

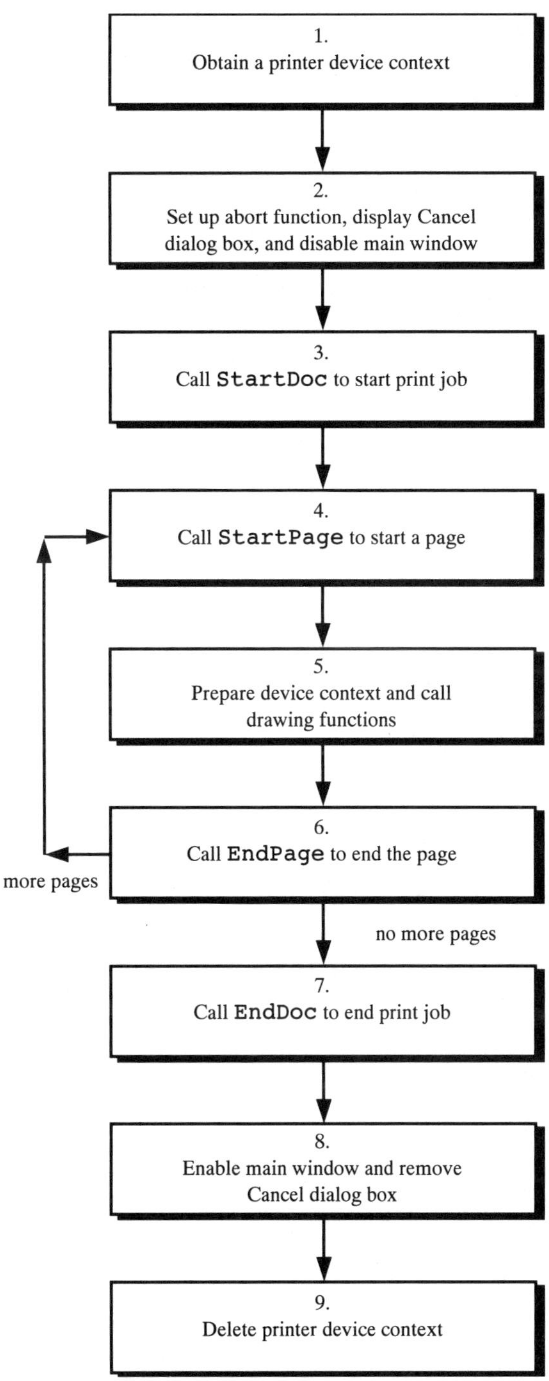

Figure 7.1:   The nine basic steps for printing graphics

Normally, your program displays graphics on the current *default* Windows printer (unless the program allows the user to choose a different printer). The name of the default printer is stored in the Win.ini initialization file. The printer name is at the beginning of the `device` string within the [windows] section of the initialization file. You can obtain this string by calling the `GetProfileString` API function.

As an example, the following code calls `GetProfileString` to obtain the device string from the initialization file, extracts the default printer name from this string, and then passes the printer name to `CreateDC` to create a printer device context:

```
char PrnInfo [128];
GetProfileString
    ("windows",
    "device",
    "",
    PrnInfo,
    sizeof (PrnInfo));
char *PPrnDevice = strtok (PrnInfo, ",");
HDC HDCPrn = CreateDC (0, PPrnDevice, 0, 0);
```

The `device` string contains the name of the printer followed by a comma and some additional information. The `strtok` run-time library function extracts the name by placing a `NULL` character after it and returning the address of the beginning of the name.

TIP If you merely want to obtain information on the printer, you can call the more efficient `CreateIC` API function rather than `CreateDC` The parameters passed to `CreateIC` are the same as those passed to `CreateDC`, and the handle that `CreateIC` returns can be used for any purpose except to generate output.

Rather than calling `CreateDC` to obtain a device context for a specific printer, you can display the standard Print dialog box, which allows the user to *select* a printer and choose print settings (see Figure 7.2). To display the Print dialog box, you call the `PrintDlg` API function,

```
BOOL PrintDlg (LPPRINTDLG lppd);
```

where `lppd` is a pointer to a `PRINTDLG` structure. You must first assign values to the fields of the `PRINTDLG` structure to tell `PrintDlg` how to initialize the dialog box. You then pass this structure to `PrintDlg`, which displays the

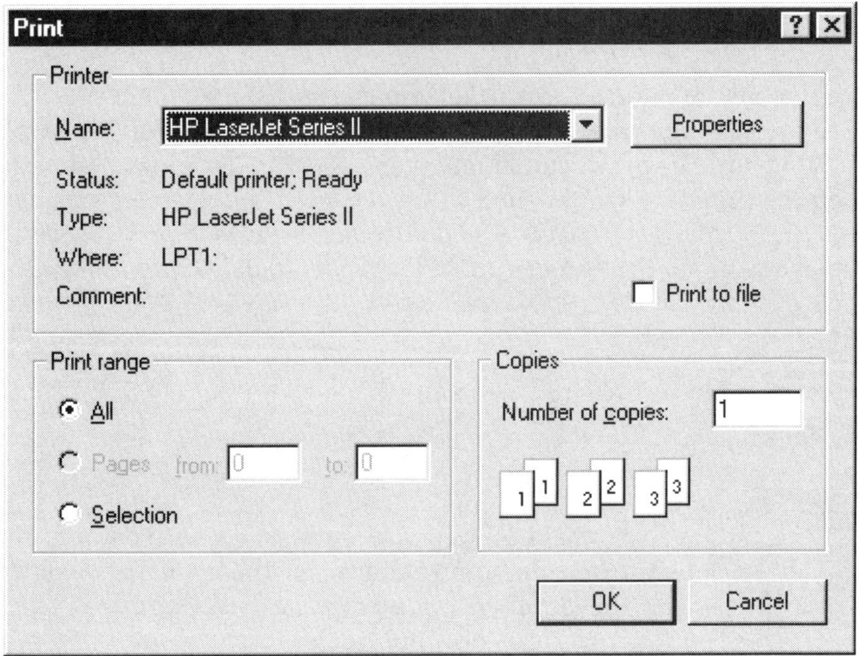

Figure 7.2:   The standard Print dialog box displayed by calling the `PrintDlg` API function

Print dialog box. After `PrintDlg` returns, the `PRINTDLG` structure will contain information based upon the choices that the user made in the dialog box. Most important, the `hDC` field of the `PRINTDLG` structure will contain the handle of a printer device context. You can then use this device context in the same way that you use one returned by `CreateDC`.

As an example, the following code assigns minimal initialization information to the fields of a `PRINTDLG` structure and then calls `PrintDlg`:

```
PRINTDLG PD;

// set all PRINTDLG fields to 0:
memset (&PD, 0, sizeof (PD));

// assign minimal initialization information:
PD.lStructSize = sizeof(PD); // size of structure
PD.Flags = PD RETURNDC;      // request a printer DC
PD.hwndOwner = HWnd;         // handle of program window

// display Print dialog box:
PrintDlg (&PD);
```

```
// PD.hDC now contains the handle of a printer device context
// based upon the user's choices in the Print dialog box
```

Note that before calling `PrintDlg`, you can assign the `PRINTDLG` structure a large variety of optional flags and values to specify various features of the Print dialog box. See the documentation on `PRINTDLG` for more information.

When the program has finished using the printer device context obtained from `CreateDC` or `PrintDlg`, it should release the system resources that it consumes by calling the `DeleteDC` API function to delete it:

```
BOOL DeleteDC (HDC hdc);
```

(The program should *not* call `ReleaseDC`, which releases a *display* device context.)

TIP　　Once you have obtained a printer device context, you can obtain extensive information on the associated device by calling the `GetDeviceCaps` or `DeviceCapabilities` API function. You can find out, for example, the specific graphics operations that the device can perform.

FYI　　The following are related API functions: `DocumentProperties` and `ResetDC`.

THE ABORT FUNCTION AND THE CANCEL DIALOG BOX

This section covers steps 2 and 8 of the process for printing graphics: setting up the abort function, displaying the Cancel dialog box, and disabling the main program window (step 2); and then later reenabling the main window and removing the Cancel dialog box (step 8).

A program that supports printing normally has a Print command on its File menu (as does DrawIt Version 4). When the user chooses this command, the program window receives a `WM_COMMAND` message. In response to this message, the program prints the document. A problem with this mechanism, however, is that the program cannot return from processing the message until it has finished printing, which can take a long time, especially if the document consists of several pages. Consequently, during printing, the program cannot process additional messages that the window receives. An important implication of this situation is that the user will be unable to cancel the print job. Even if the program provides a command for canceling printing, it will be unable to respond to the message generated by the command.

The solution to this problem is to install an *abort function* (also commonly called an *abort procedure*). If you write and install an abort function prior to printing a document, Windows will call this function periodically while it is printing (specifically, during processing of the `EndPage` function, which is the most time-consuming of the print functions because it sends the stored output for an entire page to the printer, as described later). If the abort function contains a message-processing loop, the program will be able to keep processing messages *during* printing. As you will see, the abort function can also cancel the print job.

To install an abort function, you call the `SetAbortProc` API function,

```
int SetAbortProc (HDC hdc, ABORTPROC lpAbortProc);
```

where `hdc` is the handle of the printer device context and `lpAbortProc` is the address of the abort function that you have written. The following is an example of an abort function (this is the one defined by DrawIt in the file Document.cpp):

```
BOOL CALLBACK AbortProc (HDC HDc, int Code)
   {
   // process any pending messages:
   MSG Msg;
   while (PeekMessage ((LPMSG)&Msg, (HWND)NULL, 0, 0, PM    REMOVE))
      {
      // process messages for Cancel modeless dialog box:
      if (!IsDialogMessage (CancelDlg.mHDlg, (LPMSG)&Msg))
         // dispatch other messages:
         DispatchMessage ((LPMSG) &Msg);
      }

   return Document.mContinuePrint;
   }
```

An abort function that you write must have the same return and parameter types as this example has; however, you can choose the function name and the statements that it contains. The message loop in `AbortProc` is different from the main message loops found in the example programs in this book, in the following two ways:

- Rather than calling `GetMessage`, it calls `PeekMessage`. If there are no pending messages, `PeekMessage` immediately returns the value `FALSE`, allowing `AbortProc` to return and printing to resume.

- It includes a call to the `IsDialogMessage` API function, which processes messages sent to the Cancel modeless dialog box (which will be explained shortly).

If the abort function returns `TRUE`, printing continues; if, however, it returns `FALSE`, Windows cancels the print job (and control returns immediately from `EndPage`). `AbortProc` returns the value of the *continue* flag `Document.mContinuePrint`; you will see shortly how this flag is set.

In addition to installing an abort function, the program should also provide a command for canceling the print job. The most common way to provide such a command is to display a modeless dialog box containing a Cancel button. When the user clicks the Cancel button, the dialog box procedure can set a *continue* flag to `FALSE`, which signals the abort function to return `FALSE` and thereby terminate the print job. An example is the `Document.mContinuePrint` flag used in the DrawIt program. For an example of all of the code required to display and manage a Cancel modeless dialog box, see the class `CCancelDlg`, which is defined in Dialog.h and implemented in Dialog.cpp, in the DrawIt Version 4 listings provided on the companion disk.

FYI   You display a *modeless* dialog box by calling the `CreateDialog` API function, which immediately returns control to the program, leaving the dialog box displayed. To remove a modeless dialog box, you pass its handle to the `DestroyWindow` API function. In contrast, when you call the `DialogBox` API function to display a *modal* dialog box as explained in Chapter 1, control does not return until the user closes the dialog box. A modal dialog box is thus unsuitable for display during printing.

The Cancel dialog box procedure is able to process messages sent to the Cancel dialog box during printing because of the message loop in the abort function. This message loop also allows the main window procedure to receive messages if the user chooses menu commands or presses keyboard commands. During printing, however, a program typically does not want the user to be able to issue other program commands (for example, while a document is being printed, the user should not be allowed to modify it or to quit the program). To prevent the user from issuing menu or keyboard commands, the print routine can *disable* the main program window by passing `FALSE` to the `EnableWindow` API function:

```
BOOL EnableWindow (HWND hWnd, BOOL bEnable);
```

When printing is complete, it can reenable the main window by passing `TRUE` to `EnableWindow`.

The following code sets the *continue* flag to `TRUE`, installs the abort function, displays the Cancel dialog box, and disables the main program window. This code is from DrawIt (the `CDocument::OnFilePrint` function in the Document.cpp file), and it constitutes step 2 of the printing process:

```
mContinuePrint = TRUE;
SetAbortProc (HDCPrn, AbortProc);
CancelDlg.Create ();
EnableWindow (MainWnd.mHWnd, FALSE);
```

The following code enables the main program window and removes the Cancel dialog box. `CDocument::OnFilePrint` issues these statements after the document has been printed; the statements constitute step 8 of the printing process:

```
EnableWindow (MainWnd.mHWnd, TRUE);
DestroyWindow (CancelDlg.mHDlg);
```

TIP　　　You should enable the main program window *before* removing the Cancel dialog box, so that Windows activates your main program window. Otherwise, Windows will activate the window of *another* program because it cannot activate a disabled window.

MANAGING THE PRINT JOB

This section discusses steps 3 through 7 of the printing process: starting the print job, starting the page, preparing the device context and calling the drawing functions, ending the page, and ending the print job.

To start the print job, call the `StartDoc` API function:

```
int StartDoc (HDC hdc, CONST DOCINFO *lpdi);
```

The parameter `hdc` is the handle of the printer device context, and `lpdi` is a pointer to a `DOCINFO` structure:

```
typedef struct
   {int     cbSize;
```

```
    LPCTSTR lpszDocName;
    LPCTSTR lpszOutput;
    LPCTSTR lpszDatatype;
    DWORD   fwType;}
DOCINFO;
```

You should assign `sizeof (DOCINFO)` to the `cbSize` field of this structure, and you should assign a string describing the document you are printing to the `lpszDocName` field. You can assign 0 to the last three fields.

TIP   If you assign the name of a disk file to the `lpszOutput` field of the `DOCINFO` structure, the output will be sent to the disk file rather than the printer. See the documentation on `DOCINFO` for information on the last two fields.

For example, the following code from DrawIt starts a print job:

```
DOCINFO DocInfo =
    {sizeof (DOCINFO),
    "DrawIt Drawing",
    0, 0, 0};
StartDoc (HDCPrn, &DocInfo);
```

To start each page that you want to print, call the `StartPage` API function:

```
int StartPage (HDC hDC);
```

You should then prepare the device context and call the drawing functions as follows:

- Set drawing attributes.
- Create and select graphic objects.
- Call drawing functions.
- Deselect and destroy graphic objects.

(Note that these actions constitute steps 2 through 5 of the basic process for displaying graphics that were described in Chapter 2.) To perform these actions, follow the instructions that were given in the previous chapters.

When you have finished drawing graphics on the current page, call the `EndPage` API function:

```
int EndPage (HDC hdc);
```

If you have another page to print, you should again call `BeginPage`, prepare the device context, and call the drawing functions (see Figure 7.3).

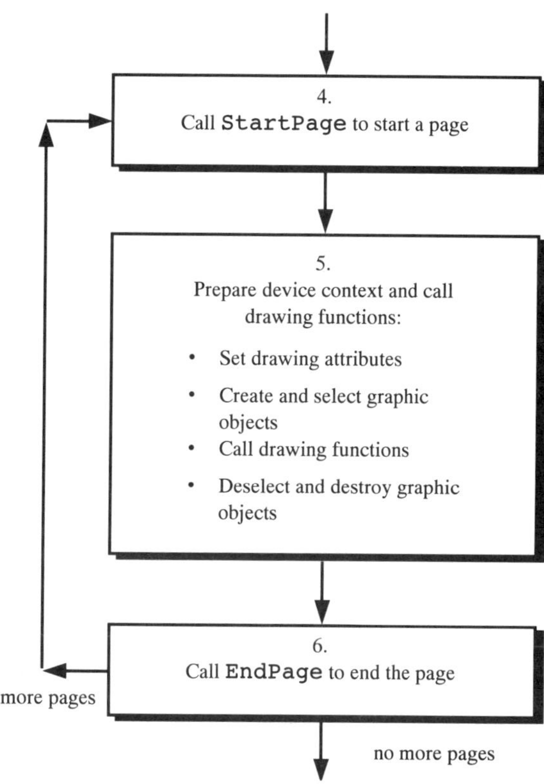

Figure 7.3:   A more detailed description of steps 4, 5, and 6 of the process for printing graphics

Note that when you call the drawing functions to display graphics on a page, the output is stored in memory; it is not actually sent to the printer until you have completed the entire page and called EndPage. Therefore,

FYI   You might think it would be easier to set drawing attributes and select graphic objects only once, before printing all of the pages. However, after you print each page, Windows automatically restores all default drawing attributes and graphic objects. You must therefore set the attributes and select the objects before printing each page. However, to increase the efficiency of your program, you can *create* the graphic objects only once before printing the pages, and then delete them after all pages have been printed.

until you call `EndPage` you can draw graphics at any position on the page, overwrite or erase graphics you have drawn, and so on, just as if you were drawing on a screen.

If a graphics document that your program has created does not fit on a single page, you will have to print it on several pages. To print the first page, you can pass the normal coordinates for each figure; any graphics that fall outside of the page will be clipped. To print each additional page, you can adjust the coordinates of each figure so that unprinted figures are "shifted" onto the page. Alternatively, you can shift the relative position of the figures by calling the `SetViewportOrgEx` API function to move the viewport origin, as explained in Chapter 6 ("Setting the Origins").

TIP   To determine the width and height of the printed page in device units (pixels), you can pass the HORZRES and VERTRES values to the `GetDeviceCaps` API function. To get the width and height in millimeters, pass HORZSIZE and VERTSIZE. Also, you can call the `PtVisible` or `RectVisible` API function (described in the section "Managing a Clipping Region" in Chapter 5) to determine whether a point or rectangle at a particular set of coordinates falls within the boundaries of the page.

FYI   The following are related API functions: `Escape`, `ExtEscape`, and `AbortDoc`.

DRAWIT VERSION 4

DrawIt Version 4 adds the capability of printing the drawing that you create. To start the program, run the file DrawIt.exe in the DrawIt4 subfolder of the folder in which you installed your companion disk.

To print a drawing, choose the Print... command on the File menu, and then choose one of the two scaling options that DrawIt displays (see Figure 7.4):

- Choose "Size on screen" to have DrawIt scale the drawing so that it has the same size and proportions on the printed page that it has on the screen.

- Choose "Full printed page" to have DrawIt scale the drawing so that it fills the entire printed page. This option may change the proportions of figures.

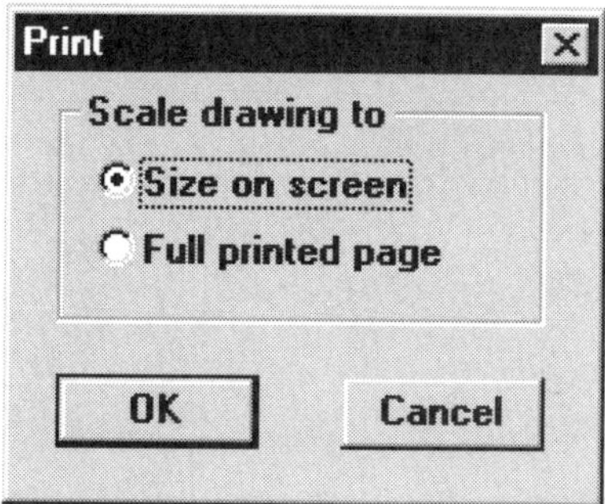

Figure 7.4:   Choosing a scaling option before printing a drawing

While DrawIt is printing the drawing, it displays the Printing dialog box (see Figure 7.5). To stop printing the drawing, click the Cancel Printing button.

For instructions on using the other features of DrawIt, see the DrawIt sections in previous chapters.

The DrawIt Version 4 Program Classes

In addition to the classes included in the previous two DrawIt versions (described in the section "The DrawIt Version 2 Program Classes" in Chapter 4), DrawIt Version 4 defines two classes, listed in Table 7.1.

Scaling Printed Graphics

For simplicity, all versions of the DrawIt program display graphics in the program window using the default `MM_TEXT` mapping mode. As discussed in Chapter 6, if the program also *printed* the graphics using this mapping mode,

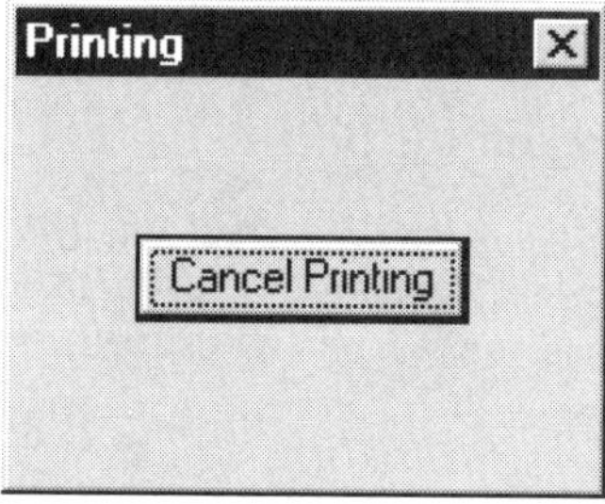

Figure 7.5:   The modeless dialog box displayed during printing, which allows one to cancel the print job

Table 7.1: Additional program classes in DrawIt Version 4

Class	Header and Implementation Files	Purpose
`CCancelDlg`	Dialog.h Dialog.cpp	Manages the Printing modeless dialog box, which is displayed during printing and contains a Cancel Printing button that allows the user to stop printing
`CPrintDlg`	Dialog.h Dialog.cpp	Manages the Print dialog box, which is displayed before printing and allows the user to choose a scaling option

the size of the drawing would vary according to the resolution of the printer; on a laser printer with a resolution of 300 dots per inch or greater, the drawing would be quite small. To avoid this problem, the DrawIt program *scales* the drawing when it is printed so that it has a reasonable size.

To scale the drawing, DrawIt prints using the `MM_ANISOTROPIC` mapping mode (changing the mapping mode is one of the scaling techniques that was discussed in Chapter 6). If the user chooses to scale the drawing so that it has the same size both on the screen and on the printed page, the DrawIt printing function (`CDocument::OnFilePrint` in Document.cpp) executes the following routine:

```
// get pixels per logical inch for screen:
HDC HDCWin = GetDC (MainWnd.mHWnd);
int LogPixelsXWin = GetDeviceCaps (HDCWin, LOGPIXELSX);
int LogPixelsYWin = GetDeviceCaps (HDCWin, LOGPIXELSY);
ReleaseDC (MainWnd.mHWnd, HDCWin);

// get pixels per logical inch for printer:
int LogPixelsXPrn = GetDeviceCaps (HDCPrn, LOGPIXELSX);
int LogPixelsYPrn = GetDeviceCaps (HDCPrn, LOGPIXELSY);

// set mapping mode for printer device context:
SetMapMode (HDCPrn, MM_ANISOTROPIC);
// map this many logical units,
SetWindowExtEx (HDCPrn, LogPixelsXWin, LogPixelsYWin, NULL);
// onto this many device units:
SetViewportExtEx (HDCPrn, LogPixelsXPrn, LogPixelsYPrn, NULL);
```

This routine first uses the API function `GetDeviceCaps` to obtain the number of pixels per inch on the screen and the number of pixels per inch on the printed page. It then passes the screen values to `SetWindowExtEx` and the printer values to `SetViewportExtEx`, so that Windows will transform an inch on the screen to an inch on the printed page. As a result, a figure on the printed page will have the same size and proportions as the figure on the screen.

<table>
<tr><td>**FYI**</td><td>For information on using the `MM_ANISOTROPIC` mapping mode and setting the window and viewport extents, see the section "Using the `MM_ANISOTROPIC` and `MM_ISOTROPIC` Mapping Modes" in Chapter 6.</td></tr>
</table>

If the user chooses to scale the drawing so that it fills the entire printed page, the DrawIt printing function executes the following routine rather than the one above:

```
// get dimensions of drawing (client area of window) in pixels:
RECT RectClient;
GetClientRect (MainWnd.mHWnd, &RectClient);

// get dimensions of printed page in pixels:
int XPrinter = GetDeviceCaps (HDCPrn, HORZRES);
int YPrinter = GetDeviceCaps (HDCPrn, VERTRES);

// set mapping mode for printer device context:
SetMapMode (HDCPrn, MM_ANISOTROPIC);
// map this many logical units,
SetWindowExtEx (HDCPrn, RectClient.right,
   RectClient.bottom, NULL);
// onto this many device units:
SetViewportExtEx (HDCPrn, XPrinter, YPrinter, NULL);
```

DrawIt assumes that the drawing includes the entire client area of the program window regardless of the portion of the window that actually contains figures. The routine first obtains the size of the drawing (that is, the size of the client area of the window) and the size of the printed page, both in pixels. It then passes the figure size to `SetWindowExtEx` and the page size to `SetViewportExtEx`, so that Windows will transform the drawing dimensions into the dimensions of the printed page, causing the drawing to be scaled to fill the entire printed page.

The beauty of these two methods is that the coordinates stored in each drawing object and passed to the drawing functions do not need to be changed. By setting the appropriate mapping mode, the program causes Windows to perform all necessary scaling transformations internally.

The Source Code for the DrawIt Version 4 Printing Functions

The following are the source code listings for the DrawIt Version 4 printing functions: CDocument::OnFilePrint and AbortProc. Both of these functions are defined in the Document.cpp file. Because the code additions to DrawIt Version 4 are relatively minor, this chapter lists only the printing functions. You will find a complete copy of the source code files in the DrawIt4 subfolder of the folder in which you installed the companion disk. You can also refer to the complete printed listings of DrawIt Version 5, given at the end of Chapter 8.

Listing 7.1:   The CDocument::OnFilePrint function from Document.cpp

```
LRESULT CDocument::OnFilePrint (void)
// processes WM_COMMAND / ID_FILE_PRINT messages
   {
   // Step 1: obtain printer device context

   // display the Print dialog box:
   if (PrnDlg.Show () == IDCANCEL)
      return NULL;

   // get description of default printer:
   char PrnInfo [128];
   GetProfileString
      ("windows",
      "device",
      "",
      PrnInfo,
      sizeof (PrnInfo));
   char *PPrnDevice = strtok (PrnInfo, ",");

   // create printer device context:
   HDC HDCPrn = CreateDC (0, PPrnDevice, 0, 0);

   // Step 2: setup abort function, display Cancel dialog box,
   // and disable main window

   mContinuePrint = TRUE; // set "continue" flag
   SetAbortProc (HDCPrn, AbortProc);
   CancelDlg.Create ();
   EnableWindow (MainWnd.mHWnd, FALSE);

   // Step 3: call StartDoc to start print job

   DOCINFO DocInfo =
      {sizeof (DOCINFO),
      "DrawIt Drawing",
      0, 0, 0};
   StartDoc (HDCPrn, &DocInfo);
```

```
// Step 4: call StartPage to start page

StartPage (HDCPrn);

// Step 5: set drawing attributes, select graphic objects,
// and call drawing functions

// scale drawing by setting mapping mode:

// user chose to scale drawing to screen size:
if (PrnDlg.mScreenSize)
    {
    // get pixels per logical inch for screen:
    HDC HDCWin = GetDC (MainWnd.mHWnd);
    int LogPixelsXWin = GetDeviceCaps (HDCWin, LOGPIXELSX);
    int LogPixelsYWin = GetDeviceCaps (HDCWin, LOGPIXELSY);
    ReleaseDC (MainWnd.mHWnd, HDCWin);

    // get pixels per logical inch for printer:
    int LogPixelsXPrn = GetDeviceCaps (HDCPrn, LOGPIXELSX);
    int LogPixelsYPrn = GetDeviceCaps (HDCPrn, LOGPIXELSY);

    // set mapping mode for printer device context:
    SetMapMode (HDCPrn, MM_ANISOTROPIC);
    // map this many logical units,
    SetWindowExtEx (HDCPrn, LogPixelsXWin, LogPixelsYWin,
        NULL);
    // onto this many device units:
    SetViewportExtEx (HDCPrn, LogPixelsXPrn, LogPixelsYPrn,
        NULL);
    }

// user chose to scale drawing to size of full printed page:
else
    {
    // get dimensions of drawing (client area of window) in
    // pixels:
    RECT RectClient;
    GetClientRect (MainWnd.mHWnd, &RectClient);

    // get dimensions of printed page in pixels:
    int XPrinter = GetDeviceCaps (HDCPrn, HORZRES);
    int YPrinter = GetDeviceCaps (HDCPrn, VERTRES);

    // set mapping mode for printer device context:
    SetMapMode (HDCPrn, MM_ANISOTROPIC);
    // map this many logical units,
    SetWindowExtEx (HDCPrn, RectClient.right,
        RectClient.bottom, NULL);
    // onto this many device units:
    SetViewportExtEx (HDCPrn, XPrinter, YPrinter, NULL);
    }
```

```cpp
// draw all figures stored in document:
FigCell *PCell = mPFirstFig;
while (PCell)
   {
   PCell->PFigure->Draw (HDCPrn);
   PCell = PCell->PNextFig;
   }

// Step 6: call EndPage to end page

EndPage (HDCPrn);

// Step 7: call EndDoc to end print job

EndDoc (HDCPrn);

// Step 8: enable main window and remove Cancel dialog box

EnableWindow (MainWnd.mHWnd, TRUE);
DestroyWindow (CancelDlg.mHDlg);

// Step 9: delete printer device context

DeleteDC (HDCPrn);
return NULL;
}
```

Listing 7.2:　The `AbortProc` function from Document.cpp

```cpp
// "Abort Function" for printing:

BOOL CALLBACK AbortProc (HDC HDc, int Code)
   {
   // process any pending messages:
   MSG Msg;
   while (PeekMessage ((LPMSG)&Msg, (HWND)NULL, 0, 0, PM_REMOVE))
      {
      // process messages for Cancel modeless dialog box:
      if (!IsDialogMessage (CancelDlg.mHDlg, (LPMSG)&Msg))
         // dispatch other messages:
         DispatchMessage ((LPMSG) &Msg);
      }
   return Document.mContinuePrint;
   }
```

CHAPTER **8**

STORING GRAPHICS IN ENHANCED METAFILES

A *metafile* is a Windows data structure that stores graphics in memory or in a disk file. It consists of a series of records that describe each of the graphics API function calls required to generate the graphics. You can use a metafile to store graphics temporarily in memory or permanently in a disk file, or to exchange graphics with other programs through the Windows Clipboard.

Windows 95 provides two types of metafile: *Windows* and *enhanced*. Windows metafiles are those that were provided by previous versions of Windows. Enhanced metafiles are new to the Win32 API; they support the new graphics features such as paths and Bézier curves, and also store additional information that makes it possible to display graphics in a device-independent manner. This chapter discusses only enhanced metafiles; throughout the chapter, the term *metafile* refers to *enhanced metafile* unless it is otherwise qualified.

The chapter also presents the fifth and final version of the DrawIt program, which provides standard New, Open, Save, and Save As commands on its File menu for saving and retrieving drawings from disk files. The drawings are stored on disk in the enhanced metafile format.

RECORDING AN ENHANCED METAFILE

To create a metafile, you *record* a series of calls to API drawing functions, using the following procedure:

1. Call `CreateEnhMetaFile`, which returns a handle to a metafile device context.
2. Call all of the API graphics functions that are required to generate the graphics that you want to store in the metafile. Pass each function the metafile device context handle that you obtained in step 1.
3. Call `CloseEnhMetaFile` to delete the metafile device context.

`CreateEnhMetaFile` has the following form:

```
HDC CreateEnhMetaFile
   (HDC hdcRef,
    LPCTSTR lpFilename,
    CONST RECT *lpRect,
    LPCTSTR lpDescription);
```

The `hdcRef` parameter is the handle of a *reference* device context, which is a device context for the device on which you normally display the graphics that you are now storing. Passing `NULL` is equivalent to passing the handle of a device context for the current display device. For example, because DrawIt normally displays graphics on the screen, it passes the value `NULL`.

If you want to store the metafile permanently in a disk file, assign the `lpFileName` parameter the address of a string containing the name of the file. You should give the file the .emf extension so that other Windows programs that read metafiles will recognize it as an enhanced metafile (in contrast, Windows metafiles are normally given the extension .wmf). If you want to store the metafile temporarily in memory, assign `NULL` to the `lpFileName` parameter.

You can assign the `lpRect` parameter the address of a `RECT` structure containing the overall dimensions of the drawing you are storing in the metafile. You must specify the dimensions in 0.01 mm units. Recall from Chapter 6 that these are the units used by the `MM_HIMETRIC` mapping mode. If you are using the `MM_TEXT` mapping mode, you can call the `GetDeviceCaps` API function to obtain the number of pixels per millimeter on the device surface (pass `HORZRES` and `VERTRES` to obtain the number of pixels, and pass `HORZSIZE` and `VERTSIZE` to obtain the number of millimeters). Alternatively, if you assign `NULL` to `lpRect`, Windows will calculate the dimensions of the smallest rectangle bounding the graphics that you store in the metafile.

Windows stores the resolution of the reference device and the overall size of the graphics within the first record of the metafile (the *header*) in both pixels and millimeters. This information is derived from the values that you pass to the hdcRef and lpRect parameters. In general, this information allows Windows and application programs to display and process the metafile in a device-independent manner (later, you will see how a program can extract this information from a metafile).

Finally, you can assign the lpDescription parameter a string containing a description of the metafile. This description should consist of the name of the application, followed by a NULL character, followed by a name describing the drawing you are saving, followed by two NULL characters. For example, when the DrawIt program records a metafile, it passes the string Description, which it defines as follows:

```
static const char Description [] =
    "Windows95 DrawIt Program\0DrawIt Drawing\0";
```

(C++ automatically appends a second NULL character to the end of the string.) DrawIt assigns this description to all metafiles that it saves so that when it opens a metafile it can determine whether the metafile is one that it has created. If you do not want to specify a metafile description, assign NULL to lpDescription.

CreateEnhMetaFile returns a handle to a metafile device context. You should now call all graphics API functions that are required to generate the graphics that you want to store in the metafile, passing each the metafile device context handle. You can set drawing attributes, create and select graphic objects, call drawing functions, and then deselect and delete graphic objects (that is, you can perform steps 2 through 5 of the basic procedure for drawing graphics described in Chapter 2). Use the techniques that were given in the previous chapters. Rather than generating graphics output on a device, however, each function call adds a record to the metafile. The DrawIt program, for example, stores the current drawing in a metafile by passing the metafile device context handle to the Draw member function of each of the C++ figure objects that it stores (Draw is the *same* function that DrawIt calls to display a figure in the window or to print it).

When you have finished generating the metafile, delete the metafile device context by passing its handle to the CloseEnhMetaFile API function:

```
HENHMETAFILE CloseEnhMetaFile (HDC hdc);
```

`CloseEnhMetaFile` returns a handle to the *metafile itself* (do not confuse a handle to a metafile device context with a handle to a metafile). You can use this handle to display the metafile and perform other operations on it, as described later in the chapter (in the section "Using an Enhanced Metafile").

When you are done using the metafile, you should pass its handle to the `DeleteEnhMetaFile` API function:

```
BOOL DeleteEnhMetaFile (HENHMETAFILE hemf);
```

If the metafile is stored in memory, `DeleteEnhMetaFile` deletes it. If, however, the metafile is stored in a disk file, `DeleteEnhMetaFile` releases the handle but *does not delete the metafile disk file*. In either case, you can no longer use the handle.

In the DrawIt Version 5 program (given at the end of the chapter), when the user chooses the Save or Save As... command on the File menu, the program creates a metafile on disk, which stores all of the figures currently displayed in the program window. The code that creates the metafile is in the `CDocument::Save` function in the Document.cpp source file.

FYI   The following is a related API function: `GdiComment`.

Opening an Enhanced Metafile

If a metafile has been stored in a disk file, any program can obtain a handle to it by calling the `GetEnhMetaFile` API function,

```
HENHMETAFILE GetEnhMetaFile (LPCTSTR lpszMetaFile);
```

where `lpszMetaFile` is the address of a string containing the name of the disk file. The handle that `GetEnhMetaFile` returns is the same as a metafile handle returned by `CloseEnhMetaFile`. That is, you can use it to display or perform other operations on the metafile, and you should pass it to `DeleteEnhMetaFile` when you are done with it.

In the DrawIt Version 5 program, when the user chooses the Open... command on the File menu, the program calls `GetEnhMetaFile` to open the specified metafile disk file. The code that calls `GetEnhMetaFile` is in the `CDocument::OnFileOpen` function in Document.cpp.

USING AN ENHANCED METAFILE

Once you have obtained a handle to a metafile, you can use it to display the metafile, obtain a copy of the metafile data, obtain a copy of the metafile header, and perform other operations on the metafile.

To display a metafile, call the `PlayEnhMetaFile` API function:

```
BOOL PlayEnhMetaFile
   (HDC hdc,
    HENHMETAFILE hemf,
    CONST RECT *lpRect);
```

The parameter `hdc` is the handle of the device context on which you want to display the metafile, `hemf` is the handle of the metafile, and `lpRect` is a pointer to a `RECT` structure that contains the logical coordinates of the area on the device in which you want to display the metafile. `PlayEnhMetaFile` will execute all of the function calls stored in the metafile, scaling the graphics as necessary to fit the drawing within the area you specified in the `lpRect` parameter.

FYI

The metafile that you play may contain records that set drawing attributes, create graphic objects, or select graphic objects. When `PlayEnhMetaFile` has finished executing the metafile functions, however, it *restores* all of the device context's drawing attributes and graphic objects to their former states. Also, if the metafile creates a graphic object but does not call `DeleteObject` to delete it, `PlayEnhMetaFile` automatically deletes the object.

When a program has a metafile handle, Windows stores internally all of the data for the metafile (that is, the binary data for the metafile records). You can obtain a copy of this data by calling the API function `GetEnhMetaFileBits`,

```
UINT GetEnhMetaFileBits
   (HENHMETAFILE hemf,
    UINT cbBuffer,
    LPBYTE lpbBuffer);
```

where `hemf` is the handle of the metafile, `lpbBuffer` is the address of the memory buffer that receives the data, and `cbBuffer` is the size of this buffer in bytes. If you assign 0 to `lpbBuffer`, the function will return the buffer size that is required to hold the metafile data.

Obtaining the binary data for a metafile allows your program to store the metafile as part of a document's data in memory or on disk (rather than storing it in a separate .emf file). For example, if a word processor document contained graphics in metafile format, the program can store the metafile data as an integral part of the document data. You can later use the metafile data to obtain a metafile handle by calling the API function `SetEnhMetaFileBits`:

```
HENHMETAFILE SetEnhMetaFileBits
   (UINT cbBuffer,
    CONST BYTE *lpData);
```

The parameter `lpData` is the address of the memory area containing the metafile data, and the parameter `cbBuffer` is the size of this data in bytes. `SetEnhMetaFileBits` creates a metafile that is stored *in memory* (not in a disk file) and returns a handle to it.

The first record in a metafile (known as the *header*) contains general information such as the original size of the graphics stored in the metafile, the size of the metafile and the number of records in it, the description specified when the metafile was created (if any), and the resolution of the reference device specified when the metafile was created. You can obtain a copy of this record by calling the `GetEnhMetaFileHeader` API function,

```
UINT GetEnhMetaFileHeader
   (HENHMETAFILE hemf,
    UINT cbBuffer,
    LPENHMETAHEADER lpemh);
```

where `hemf` is the metafile handle, `lpemh` is a pointer to a `ENHMETAHEADER` structure defined in your program, and `cbBuffer` is the size of this structure. `GetEnhMetaFileHeader` will copy the first metafile record to the `ENHMETAHEADER` structure. See the documentation on `ENHMETAHEADER` for an explanation of each field.

You can obtain a copy of the metafile description, if any, that is stored in the first record by calling the `GetEnhMetaFileDescription` API function:

```
UINT GetEnhMetaFileDescription
   (HENHMETAFILE hemf,
    UINT cchBuffer,
    LPTSTR lpszDescription);
```

This function copies characters from the metafile description to the buffer pointed to by the `lpszDescription` parameter, until it has reached the end of the description or has copied the number of characters specified by the `cchBuffer` parameter. It returns the number of characters it has copied, or 0 if no description was specified when the metafile was created.

The format of the metafile description was described previously (in the section "Recording an Enhanced Metafile"). For example, when the DrawIt program first opens a metafile contained in a disk file (in response to the Open command on the File menu), it calls `GetEnhMetaFileDescription` to obtain the metafile description. It then compares this description to the standard description that it specifies when it creates a metafile. If the descriptions do not match, DrawIt refuses to open the metafile (the reason that DrawIt does not open metafiles created by other applications is explained in the next section). The code that calls `GetEnhMetaFileDescription` is in the function `CDocument::OnFileOpen` in Document.cpp.

The API provides several other functions for working with metafiles. For example, you can call `CopyEnhMetaFile` to obtain a handle to a copy of a metafile. Also, you can convert an enhanced metafile to a Windows metafile by calling `GetWinMetaFileBits`, and you can convert a Windows metafile to an enhanced metafile by calling `SetWinMetaFileBits`.

FYI The following is a related API function: `GetEnhMetaFilePalletteEntries`.

EDITING AN ENHANCED METAFILE

Although creating and displaying a metafile is easy, editing its contents can be a complex undertaking. Directly modifying the metafile data is a difficult way to edit a metafile because it requires intimate knowledge of the metafile data format. The DrawIt Version 5 program uses a different approach, which can be summarized in the following steps:

1. When the user opens a metafile disk file, DrawIt converts the metafile graphics to the native DrawIt format (that is, a linked list containing a C++ object for each figure).

2. As the user adds, deletes, or modifies the figures, DrawIt modifies the graphic data that is stored in the native DrawIt format (as in previous versions of the program).

3. When the user saves the drawing, DrawIt converts the drawing back to metafile format by calling `CreateEnhMetaFile` to create a new metafile that overwrites the original disk file; then DrawIt passes the metafile device context handle to the Draw function for each graphic object (this step takes place in the `CDocument::Save` function in Document.cpp).

The remainder of this section discusses step 1: converting the metafile to the native DrawIt data format. DrawIt does this by reading each metafile record and creating a C++ figure object for each function call recorded in the metafile that draws a figure.

To read the metafile records, the `CDocument::OnFileOpen` function (in Document.cpp) passes the handle of the metafile that it has opened to the `EnumEnhMetaFile` API function. For each record in the metafile, `EnumEnhMetaFile` calls the `ConvertRecord` callback function (also defined in Document.cpp), passing it the metafile record data.

The records in a metafile have variable lengths and data types. Every record, however, begins with a `DWORD` code that indicates the type of the record (the API header file Wingdi.h, which is included in the standard Windows.h header file, defines a constant for each possible record code). The first metafile record has the code `EMR_HEADER`. For most of the other records in the metafile, the code indicates the specific graphics function call that is stored in each record. For example, a record with the `EMR_SETROP2` code stores a call to the `SetRop2` function, an `EMR_CREATEBRUSHINDIRECT` record stores a `CreateBrushIndirect` function call, a `EMR_ELLIPSE` record stores an `Ellipse` function call, and so on.

In each metafile record that stores a graphics function, the `DWORD` record code is followed by the size of the record and the values of the parameters that were passed to the function when the metafile was recorded. For each record type, Wingdi.h defines a structure (and a pointer to the structure) that programs can use to access the parameter values. For example, to access the values in an `EMR_ELLIPSE` metafile record, it defines the following types:

```
typedef struct tagEMRELLIPSE
    {
    EMR    emr;
    RECTL rclBox;
    }
EMRELLIPSE, *PEMRELLIPSE;
```

The `emr` field stores the `DWORD` record code (in `emr.iType`) and the `DWORD` value containing the size of the record (in `emr.nSize`). (The `emr` field is common to all of the metafile structures.) The `rclBox` field stores the two pairs of coordinates that were passed to the `Ellipse` function.

The DrawIt `ConvertRecord` function uses a `switch` statement to test the value of the record code and branch to the appropriate routine for handling the record (as discussed shortly, it does not handle all of the record types). The routine that handles the record performs one of the following three actions, depending upon the type of graphics function that is stored in the record:

- If the function sets a drawing attribute, `ConvertRecord` stores the value of the attribute.

- If the function creates a graphic object (that is, a pen or brush), `ConvertRecord` stores the features of that object.

- If the function draws a figure, `ConvertRecord` creates an object of the appropriate C++ class (for example, an instance of `CEllipse` for the `Ellipse` function) and saves this object in the drawing, just as if the user had drawn the figure. It stores within this object the drawing function parameter values as well as the previously saved drawing attributes and graphic object features (saved in the two steps above).

Notice that the `ConvertRecord` function in the DrawIt program processes *only* those metafile records that set drawing attributes, create graphic objects, or draw figures that the program normally supports. DrawIt refuses to read a metafile that has been created by another application because such a metafile would likely contain records that DrawIt cannot process (resulting in a drawing that would not contain all of the figures or features stored in the metafile). A program that could read and edit *any* metafile would have to support virtually every drawing attribute, graphic object, and figure that can be generated with the Win32 API; writing such a program would be a substantial task.

FYI   The following is a related API function:
`PlayEnhMetaFileRecord`.

DRAWIT VERSION 5

DrawIt Version 5 adds the standard file I/O commands to the File menu. To run the program, execute the file DrawIt.exe in the DrawIt5 subfolder within the folder in which you installed the companion disk file.

You use the new commands on the File menu as follows:

- Choose the New command to create a new, blank drawing and discard any drawing currently displayed in the window.
- Choose Open... to open an existing drawing file. DrawIt will display the standard Open dialog box (Figure 8.1). The file you select must be a metafile that was created previously by DrawIt.
- Choose Save to save the current drawing under its existing file name (if the file has not already been saved, DrawIt will perform the Save As command).
- Choose Save As... to save a copy of the current drawing under a new file name. DrawIt will display the standard Save As dialog box, which allows you to choose a file name and location.

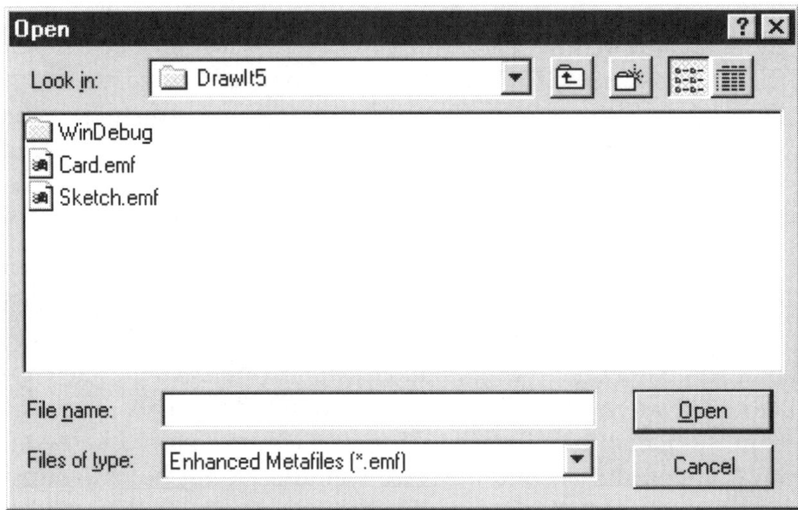

Figure 8.1:   The standard Open dialog box that DrawIt displays in response to the Open command on the File menu. You must choose a metafile that was created by DrawIt.

If performing any of the above operations, or quitting the program, will cause you to lose unsaved data, DrawIt will warn you and give you the opportunity to save your work.

The DrawIt Version 5 Source Code

The following are the DrawIt Version 5 source code listings. You will find a copy of these listings in the DrawIt5 subfolder of the folder containing your companion disk files.

Listing 8.1:   DrawIt.cpp

```
//////////////////////////////////////////////////////////////////////////////
//                                                                            //
// DrawIt.cpp: Main program object declarations and WinMain                   //
//             program entry function.                                        //
//                                                                            //
//////////////////////////////////////////////////////////////////////////////

#define STRICT
#include <windows.h>

// header files for main program classes:
#include "app.h"
```

```cpp
#include "figure.h"
#include "mainwnd.h"
#include "document.h"
#include "dialog.h"

// main program objects:
CApp       App;
CMainWnd   MainWnd;
CDocument  Document;
CAboutDlg  AboutDlg;
CAttrDlg   AttrDlg;
CBrushDlg  BrushDlg;
CCancelDlg CancelDlg;
CPenDlg    PenDlg;
CPrintDlg  PrnDlg;

/////////////////////////////////////////////////////////////////////////
// program entry function:                                              //
/////////////////////////////////////////////////////////////////////////

int APIENTRY WinMain
   (HINSTANCE HInstCurrent,
    HINSTANCE HInstPrevious,
    LPSTR     CmdLine,
    int       CmdShow)
    {
    MSG Msg;

    // store program informaton in application object:
    App.Initialize (HInstCurrent, CmdLine);

    // register class for main program window:
    if (!MainWnd.RegisterClass ())
       return 0;

    // create and display main program window:
    if (!MainWnd.Create ())
       return 0;

    // main message loop:
    while (GetMessage (&Msg, NULL, NULL, NULL))
       {
       TranslateMessage (&Msg);
       DispatchMessage (&Msg);
       }

    // return "application-defined exit code":
    return Msg.wParam;
    }
```

Listing 8.2:   App.h

```cpp
///////////////////////////////////////////////////////////////////////
//                                                                     //
// App.h: Header file for application class.                           //
//                                                                     //
///////////////////////////////////////////////////////////////////////

class CApp
{
public:
   HINSTANCE mHInstance; // handle of program instance
   LPSTR     mCmdLine;   // pointer to program command line

   void Initialize (HINSTANCE HInstCurrent, LPSTR CmdLine)
   // saves application values
      {
      mHInstance = HInstCurrent;
      mCmdLine = CmdLine;
      }
};
```

Listing 8.3:   MainWnd.h

```cpp
///////////////////////////////////////////////////////////////////////
//                                                                     //
// MainWnd.h: Header file for main window class.                       //
//                                                                     //
///////////////////////////////////////////////////////////////////////

#define WINWIDTH   350  // dimensions of main program window
#define WINHEIGHT  400
#define SIZEHANDLE 10   // size of scaling handle

class CMainWnd
{
public:
   enum // current drawing mode
      {
      ModeNone,
      ModeDragging,
      ModeMark1,
      ModeMark2,
      ModeMoving,
      ModeScaling
      }
   mMode;

   CFigure *mCurrentFig;  // pointer to current figure object
   HPEN mHPenDotted;       // handle to dotted pen
```

```cpp
    HWND mHWnd;                // main window handle
    CFigure *mSelectedFig; // currently selected figure (if any)
    BOOL mSelecting;          // Figure / Select menu command chosen

    CMainWnd (void);
    void CancelDrag (void);
    BOOL Create (void);
    BOOL RegisterClass (void);

    // message-handling functions:
    LRESULT OnClose (void);
    LRESULT OnDestroy (void);
    LRESULT OnFigure (WORD MenuCommandID);
    LRESULT OnHelpAbout (void);
    LRESULT OnInitMenuPopup (HMENU HMenu, UINT MenuPosition);
    LRESULT OnKeyDown (int VirtKeyCode);
    LRESULT OnKillFocus (void);
    LRESULT OnLButtonDown (WORD XCursor, WORD YCursor);
    LRESULT OnLButtonUp (WORD XCursor, WORD YCursor);
    LRESULT OnMouseMove (WORD XCursor, WORD YCursor);
    LRESULT OnOptionsAttributes (void);
    LRESULT OnOptionsBrush (void);
    LRESULT OnOptionsPen (void);
    LRESULT OnPaint (void);
    LRESULT OnQueryEndSession (void);

protected:
    UINT mCurrentFigID;     // ID of menu command for curr. figure
    RECT mRectPrev;         // previous rectangle in moving figure
    int mXOrig, mYOrig;     // original point when moving figure
    int mXPrev, mYPrev;     // previous point when moving figure

    void DrawSelection (void);
    void DrawSelectRect (HDC HDc, RECT *PRect);
};
```

Listing 8.4:   MainWnd.cpp

```cpp
///////////////////////////////////////////////////////////////////////
//                                                                     //
// MainWnd.cpp: Implementation file for main window class.             //
//                                                                     //
///////////////////////////////////////////////////////////////////////

#define STRICT
#include <windows.h>
#include <afxres.h>
```

```cpp
#include "resource.h"

#include "app.h"
#include "figure.h"
#include "mainwnd.h"
#include "document.h"
#include "dialog.h"

extern CApp      App;
extern CMainWnd  MainWnd;
extern CDocument Document;
extern CAboutDlg AboutDlg;
extern CAttrDlg  AttrDlg;
extern CBrushDlg BrushDlg;
extern CPenDlg   PenDlg;

LRESULT CALLBACK MainWndProc (HWND HWnd, UINT Msg, WPARAM WParam,
   LPARAM LParam);

/////////////////////////////////////////////////////////////////////////////
// CMainWnd constructor:                                                     //
/////////////////////////////////////////////////////////////////////////////

CMainWnd::CMainWnd (void)
   {
   mCurrentFig = new CLine;
   mCurrentFigID = ID_FIGURE_LINE;
   mHPenDotted = CreatePen (PS_DOT, 1, RGB (0,0,0));
   mMode = ModeNone;
   mSelectedFig = 0;
   mSelecting = FALSE;
   }

/////////////////////////////////////////////////////////////////////////////
// CMainWnd public member functions:                                         //
/////////////////////////////////////////////////////////////////////////////

void CMainWnd::CancelDrag (void)
// stops a figure move operation; called only if mSelecting is
// TRUE
   {
   if (mMode != ModeMoving)
      return;

   // end drag operation:
   ReleaseCapture ();
   ClipCursor (NULL);

   // erase temporary bounding rectangle:
   InvalidateRect (mHWnd, &mRectPrev, TRUE);
   RECT Rect = mSelectedFig->GetBoundRect ();
   InvalidateRect (mHWnd, &Rect, TRUE);
```

```cpp
    mMode = ModeNone;
    return;
    };

BOOL CMainWnd::Create (void)
// creates and displays main program window; returns TRUE on
// success or FALSE on error
    {
    // create main program window and save handle:
    mHWnd = CreateWindow
        ("DemoClass",
        "DrawIt - untitled",
        WS_OVERLAPPED | WS_SYSMENU | WS_MINIMIZEBOX,
        CW_USEDEFAULT,
        CW_USEDEFAULT,
        WINWIDTH,
        WINHEIGHT,
        NULL,
        NULL,
        App.mHInstance,
        NULL);
    if (!mHWnd)
        return FALSE;

    // display window:
    ShowWindow
        (mHWnd,
        SW_SHOWDEFAULT);
    return TRUE;
    }

BOOL CMainWnd::RegisterClass (void)
// registers class for main program window; returns TRUE on
// success or FALSE on error
    {
    WNDCLASS WC;

    // specify class information:
    WC.style = CS_DBLCLKS;
    WC.lpfnWndProc = MainWndProc;
    WC.cbClsExtra = 0;
    WC.cbWndExtra = 0;
    WC.hInstance = App.mHInstance;
    WC.hIcon = LoadIcon (App.mHInstance,
        MAKEINTRESOURCE (IDI_ICON1));
    WC.hCursor = 0;
    WC.hbrBackground = (HBRUSH)GetStockObject (WHITE_BRUSH);
    WC.lpszMenuName = MAKEINTRESOURCE (IDR_MENU1);
    WC.lpszClassName = "DemoClass";

    // register class:
    return (BOOL)::RegisterClass (&WC);
    }
```

```cpp
void CMainWnd::DrawSelection (void)
// obtains device context and draws selection rectangle around
// bounding rectangle of currently selected figure; second call
// erases rectangle
    {
    if (!mSelectedFig)
       return;

    RECT Rect = mSelectedFig->GetBoundRect ();
    HDC HDc = GetDC (mHWnd);
    DrawSelectRect (HDc, &Rect);
    ReleaseDC (mHWnd, HDc);
    return;
    }

void CMainWnd::DrawSelectRect (HDC HDc, RECT *PRect)
// draws the selection rectangle and scaling handle
    {
    // draw selection rectangle:
    DrawFocusRect (HDc, PRect);

    // draw sizing handle:
    SetROP2 (HDc, R2_NOT);
    Rectangle
       (HDc,
        PRect->right - SIZEHANDLE,
        PRect->bottom - SIZEHANDLE,
        PRect->right,
        PRect->bottom);
    return;
    }

//////////////////////////////////////////////////////////////////////////////
// window procedure for main window:                                         //
//////////////////////////////////////////////////////////////////////////////

LRESULT CALLBACK MainWndProc
    (HWND   HWnd,
     UINT   Msg,
     WPARAM WParam,
     LPARAM LParam)
    {
    switch (Msg)
       {
       case WM_CLOSE: // user chose Close command or button
          return MainWnd.OnClose ();

       case WM_COMMAND: // user chose a menu command
          switch (LOWORD (WParam))
             {
             case ID_HELP  ABOUT: // user chose Help/About
                return MainWnd.OnHelpAbout ();

             case ID_FIGURE_SELECT: // user chose command on
```

```cpp
            case ID_FIGURE_ARC:  // Figure menu
            case ID_FIGURE_BEZIER:
            case ID_FIGURE_CHORD:
            case ID_FIGURE_ELLIPSE:
            case ID_FIGURE_LINE:
            case ID_FIGURE_PIE:
            case ID_FIGURE_POLYGON:
            case ID_FIGURE_POLYLINE:
            case ID_FIGURE_RECTANGLE:
            case ID_FIGURE_ROUNDRECT:
                return MainWnd.OnFigure (LOWORD (WParam));

            case ID_FILE_NEW:  // user chose File/New
                return Document.OnFileNew ();

            case ID_FILE_OPEN: // user chose File/Open
                return Document.OnFileOpen ();

            case ID_FILE_PRINT: // user chose File/Print
                return Document.OnFilePrint ();

            case ID_FILE_SAVE: // user chose File/Save
                return Document.OnFileSave ();

            case ID_FILE_SAVE_AS: // user chose File/Save As...
                return Document.OnFileSaveAs ();

            case ID_OPTIONS_ATTRIBUTES: // user chose
                                        // Options/Attributes
                return MainWnd.OnOptionsAttributes ();

            case ID_OPTIONS_BRUSH: // user chose Options/Brush
                return MainWnd.OnOptionsBrush ();

            case ID_OPTIONS_PEN: // user chose Options/Pen
                return MainWnd.OnOptionsPen ();

            default:
                // default processing for other commands:
                return DefWindowProc (HWnd, Msg, WParam, LParam);
        }

    case WM_DESTROY: // DestroyWindow was called
        return MainWnd.OnDestroy ();

    case WM_INITMENUPOPUP: // user opened a popup menu
        return MainWnd.OnInitMenuPopup ((HMENU)WParam,
            (UINT)LOWORD(LParam));

    case WM_KEYDOWN: // user pressed a key
        return MainWnd.OnKeyDown ((int)WParam);

    case WM_KILLFOCUS: // program window has lost focus
```

```
        return MainWnd.OnKillFocus ();

    case WM_LBUTTONDBLCLK: // user double-clicked left mouse
                           // button
        return MainWnd.mCurrentFig->OnLButtonDblClk
           (LOWORD (LParam), HIWORD (LParam));

    case WM_LBUTTONDOWN: // user pressed left button
        return MainWnd.OnLButtonDown
           (LOWORD (LParam), HIWORD (LParam));

    case WM_LBUTTONUP:  // user released left button
        return MainWnd.OnLButtonUp
           (LOWORD (LParam), HIWORD (LParam));

    case WM_MOUSEMOVE:  // user moved mouse pointer
        return MainWnd.OnMouseMove
           (LOWORD (LParam), HIWORD (LParam));

    case WM_PAINT: // window needs painting or repainting
        return MainWnd.OnPaint ();

    case WM_QUERYENDSESSION: // user wants to quit Windows
        return MainWnd.OnQueryEndSession ();

    default:
        // default processing for all other messages:
        return DefWindowProc (HWnd, Msg, WParam, LParam);
    }
  }

////////////////////////////////////////////////////////////////////////////
// CMainWnd message handling member functions:                            //
////////////////////////////////////////////////////////////////////////////

LRESULT CMainWnd::OnClose (void)
// processes WM_CLOSE messages
   {
   // allow user to save any unsaved data; destroy window if
   // user does not cancel operation:
   if (Document.CheckSave ())
      DestroyWindow (mHWnd);
   return NULL;
   }

LRESULT CMainWnd::OnDestroy (void)
// processes WM_DESTROY messages
   {
   PostQuitMessage (0);    // post a WM_QUIT message to
   return NULL;            // cause message loop to exit
   }

LRESULT CMainWnd::OnFigure (WORD MenuCommandID)
// processes WM_COMMAND messages from ALL commands on Figure menu
```

```cpp
{
// exit if user chose same command previously chosen:
if (mCurrentFigID == MenuCommandID)
   return NULL;

// move check mark to chosen command:
CheckMenuItem (GetMenu (mHWnd), mCurrentFigID, MF_UNCHECKED);
mCurrentFigID = MenuCommandID;
CheckMenuItem (GetMenu (mHWnd), mCurrentFigID, MF_CHECKED);

// cancel any drawing or drag operation:
if (mSelecting)
   CancelDrag ();
else
   mCurrentFig->Cancel ();

// cancel current selection, if any:
DrawSelection ();
mSelectedFig = 0;

// if user chose Select command, set flag and exit:
if (MenuCommandID == ID_FIGURE_SELECT)
   {
   mSelecting = TRUE;
   return NULL;
   }

// a figure command was chosen; start by setting mSelecting
// flag to FALSE:
mSelecting = FALSE;

// delete figure object:
delete mCurrentFig;

// create figure object for new figure type:
switch (MenuCommandID)
   {
   case ID_FIGURE_ARC:
      mCurrentFig = new CArc;
      break;

   case ID_FIGURE_BEZIER:
      mCurrentFig = new CBezier;
      break;

   case ID_FIGURE_CHORD:
      mCurrentFig = new CChord;
      break;

   case ID_FIGURE_ELLIPSE:
      mCurrentFig = new CEllipse;
      break;
```

```
      case ID_FIGURE_LINE:
         mCurrentFig = new CLine;
         break;

      case ID_FIGURE_PIE:
         mCurrentFig = new CPie;
         break;

      case ID_FIGURE_POLYGON:
         mCurrentFig = new CPolygon;
         break;

      case ID_FIGURE_POLYLINE:
         mCurrentFig = new CPolyline;
         break;

      case ID_FIGURE_RECTANGLE:
         mCurrentFig = new CRectangle;
         break;

      case ID_FIGURE_ROUNDRECT:
         mCurrentFig = new CRoundRect;
         break;
      }
   return NULL;
   }

LRESULT CMainWnd::OnHelpAbout (void)
// processes WM_COMMAND / ID_HELP_ABOUT messages
   {
   AboutDlg.Show (); // display About dialog box
   return NULL;
   }

LRESULT CMainWnd::OnInitMenuPopup (HMENU HMenu,
   UINT MenuPosition)
// processes WM_INITMENUPOPUP messages
   {
   if (MenuPosition != 2)
      return NULL;

   // modify Options menu commands based upon whether a figure
   // is selected and type of figure selected:
   if (mSelectedFig)
      {
      if (mSelectedFig->IsBrush ())
         ModifyMenu (HMenu, ID_OPTIONS_BRUSH, MF_STRING |
         MF_ENABLED, ID_OPTIONS_BRUSH, "Figure Brush...");
      else
         ModifyMenu (HMenu, ID_OPTIONS_BRUSH,
         MF_STRING | MF_GRAYED, ID_OPTIONS_BRUSH, "Brush...");
      ModifyMenu (HMenu, ID_OPTIONS_PEN, MF_STRING,
         ID_OPTIONS_PEN, "Figure Pen...");
```

```cpp
      ModifyMenu (HMenu, ID_OPTIONS_ATTRIBUTES, MF_STRING,
         ID_OPTIONS_ATTRIBUTES, "Figure Attributes...");
      }
   else
      {
      ModifyMenu (HMenu, ID_OPTIONS_BRUSH, MF_STRING |
         MF_ENABLED, ID_OPTIONS_BRUSH, "Default Brush...");
      ModifyMenu (HMenu, ID_OPTIONS_PEN, MF_STRING,
         ID_OPTIONS_PEN, "Default Pen...");
      ModifyMenu (HMenu, ID_OPTIONS_ATTRIBUTES, MF_STRING,
         ID_OPTIONS_ATTRIBUTES, "Default Attributes...");
      }
   return NULL;
   }

LRESULT CMainWnd::OnKeyDown (int VirtKeyCode)
// processes WM_KEYDOWN messages
   {
   // user pressed Esc when not in selecting mode:
   if (VirtKeyCode == VK_ESCAPE && !mSelecting)
      {
      mCurrentFig->Cancel (); // cancel drawing operation
      }

   // user pressed Tab in selecting mode but is NOT dragging a
   // figure:
   else if (VirtKeyCode == VK_TAB && mSelecting &&
           mMode == ModeNone)
      {
      // if figure is currently selected get next/previous one:
      if (mSelectedFig)
         {
         DrawSelection (); // erase old selection rectangle

         // if Shift is pressed, select previous figure:
         if (GetKeyState (VK_SHIFT) < 0)
            mSelectedFig = Document.GetPreviousFig(mSelectedFig);

         // if Shift not pressed, select next figure:
         else
            mSelectedFig = Document.GetNextFig (mSelectedFig);
         }

      // if no figure selected, select the first one, if any:
      else if (Document.mPFirstFig)
         mSelectedFig = Document.mPFirstFig->PFigure;

      // draw the selection rectangle:
      DrawSelection ();
      }

   // user pressed Delete key, a figure is selected, and user is
   // NOT dragging a figure:
```

```cpp
    else if (VirtKeyCode == VK_DELETE && mSelectedFig &&
            mMode == ModeNone)
      {
      // erase the figure from window:
      RECT Rect = mSelectedFig->GetBoundRect ();
      InvalidateRect (mHWnd, &Rect, TRUE);

      // remove figure object from linked list and delete it:
      Document.DeleteFigure (mSelectedFig);
      delete mSelectedFig;
      mSelectedFig = 0;
      }
   return NULL;
   }

LRESULT CMainWnd::OnKillFocus (void)
// processes WM_KILLFOCUS messages
   {
   // cancel any drawing or drag operation:
   if (mSelecting)
      CancelDrag ();
   else
      mCurrentFig->Cancel ();
   return NULL;
   }

LRESULT CMainWnd::OnLButtonDown (WORD XCursor, WORD YCursor)
// processes WM_LBUTTONDOWN messages
   {
   // if Figure/Select command not chosen, have current figure
   // object handle the message:
   if (!mSelecting)
      return mCurrentFig->OnLButtonDown (XCursor, YCursor);

   POINT Point = {XCursor, YCursor};
   RECT RectBound;

   // if a selected figure is under the cursor, begin a move
   // or scale operation:
   if (mSelectedFig)
      {
      RectBound = mSelectedFig->GetBoundRect ();
      if (PtInRect (&RectBound, Point))
         {
         // save current coordinates:
         mRectPrev = RectBound;
         mXOrig = XCursor; mYOrig = YCursor;
         mXPrev = XCursor; mYPrev = YCursor;

         // start drag:
         SetCapture (mHWnd);
         RECT RectClip;
         GetClientRect (mHWnd, &RectClip);
```

```cpp
        // if cursor in scaling handle, start scaling;
        // otherwise, start moving:
        RECT RectHandle =
            {RectBound.right - SIZEHANDLE,
             RectBound.bottom - SIZEHANDLE,
             RectBound.right,
             RectBound.bottom};
        if (PtInRect (&RectHandle, Point))
            {
            // adjust clipping rectangle to keep user from
            // dragging scaling handle to left or above figure:
            RectClip.left = RectBound.left + XCursor -
                RectHandle.left;
            RectClip.top = RectBound.top + YCursor -
                RectHandle.top;
            mMode = ModeScaling;
            }
        else
            mMode = ModeMoving;

        // clip cursor:
        ClientToScreen (mHWnd, (LPPOINT)&RectClip);
        ClientToScreen (mHWnd, (LPPOINT)&RectClip.right);
        ClipCursor (&RectClip);

        return NULL;
        }
    // cancel existing selection:
    DrawSelection ();
    mSelectedFig = 0;
    }

// no selected figure is under cursor; therefore, select the
// figure under cursor, if any:

// perform hit test on all figures stored in document:
FigCell *PCell = Document.mPFirstFig;
while (PCell)
    {
    RectBound = PCell->PFigure->GetBoundRect ();
    // if figure found under cursor, select it:
    if (PtInRect (&RectBound, Point))
        {
        mSelectedFig = PCell->PFigure;
        DrawSelection ();
        return NULL;
        }
    PCell = PCell->PNextFig;
    }
return NULL;
}


LRESULT CMainWnd::OnLButtonUp (WORD XCursor, WORD YCursor)
```

```cpp
// processes WM_LBUTTONUP messages
   {
   // if Figure/Select command not chosen, have current figure
   // object handle the message:
   if (!mSelecting)
      return mCurrentFig->OnLButtonUp (XCursor, YCursor);

   // if user was moving or scaling a figure, end operation:
   if (mMode == ModeMoving   mMode == ModeScaling)
      {
      // end drag:
      ReleaseCapture ();
      ClipCursor (NULL);

      // erase previous temporary rectangle:
      HDC HDc = GetDC (mHWnd);
      DrawSelectRect (HDc, &mRectPrev);
      ReleaseDC (mHWnd, HDc);

      // move or scale the figure and force redrawing of affected
      // areas:
      RECT Rect = mSelectedFig->GetBoundRect ();
      InvalidateRect (mHWnd, &Rect, TRUE);
      if (mMode == ModeMoving)
         {
         mSelectedFig->Move (XCursor - mXOrig, YCursor - mYOrig);
         // place moved figure on top (i.e., at end of list):
         Document.AddFigure (mSelectedFig, FALSE);
         Document.DeleteFigure (mSelectedFig);
         }
      else
         mSelectedFig->Scale(XCursor - mXOrig, YCursor - mYOrig);
      Rect = mSelectedFig->GetBoundRect ();
      InvalidateRect (mHWnd, &Rect, TRUE);

      mMode = ModeNone;
      }
   return NULL;
   }

LRESULT CMainWnd::OnMouseMove (WORD XCursor, WORD YCursor)
// processes WM_MOUSEMOVE messages
   {
   // if Figure/Select command not chosen, have current figure
   // object handle the message:
   if (!mSelecting)
      {
      SetCursor (LoadCursor (NULL, IDC_CROSS));
      return mCurrentFig->OnMouseMove (XCursor, YCursor);
      }

   // if user is moving or scaling a figure, update selection
   // rectangle and set cursor:
```

```cpp
   if (mMode == ModeMoving || mMode == ModeScaling)
      {
      HDC HDc = GetDC (mHWnd);
      DrawSelectRect (HDc, &mRectPrev);
      mRectPrev.right += XCursor - mXPrev;
      mRectPrev.bottom += YCursor - mYPrev;

      if (mMode == ModeMoving)
         {
         mRectPrev.left += XCursor - mXPrev;
         mRectPrev.top += YCursor - mYPrev;
         SetCursor (LoadCursor (NULL, IDC_SIZE));
         }
      else
         SetCursor (LoadCursor (NULL, IDC_SIZENWSE));

      DrawSelectRect (HDc, &mRectPrev);
      mXPrev = XCursor;
      mYPrev = YCursor;
      ReleaseDC (mHWnd, HDc);
      return NULL;
      }

   // user is not moving or scaling a figure, just set cursor:

   // if a figure is selected, must test for cursor within
   // bounding rectangle or scaling box:
   if (mSelectedFig)
      {
      // test for cursor in bounding rectangle:
      RECT Rect = mSelectedFig->GetBoundRect ();
      POINT Point = {XCursor, YCursor};
      if (PtInRect (&Rect, Point))
         {
         // test for cursor in scaling handle:
         Rect.left = Rect.right - SIZEHANDLE;
         Rect.top = Rect.bottom - SIZEHANDLE;
         if (PtInRect (&Rect, Point))
            SetCursor (LoadCursor (NULL, IDC_SIZENWSE));
         else
            SetCursor (LoadCursor (NULL, IDC_SIZE));
         return NULL;
         }
      }

   // in selecting mode, but cursor not within selected figure:
   SetCursor (LoadCursor (NULL, IDC_ARROW));
   return NULL;
   }

LRESULT CMainWnd::OnOptionsAttributes (void)
// processes WM_COMMAND / ID_OPTIONS_ATTRIBUTES messages
   {
```

```cpp
   AttrDlg.Show (); // display Attributes dialog box
   return NULL;
   }

LRESULT CMainWnd::OnOptionsBrush (void)
// processes WM_COMMAND / ID_OPTIONS_BRUSH messages
   {
   BrushDlg.Show (); // display Brush dialog box
   return NULL;
   }

LRESULT CMainWnd::OnOptionsPen (void)
// processes WM_COMMAND / ID_OPTIONS_PEN messages
   {
   PenDlg.Show (); // display Pen dialog box
   return NULL;
   }

LRESULT CMainWnd::OnPaint (void)
// processes WM_PAINT messages
   {
   HDC HDCPaint;
   PAINTSTRUCT PaintStruct;
   RECT RectBound;

   // cancel any drawing or drag operation:
   if (mSelecting)
      CancelDrag ();
   else
      mCurrentFig->Cancel ();

   // initiate painting and obtain a device context:
   HDCPaint = BeginPaint (mHWnd, &PaintStruct);

   // save state of device context:
   SaveDC (HDCPaint);

   // draw all figures stored in document:
   FigCell *PCell = Document.mPFirstFig;
   while (PCell)
      {
      RectBound = PCell->PFigure->GetBoundRect ();
      if (RectVisible (HDCPaint, &RectBound))
         PCell->PFigure->Draw (HDCPaint);
      PCell = PCell->PNextFig;
      }

   // restore the saved device context:
   RestoreDC (HDCPaint, -1);

   if (mSelectedFig)
      {
      RectBound = mSelectedFig->GetBoundRect ();
```

```
         DrawSelectRect (HDCPaint, &RectBound);
         }

   // terminate painting and release device context:
   EndPaint (mHWnd, &PaintStruct);
   return NULL;
   }


LRESULT CMainWnd::OnQueryEndSession (void)
// processes WM_QUERYENDSESSION messages
   {
   // allow user to save unsaved data; if user cancels operation,
   // stop the Windows termination:
   return Document.CheckSave ();
   }
```

Listing 8.5:   Figure.h

```
///////////////////////////////////////////////////////////////////////
//                                                                     //
// Figure.h: Header file for figure classes.                          //
//                                                                     //
///////////////////////////////////////////////////////////////////////

class CFigure // abstract base class for all figure classes
{
public:
   // description of pen used to draw figure:
   COLORREF mPenColor;
   DWORD mPenStyle;
   DWORD mPenType;
   DWORD mPenWidth;

   // drawing attributes:
   COLORREF mBkColor;
   int mBkMode;
   int mBrushXOrg;
   int mBrushYOrg;
   int mFillMode;
   int mMixMode;

   // basic figure dimensions:
   int mX1, mY1, mX2, mY2;

   CFigure (void);
   void Cancel (void);
   virtual CFigure *CreateObject (void) = 0;
   virtual void DefineBrush (COLORREF BrushColor,
      LONG BrushHatchPattern, DWORD BrushStyle)
      {
      return;
```

```cpp
        }
    virtual void Draw (HDC HDc);
    virtual RECT GetBoundRect (void);
    virtual void GetBrushDescription (COLORREF *PBrushColor,
       LONG *PBrushHatchPattern, DWORD *PBrushStyle)
        {
        return;
        }
    virtual BOOL IsBrush (void)
        {
        return FALSE;
        }
    virtual void Move (int DeltaX, int DeltaY);
    virtual void PureDraw (HDC HDc) = 0;
    virtual void Scale (int DeltaX, int DeltaY);

    // message-handling functions:
    virtual LRESULT OnLButtonDblClk (WORD XCursor, WORD YCursor)
        {
        return NULL;
        }
    virtual LRESULT OnLButtonDown (WORD XCursor, WORD YCursor) =0;
    virtual LRESULT OnLButtonUp (WORD XCursor, WORD YCursor) = 0;
    virtual LRESULT OnMouseMove (WORD XCursor, WORD YCursor) = 0;

protected:
    virtual HBRUSH GetBrush (void)
        {
        return 0;
        }
    HDC GetTempDC (void);
    int Max4 (int A, int B, int C, int D)
        {
        return max (max (max (A, B), C), D);
        }
    int Min4 (int A, int B, int C, int D)
        {
        return min (min (min (A, B), C), D);
        }
    void StartDrag (void);
};

class CArc : public CFigure
{
public:
    int mX3, mY3, mX4, mY4; // additional arc dimensions

    virtual CFigure *CreateObject (void)
        {
        return new CArc;
        }
    virtual RECT GetBoundRect (void);
    virtual void Move (int DeltaX, int DeltaY);
```

```cpp
   virtual void PureDraw (HDC HDc);
   virtual void Scale (int DeltaX, int DeltaY);

   // message-handling functions:
   virtual LRESULT OnLButtonDown (WORD XCursor, WORD YCursor);
   virtual LRESULT OnLButtonUp (WORD XCursor, WORD YCursor);
   virtual LRESULT OnMouseMove (WORD XCursor, WORD YCursor);
};

class CChord : public CArc
{
public:
   virtual CFigure *CreateObject (void)
      {
      return new CChord;
      }
   virtual void DefineBrush (COLORREF BrushColor,
      LONG BrushHatchPattern, DWORD BrushStyle)
      {
      mBrushColor = BrushColor;
      mBrushHatchPattern = BrushHatchPattern;
      mBrushStyle = BrushStyle;
      }
   virtual void GetBrushDescription (COLORREF *PBrushColor,
      LONG *PBrushHatchPattern, DWORD *PBrushStyle)
      {
      *PBrushColor = mBrushColor;
      *PBrushHatchPattern = mBrushHatchPattern;
      *PBrushStyle = mBrushStyle;
      return;
      }
   virtual BOOL IsBrush (void)
      {
      return TRUE;
      }
   virtual void PureDraw (HDC HDc);

protected:
   // description of brush used to draw figure:
   COLORREF mBrushColor;
   LONG mBrushHatchPattern;
   DWORD mBrushStyle;

   virtual HBRUSH GetBrush (void);
};

class CPie : public CChord
{
public:
   virtual CFigure *CreateObject (void)
      {
      return new CPie;
      }
```

```cpp
    virtual void PureDraw (HDC HDc);
};

class CBezier : public CFigure
{
public:
    int mX3, mY3, mX4, mY4; // additional bezier curve dimensions

    virtual CFigure *CreateObject (void)
        {
        return new CBezier;
        }
    virtual RECT GetBoundRect (void);
    virtual void Move (int DeltaX, int DeltaY);
    virtual void PureDraw (HDC HDc);
    virtual void Scale (int DeltaX, int DeltaY);

    // message-handling functions:
    virtual LRESULT OnLButtonDown (WORD XCursor, WORD YCursor);
    virtual LRESULT OnLButtonUp (WORD XCursor, WORD YCursor);
    virtual LRESULT OnMouseMove (WORD XCursor, WORD YCursor);
};

class CLine : public CFigure
{
public:
    virtual CFigure *CreateObject (void)
        {
        return new CLine;
        }
    virtual void PureDraw (HDC HDc);

    // message-handling functions:
    virtual LRESULT OnLButtonDown (WORD XCursor, WORD YCursor);
    virtual LRESULT OnLButtonUp (WORD XCursor, WORD YCursor);
    virtual LRESULT OnMouseMove (WORD XCursor, WORD YCursor);
};

class CRectangle : public CLine
{
public:
    virtual CFigure *CreateObject (void)
        {
        return new CRectangle;
        }
    virtual void DefineBrush (COLORREF BrushColor,
        LONG BrushHatchPattern, DWORD BrushStyle)
        {
        mBrushColor = BrushColor;
        mBrushHatchPattern = BrushHatchPattern;
        mBrushStyle = BrushStyle;
        }
    virtual void GetBrushDescription (COLORREF *PBrushColor,
```

```
          LONG *PBrushHatchPattern, DWORD *PBrushStyle)
          {
          *PBrushColor = mBrushColor;
          *PBrushHatchPattern = mBrushHatchPattern;
          *PBrushStyle = mBrushStyle;
          return;
          }
    virtual BOOL IsBrush (void)
          {
          return TRUE;
          }
    virtual void PureDraw (HDC HDc);

protected:
    // description of brush used to draw figure:
    COLORREF mBrushColor;
    LONG mBrushHatchPattern;
    DWORD mBrushStyle;
    virtual HBRUSH GetBrush (void);
};

class CRoundRect : public CRectangle
{
public:
    virtual CFigure *CreateObject (void)
        {
        return new CRoundRect;
        }
    virtual void PureDraw (HDC HDc);
};

class CEllipse : public CRectangle
{
public:
    virtual CFigure *CreateObject (void)
        {
        return new CEllipse;
        }
    virtual void PureDraw (HDC HDc);
};

#define MAXPOINTS 25 // maximum number of vertices in polyline

class CPolyline : public CFigure
{
public:
    int mNumPoints;              // number of points stored
    POINT mPoints [MAXPOINTS]; // stores coordinates of vertices

    virtual CFigure *CreateObject (void)
        {
        return new CPolyline;
        }
```

```cpp
   virtual RECT GetBoundRect (void);
   virtual void Move (int DeltaX, int DeltaY);
   virtual void PureDraw (HDC HDc);
   virtual void Scale (int DeltaX, int DeltaY);

   // message-handling functions:
   virtual LRESULT OnLButtonDblClk (WORD XCursor, WORD YCursor);
   virtual LRESULT OnLButtonDown (WORD XCursor, WORD YCursor);
   virtual LRESULT OnLButtonUp (WORD XCursor, WORD YCursor);
   virtual LRESULT OnMouseMove (WORD XCursor, WORD YCursor);

};

class CPolygon : public CPolyline
{
public:
   virtual CFigure *CreateObject (void)
       {
       return new CPolygon;
       }
   virtual void DefineBrush (COLORREF BrushColor,
       LONG BrushHatchPattern, DWORD BrushStyle)
       {
       mBrushColor = BrushColor;
       mBrushHatchPattern = BrushHatchPattern;
       mBrushStyle = BrushStyle;
       }
   virtual void GetBrushDescription (COLORREF *PBrushColor,
       LONG *PBrushHatchPattern, DWORD *PBrushStyle)
       {
       *PBrushColor = mBrushColor;
       *PBrushHatchPattern = mBrushHatchPattern;
       *PBrushStyle = mBrushStyle;
       return;
       }
   virtual BOOL IsBrush (void)
       {
       return TRUE;
       }
   virtual void PureDraw (HDC HDc);

protected:
   // description of brush used to draw figure:
   COLORREF mBrushColor;
   LONG mBrushHatchPattern;
   DWORD mBrushStyle;

   virtual HBRUSH GetBrush (void);
};
```

Listing 8.6:   Figure.cpp

```cpp
////////////////////////////////////////////////////////////////////////
//                                                                      //
// Figure.cpp: Implementaton file for figure classes.                   //
//                                                                      //
////////////////////////////////////////////////////////////////////////

#define STRICT
#include <windows.h>
#include <limits.h>
#include <math.h>
#include "resource.h"

#include "figure.h"
#include "mainwnd.h"
#include "document.h"

extern CMainWnd MainWnd;
extern CDocument Document;

#define PI 3.14159265

////////////////////////////////////////////////////////////////////////
// CFigure:                                                             //
////////////////////////////////////////////////////////////////////////

CFigure::CFigure (void)
   {
   mPenWidth = 1;
   }

void CFigure::Cancel (void)
// cancels a drawing operation
   {
   if (MainWnd.mMode == MainWnd.ModeNone)
      return;

   // erase temporary line(s) and redraw affected area of window:
   RECT Rect = GetBoundRect ();
   InvalidateRect (MainWnd.mHWnd, &Rect, TRUE);

   // end dragging operation:
   if (MainWnd.mMode == MainWnd.ModeDragging)
      {
      ReleaseCapture ();
      ClipCursor (NULL);
      }
   MainWnd.mMode = MainWnd.ModeNone;
   return;
   }

void CFigure::Draw (HDC HDc)
```

```cpp
// prepares the device context AND draws the current object
    {
    // set drawing attributes:
    SetBkColor (HDc, mBkColor);
    SetBkMode (HDc, mBkMode);
    SetBrushOrgEx (HDc, mBrushXOrg, mBrushYOrg, NULL);
    SetPolyFillMode (HDc, mFillMode);
    SetROP2 (HDc, mMixMode);

    // create and select object's pen:
    LOGBRUSH LogBrush = {BS_SOLID, mPenColor, 0};
    HPEN HPen = ExtCreatePen
        (mPenType | mPenStyle,
        mPenWidth,
        &LogBrush,
        0,
        0);
    HPEN HPenOld = (HPEN)SelectObject (HDc, HPen);

    // get and select object's brush, if any:
    HBRUSH HBrush = GetBrush ();
    HBRUSH HBrushOld;
    if (HBrush)
        HBrushOld = (HBRUSH)SelectObject (HDc, HBrush);

    // call the appropriate drawing function for the object:
    PureDraw (HDc);

    // deselect and destroy brush, if any:
    if (HBrush)
        {
        SelectObject (HDc, HBrushOld);
        DeleteObject (HBrush);
        }

    // deselect and destroy pen:
    SelectObject (HDc, HPenOld);
    DeleteObject (HPen);
    return;
    }

RECT CFigure::GetBoundRect (void)
// returns rectangle bounding figure
    {
    RECT Rect =
        {min (mX1, mX2),
         min (mY1, mY2),
         max (mX1, mX2),
         max (mY1, mY2)};

    // expand rectangle to accommodate wide lines and margin:
    int LineAdd = (mPenWidth-1) / 2 + (mPenWidth-1) % 2 + 3;
    InflateRect (&Rect, LineAdd, LineAdd);
```

```cpp
   // make rectangle at least as large as scaling handle:
   Rect.right = max (Rect.right, Rect.left + SIZEHANDLE);
   Rect.bottom = max (Rect.bottom, Rect.top + SIZEHANDLE);

   return Rect;
   }

HDC CFigure::GetTempDC (void)
// returns a device-context handle for drawing temporary lines
   {
   HDC HDCClient = GetDC (MainWnd.mHWnd);
   SetROP2 (HDCClient, R2_NOT);
   HPEN HPenOld = (HPEN)SelectObject
      (HDCClient, MainWnd.mHPenDotted);
   SetBkMode (HDCClient, TRANSPARENT);
   SelectObject (HDCClient, GetStockObject (NULL_BRUSH));
   return HDCClient;
   }

void CFigure::Move (int DeltaX, int DeltaY)
// moves the figure by the specified offsets
   {
   mX1 += DeltaX;
   mY1 += DeltaY;
   mX2 += DeltaX;
   mY2 += DeltaY;

   // set modified flag:
   Document.mModified = TRUE;
   return;
   }

void CFigure::Scale (int DeltaX, int DeltaY)
// scales the figure by the specified offsets
   {
   if (mX1 < mX2)
      mX2 += DeltaX;
   else if (mX2 < mX1)
      mX1 += DeltaX;

   if (mY1 < mY2)
      mY2 += DeltaY;
   else if (mY2 < mY1)
      mY1 += DeltaY;

   // set modified flag:
   Document.mModified = TRUE;
   return;
   }

void CFigure::StartDrag (void)
// initializes a drag operation for drawing a figure
   {
```

```cpp
    // capture mouse messages:
    SetCapture (MainWnd.mHWnd);

    // confine mouse cursor to client area of window:
    RECT Rect;
    GetClientRect (MainWnd.mHWnd, &Rect);
    ClientToScreen (MainWnd.mHWnd, (LPPOINT)&Rect);
    ClientToScreen (MainWnd.mHWnd, (LPPOINT)&Rect.right);
    ClipCursor (&Rect);
    return;
    }

////////////////////////////////////////////////////////////////////////
// CArc:                                                                //
////////////////////////////////////////////////////////////////////////

RECT CArc::GetBoundRect (void)
// returns rectangle bounding arc
    {
    // store dimensions of rectangle bounding the full ellipse:
    RECT Rect =
        {min (mX1, mX2),
         min (mY1, mY2),
         max (mX1, mX2),
         max (mY1, mY2)};

    // if user has completed drawing the figure, calculate the
    // rectangle that bounds only those quadrants of the ellipse
    // that contain the figure:
    if (MainWnd.mSelecting   MainWnd.mMode == MainWnd.ModeNone)
        {
        BOOL ContainsEnd, ContainsStart;
        BOOL Started = FALSE;

        // calculate midpoint of ellipse:
        int XMid = (Rect.left + Rect.right) / 2;
        int YMid = (Rect.top + Rect.bottom) / 2;

        // store information on the four ellipse quadrants:
        struct
            {
            double StartAngle; // starting angle of quadrant
            double EndAngle;   // ending angle of quadrant
            RECT Rect;         // dimensions of quadrant
            }
        Quadrants [4] =
            {{-PI,      -PI/2.0, {Rect.left,YMid,XMid,Rect.bottom}},
             {-PI/2.0, 0.0,      {XMid,YMid,Rect.right,Rect.bottom}},
             {0.0,      PI/2.0,  {XMid,Rect.top,Rect.right,YMid}},
             {PI/2.0,   PI,      {Rect.left,Rect.top,XMid,YMid}}};

        // calculate angles of starting and ending lines of arc:
        double ThetaStart = atan2 (YMid - mY3, mX3 - XMid);
        double ThetaEnd   = atan2 (YMid - mY4, mX4 - XMid);
```

```cpp
      // initialize bounding rectangle to null:
      Rect.left = Rect.top = Rect.right = Rect.bottom = 0;

      // find the ellipse quadrant that contains starting line:
      for (int Q = 0; Q <= 3; ++Q)
         {
         ContainsStart = ThetaStart>=Quadrants [Q].StartAngle &&
            ThetaStart < Quadrants [Q].EndAngle;
         if (ContainsStart)
            break;
         }

      // add ellipse quadrants to bounding rectangle until the
      // ending line is encountered:
      for (int i = 1; i <= 3; ++i)
         {
         UnionRect (&Rect, &Rect, &Quadrants [Q].Rect);
         ContainsEnd = ThetaEnd >= Quadrants [Q].StartAngle &&
            ThetaEnd < Quadrants [Q].EndAngle;
         if (ContainsEnd && !(i == 1 && ThetaEnd <= ThetaStart))
            break;
         Q = (Q + 1) % 4;
         }
      }

   // expand rectangle to accommodate wide lines and margin:
   int LineAdd = (mPenWidth-1) / 2 + (mPenWidth-1) % 2 + 3;
   InflateRect (&Rect, LineAdd, LineAdd);

   return Rect;
   }

void CArc::Move (int DeltaX, int DeltaY)
// moves the arc by the specified offsets
   {
   mX1 += DeltaX;
   mY1 += DeltaY;
   mX2 += DeltaX;
   mY2 += DeltaY;
   mX3 += DeltaX;
   mY3 += DeltaY;
   mX4 += DeltaX;
   mY4 += DeltaY;

   // set modified flag:
   Document.mModified = TRUE;
   return;
   }

void CArc::PureDraw (HDC HDc)
// draws the arc
   {
   Arc (HDc, mX1, mY1, mX2, mY2, mX3, mY3, mX4, mY4);
```

```cpp
    return;
    }

void CArc::Scale (int DeltaX, int DeltaY)
// scales the arc by the specified offsets
    {
    int *PXMin, *PXMax, *PYMin, *PYMax;

    // get pointers to max and min coordinates of bounding rect:
    if (mX2 > mX1)
        {
        PXMin = &mX1;
        PXMax = &mX2;
        }
    else
        {
        PXMin = &mX2;
        PXMax = &mX1;
        }
    if (mY2 > mY1)
        {
        PYMin = &mY1;
        PYMax = &mY2;
        }
    else
        {
        PYMin = &mY2;
        PYMax = &mY1;
        }

    // calculate the angles of the starting and ending lines:
    int XMid = (*PXMin + *PXMax) / 2;
    int YMid = (*PYMin + *PYMax) / 2;
    double ThetaStart = atan2 (YMid - mY3, mX3 - XMid);
    double ThetaEnd   = atan2 (YMid - mY4, mX4 - XMid);

    // assign new values to coordinates of bounding rectangle,
    // preserving the size of scaling rectangle:
    RECT Rect = GetBoundRect ();
    if (Rect.left < *PXMin && Rect.right > *PXMax)
        {
        *PXMax += DeltaX;
        }
    else if (Rect.left < *PXMin)
        {
        *PXMax += 2 * DeltaX;
        }
    else
        {
        *PXMin -= DeltaX;
        *PXMax += DeltaX;
        }

    if (Rect.top < *PYMin && Rect.bottom > *PYMax)
```

```
          {
          *PYMax += DeltaY;
          }
      else if (Rect.top < *PYMin)
          {
          *PYMax += 2 * DeltaY;
          }
      else
          {
          *PYMin -= DeltaY;
          *PYMax += DeltaY;
          }

      // assign new starting and ending points so that the starting
      // and ending lines have the SAME angles as before scaling:
      XMid = (*PXMin + *PXMax) / 2;
      YMid = (*PYMin + *PYMax) / 2;

      mX3 = XMid + (int)(100.0 * cos (ThetaStart));
      mY3 = YMid - (int)(100.0 * sin (ThetaStart));

      mX4 = XMid + (int)(100.0 * cos (ThetaEnd));
      mY4 = YMid - (int)(100.0 * sin (ThetaEnd));

      // set modified flag:
      Document.mModified = TRUE;
      return;
      }

LRESULT CArc::OnLButtonDown (WORD XCursor, WORD YCursor)
// processes WM_LBUTTONDOWN messages
   {
   switch (MainWnd.mMode)
      {
      case MainWnd.ModeNone:    // draw bounding ellipse
         StartDrag ();
         mX1 = XCursor; mY1 = YCursor;
         mX2 = XCursor; mY2 = YCursor;
         MainWnd.mMode = MainWnd.ModeDragging;
         break;

      case MainWnd.ModeMark1:  // mark start of arc
         mX3 = XCursor; mY3 = YCursor;
         MainWnd.mMode = MainWnd.ModeMark2;
         break;

      case MainWnd.ModeMark2:  // mark end of arc
         // erase temporary ellipse:
         HDC HDCClient = GetTempDC ();
         Ellipse (HDCClient, mX1, mY1, mX2, mY2);

         // add arc to document:
         mX4 = XCursor; mY4 = YCursor;
```

```
          Document.AddFigure (this, TRUE);
          MainWnd.mCurrentFig = CreateObject ();

          // draw arc:
          Draw (HDCClient);
          ReleaseDC (MainWnd.mHWnd, HDCClient);

          MainWnd.mMode = MainWnd.ModeNone;
          break;
      }
   return NULL;
   }

LRESULT CArc::OnLButtonUp (WORD XCursor, WORD YCursor)
// processes WM_LBUTTONUP messages
   {
   if (MainWnd.mMode != MainWnd.ModeDragging)
      return NULL;

   // end drag operation:
   ReleaseCapture ();
   ClipCursor (NULL);

   // erase old temporary ellipse / draw new temporary ellipse:
   HDC HDCClient = GetTempDC ();
   Ellipse (HDCClient, mX1, mY1, mX2, mY2);
   Ellipse (HDCClient, mX1, mY1, XCursor, YCursor);
   ReleaseDC (MainWnd.mHWnd, HDCClient);

   // save new coordinates / stop drawing if ellipse is trivial:
   mX2 = XCursor; mY2 = YCursor;
   if (mX1 == mX2 && mY1 == mY2)
      MainWnd.mMode = MainWnd.ModeNone;
   else
      MainWnd.mMode = MainWnd.ModeMark1;
   return NULL;
   }

LRESULT CArc::OnMouseMove (WORD XCursor, WORD YCursor)
// processes WM_MOUSEMOVE messages
   {
   if (MainWnd.mMode != MainWnd.ModeDragging)
      return NULL;

   // erase old temporary ellipse / draw new temporary ellipse:
   HDC HDCClient = GetTempDC ();
   Ellipse (HDCClient, mX1, mY1, mX2, mY2);
   Ellipse (HDCClient, mX1, mY1, XCursor, YCursor);
   ReleaseDC (MainWnd.mHWnd, HDCClient);

   // save new coordinates:
   mX2 = XCursor; mY2 = YCursor;
   return NULL;
 }
```

```
//////////////////////////////////////////////////////////////////////
// CChord:                                                            //
//////////////////////////////////////////////////////////////////////

HBRUSH CChord::GetBrush (void)
   // returns a handle to a brush for the chord
   {
   LOGBRUSH LB =
      {mBrushStyle,
       mBrushColor,
       mBrushHatchPattern};
   return CreateBrushIndirect (&LB);
   }

void CChord::PureDraw (HDC HDc)
// draws the chord
   {
   Chord (HDc, mX1, mY1, mX2, mY2, mX3, mY3, mX4, mY4);
   return;
   }


//////////////////////////////////////////////////////////////////////
// CPie:                                                              //
//////////////////////////////////////////////////////////////////////

void CPie::PureDraw (HDC HDc)
// draws the pie
   {
   Pie (HDc, mX1, mY1, mX2, mY2, mX3, mY3, mX4, mY4);
   return;
   }


//////////////////////////////////////////////////////////////////////
// CBezier:                                                           //
//////////////////////////////////////////////////////////////////////

RECT CBezier::GetBoundRect (void)
// returns rectangle bounding the Bezier curve
   {
   RECT Rect =
      {Min4 (mX1, mX2, mX3, mX4),
       Min4 (mY1, mY2, mY3, mY4),
       Max4 (mX1, mX2, mX3, mX4),
       Max4 (mY1, mY2, mY3, mY4)};

   // expand rectangle to accommodate wide lines and margin:
   int LineAdd = (mPenWidth-1) / 2 + (mPenWidth-1) % 2 + 3;
   InflateRect (&Rect, LineAdd, LineAdd);
   return Rect;
   }

void CBezier::Move (int DeltaX, int DeltaY)
// moves the bezier curve by the specified offsets
   {
```

```cpp
   mX1 += DeltaX;
   mY1 += DeltaY;
   mX2 += DeltaX;
   mY2 += DeltaY;
   mX3 += DeltaX;
   mY3 += DeltaY;
   mX4 += DeltaX;
   mY4 += DeltaY;

   // set modified flag:
   Document.mModified = TRUE;
   return;
   }

void CBezier::PureDraw (HDC HDc)
// draws the Bezier curve
   {
   POINT Points [4] =
      {{mX1, mY1},
       {mX2, mY2},
       {mX3, mY3},
       {mX4, mY4}};
   PolyBezier (HDc, Points, 4);
   return;
   }

void CBezier::Scale (int DeltaX, int DeltaY)
// scales the bezier curve by the specified offsets
   {
   // get minimum and maximum coordinates:
   int XMin = Min4 (mX1, mX2, mX3, mX4);
   int XMax = Max4 (mX1, mX2, mX3, mX4);
   int YMin = Min4 (mY1, mY2, mY3, mY4);
   int YMax = Max4 (mY1, mY2, mY3, mY4);

   // calculate scaling factors:
   double XScaleFact = (double)(XMax - XMin + DeltaX) /
                       (double)(XMax - XMin);
   double YScaleFact = (double)(YMax - YMin + DeltaY) /
                       (double)(YMax - YMin);

   // use scaling factors to calculate new positions of points:
   mX1 = (int)(XMin + XScaleFact * (mX1 - XMin));
   mX2 = (int)(XMin + XScaleFact * (mX2 - XMin));
   mX3 = (int)(XMin + XScaleFact * (mX3 - XMin));
   mX4 = (int)(XMin + XScaleFact * (mX4 - XMin));

   mY1 = (int)(YMin + YScaleFact * (mY1 - YMin));
   mY2 = (int)(YMin + YScaleFact * (mY2 - YMin));
   mY3 = (int)(YMin + YScaleFact * (mY3 - YMin));
   mY4 = (int)(YMin + YScaleFact * (mY4 - YMin));

   // set modified flag:
   Document.mModified = TRUE;
```

```
   return;
   }

LRESULT CBezier::OnLButtonDown (WORD XCursor, WORD YCursor)
// processes WM_LBUTTONDOWN messages
   {
   HDC HDCClient;

   switch (MainWnd.mMode)
   {
      case MainWnd.ModeNone: // draw straight line
         StartDrag ();
         mX1 = XCursor; mY1 = YCursor;
         mX2 = XCursor; mY2 = YCursor;
         mX3 = XCursor; mY3 = YCursor;
         mX4 = XCursor; mY4 = YCursor;

         MainWnd.mMode = MainWnd.ModeDragging;
         break;

      case MainWnd.ModeMark1: // mark first control point
         // erase straight line / draw temporary bezier:
         HDCClient = GetTempDC ();
         MoveToEx (HDCClient, mX1, mY1, 0);
         LineTo (HDCClient, mX4, mY4);
         mX2 = XCursor; mY2 = YCursor;
         mX3 = XCursor; mY3 = YCursor;
         PureDraw (HDCClient);
         ReleaseDC (MainWnd.mHWnd, HDCClient);

         MainWnd.mMode = MainWnd.ModeMark2;
         break;

      case MainWnd.ModeMark2: // mark second control point
         // erase temporary bezier:
         HDCClient = GetTempDC ();
         PureDraw (HDCClient);

         // add bezier to document and draw it:
         mX3 = XCursor; mY3 = YCursor;
         Document.AddFigure (this, TRUE);
         MainWnd.mCurrentFig = CreateObject ();
         Draw (HDCClient);
         ReleaseDC (MainWnd.mHWnd, HDCClient);

         MainWnd.mMode = MainWnd.ModeNone;
         break;
      }
   return NULL;
   }

LRESULT CBezier::OnLButtonUp (WORD XCursor, WORD YCursor)
// processes WM_LBUTTONUP messages
   {
```

```cpp
   if (MainWnd.mMode != MainWnd.ModeDragging)
      return NULL;

   // end drag operation:
   ReleaseCapture ();
   ClipCursor (NULL);

   // erase old temp. straight line / draw new one:
   HDC HDCClient = GetTempDC ();
   MoveToEx (HDCClient, mX1, mY1, 0);
   LineTo    (HDCClient, mX4, mY4);
   MoveToEx (HDCClient, mX1, mY1, 0);
   LineTo    (HDCClient, XCursor, YCursor);
   ReleaseDC (MainWnd.mHWnd, HDCClient);

   // save new coordinates / stop drawing if line is trivial:
   mX4 = XCursor; mY4 = YCursor;
   if (mX1 == mX4 && mY1 == mY4)
      MainWnd.mMode = MainWnd.ModeNone;
   else
      MainWnd.mMode = MainWnd.ModeMark1;
   return NULL;
   }

LRESULT CBezier::OnMouseMove (WORD XCursor, WORD YCursor)
// processes WM_MOUSEMOVE messages
   {
   if (MainWnd.mMode != MainWnd.ModeDragging)
      return NULL;

   // erase old temporary straight line / draw new one:
   HDC HDCClient = GetTempDC ();
   MoveToEx (HDCClient, mX1, mY1, 0);
   LineTo    (HDCClient, mX4, mY4);
   MoveToEx (HDCClient, mX1, mY1, 0);
   LineTo    (HDCClient, XCursor, YCursor);
   mX4 = XCursor; mY4 = YCursor;
   ReleaseDC (MainWnd.mHWnd, HDCClient);
   return NULL;
   }

//////////////////////////////////////////////////////////////////////
// CLine:                                                            //
//////////////////////////////////////////////////////////////////////

void CLine::PureDraw (HDC HDc)
// draws the line
   {
   MoveToEx (HDc, mX1, mY1, 0);
   LineTo    (HDc, mX2, mY2);
   return;
   }
```

```cpp
LRESULT CLine::OnLButtonDown (WORD XCursor, WORD YCursor)
// processes WM_LBUTTONDOWN messages
   {
   StartDrag ();
   mX1 = XCursor; mY1 = YCursor;
   mX2 = XCursor; mY2 = YCursor;
   MainWnd.mMode = MainWnd.ModeDragging;
   return NULL;
   }

LRESULT CLine::OnLButtonUp (WORD XCursor, WORD YCursor)
// processes WM_LBUTTONUP messages
   {
   if (MainWnd.mMode != MainWnd.ModeDragging)
      return NULL;

   // end drag operation:
   ReleaseCapture ();
   ClipCursor (NULL);

   // erase temporary line:
   HDC HDCClient = GetTempDC ();
   PureDraw (HDCClient);

   // if line is not trivial, add it to document and draw it:
   mX2 = XCursor; mY2 = YCursor;
   if (mX1 != mX2 || mY1 != mY2)
      {
      Document.AddFigure (this, TRUE);
      MainWnd.mCurrentFig = CreateObject ();
      Draw (HDCClient);
      }
   ReleaseDC (MainWnd.mHWnd, HDCClient);
   MainWnd.mMode = MainWnd.ModeNone;
   return NULL;
   }

LRESULT CLine::OnMouseMove (WORD XCursor, WORD YCursor)
// processes WM_MOUSEMOVE messages
   {
   if (MainWnd.mMode != MainWnd.ModeDragging)
      return NULL;

   // erase old temporary line / draw new one:
   HDC HDCClient = GetTempDC ();
   PureDraw (HDCClient);
   mX2 = XCursor; mY2 = YCursor;
   PureDraw (HDCClient);
   ReleaseDC (MainWnd.mHWnd, HDCClient);
   return NULL;
   }
```

```cpp
////////////////////////////////////////////////////////////////////////////
// CRectangle:                                                             //
////////////////////////////////////////////////////////////////////////////

void CRectangle::PureDraw (HDC HDc)
// draws the rectangle
   {
   Rectangle (HDc, mX1, mY1, mX2, mY2);
   return;
   }

   HBRUSH CRectangle::GetBrush (void)
   // returns a handle to a brush for the rectangle
   {
   LOGBRUSH LB =
      {mBrushStyle,
      mBrushColor,
      mBrushHatchPattern};
   return CreateBrushIndirect (&LB);
   }

////////////////////////////////////////////////////////////////////////////
// CRoundRect:                                                             //
////////////////////////////////////////////////////////////////////////////

void CRoundRect::PureDraw (HDC HDc)
// draws the rounded rectangle
   {
   int RoundDiameter = (mX2 - mX1 + mY2 - mY2) / 6;
   RoundRect (HDc, mX1, mY1, mX2, mY2, RoundDiameter,
      RoundDiameter);
   return;
   }

////////////////////////////////////////////////////////////////////////////
// CEllipse:                                                               //
////////////////////////////////////////////////////////////////////////////

void CEllipse::PureDraw (HDC HDc)
   // draws the ellipse
   {
   Ellipse (HDc, mX1, mY1, mX2, mY2);
   return;
   }

////////////////////////////////////////////////////////////////////////////
// CPolyline:                                                              //
////////////////////////////////////////////////////////////////////////////

RECT CPolyline::GetBoundRect (void)
// returns rectangle bounding all lines
   {
   int NP = mNumPoints;
   RECT Rect = {0,0,0,0};
```

```cpp
   // if dragging, must include the new point not yet added:
   if (MainWnd.mMode == MainWnd.ModeDragging)
      ++NP;

   if (NP < 2)      // if less than 2 points, return empty
      return Rect; // rectangle

   // obtain dimensions of bounding rectangle:
   Rect.left = INT_MAX;
   Rect.top = INT_MAX;
   Rect.right = INT_MIN;
   Rect.bottom = INT_MIN;
   for (int i = 0; i < NP; ++i)
      {
      Rect.left   = min (Rect.left,   mPoints [i].x);
      Rect.top    = min (Rect.top,    mPoints [i].y);
      Rect.right  = max (Rect.right,  mPoints [i].x);
      Rect.bottom = max (Rect.bottom, mPoints [i].y);
      }

   // expand rectangle to accommodate wide lines and margin:
   int LineAdd = (mPenWidth-1) / 2 + (mPenWidth-1) % 2 + 3;
   InflateRect (&Rect, LineAdd, LineAdd);

   return Rect;
   }

void CPolyline::Move (int DeltaX, int DeltaY)
// moves the polyline by the specified offsets
   {
   for (int i = 0; i < mNumPoints; ++i)
      {
      mPoints [i].x += DeltaX;
      mPoints [i].y += DeltaY;
      }

   // set modified flag:
   Document.mModified = TRUE;
   return;
   }

void CPolyline::PureDraw (HDC HDc)
// draws the connected lines:
   {
   Polyline (HDc, mPoints, mNumPoints);
   return;
   }

void CPolyline::Scale (int DeltaX, int DeltaY)
// scales the polyline by the specified offsets
   {
   // calculate the maximum and minimum X and Y coordinates:
   int XMax = INT_MIN;
```

```cpp
int XMin = INT_MAX;
int YMax = INT_MIN;
int YMin = INT_MAX;
for (int i = 0; i < mNumPoints; ++i)
    {
    XMin = min (XMin, mPoints [i].x);
    XMax = max (XMax, mPoints [i].x);
    YMin = min (YMin, mPoints [i].y);
    YMax = max (YMax, mPoints [i].y);
    }

// calculate the X and Y scaling factors:
double XScaleFact = (double)(XMax - XMin + DeltaX) /
                    (double)(XMax - XMin);
double YScaleFact = (double)(YMax - YMin + DeltaY) /
                    (double)(YMax - YMin);

// use the scaling factors to adjust all the points:
for (i = 0; i < mNumPoints; ++i)
    {
    mPoints [i].x = (int)(XMin + XScaleFact *
        (mPoints [i].x - XMin));
    mPoints [i].y = (int)(YMin + YScaleFact *
        (mPoints [i].y - YMin));
    }

// set modified flag:
Document.mModified = TRUE;
return;
}

LRESULT CPolyline::OnLButtonDblClk (WORD XCursor, WORD YCursor)
// processes WM_LBUTTONDBLCLK messages
    {
    // if more than 1 point marked, add polyline figure to
    // document and draw it:
    if (mNumPoints > 1)
        {
        Document.AddFigure (this, TRUE);
        MainWnd.mCurrentFig = CreateObject ();
        HDC HDCClient = GetDC (MainWnd.mHWnd);
        Draw (HDCClient);
        ReleaseDC (MainWnd.mHWnd, HDCClient);
        }
    MainWnd.mMode = MainWnd.ModeNone;
    return NULL;
    }

LRESULT CPolyline::OnLButtonDown (WORD XCursor, WORD YCursor)
// processes WM_LBUTTONDOWN messages
    {
    // initialize first point:
    if (MainWnd.mMode == MainWnd.ModeNone)
```

```
      {
      mNumPoints = 1;
      mPoints [0].x = XCursor;
      mPoints [0].y = YCursor;
      }

   // save coordinates:
   mPoints [mNumPoints].x = XCursor;
   mPoints [mNumPoints].y = YCursor;

   // draw temporary line back to previous point:
   HDC HDCClient = GetTempDC ();
   MoveToEx (HDCClient, mPoints [mNumPoints-1].x,
      mPoints [mNumPoints-1].y, 0);
   LineTo (HDCClient, mPoints [mNumPoints].x,
      mPoints [mNumPoints].y);
   ReleaseDC (MainWnd.mHWnd, HDCClient);

   StartDrag ();
   MainWnd.mMode = MainWnd.ModeDragging;
   return NULL;
   }

LRESULT CPolyline::OnLButtonUp (WORD XCursor, WORD YCursor)
// processes WM_LBUTTONUP messages
   {
   if (MainWnd.mMode != MainWnd.ModeDragging)
      return NULL;

   // end drag operation:
   ReleaseCapture ();
   ClipCursor (NULL);

   // erase old temporary line / draw new one:
   HDC HDCClient = GetTempDC ();
   MoveToEx (HDCClient, mPoints [mNumPoints-1].x,
      mPoints [mNumPoints-1].y, 0);
   LineTo   (HDCClient, mPoints [mNumPoints].x,
      mPoints [mNumPoints].y);
   MoveToEx (HDCClient, mPoints [mNumPoints-1].x,
      mPoints [mNumPoints-1].y, 0);
   LineTo   (HDCClient, XCursor, YCursor);
   ReleaseDC (MainWnd.mHWnd, HDCClient);

   mPoints [mNumPoints].x = XCursor;
   mPoints [mNumPoints].y = YCursor;

   // if new point is not on top of previous point, increment
   // number of points:
   if (mPoints [mNumPoints].x != mPoints [mNumPoints-1].x
       mPoints [mNumPoints].y != mPoints [mNumPoints-1].y)
      ++mNumPoints;
```

```cpp
   // if maximum number of points has been used, end drawing now:
   if (mNumPoints == MAXPOINTS)
      OnLButtonDblClk (XCursor, YCursor);

   MainWnd.mMode = MainWnd.ModeMark1;
   return NULL;
   }

LRESULT CPolyline::OnMouseMove (WORD XCursor, WORD YCursor)
// processes WM_MOUSEMOVE messages
   {
   if (MainWnd.mMode != MainWnd.ModeDragging)
      return NULL;

   // erase old temporary line / draw new one:
   HDC HDCClient = GetTempDC ();
   MoveToEx (HDCClient, mPoints [mNumPoints-1].x,
      mPoints [mNumPoints-1].y, 0);
   LineTo   (HDCClient, mPoints [mNumPoints].x,
      mPoints [mNumPoints].y);
   MoveToEx (HDCClient, mPoints [mNumPoints-1].x,
      mPoints [mNumPoints-1].y, 0);
   LineTo   (HDCClient, XCursor, YCursor);
   ReleaseDC (MainWnd.mHWnd, HDCClient);

   // save new coordinates:
   mPoints [mNumPoints].x = XCursor;
   mPoints [mNumPoints].y = YCursor;
   return NULL;
   }

///////////////////////////////////////////////////////////////////////////
// CPolygon:                                                              //
///////////////////////////////////////////////////////////////////////////

HBRUSH CPolygon::GetBrush (void)
// returns a handle to a brush for the polygon
   {
   LOGBRUSH LB =
      {mBrushStyle,
      mBrushColor,
      mBrushHatchPattern};
   return CreateBrushIndirect (&LB);
   }

void CPolygon::PureDraw (HDC HDc)
// draws the polygon:
   {
   Polygon (HDc, mPoints, mNumPoints);
   return;
   }
```

Listing 8.7:   Document.h

```cpp
////////////////////////////////////////////////////////////////////
//                                                                  //
// Document.h: Header file for document class.                      //
//                                                                  //
////////////////////////////////////////////////////////////////////

struct FigCell          // element of linked list storing figures
{
   FigCell *PNextFig; // pointer to next element in list
   CFigure *PFigure;  // pointer to figure object
};

class CDocument
{
public:
   BOOL mContinuePrint; // TRUE to continue print job
   BOOL mModified;      // TRUE if document has unsaved changes
   FigCell *mPFirstFig; // pointer to start of linked list

   CDocument (void);
   void AddFigure (CFigure *PFigure, BOOL StoreDefaults);
   BOOL CheckSave (void);
   void DeleteAll (void);
   void DeleteFigure (CFigure *PFigure);
   CFigure *GetNextFig (CFigure *PFigure);
   CFigure *GetPreviousFig (CFigure *PFigure);
   void Save (void);
   BOOL SaveAs (void);

   // message-handling functions:
   LRESULT OnFileNew (void);
   LRESULT OnFileOpen (void);
   LRESULT OnFilePrint (void);
   LRESULT OnFileSave (void);
   LRESULT OnFileSaveAs (void);

protected:
   char mFileName [256]; // document file name
};
```

Listing 8.8:   Document.cpp

```cpp
////////////////////////////////////////////////////////////////////
//                                                                  //
// Document.cpp: Implementation file for document class.            //
//                                                                  //
////////////////////////////////////////////////////////////////////
```

```cpp
#define STRICT
#include <windows.h>
#include <stdio.h>
#include <string.h>

#include "figure.h"
#include "mainwnd.h"
#include "document.h"
#include "dialog.h"

extern CMainWnd MainWnd;
extern CDocument Document;
extern CAttrDlg AttrDlg;
extern CBrushDlg BrushDlg;
extern CPenDlg PenDlg;
extern CCancelDlg CancelDlg;
extern CPrintDlg PrnDlg;

static const char Description [] =  // metafile description
   "Windows95 DrawIt Program\0DrawIt Drawing\0";

//////////////////////////////////////////////////////////////////////////
// Callback functions:                                                    //
//////////////////////////////////////////////////////////////////////////

BOOL CALLBACK AbortProc (HDC HDc, int Code)
// "abort procedure" for printing
   {
   // process any pending messages:
   MSG Msg;
   while (PeekMessage ((LPMSG)&Msg, (HWND)NULL, 0, 0, PM_REMOVE))
      {
      // process messages for Cancel modeless dialog box:
      if (!IsDialogMessage (CancelDlg.mHDlg, (LPMSG)&Msg))
         // dispatch other messages:
         DispatchMessage ((LPMSG) &Msg);
      }

   return Document.mContinuePrint;
   }


int CALLBACK ConvertRecord (HDC HDc, HANDLETABLE FAR *PHTable,
   CONST ENHMETARECORD *PRec, int NumObjects, LPARAM PData)
// callback function called by EnumEnhMetaFile API function,
// once for each metafile record; converts metafile records
// into a DrawIt drawing
   {
   int i;
   CFigure *PFigure;

   // store drawing attributes and GDI object features; assign
   // default values:
   static COLORREF BkColor = RGB (255,255,255);
   static int BkMode = OPAQUE;
```

```cpp
static COLORREF BrushColor = RGB (255,255,255);
static LONG BrushHatchPattern = HS_VERTICAL;
static DWORD BrushStyle = BS_SOLID;
static int BrushXOrg = 0;
static int BrushYOrg = 0;
static int FillMode = ALTERNATE;
static int MixMode = R2_COPYPEN;
static COLORREF PenColor = RGB (0,0,0);
static DWORD PenStyle = PS_SOLID;
static DWORD PenType = PS_COSMETIC;
static DWORD PenWidth = 1;
static int XCurr = 0, YCurr = 0;

// switch on type of metafile record:
switch (PRec->iType)
{
   case EMR_ARC: // call to Arc
      PFigure = new CArc;
      PFigure->mX1 = ((PEMRARC)PRec)->rclBox.left;
      PFigure->mY1 = ((PEMRARC)PRec)->rclBox.top;
      PFigure->mX2 = ((PEMRARC)PRec)->rclBox.right + 1;
      PFigure->mY2 = ((PEMRARC)PRec)->rclBox.bottom + 1;
      ((CArc *)PFigure)->mX3 = ((PEMRARC)PRec)->ptlStart.x;
      ((CArc *)PFigure)->mY3 = ((PEMRARC)PRec)->ptlStart.y;
      ((CArc *)PFigure)->mX4 = ((PEMRARC)PRec)->ptlEnd.x;
      ((CArc *)PFigure)->mY4 = ((PEMRARC)PRec)->ptlEnd.y;
      break;

   case EMR_CHORD: // call to Chord
      PFigure = new CChord;
      PFigure->mX1 = ((PEMRCHORD)PRec)->rclBox.left;
      PFigure->mY1 = ((PEMRCHORD)PRec)->rclBox.top;
      PFigure->mX2 = ((PEMRCHORD)PRec)->rclBox.right + 1;
      PFigure->mY2 = ((PEMRCHORD)PRec)->rclBox.bottom + 1;
      ((CChord *)PFigure)->mX3 =((PEMRCHORD)PRec)->ptlStart.x;
      ((CChord *)PFigure)->mY3 =((PEMRCHORD)PRec)->ptlStart.y;
      ((CChord *)PFigure)->mX4 =((PEMRCHORD)PRec)->ptlEnd.x;
      ((CChord *)PFigure)->mY4 =((PEMRCHORD)PRec)->ptlEnd.y;
      break;

   case EMR_CREATEBRUSHINDIRECT:// call to CreateBrushIndirect
      BrushColor =((PEMRCREATEBRUSHINDIRECT)PRec)->lb.lbColor;
      BrushHatchPattern =
         ((PEMRCREATEBRUSHINDIRECT)PRec)->lb.lbHatch;
      BrushStyle =((PEMRCREATEBRUSHINDIRECT)PRec)->lb.lbStyle;
      return 1;

   case EMR_CREATEPEN: // call to ExtCreatePen
      PenColor = ((PEMRCREATEPEN)PRec)->lopn.lopnColor;
      PenStyle = ((PEMRCREATEPEN)PRec)->lopn.lopnStyle;
      if (((PEMRCREATEPEN)PRec)->lopn.lopnWidth.x == 0)
          {
          PenType = PS_COSMETIC;
```

```cpp
            PenWidth = 1;
            }
        else
            {
            PenType = PS_GEOMETRIC;
            PenWidth = ((PEMRCREATEPEN)PRec)->lopn.lopnWidth.x;
            }
        return 1;

case EMR_ELLIPSE: // call to Ellipse
    PFigure = new CEllipse;
    PFigure->mX1 = ((PEMRELLIPSE)PRec)->rclBox.left;
    PFigure->mY1 = ((PEMRELLIPSE)PRec)->rclBox.top;
    PFigure->mX2 = ((PEMRELLIPSE)PRec)->rclBox.right + 1;
    PFigure->mY2 = ((PEMRELLIPSE)PRec)->rclBox.bottom + 1;
    break;

case EMR_LINETO: // call to LineTo
    PFigure = new CLine;
    PFigure->mX1 = XCurr;
    PFigure->mY1 = YCurr;
    PFigure->mX2 = ((PEMRLINETO)PRec)->ptl.x;
    PFigure->mY2 = ((PEMRLINETO)PRec)->ptl.y;
    break;

case EMR_MOVETOEX: // call to MoveToEx
    XCurr = ((PEMRMOVETOEX)PRec)->ptl.x;
    YCurr = ((PEMRMOVETOEX)PRec)->ptl.y;
    return 1;

case EMR_PIE: // call to Pie
    PFigure = new CPie;
    PFigure->mX1 = ((PEMRPIE)PRec)->rclBox.left;
    PFigure->mY1 = ((PEMRPIE)PRec)->rclBox.top;
    PFigure->mX2 = ((PEMRPIE)PRec)->rclBox.right + 1;
    PFigure->mY2 = ((PEMRPIE)PRec)->rclBox.bottom + 1;
    ((CPie *)PFigure)->mX3 = ((PEMRPIE)PRec)->ptlStart.x;
    ((CPie *)PFigure)->mY3 = ((PEMRPIE)PRec)->ptlStart.y;
    ((CPie *)PFigure)->mX4 = ((PEMRPIE)PRec)->ptlEnd.x;
    ((CPie *)PFigure)->mY4 = ((PEMRPIE)PRec)->ptlEnd.y;
    break;

case EMR_POLYBEZIER16: // call to PolyBezier
    PFigure = new CBezier;
    PFigure->mX1 = ((PEMRPOLYBEZIER16)PRec)->apts [0].x;
    PFigure->mY1 = ((PEMRPOLYBEZIER16)PRec)->apts [0].y;
    PFigure->mX2 = ((PEMRPOLYBEZIER16)PRec)->apts [1].x;
    PFigure->mY2 = ((PEMRPOLYBEZIER16)PRec)->apts [1].y;
    ((CBezier *)PFigure)->mX3 =
        ((PEMRPOLYBEZIER16)PRec)->apts [2].x;
    ((CBezier *)PFigure)->mY3 =
        ((PEMRPOLYBEZIER16)PRec)->apts [2].y;
    ((CBezier *)PFigure)->mX4 =
```

```
                ((PEMRPOLYBEZIER16)PRec)->apts [3].x;
            ((CBezier *)PFigure)->mY4 =
                ((PEMRPOLYBEZIER16)PRec)->apts [3].y;
            break;

    case EMR_POLYGON16: // call to Polygon
        {
        CPolygon *PPolygon = new CPolygon;
        PPolygon->mNumPoints = ((PEMRPOLYGON16)PRec)->cpts;
        for (i = 0; i < PPolygon->mNumPoints; ++i)
            {
            PPolygon->mPoints [i].x =
                ((PEMRPOLYGON16)PRec)->apts [i].x;
            PPolygon->mPoints [i].y =
                ((PEMRPOLYGON16)PRec)->apts [i].y;
            }
        PFigure = (CFigure *)PPolygon;
        break;
        }

    case EMR_POLYLINE16: // call to Polyline
        {
        CPolyline *PPolyline = new CPolyline;
        PPolyline->mNumPoints = ((PEMRPOLYLINE16)PRec)->cpts;
        for (i = 0; i < PPolyline->mNumPoints; ++i)
            {
            PPolyline->mPoints [i].x =
                ((PEMRPOLYLINE16)PRec)->apts [i].x;
            PPolyline->mPoints [i].y =
                ((PEMRPOLYLINE16)PRec)->apts [i].y;
            }
        PFigure = (CFigure *)PPolyline;
        break;
        }

    case EMR_RECTANGLE: // call to Rectangle
        PFigure = new CRectangle;
        PFigure->mX1 = ((PEMRRECTANGLE)PRec)->rclBox.left;
        PFigure->mY1 = ((PEMRRECTANGLE)PRec)->rclBox.top;
        PFigure->mX2 = ((PEMRRECTANGLE)PRec)->rclBox.right + 1;
        PFigure->mY2 = ((PEMRRECTANGLE)PRec)->rclBox.bottom + 1;
        break;

    case EMR_ROUNDRECT: // call to RoundRect
        PFigure = new CRoundRect;
        PFigure->mX1 = ((PEMRROUNDRECT)PRec)->rclBox.left;
        PFigure->mY1 = ((PEMRROUNDRECT)PRec)->rclBox.top;
        PFigure->mX2 = ((PEMRROUNDRECT)PRec)->rclBox.right + 1;
        PFigure->mY2 = ((PEMRROUNDRECT)PRec)->rclBox.bottom + 1;
        break;

    case EMR_SETBKCOLOR: // call to SetBkColor
        BkColor = ((PEMRSETBKCOLOR)PRec)->crColor;
        return 1;
```

```cpp
    case EMR_SETBKMODE: // call to SetBkMode
        BkMode = ((PEMRSETBKMODE)PRec)->iMode;
        return 1;

    case EMR_SETBRUSHORGEX: // call to SetBrushOrgEx
        BrushXOrg = ((PEMRSETBRUSHORGEX)PRec)->ptlOrigin.x;
        BrushYOrg = ((PEMRSETBRUSHORGEX)PRec)->ptlOrigin.y;
        return 1;

    case EMR_SETPOLYFILLMODE: // call to SetPolyFillMode
        FillMode = ((PEMRSETPOLYFILLMODE)PRec)->iMode;
        return 1;

    case EMR_SETROP2: // call to SetROP2
        MixMode = ((PEMRSETROP2)PRec)->iMode;
        return 1;

    default:
        return 1;
    }

// a metafile record has drawn a new figure; store drawing
// attributes and GDI object features in figure object and add
// object to document:
PFigure->mBkColor = BkColor;
PFigure->mBkMode = BkMode;
PFigure->mBrushXOrg = BrushXOrg;
PFigure->mBrushYOrg = BrushYOrg;
PFigure->mFillMode = FillMode;
PFigure->mMixMode = MixMode;
PFigure->mPenColor = PenColor;
PFigure->mPenStyle = PenStyle;
PFigure->mPenType = PenType;
PFigure->mPenWidth = PenWidth;
PFigure->DefineBrush (BrushColor, BrushHatchPattern,
    BrushStyle);
Document.AddFigure (PFigure, FALSE);

// after saving the new figure, restore all drawing
// attributes and graphic object features to their
// default values to initialize the next figure:

BkColor = RGB (255,255,255);
BkMode = OPAQUE;
BrushColor = RGB (255,255,255);
BrushHatchPattern = HS_VERTICAL;
BrushStyle = BS_SOLID;
BrushXOrg = 0;
BrushYOrg = 0;
FillMode = ALTERNATE;
MixMode = R2_COPYPEN;
PenColor = RGB (0,0,0);
```

```cpp
   PenStyle = PS_SOLID;
   PenType = PS_COSMETIC;
   PenWidth = 1;
   XCurr = 0, YCurr = 0;

   return 1; // returning nonzero continues enumeration
   }

//////////////////////////////////////////////////////////////////////////
// CDocument member functions:                                           //
//////////////////////////////////////////////////////////////////////////

CDocument::CDocument (void)
   {
   mFileName [0] = '\0';
   mModified = FALSE;
   mPFirstFig = 0;
   return;
   }

void CDocument::AddFigure (CFigure *PFigure, BOOL StoreDefaults)
// adds a new figure to end of linked list; if StoreDefaults is
// TRUE, stores the default attributes & drawing tools in object
   {
   FigCell *PCell;

   if (StoreDefaults)
      {
      // save default brush features:
      PFigure->DefineBrush (BrushDlg.mBrushColor,
         BrushDlg.mBrushHatchPattern, BrushDlg.mBrushStyle);

      // save default pen features:
      PFigure->mPenColor = PenDlg.mPenColor;
      PFigure->mPenStyle = PenDlg.mPenStyle;
      PFigure->mPenType = PenDlg.mPenType;
      PFigure->mPenWidth = PenDlg.mPenWidth;

      // save default drawing attributes:
      PFigure->mBkColor = AttrDlg.mBkColor;
      PFigure->mBkMode = AttrDlg.mBkMode;
      PFigure->mBrushXOrg = AttrDlg.mBrushXOrg;
      PFigure->mBrushYOrg = AttrDlg.mBrushYOrg;
      PFigure->mFillMode = AttrDlg.mFillMode;
      PFigure->mMixMode = AttrDlg.mMixMode;
      }

   // set PCell to new cell at end of list:
   if (mPFirstFig == 0)
      {
      mPFirstFig = new FigCell;
      PCell = mPFirstFig;
      }
   else
```

```cpp
      {
   PCell = mPFirstFig;
   while (PCell->PNextFig != 0)
      PCell = PCell->PNextFig;
   PCell->PNextFig = new FigCell;
   PCell = PCell->PNextFig;
      }

   // assign values to new cell:
   PCell->PNextFig = 0;
   PCell->PFigure = PFigure;

   // set modified flag:
   mModified = TRUE;
   return;
      }

BOOL CDocument::CheckSave (void)
// if document contains unsaved data, allows user to save it;
// returns TRUE to proceed with operation, or FALSE to cancel
// operation
      {
   if (!mModified)
      return TRUE;
   int Result = MessageBox
      (MainWnd.mHWnd,
      "Save changes to drawing?",
      "DrawIt",
      MB_ICONQUESTION | MB_YESNOCANCEL);

   if (Result == IDNO)
      return TRUE;

   if (Result == IDCANCEL)
      return FALSE;
   if (mFileName [0])
      {
      Save ();
      return TRUE;
      }
   if (SaveAs ())
      {
      Save ();
      return TRUE;
      }
   return FALSE;
      }

void CDocument::DeleteAll (void)
      {
   // cancel any drawing or drag operation, or selection:
   if (MainWnd.mSelecting)
      MainWnd.CancelDrag ();
```

```cpp
   else
      MainWnd.mCurrentFig->Cancel ();
   MainWnd.mSelectedFig = 0;

   // delete all cell and figure objects:
   FigCell *PCellTemp;
   FigCell *PCell = mPFirstFig;
   while (PCell)
      {
      delete PCell->PFigure;
      PCellTemp = PCell;
      PCell = PCell->PNextFig;
      delete PCellTemp;
      }

   mPFirstFig = 0;
   return;
   }

void CDocument::DeleteFigure (CFigure *PFigure)
// deletes the linked-list cell that points to the figure object
// pointed to by PFigure; does not delete the figure object
// itself; assumes that the list DOES CONTAIN this cell
   {
   FigCell *PCell;

   // test first cell in list:
   if (mPFirstFig->PFigure == PFigure)
      {
      PCell = mPFirstFig;
      mPFirstFig = mPFirstFig->PNextFig;
      delete PCell;
      return;
      }

   // test remaining cells in list:
   FigCell *PPrevCell = mPFirstFig;
   PCell = mPFirstFig->PNextFig;
   while (PCell)
      {
      if (PCell->PFigure == PFigure)
         {
         PPrevCell->PNextFig = PCell->PNextFig;
         delete PCell;
         return;
         }
      PPrevCell = PCell;
      PCell = PCell->PNextFig;
      }

   // set modified flag:
   mModified = TRUE;
   return;
   }
```

```
CFigure *CDocument::GetNextFig (CFigure *PFigure)
// returns a pointer to the CFigure object that immediately
// FOLLOWS the object pointed to by PFigure in the linked list;
// if there is only 1 object in the list, it returns a pointer to
// that object
   {
   FigCell *PCell = mPFirstFig;

   while (PCell)
      {
      if (PCell->PFigure == PFigure)
         break;
      PCell = PCell->PNextFig;
      }
   if (PCell->PNextFig == 0)
      return mPFirstFig->PFigure;
   else
      return PCell->PNextFig->PFigure;
   }

CFigure *CDocument::GetPreviousFig (CFigure *PFigure)
// returns a pointer to the CFigure object that immediately
// PRECEDES the object pointed to by PFigure in the linked list;
// if there is only 1 object in the list, it returns a pointer to
// that object
   {
   FigCell *PCell = mPFirstFig;
   FigCell *PPrevFig;

   // get pointer to last cell in list:
   while (PCell)
      {
      if (PCell->PNextFig == 0)
         PPrevFig = PCell;
      PCell = PCell->PNextFig;
      }

   // search list from beginning for match:
   PCell = mPFirstFig;
   while (PCell)
      {
      if (PCell->PFigure == PFigure)
         return PPrevFig->PFigure;
      PPrevFig = PCell;
      PCell = PCell->PNextFig;
      }
   return 0;
   }

LRESULT CDocument::OnFileNew (void)
// processes WM_COMMAND / ID_FILE_NEW messages
   {
   // check for unsaved data:
```

```cpp
   if (!CheckSave ())
      return NULL;
   // delete existing document data:
   DeleteAll ();

   // reset mFileName, update title bar, and erase window:
   mFileName [0] = '\0';
   SetWindowText (MainWnd.mHWnd, "DrawIt - untitled");
   InvalidateRect (MainWnd.mHWnd, NULL, TRUE);

   // reset modified flag:
   mModified = FALSE;
   return NULL;
   }

LRESULT CDocument::OnFileOpen (void)
// processes WM_COMMAND / ID_FILE_OPEN messages
   {
   // check for unsaved data:
   if (!CheckSave ())
      return NULL;

   // display Open common dialog box:
   char Filter [] = "Enhanced Metafiles (*.emf)\0*.emf\0";
   char FileName [256] = {'\0'};
   OPENFILENAME OFName;
   memset (&OFName, 0, sizeof (OPENFILENAME));
   OFName.lStructSize = sizeof (OPENFILENAME);
   OFName.hwndOwner = MainWnd.mHWnd;
   OFName.lpstrFilter = Filter;
   OFName.lpstrFile = FileName;
   OFName.nMaxFile = sizeof (FileName);
   OFName.Flags = OFN_FILEMUSTEXIST | OFN_HIDEREADONLY;
   OFName.lpstrDefExt = "emf";
   if (GetOpenFileName (&OFName) == FALSE)
      return NULL;

   // open metafile and get handle:
   HENHMETAFILE HMetaFile = GetEnhMetaFile (FileName);
   if (!HMetaFile)
      {
      MessageBox
         (NULL,
         "Sorry, cannot open file because it is not a valid"
         " enhanced metafile.",
         "Open",
         MB_ICONHAND | MB_OK);
      return NULL;
      }

   // make sure metafile was created by DrawIt:
   char Buffer [sizeof (Description)] = "";
   GetEnhMetaFileDescription
```

```cpp
         (HMetaFile,
         sizeof (Buffer),
         Buffer);
      for (int i = 0; i < sizeof (Description); ++i)
         if (Buffer [i] != Description [i])
            {
            MessageBox
               (NULL,
               "Sorry, cannot open this metafile because it was not"
               " created by DrawIt.",
               "Open",
               MB_ICONHAND | MB_OK);
            DeleteEnhMetaFile (HMetaFile);
            return NULL;
            }

   // before generating new data, delete existing document:
   DeleteAll ();

   // convert metafile to a DrawIt drawing:
   EnumEnhMetaFile
      (NULL,            // dc: none needed
      HMetaFile,        // handle of metafile
      ConvertRecord,    // callback funct. to process each record
      NULL,             // callback funct. data: none
      NULL);            // picture rectangle: none needed

   // redraw the window:
   InvalidateRect (MainWnd.mHWnd, NULL, TRUE);

   // close metafile handle:
   DeleteEnhMetaFile (HMetaFile);

   // write file name to title bar and save file name:
   char Title [128];
   sprintf (Title, "DrawIt - %s", FileName + OFName.nFileOffset);
   SetWindowText (MainWnd.mHWnd, Title);
   lstrcpy (mFileName, FileName);

   // reset modified flag:
   mModified = FALSE;
   return NULL;
   }

LRESULT CDocument::OnFilePrint (void)
// processes WM_COMMAND / ID_FILE_PRINT messages
   {
   // Step 1: obtain printer device context

   // display the Print dialog box:
   if (PrnDlg.Show () == IDCANCEL)
      return NULL;
```

```cpp
// get description of default printer:
char PrnInfo [128];
GetProfileString
   ("windows",
   "device",
   "",
   PrnInfo,
   sizeof (PrnInfo));
char *PPrnDevice = strtok (PrnInfo, ",");

// create printer device context:
HDC HDCPrn = CreateDC (0, PPrnDevice, 0, 0);

// Step 2: setup abort function, display Cancel dialog box,
// and disable main window

mContinuePrint = TRUE; // set "continue" flag
SetAbortProc (HDCPrn, AbortProc);
CancelDlg.Create ();
EnableWindow (MainWnd.mHWnd, FALSE);

// Step 3: call StartDoc to start print job

DOCINFO DocInfo =
   {sizeof (DOCINFO),
   "DrawIt Drawing",
   0, 0, 0};
StartDoc (HDCPrn, &DocInfo);

// Step 4: call StartPage to start page

StartPage (HDCPrn);

// Step 5: set drawing attributes, select graphic objects,
// and call drawing functions

// scale drawing by setting mapping mode:
// user chose to scale drawing to screen size:
if (PrnDlg.mScreenSize)
   {
   // get pixels per logical inch for screen:
   HDC HDCWin = GetDC (MainWnd.mHWnd);
   int LogPixelsXWin = GetDeviceCaps (HDCWin, LOGPIXELSX);
   int LogPixelsYWin = GetDeviceCaps (HDCWin, LOGPIXELSY);
   ReleaseDC (MainWnd.mHWnd, HDCWin);

   // get pixels per logical inch for printer:
   int LogPixelsXPrn = GetDeviceCaps (HDCPrn, LOGPIXELSX);
   int LogPixelsYPrn = GetDeviceCaps (HDCPrn, LOGPIXELSY);

   // set mapping mode for printer device context:
   SetMapMode (HDCPrn, MM_ANISOTROPIC);
   // map this many logical units,
```

```cpp
SetWindowExtEx (HDCPrn, LogPixelsXWin, LogPixelsYWin,
    NULL);
// onto this many device units:
SetViewportExtEx (HDCPrn, LogPixelsXPrn, LogPixelsYPrn,
    NULL);
}

// user chose to scale drawing to size of full printed page:
else
    {
    // get dimensions of drawing (client area of window) in
    // pixels:
    RECT RectClient;
    GetClientRect (MainWnd.mHWnd, &RectClient);

    // get dimensions of printed page in pixels:
    int XPrinter = GetDeviceCaps (HDCPrn, HORZRES);
    int YPrinter = GetDeviceCaps (HDCPrn, VERTRES);

    // set mapping mode for printer device context:
    SetMapMode (HDCPrn, MM_ANISOTROPIC);
    // map this many logical units,
    SetWindowExtEx (HDCPrn, RectClient.right,
        RectClient.bottom, NULL);
    // onto this many device units:
    SetViewportExtEx (HDCPrn, XPrinter, YPrinter, NULL);
    }

// draw all figures stored in document:
FigCell *PCell = mPFirstFig;
while (PCell)
    {
    PCell->PFigure->Draw (HDCPrn);
    PCell = PCell->PNextFig;
    }

// Step 6: call EndPage to end page

EndPage (HDCPrn);

// Step 7: call EndDoc to end print job

EndDoc (HDCPrn);

// Step 8: enable main window and remove Cancel dialog box

EnableWindow (MainWnd.mHWnd, TRUE);
DestroyWindow (CancelDlg.mHDlg);

// Step 9: delete printer device context

DeleteDC (HDCPrn);
return NULL;
}
```

```cpp
LRESULT CDocument::OnFileSave (void)
// processes WM_COMMAND / ID_FILE_SAVE messages
   {
   if (!mFileName [0])
      if (!SaveAs ())
         return NULL;
   Save ();
   return NULL;
   }


LRESULT CDocument::OnFileSaveAs (void)
// processes WM_COMMAND / ID_FILE_SAVE_AS messages
   {
   // get save file name; if user does not cancel, save file:
   if (SaveAs ())
      Save ();
   return NULL;
   }


void CDocument::Save (void)
// saves the drawing under the current file name
   {
   // create the metafile and obtain DC handle:
   HDC HDCMeta = CreateEnhMetaFile
      (NULL,         // reference DC; use current display device
      mFileName,     // name of file for storing metafile
      NULL,          // picture dimensions: use smallest bound.rect.
      Description); // drawing description

   // draw all figures into the metafile:
   FigCell *PCell = Document.mPFirstFig;
   while (PCell)
      {
      PCell->PFigure->Draw (HDCMeta);
      PCell = PCell->PNextFig;
      }

   // close metafile device context and metafile handle:
   DeleteEnhMetaFile (CloseEnhMetaFile (HDCMeta));

   // reset modified flag:
   mModified = FALSE;
   return;
   }


BOOL CDocument::SaveAs (void)
// displays the Save As common dialog box to allow user to
// specify the name of save file; returns TRUE to continue save
// operation, or FALSE if user cancels save operation
   {
   // prepare data to pass GetSaveFileName:
   char Filter [] = "Enhanced Metafiles (*.emf)\x0*.emf\x0";
   OPENFILENAME OFName;
```

```
memset (&OFName, 0, sizeof (OPENFILENAME));
OFName.lStructSize = sizeof (OPENFILENAME);
OFName.hwndOwner = MainWnd.mHWnd;
OFName.lpstrFilter = Filter;
OFName.lpstrFile = mFileName;
OFName.nMaxFile = sizeof (mFileName);
OFName.Flags = OFN_OVERWRITEPROMPT | OFN_HIDEREADONLY;
OFName.lpstrDefExt = "emf";

// display Save As common dialog box:
if (GetSaveFileName (&OFName))
   // user clicked OK button:
   {
   // write file name to title bar:
   char Title [128];
   sprintf (Title, "DrawIt - %s", mFileName +
      OFName.nFileOffset);
   SetWindowText (MainWnd.mHWnd, Title);
   return TRUE;
   }

// user clicked Cancel button:
else
   return FALSE;
}
```

Listing 8.9:   Dialog.h

```
/////////////////////////////////////////////////////////////////////////
//                                                                     //
// Dialog.h: Header file for the dialog box classes.                   //
//                                                                     //
/////////////////////////////////////////////////////////////////////////

class CAboutDlg
{
public:
   int Show (void);

   // message-handling functions:
   BOOL OnCancel (HWND HDlg);
   BOOL OnCtlColor (HDC HDc);
   BOOL OnInitDialog (void);
   BOOL OnOK (HWND HDlg);
};

class CAttrDlg
{
public:
   // store default drawing attributes:
```

```cpp
    COLORREF mBkColor;
    int mBkMode;
    int mBrushXOrg;
    int mBrushYOrg;
    int mFillMode;
    int mMixMode;

    CAttrDlg (void);
    int Show (void);

    // message-handling functions:
    BOOL OnCancel (HWND HDlg);
    BOOL OnCtlColor (HDC HDc);
    BOOL OnInitDialog (HWND HDlg);
    BOOL OnOK (HWND HDlg);
    BOOL OnSetColor (HWND HDlg);

protected:
    // store temporary drawing attributes:
    COLORREF mTBkColor;
    int mTBkMode;
    int mTBrushXOrg;
    int mTBrushYOrg;
    int mTFillMode;
    int mTMixMode;

    // saves custom colors user chooses in Color dialog box:
    DWORD mCustColors [16];
};

class CBrushDlg
{
public:
    // store default brush description:
    COLORREF mBrushColor;
    DWORD mBrushStyle;
    LONG mBrushHatchPattern;

    CBrushDlg (void);
    int Show (void);

    // message-handling functions:
    BOOL OnCancel (HWND HDlg);
    BOOL OnCtlColor (HDC HDc);
    BOOL OnInitDialog (HWND HDlg);
    BOOL OnOK (HWND HDlg);
    BOOL OnSetColor (HWND HDlg);

protected:
    // store temporary brush description:
    COLORREF mTBrushColor;
    DWORD mTBrushStyle;
    LONG mTBrushHatchPattern;
```

```cpp
    // saves custom colors user chooses in Color dialog box:
    DWORD mCustColors [16];
};

class CCancelDlg
{
public:
    HWND mHDlg;
    void Create (void);

    // message-handling functions:
    BOOL OnCancel (void);
    BOOL OnCtlColor (HDC HDc);
    BOOL OnInitDialog (void);
};

class CPenDlg
{
public:
    // store default pen description:
    COLORREF mPenColor;
    DWORD mPenStyle;
    DWORD mPenType;
    DWORD mPenWidth;

    CPenDlg (void);
    int Show (void);

    // message-handling functions:
    BOOL OnCancel (HWND HDlg);
    BOOL OnCtlColor (HDC HDc);
    BOOL OnInitDialog (HWND HDlg);
    BOOL OnOK (HWND HDlg);
    BOOL OnSetColor (HWND HDlg);

protected:
    // store temporary pen description:
    COLORREF mTPenColor;
    DWORD mTPenStyle;
    DWORD mTPenType;
    DWORD mTPenWidth;

    // saves custom colors user chooses in Color dialog box:
    DWORD mCustColors [16];
};

class CPrintDlg
{
public:
    BOOL mScreenSize; // TRUE to scale drawing to screen size

    CPrintDlg ()
        {
```

```
      mScreenSize = TRUE;
      }
   int Show (void);

   // message-handling functions:
   BOOL OnCancel (HWND HDlg);
   BOOL OnCtlColor (HDC HDc);
   BOOL OnInitDialog (HWND HDlg);
   BOOL OnOK (HWND HDlg);
};
```

Listing 8.10:   Dialog.cpp

```cpp
///////////////////////////////////////////////////////////////////////////
//                                                                       //
// Dialog.cpp: Implementation file for the dialog box classes.           //
//                                                                       //
///////////////////////////////////////////////////////////////////////////

#define STRICT
#include <windows.h>
#include "resource.h"

#include "app.h"
#include "figure.h"
#include "mainwnd.h"
#include "document.h"
#include "dialog.h"

#include <memory.h>

extern CApp       App;
extern CMainWnd   MainWnd;
extern CDocument  Document;
extern CAboutDlg  AboutDlg;
extern CAttrDlg   AttrDlg;
extern CBrushDlg  BrushDlg;
extern CCancelDlg CancelDlg;
extern CPenDlg    PenDlg;
extern CPrintDlg  PrnDlg;

BOOL CALLBACK AboutDialogProc (HWND HDlg, UINT Msg,
   WPARAM WParam, LPARAM LParam);
BOOL CALLBACK AttrDialogProc (HWND HDlg, UINT Msg, WPARAM WParam,
   LPARAM LParam);
BOOL CALLBACK BrushDialogProc (HWND HDlg, UINT Msg,
   WPARAM WParam, LPARAM LParam);
BOOL CALLBACK CancelDialogProc (HWND HDlg, UINT Msg,
   WPARAM WParam, LPARAM LParam);
BOOL CALLBACK PenDialogProc (HWND HDlg, UINT Msg, WPARAM WParam,
```

```c
    LPARAM LParam);
BOOL CALLBACK PrintDialogProc (HWND HDlg, UINT Msg,
    WPARAM WParam, LPARAM LParam);

////////////////////////////////////////////////////////////////////////////
// global tables for combo box data:                                        //
////////////////////////////////////////////////////////////////////////////

static struct  // stores strings and color values for all
{              // elements to be added to Color combo box
    char *ColorName;
    COLORREF ColorValue;
}
ColorTable [10] =
    {{"Black",     RGB (0,0,0)},
     {"Gray",      RGB (192,192,192)},
     {"White",     RGB (255,255,255)},
     {"Red",       RGB (255,0,0)},
     {"Green",     RGB (0,255,0)},
     {"Blue",      RGB (0,0,255)},
     {"Yellow",    RGB (255,255,0)},
     {"Cyan",      RGB (0,255,255)},
     {"Magenta",   RGB (255,0,255)},
     {"<Custom>",  RGB (0,0,0)}};

static struct  // stores strings and IDs for all elements to be
{              // added to Hatch Pattern combo box
    char *HatchName;
    LONG HatchID;
}
HatchTable [6] =
    {{"Vertical",            HS_VERTICAL},
     {"Horizontal",         HS_HORIZONTAL},
     {"Up Diagonal",        HS_BDIAGONAL},
     {"Down Diagonal",      HS_FDIAGONAL},
     {"Crosshatch",         HS_CROSS},
     {"Diagonal crosshatch", HS_DIAGCROSS}};

static struct  // stores strings and IDs for all elements to be
{              // added to Mix Mode combo box
    char *MixModeName;
    int MixModeID;
}
MixModeTable [16] =
    {{"R2_BLACK",         R2_BLACK},
     {"R2_COPYPEN",       R2_COPYPEN},
     {"R2_MASKNOTPEN",    R2_MASKNOTPEN},
     {"R2_MASKPEN",       R2_MASKPEN},
     {"R2_MASKPENNOT",    R2_MASKPENNOT},
     {"R2_MERGENOTPEN",   R2_MERGENOTPEN},
     {"R2_MERGEPEN",      R2_MERGEPEN},
     {"R2_MERGEPENNOT",   R2_MERGEPENNOT},
     {"R2_NOP",           R2_NOP},
     {"R2_NOT",           R2_NOT},
```

```
      {"R2_NOTCOPYPEN",   R2_NOTCOPYPEN},
      {"R2_NOTMASKPEN",   R2_NOTMASKPEN},
      {"R2_NOTMERGEPEN",  R2_NOTMERGEPEN},
      {"R2_NOTXORPEN",    R2_NOTXORPEN},
      {"R2_WHITE",        R2_WHITE},
      {"R2_XORPEN",       R2_XORPEN}};

static struct  // stores strings and IDs for all elements to be
{              // added to Style combo box
   char *StyleName;
   DWORD StyleID;
}
StyleTable [7] =
   {{"Solid",         PS_SOLID},
    {"Dash",          PS_DASH},
    {"Dot",           PS_DOT},
    {"Dash-Dot",      PS_DASHDOT},
    {"Dash-Dot-Dot",  PS_DASHDOTDOT},
    {"Null",          PS_NULL},
    {"Inside-Frame",  PS_INSIDEFRAME}};

//////////////////////////////////////////////////////////////////////
// About dialog box:                                                 //
//////////////////////////////////////////////////////////////////////

//////////////////////////////////////////////////////////////////////
// CAboutDlg public member function:                                 //
//////////////////////////////////////////////////////////////////////

int CAboutDlg::Show (void)
// displays About dialog box
   {
   return DialogBox
      (App.mHInstance,
      MAKEINTRESOURCE (IDD_ABOUT),
      MainWnd.mHWnd,
      AboutDialogProc);
 }

//////////////////////////////////////////////////////////////////////
// About dialog box procedure:                                       //
//////////////////////////////////////////////////////////////////////

BOOL CALLBACK AboutDialogProc
   (HWND   HDlg,
    UINT   Msg,
    WPARAM WParam,
    LPARAM LParam)
    {
    switch (Msg)
       {
       case WM_INITDIALOG: // dialog box was just created
          return AboutDlg.OnInitDialog ();
```

```cpp
      case WM_COMMAND:      // user issued a command
        switch (LOWORD (WParam))
        {
        case IDCANCEL: // user chose Close or pressed Esc
           return AboutDlg.OnCancel (HDlg);

        case IDOK:       // user clicked OK or pressed Enter
           return AboutDlg.OnOK (HDlg);

        default:
           return FALSE; // default message processing
        }

      case WM_CTLCOLORDLG:    // dialog box about to be painted;
      case WM_CTLCOLORSTATIC: // text about to be painted
        return AboutDlg.OnCtlColor ((HDC)WParam);

      default:         // request default processing for all
        return FALSE; // other messages
      }
  }

////////////////////////////////////////////////////////////////////////
// CAboutDlg message handling member functions:                        //
////////////////////////////////////////////////////////////////////////

BOOL CAboutDlg::OnCancel (HWND HDlg)
// processes WM_COMMAND / IDCANCEL messages
  {
  // close the dialog box:
  EndDialog (HDlg, IDCANCEL);
  return TRUE;
  }

BOOL CAboutDlg::OnCtlColor (HDC HDc)
// processes WM_CTLCOLORDLG and WM_CTLCOLORSTATIC messages
  {
  // set text background to light gray:
  SetBkColor (HDc, RGB (192,192,192));

  // supply a handle to a light-gray brush:
  return (BOOL)GetStockObject (LTGRAY_BRUSH);
  }

BOOL CAboutDlg::OnInitDialog (void)
// processes WM_INITDIALOG messages
  {
  // return TRUE to set focus to first control:
  return TRUE;
  }

BOOL CAboutDlg::OnOK (HWND HDlg)
// processes WM_COMMAND / IDOK messages
```

```
   {
   // close the dialog box:
   EndDialog (HDlg, IDOK);
   return TRUE;
   }

//////////////////////////////////////////////////////////////////////////
// Attributes dialog box:                                                 //
//////////////////////////////////////////////////////////////////////////

//////////////////////////////////////////////////////////////////////////
// CAttrDlg public member functions:                                      //
//////////////////////////////////////////////////////////////////////////

CAttrDlg::CAttrDlg (void)
   {
   mBkColor = RGB (255,255,255);
   mBkMode = OPAQUE;
   mBrushXOrg = 0;
   mBrushYOrg = 0;
   mFillMode = ALTERNATE;
   mMixMode = R2_COPYPEN;
   memset (mCustColors, 0, sizeof (mCustColors));
   return;
   }

int CAttrDlg::Show (void)
// displays Attributes dialog box
   {
   return DialogBox
      (App.mHInstance,
       MAKEINTRESOURCE (IDD_ATTR),
       MainWnd.mHWnd,
       AttrDialogProc);
   }

//////////////////////////////////////////////////////////////////////////
// Attributes dialog box procedure:                                       //
//////////////////////////////////////////////////////////////////////////

BOOL CALLBACK AttrDialogProc
   (HWND   HDlg,
    UINT   Msg,
    WPARAM WParam,
    LPARAM LParam)
   {
   switch (Msg)
      {
      case WM_INITDIALOG: // dialog box was just created
         return AttrDlg.OnInitDialog (HDlg);

      case WM_COMMAND:    // user issued a command
         switch (LOWORD (WParam))
            {
```

```cpp
            case IDC_SETCOLOR: // user clicked Set Custom Color
               return AttrDlg.OnSetColor (HDlg);

            case IDCANCEL: // user chose Close or pressed Esc
               return AttrDlg.OnCancel (HDlg);

            case IDOK:  // user clicked OK or pressed Enter
               return AttrDlg.OnOK (HDlg);

            default:
               return FALSE; // default message processing
            }
      case WM_CTLCOLORBTN:     // button is about to be painted;
      case WM_CTLCOLORDLG:     // dialog box about to be painted;
      case WM_CTLCOLORSTATIC: // dialog text about to be painted
         return AttrDlg.OnCtlColor ((HDC)WParam);

      default:           // request default processing for all
         return FALSE; // other messages
      }
   }

//////////////////////////////////////////////////////////////////////////
// CAttrDlg message handling member functions:                          //
//////////////////////////////////////////////////////////////////////////

BOOL CAttrDlg::OnCancel (HWND HDlg)
// processes WM_COMMAND / IDCANCEL messages
   {
   // close the dialog box:
   EndDialog (HDlg, IDCANCEL);
   return TRUE;
   }

BOOL CAttrDlg::OnCtlColor (HDC HDc)
// processes WM_CTLCOLORBTN, WM_CTLCOLORDLG, and
// WM_CTLCOLORSTATIC messages
   {
   // set text background to light gray:
   SetBkColor (HDc, RGB (192,192,192));

   // supply a handle to a light-gray brush:
   return (BOOL)GetStockObject (LTGRAY_BRUSH);
   }

BOOL CAttrDlg::OnInitDialog (HWND HDlg)
// processes WM_INITDIALOG messages
   {
   // obtain current attributes from selected figure or defaults:
   if (MainWnd.mSelectedFig) // figure is selected
      {
      mTBkColor = MainWnd.mSelectedFig->mBkColor;
      mTBkMode = MainWnd.mSelectedFig->mBkMode;
```

```cpp
    mTBrushXOrg = MainWnd.mSelectedFig->mBrushXOrg;
    mTBrushYOrg = MainWnd.mSelectedFig->mBrushYOrg;
    mTFillMode = MainWnd.mSelectedFig->mFillMode;
    mTMixMode = MainWnd.mSelectedFig->mMixMode;
    SetWindowText (HDlg, "Figure Attributes");
    }
else                           // no figure selected
    {
    mTBkColor = mBkColor;
    mTBkMode = mBkMode;
    mTBrushXOrg = mBrushXOrg;
    mTBrushYOrg = mBrushYOrg;
    mTFillMode = mFillMode;
    mTMixMode = mMixMode;
    }

// initialize Mix Mode combo box and select current value:
for (int i = 0; i < 16; ++i)
    {
    SendDlgItemMessage (HDlg, IDC_MIXMODE, CB_ADDSTRING,
        0, (LPARAM)(LPCSTR)MixModeTable [i].MixModeName);
    if (MixModeTable [i].MixModeID == mTMixMode)
        SendDlgItemMessage (HDlg, IDC_MIXMODE, CB_SETCURSEL,
            (WPARAM)i, 0);
    }

// check Background Mode radio button:
CheckDlgButton
    (HDlg,
    mTBkMode == TRANSPARENT ? IDC_TRANSPARENT : IDC_OPAQUE,
    1);

// initialize Color combo box and select current value:
BOOL Selected = FALSE;
for (i = 0; i < 10; ++i)
    {
    SendDlgItemMessage (HDlg, IDC_COLOR, CB_ADDSTRING, 0,
        (LPARAM)(LPCSTR)ColorTable [i].ColorName);
    if (!Selected && ColorTable [i].ColorValue == mTBkColor)
        {
        SendDlgItemMessage (HDlg, IDC_COLOR, CB_SETCURSEL,
            (WPARAM)i, 0);
        Selected = TRUE;
        }
    }
if (!Selected)
{
    ColorTable [9].ColorValue = mTBkColor;
    SendDlgItemMessage (HDlg, IDC_COLOR, CB_SETCURSEL,
        (WPARAM)9, 0);
    }
```

```cpp
   // check Polygon Fill Mode radio button:
   CheckDlgButton
      (HDlg,
      mTFillMode == ALTERNATE ? IDC_ALTERNATE : IDC_WINDING,
      1);

   // set values of Brush Origin edit controls:
   SetDlgItemInt (HDlg, IDC_XORG, mTBrushXOrg, TRUE);
   SetDlgItemInt (HDlg, IDC_YORG, mTBrushYOrg, TRUE);

   // return TRUE to set focus to first control:
   return TRUE;
   }

BOOL CAttrDlg::OnOK (HWND HDlg)
// processes WM_COMMAND / IDOK messages
   {
   // save selection from Mix Mode combo box:
   mTMixMode = MixModeTable [SendDlgItemMessage (HDlg,
      IDC_MIXMODE, CB_GETCURSEL, 0, 0)].MixModeID;

   // save Background Mode choice:
   mTBkMode = IsDlgButtonChecked (HDlg, IDC_TRANSPARENT) ?
      TRANSPARENT : OPAQUE;

   // save selection from Color combo box:
   mTBkColor = ColorTable [SendDlgItemMessage (HDlg,
      IDC_COLOR, CB_GETCURSEL, 0, 0)].ColorValue;

   // save Polygon Fill Mode choice:
   mTFillMode = IsDlgButtonChecked (HDlg, IDC_ALTERNATE) ?
      ALTERNATE : WINDING;

   // save Brush Origin values:
   BOOL Translated;
   mTBrushXOrg = GetDlgItemInt(HDlg, IDC_XORG, &Translated,TRUE);
   mTBrushYOrg = GetDlgItemInt(HDlg, IDC_YORG, &Translated,TRUE);

   // store values in figure or in default data members:
   if (MainWnd.mSelectedFig) // figure is selected
      {
      MainWnd.mSelectedFig->mBkColor = mTBkColor;
      MainWnd.mSelectedFig->mBkMode = mTBkMode;
      MainWnd.mSelectedFig->mBrushXOrg = mTBrushXOrg;
      MainWnd.mSelectedFig->mBrushYOrg = mTBrushYOrg;
      MainWnd.mSelectedFig->mFillMode = mTFillMode;
      MainWnd.mSelectedFig->mMixMode = mTMixMode;

      // force redrawing of figure:
      RECT Rect = MainWnd.mSelectedFig->GetBoundRect ();
      InvalidateRect (MainWnd.mHWnd, &Rect, TRUE);
      }
   else                       // no figure selected
```

```
      {
      mBkColor = mTBkColor;
      mBkMode = mTBkMode;
      mBrushXOrg = mTBrushXOrg;
      mBrushYOrg = mTBrushYOrg;
      mFillMode = mTFillMode;
      mMixMode = mTMixMode;
      }

   // close the dialog box:
   EndDialog (HDlg, IDOK);
   return TRUE;
   }

BOOL CAttrDlg::OnSetColor (HWND HDlg)
// processes WM_COMMAND / ID_SETCOLOR messages
   {
   CHOOSECOLOR CC;

   // assign values to structure to control Color dialog box:
   memset (&CC, 0, sizeof (CC));
   CC.lStructSize = sizeof (CC);
   CC.hwndOwner = HDlg;
   CC.rgbResult = ColorTable [9].ColorValue;
   CC.lpCustColors = mCustColors;
   CC.Flags = CC_RGBINIT;

   // display Color common dialog box; save selected color if
   // user clicked OK:
   if (ChooseColor (&CC))
      ColorTable [9].ColorValue = CC.rgbResult;
   return TRUE;
   }

///////////////////////////////////////////////////////////////////////////
// Brush dialog box:                                                      //
///////////////////////////////////////////////////////////////////////////

///////////////////////////////////////////////////////////////////////////
// CBrushDlg public member functions:                                     //
///////////////////////////////////////////////////////////////////////////

CBrushDlg::CBrushDlg (void)
   {
   mBrushColor = RGB (255,255,255);
   mBrushHatchPattern = HS_VERTICAL;
   mBrushStyle = BS_SOLID;
   memset (mCustColors, 0, sizeof (mCustColors));
   return;
   }

int CBrushDlg::Show (void)
// displays Brush dialog box
   {
```

```cpp
   return DialogBox
     (App.mHInstance,
     MAKEINTRESOURCE (IDD_BRUSH),
     MainWnd.mHWnd,
     BrushDialogProc);
   }

//////////////////////////////////////////////////////////////////////////
// Brush dialog box procedure:                                           //
//////////////////////////////////////////////////////////////////////////

BOOL CALLBACK BrushDialogProc
   (HWND   HDlg,
    UINT   Msg,
    WPARAM WParam,
    LPARAM LParam)
    {
    switch (Msg)
       {
       case WM_INITDIALOG: // dialog box was just created
          return BrushDlg.OnInitDialog (HDlg);

       case WM_COMMAND:     // user issued a command
          switch (LOWORD (WParam))
             {
             case IDC_SETCOLOR: // user clicked Set Custom Color
                return BrushDlg.OnSetColor (HDlg);

             case IDCANCEL: // user chose Close or pressed Esc
                return BrushDlg.OnCancel (HDlg);

             case IDOK:  // user clicked OK or pressed Enter
                return BrushDlg.OnOK (HDlg);

             default:
                return FALSE; // default message processing
             }

       case WM_CTLCOLORBTN:    // button is about to be painted;
       case WM_CTLCOLORDLG:    // dialog box about to be painted;
       case WM_CTLCOLORSTATIC: // dialog text about to be painted
          return BrushDlg.OnCtlColor ((HDC)WParam);

       default:          // request default processing for all
          return FALSE; // other messages
       }
    }

//////////////////////////////////////////////////////////////////////////
// CBrushDlg message handling member functions:                          //
//////////////////////////////////////////////////////////////////////////

BOOL CBrushDlg::OnCancel (HWND HDlg)
// processes WM_COMMAND / IDCANCEL messages
```

```
   {
   // close the dialog box:
   EndDialog (HDlg, IDCANCEL);
   return TRUE;
   }

BOOL CBrushDlg::OnCtlColor (HDC HDc)
// processes WM_CTLCOLORBTN, WM_CTLCOLORDLG, and
// WM_CTLCOLORSTATIC messages
   {
   // set text background to light gray:
   SetBkColor (HDc, RGB (192,192,192));

   // supply a handle to a light-gray brush:
   return (BOOL)GetStockObject (LTGRAY_BRUSH);
   }

BOOL CBrushDlg::OnInitDialog (HWND HDlg)
// processes WM_INITDIALOG messages
   {
   // obtain current brush description:
   if (MainWnd.mSelectedFig)  // figure is selected
      {
      MainWnd.mSelectedFig->GetBrushDescription
         (&mTBrushColor,
         &mTBrushHatchPattern,
         &mTBrushStyle);
      SetWindowText (HDlg, "Figure Brush");
      }
   else                       // no figure selected
      {
      mTBrushColor = mBrushColor;
      mTBrushHatchPattern = mBrushHatchPattern;
      mTBrushStyle = mBrushStyle;
      }

   // check Style radio button:
   switch (mTBrushStyle)
      {
      case BS_SOLID:
         CheckDlgButton (HDlg, IDC_SOLID, 1);
         break;

      case BS_HATCHED:
         CheckDlgButton (HDlg, IDC_HATCHED, 1);
         break;

      case BS_NULL:
         CheckDlgButton (HDlg, IDC_NULL, 1);
         break;
      }

   // initialize Hatch Pattern combo box / select current value:
```

```cpp
for (int i = 0; i < 6; ++i)
    {
    SendDlgItemMessage (HDlg, IDC_HATCHPATTERN, CB_ADDSTRING,
        0, (LPARAM)(LPCSTR)HatchTable [i].HatchName);
    if (HatchTable [i].HatchID == mTBrushHatchPattern)
        SendDlgItemMessage (HDlg, IDC_HATCHPATTERN,
        CB_SETCURSEL, (WPARAM)i, 0);
    }

// initialize Color combo box and select current value:
BOOL Selected = FALSE;
for (i = 0; i < 10; ++i)
    {
    SendDlgItemMessage (HDlg, IDC_COLOR, CB_ADDSTRING, 0,
        (LPARAM)(LPCSTR)ColorTable [i].ColorName);
    if (!Selected && ColorTable [i].ColorValue == mTBrushColor)
        {
        SendDlgItemMessage (HDlg, IDC_COLOR, CB_SETCURSEL,
            (WPARAM)i, 0);
        Selected = TRUE;
        }
    }
if (!Selected)
    {
    ColorTable [9].ColorValue = mTBrushColor;
    SendDlgItemMessage (HDlg, IDC_COLOR, CB_SETCURSEL,
        (WPARAM)9, 0);
    }

// return TRUE to set focus to first control:
return TRUE;
}

BOOL CBrushDlg::OnOK (HWND HDlg)
// processes WM_COMMAND / IDOK messages
    {
    // save Style choice:
    if (IsDlgButtonChecked (HDlg, IDC_SOLID))
        mTBrushStyle = BS_SOLID;
    else if (IsDlgButtonChecked (HDlg, IDC_HATCHED))
        mTBrushStyle = BS_HATCHED;
    else
        mTBrushStyle = BS_NULL;

    // save selection from Hatch Pattern combo box:
    mTBrushHatchPattern = HatchTable [SendDlgItemMessage
        (HDlg, IDC_HATCHPATTERN, CB_GETCURSEL, 0, 0)].HatchID;

    // save selection from Color combo box:
    mTBrushColor = ColorTable [SendDlgItemMessage (HDlg,
        IDC_COLOR, CB_GETCURSEL, 0, 0)].ColorValue;

    // store values in figure or in default data members:
```

```cpp
   if (MainWnd.mSelectedFig)  // figure is selected
      {
      MainWnd.mSelectedFig->DefineBrush
         (mTBrushColor,
          mTBrushHatchPattern,
          mTBrushStyle);
      // force redrawing of figure:
      RECT Rect = MainWnd.mSelectedFig->GetBoundRect ();
      InvalidateRect (MainWnd.mHWnd, &Rect, TRUE);
      }
   else                         // no figure selected
      {
      mBrushColor = mTBrushColor;
      mBrushHatchPattern = mTBrushHatchPattern;
      mBrushStyle = mTBrushStyle;
      }

   // close the dialog box:
   EndDialog (HDlg, IDOK);
   return TRUE;
   }

BOOL CBrushDlg::OnSetColor (HWND HDlg)
// processes WM_COMMAND / ID_SETCOLOR messages
   {
   CHOOSECOLOR CC;

   // assign values to structure to control Color dialog box:
   memset (&CC, 0, sizeof (CC));
   CC.lStructSize = sizeof (CC);
   CC.hwndOwner = HDlg;
   CC.rgbResult = ColorTable [9].ColorValue;
   CC.lpCustColors = mCustColors;
   CC.Flags = CC_RGBINIT;

   // display Color common dialog box; save selected color if
   // user clicked OK:
   if (ChooseColor (&CC))
      ColorTable [9].ColorValue = CC.rgbResult;
   return TRUE;
   }

//////////////////////////////////////////////////////////////////////
// Cancel print dialog box:                                          //
//////////////////////////////////////////////////////////////////////

//////////////////////////////////////////////////////////////////////
// CCancelDlg public member function:                                //
//////////////////////////////////////////////////////////////////////

void CCancelDlg::Create (void)
// creates the Cancel print modeless dialog box
   {
   mHDlg = CreateDialog
```

```cpp
        (App.mHInstance,
        MAKEINTRESOURCE (IDD_CANCEL),
        MainWnd.mHWnd,
        CancelDialogProc);
    }

/////////////////////////////////////////////////////////////////////////////
// Cancel dialog box procedure:                                             //
/////////////////////////////////////////////////////////////////////////////

BOOL CALLBACK CancelDialogProc
    (HWND    HDlg,
     UINT    Msg,
     WPARAM WParam,
     LPARAM LParam)
    {
    switch (Msg)
        {
        case WM_INITDIALOG: // dialog box was just created
            return CancelDlg.OnInitDialog ();

        case WM_COMMAND:     // user cancelled print job
            return CancelDlg.OnCancel ();

        case WM_CTLCOLORDLG:    // dialog box about to be painted;
        case WM_CTLCOLORSTATIC: // text about to be painted
            return CancelDlg.OnCtlColor ((HDC)WParam);

        default:             // request default processing for all
            return FALSE; // other messages
        }
    }

/////////////////////////////////////////////////////////////////////////////
// CCancelDlg message handling member functions:                            //
/////////////////////////////////////////////////////////////////////////////

BOOL CCancelDlg::OnCancel (void)
// processes WM_COMMAND messages
    {
    // stop printing:
    Document.mContinuePrint = FALSE;
    return TRUE;
    }

BOOL CCancelDlg::OnCtlColor (HDC HDc)
// processes WM_CTLCOLORDLG and WM_CTLCOLORSTATIC messages
    {
    // set text background to light gray:
    SetBkColor (HDc, RGB (192,192,192));

    // supply a handle to a light-gray brush:
    return (BOOL)GetStockObject (LTGRAY_BRUSH);
    }
```

```
BOOL CCancelDlg::OnInitDialog (void)
// processes WM_INITDIALOG messages
    {
    // return TRUE to set focus to first control:
    return TRUE;
    }

////////////////////////////////////////////////////////////////////////
// Pen dialog box:                                                      //
////////////////////////////////////////////////////////////////////////

////////////////////////////////////////////////////////////////////////
// CPenDlg public member functions:                                     //
////////////////////////////////////////////////////////////////////////

CPenDlg::CPenDlg (void)
    {
    mPenColor = RGB (0,0,0);
    mPenStyle = PS_SOLID;
    mPenType = PS_COSMETIC;
    mPenWidth = 1;
    memset (mCustColors, 0, sizeof (mCustColors));
    return;
    }

int CPenDlg::Show (void)
// displays Pen dialog box
    {
    return DialogBox
        (App.mHInstance,
        MAKEINTRESOURCE (IDD_PEN),
        MainWnd.mHWnd,
        PenDialogProc);
    }

////////////////////////////////////////////////////////////////////////
// Pen dialog box procedure:                                            //
////////////////////////////////////////////////////////////////////////

BOOL CALLBACK PenDialogProc
    (HWND   HDlg,
    UINT   Msg,
    WPARAM WParam,
    LPARAM LParam)
    {
    switch (Msg)
        {
        case WM_INITDIALOG: // dialog box was just created
            return PenDlg.OnInitDialog (HDlg);

        case WM_COMMAND:   // user issued a command
            switch (LOWORD (WParam))
                {
```

```
            case IDC_SETCOLOR: // user clicked Set Custom Color
               return PenDlg.OnSetColor (HDlg);

            case IDCANCEL: // user chose Close or pressed Esc
               return PenDlg.OnCancel (HDlg);

            case IDOK:  // user clicked OK or pressed Enter
               return PenDlg.OnOK (HDlg);

            default:
               return FALSE; // default message processing
            }

      case WM_CTLCOLORBTN:     // button is about to be painted;
      case WM_CTLCOLORDLG:     // dialog box about to be painted;
      case WM_CTLCOLORSTATIC: // dialog text about to be painted
         return PenDlg.OnCtlColor ((HDC)WParam);

      default:            // request default processing for all
         return FALSE; // other messages
      }
   }

/////////////////////////////////////////////////////////////////////////////
// CPenDlg message handling member functions:                              //
/////////////////////////////////////////////////////////////////////////////

BOOL CPenDlg::OnCancel (HWND HDlg)
// processes WM_COMMAND / IDCANCEL messages
   {
   // close the dialog box:
   EndDialog (HDlg, IDCANCEL);
   return TRUE;
   }

BOOL CPenDlg::OnCtlColor (HDC HDc)
// processes WM_CTLCOLORBTN, WM_CTLCOLORDLG, and
// WM_CTLCOLORSTATIC messages
   {
   // set text background to light gray:
   SetBkColor (HDc, RGB (192,192,192));

   // supply a handle to a light-gray brush:
   return (BOOL)GetStockObject (LTGRAY_BRUSH);
   }

BOOL CPenDlg::OnInitDialog (HWND HDlg)
// processes WM_INITDIALOG messages
   {
   // obtain current pen description:
   if (MainWnd.mSelectedFig)  // figure is selected
      {
      mTPenColor = MainWnd.mSelectedFig->mPenColor;
```

```cpp
      mTPenStyle = MainWnd.mSelectedFig->mPenStyle;
      mTPenType = MainWnd.mSelectedFig->mPenType;
      mTPenWidth = MainWnd.mSelectedFig->mPenWidth;
      SetWindowText (HDlg, "Figure Pen");
      }
   else                          // no figure selected
      {
      mTPenColor = mPenColor;
      mTPenStyle = mPenStyle;
      mTPenType = mPenType;
      mTPenWidth = mPenWidth;
      }

   // check Type radio button:
   CheckDlgButton
      (HDlg,
      mTPenType == PS_COSMETIC ? IDC_COSMETIC : IDC_GEOMETRIC,
      1);

   // initialize Style combo box and select current value:
   for (int i = 0; i < 7; ++i)
      {
      SendDlgItemMessage (HDlg, IDC_STYLE, CB_ADDSTRING,
         0, (LPARAM)(LPCSTR)StyleTable [i].StyleName);
      if (StyleTable [i].StyleID == mTPenStyle)
         SendDlgItemMessage (HDlg, IDC_STYLE, CB_SETCURSEL,
            (WPARAM)i, 0);
      }

   // limit Width edit control to 2 characters and set value:
   SendDlgItemMessage (HDlg, IDC_WIDTH, EM_SETLIMITTEXT,
      (WPARAM)2, 0);
   SetDlgItemInt (HDlg, IDC_WIDTH, mTPenWidth, FALSE);

   // initialize Color combo box and select current value:
   BOOL Selected = FALSE;
   for (i = 0; i < 10; ++i)
      {
      SendDlgItemMessage (HDlg, IDC_COLOR, CB_ADDSTRING, 0,
         (LPARAM)(LPCSTR)ColorTable [i].ColorName);
      if (!Selected && ColorTable [i].ColorValue == mTPenColor)
         {
         SendDlgItemMessage (HDlg, IDC_COLOR, CB_SETCURSEL,
            (WPARAM)i, 0);
         Selected = TRUE;
         }
      }
   if (!Selected)
      {
      ColorTable [9].ColorValue = mTPenColor;
      SendDlgItemMessage (HDlg, IDC_COLOR, CB_SETCURSEL,
         (WPARAM)9, 0);
      }
```

```cpp
   // return TRUE to set focus to first control:
   return TRUE;
   }

BOOL CPenDlg::OnOK (HWND HDlg)
// processes WM_COMMAND / IDOK messages
   {
   // save Type choice:
   mTPenType = IsDlgButtonChecked (HDlg, IDC_COSMETIC) ?
      PS_COSMETIC : PS_GEOMETRIC;

   // save selection from Style combo box:
   mTPenStyle = StyleTable [SendDlgItemMessage (HDlg, IDC_STYLE,
      CB_GETCURSEL, 0, 0)].StyleID;

   // save value from Width edit control:
   BOOL Translated;
   mTPenWidth = GetDlgItemInt (HDlg, IDC_WIDTH, &Translated,
      FALSE);

   // save selection from Color combo box:
   mTPenColor = ColorTable [SendDlgItemMessage (HDlg,
      IDC_COLOR, CB_GETCURSEL, 0, 0)].ColorValue;

   // store values in figure or in default data members:
   if (MainWnd.mSelectedFig)  // figure is selected
      {
      MainWnd.mSelectedFig->mPenColor = mTPenColor;
      MainWnd.mSelectedFig->mPenStyle = mTPenStyle;
      MainWnd.mSelectedFig->mPenType = mTPenType;
      MainWnd.mSelectedFig->mPenWidth = mTPenWidth;

      // force redrawing of figure:
      RECT Rect = MainWnd.mSelectedFig->GetBoundRect ();
      InvalidateRect (MainWnd.mHWnd, &Rect, TRUE);
      }
   else                       // no figure selected
      {
      mPenColor = mTPenColor;
      mPenStyle = mTPenStyle;
      mPenType = mTPenType;
      mPenWidth = mTPenWidth;
      }

   // close the dialog box:
   EndDialog (HDlg, IDOK);
   return TRUE;
   }

BOOL CPenDlg::OnSetColor (HWND HDlg)
// processes WM_COMMAND / ID_SETCOLOR messages
   {
   CHOOSECOLOR CC;
```

```cpp
   // assign values to structure to control Color dialog box:
   memset (&CC, 0, sizeof (CC));
   CC.lStructSize = sizeof (CC);
   CC.hwndOwner = HDlg;
   CC.rgbResult = ColorTable [9].ColorValue;
   CC.lpCustColors = mCustColors;
   CC.Flags = CC_RGBINIT;

   // display Color common dialog box; save selected color if
   // user clicked OK:
   if (ChooseColor (&CC))
      ColorTable [9].ColorValue = CC.rgbResult;
   return TRUE;
   }

/////////////////////////////////////////////////////////////////////////////
// Print dialog box:                                                        //
/////////////////////////////////////////////////////////////////////////////

/////////////////////////////////////////////////////////////////////////////
// CPrintDlg public member functions:                                       //
/////////////////////////////////////////////////////////////////////////////

int CPrintDlg::Show (void)
// displays Print dialog box
   {
   return DialogBox
      (App.mHInstance,
      MAKEINTRESOURCE (IDD_PRINT),
      MainWnd.mHWnd,
      PrintDialogProc);
   }

/////////////////////////////////////////////////////////////////////////////
// Print dialog box procedure:                                              //
/////////////////////////////////////////////////////////////////////////////

BOOL CALLBACK PrintDialogProc
   (HWND   HDlg,
    UINT   Msg,
    WPARAM WParam,
    LPARAM LParam)
   {
   switch (Msg)
      {
      case WM_INITDIALOG:  // dialog box was just created
         return PrnDlg.OnInitDialog (HDlg);

      case WM_COMMAND:     // user issued a command
         switch (LOWORD (WParam))
            {
            case IDCANCEL: // user chose Close or pressed Esc
               return PrnDlg.OnCancel (HDlg);
```

```cpp
            case IDOK:       // user clicked OK or pressed Enter
                return PrnDlg.OnOK (HDlg);

            default:
                return FALSE; // default message processing
            }

        case WM_CTLCOLORBTN:    // button is about to be painted;
        case WM_CTLCOLORDLG:    // dialog box about to be painted;
        case WM_CTLCOLORSTATIC: // dialog text about to be painted
            return PrnDlg.OnCtlColor ((HDC)WParam);

        default:            // request default processing for all
            return FALSE; // other messages
        }
    }

/////////////////////////////////////////////////////////////////////////////
// CPrintDlg message handling member functions:                             //
/////////////////////////////////////////////////////////////////////////////

BOOL CPrintDlg::OnCancel (HWND HDlg)
// processes WM_COMMAND / IDCANCEL messages
    {
    // close the dialog box:
    EndDialog (HDlg, IDCANCEL);
    return TRUE;
    }


BOOL CPrintDlg::OnCtlColor (HDC HDc)
// processes WM_CTLCOLORBTN, WM_CTLCOLORDLG, and
// WM_CTLCOLORSTATIC messages
    {
    // set text background to light gray:
    SetBkColor (HDc, RGB (192,192,192));

    // supply a handle to a light-gray brush:
    return (BOOL)GetStockObject (LTGRAY_BRUSH);
    }


BOOL CPrintDlg::OnInitDialog (HWND HDlg)
// processes WM_INITDIALOG messages
    {
    // check Scale radio button:
    CheckDlgButton
        (HDlg,
        mScreenSize ? IDC_SCREENSIZE : IDC_FULLPAGE,
        1);

    // return TRUE to set focus to first control:
    return TRUE;
    }
```

```
BOOL CPrintDlg::OnOK (HWND HDlg)
// processes WM_COMMAND / IDOK messages
   {
   // save Scale choice:
   mScreenSize = IsDlgButtonChecked (HDlg, IDC_SCREENSIZE);

   // close the dialog box:
   EndDialog (HDlg, IDOK);
   return TRUE;
   }
```

THE COMPANION DISK

This appendix explains how to install the companion disk provided with the book and how to run the example programs that are contained on this disk.

INSTALLING THE COMPANION DISK

To install the companion disk, do the following:

1. Insert the disk into a floppy disk drive.

2. Click the Start button on the Windows 95 taskbar and choose the Run… command. Windows will display the Run dialog box.

3. If you inserted the companion disk into drive A, type the following into the Open text box and click the OK button:

```
A:\INSTALL
```

   If you inserted the disk into a different drive, substitute the correct drive letter. The Install program window will appear on your screen.

4. If you wish, change the folder path displayed in the Target Folder text box. This box specifies the hard disk folder to which Install will

Table A.1:   The subfolders created by the Install program and the example programs they contain

Subfolder	Example Program Contained
C:\GrWin95\Clip	Clip (Chapter 5)
C:\GrWin95\DrawIt1	DrawIt Version 1 (Chapter 3)
C:\GrWin95\DrawIt2	DrawIt Version 2 (Chapter 4)
C:\GrWin95\DrawIt3	DrawIt Version 3 (Chapter 6)
C:\GrWin95\DrawIt4	DrawIt Version 4 (Chapter 7)
C:\GrWin95\DrawIt5	DrawIt Version 5 (Chapter 8)
C:\GrWin95\Region	Region (Chapter 5)
C:\GrWin95\Template	Template (Chapter 1)

copy the companion disk files. The default folder is C:\GrWin95. If you specify a different folder, be sure to enter the *full path*, including the drive specification. (You cannot use long folder names—that is, the name of each folder in the path you enter is limited to eight characters.) If the folder you specify does not exist, Install will create it.

5. Click the OK button in the Install window. The program will begin installing the companion disk files.

The Install program expands and copies all of the files from the companion disk to your hard disk. For each example program, it creates a separate subfolder within the target folder you specified in step 4 and copies the executable and source files for the program to that subfolder. Table A.1 lists the subfolders that are created, indicating the example program contained in each one.

TIP

Because the files on the companion disk are compressed, you cannot use a simple copy command to install them on your hard disk. To install *all* of the files, use the Install program as described. To copy and expand one or more individual files, you can use Microsoft Expand.exe program (Expand.exe is an MS-DOS program included with Visual C++, the Win32 Software Development Kit, and other Microsoft products). To copy a file, type `Expand` at the MS-DOS prompt, and the program will prompt you for the required information. Note that the compressed files are named by replacing the last letter of the file name with the "_" character. For example, the compressed version of Template.exe is named Template.ex_.

RUNNING THE EXAMPLE PROGRAMS

The Install program copies the executable (.exe) file for each example program to the subfolder for that program on the hard disk (see Table A.1). To run the program, simply double-click the name of the executable file in a desktop folder or in the Windows Explorer, or use any of the other methods for launching a Windows program.

INDEX

LIMITED WARRANTY AND DISCLAIMER OF LIABILITY

ACADEMIC PRESS, INC. ("AP") AND ANYONE ELSE WHO HAS BEEN INVOLVED IN THE CREATION OR PRODUCTION OF THE ACCOMPANYING CODE ("THE PRODUCT") CANNOT AND DO NOT WARRANT THE PERFORMANCE OR RESULTS THAT MAY BE OBTAINED BY USING THE PRODUCT. THE PRODUCT IS SOLD "AS IS" WITHOUT WARRANTY OF ANY KIND (EXCEPT AS HEREAFTER DESCRIBED), EITHER EXPRESSED OR IMPLIED, INCLUDING, BUT NOT LIMITED TO, ANY WARRANTY OF PERFORMANCE OR ANY IMPLIED WARRANTY OF MERCHANTABILITY OR FITNESS FOR ANY PARTICULAR PURPOSE. AP WARRANTS ONLY THAT THE MAGNETIC DISKETTE(S) ON WHICH THE CODE IS RECORDED IS FREE FROM DEFECTS IN MATERIAL AND FAULTY WORKMANSHIP UNDER THE NORMAL USE AND SERVICE FOR A PERIOD OF NINETY (90) DAYS FROM THE DATE THE PRODUCT IS DELIVERED. THE PURCHASER'S SOLE AND EXCLUSIVE REMEDY IN THE EVENT OF A DEFECT IS EXPRESSLY LIMITED TO EITHER REPLACEMENT OF THE DISKETTE(S) OR REFUND OF THE PURCHASE PRICE, AT AP'S SOLE DISCRETION.

IN NO EVENT, WHETHER AS A RESULT OF BREACH OF CONTRACT, WARRANTY OR TORT (INCLUDING NEGLIGENCE), WILL AP OR ANYONE WHO HAS BEEN INVOLVED IN THE CREATION OR PRODUCTION OF THE PRODUCT BE LIABLE TO PURCHASER FOR ANY DAMAGES, INCLUDING ANY LOST PROFITS, LOST SAVINGS OR OTHER INCIDENTAL OR CONSEQUENTIAL DAMAGES ARISING OUT OF THE USE OR INABILITY TO USE THE PRODUCT OR ANY MODIFICATIONS THEREOF, OR DUE TO THE CONTENTS OF THE CODE, EVEN IF AP HAS BEEN ADVISED OF THE POSSIBILITY OF SUCH DAMAGES, OR FOR ANY CLAIM BY ANY OTHER PARTY.

Any request for replacement of a defective diskette must be postage prepaid and must be accompanied by the original defective diskette, your mailing address and telephone number, and proof of date of purchase and purchase price. Send such requests, stating the nature of the problem, to Academic Press Customer Service, 6277 Sea Harbor Drive, Orlando, FL 32887, 1-800-321-5068. APP shall have no obligation to refund the purchase price or to replace a diskette based on claims of defects in the nature or operation of the Product.

Some states do not allow limitation on how long an implied warranty lasts, nor exclusions or limitations of incidental or consequential damage, so the above limitations and exclusions may not apply to you. This Warranty gives you specific legal rights, and you may also have other rights which vary from jurisdiction to jurisdiction.

THE RE-EXPORT OF UNITED STATES ORIGIN SOFTWARE IS SUBJECT TO THE UNITED STATES LAWS UNDER THE EXPORT ADMINISTRATION ACT OF 1969 AS AMENDED. ANY FURTHER SALE OF THE PRODUCT SHALL BE IN COMPLIANCE WITH THE UNITED STATES DEPARTMENT OF COMMERCE ADMINISTRATION REGULATIONS. COMPLIANCE WITH SUCH REGULATIONS IS YOUR RESPONSIBILITY AND NOT THE RESPONSIBILITY OF AP.